Horizons in Human Geograp

Also Available from Macmillan Education

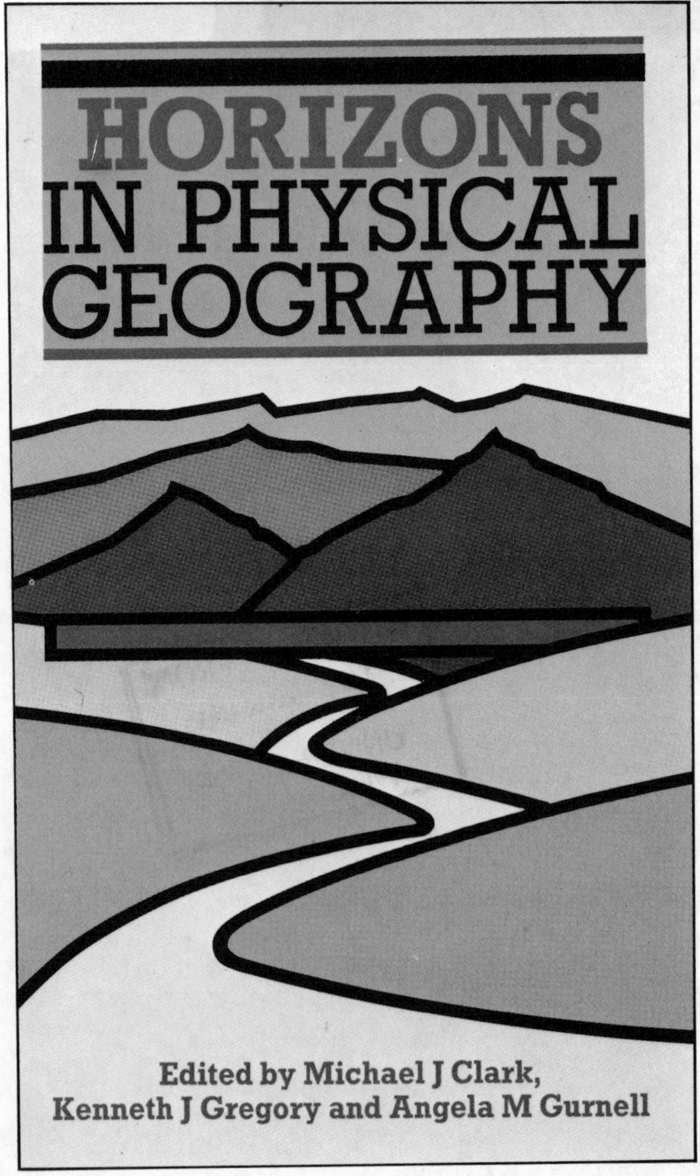

ISBN 0–333–39609–X HC
0–333–39610–3 PB

Horizons in Human Geography

Edited by

Derek Gregory and Rex Walford

First published 1989

Published by
MACMILLAN EDUCATION LTD
Houndmills, Basingstoke, Hampshire RG21 2XS
and London
Companies and representatives
throughout the world

Typeset by TecSet Ltd., Wallington, Surrey

Printed in Hong Kong

ISBN 0–333–39611–1 (hardcover)
ISBN 0–333–39612–X (paperback)

Contents

Preface

It is now more than twenty years since Richard Chorley and Peter Haggett compiled their path-breaking survey of *Frontiers in Geographical Teaching* (1965), which, together with *Models in Geography* published just two years later (1967), did so much to consolidate the foundations of what had come to be called the 'New Geography'. The intervening two decades have seen further (and, on occasion, dramatically different) developments in the discipline. Indeed, one of the lasting contributions of both *Frontiers* and *Models* was to recognise and welcome change as the very life-blood of intellectual inquiry. To be sure, many of these changes collided awkwardly with individuals, institutions and even governments which, in their various ways, sought to impose some sort of stability or direction – a semblance of order – on the shifting kaleidoscope of discovery and debate. But there can be no doubt that since 1965 geography has continued (and is continuing) to change, and *Horizons in Human Geography* and *Horizons in Physical Geography* are intended to introduce some of the most exciting challenges of the contemporary subject to a wider audience. Like *Frontiers*, the *Horizons* volumes are directed primarily at teachers, although we naturally hope for a wider readership. We regard geography in the schools and geography in the colleges, polytechnics and universities as parts of a corporate project. Their aims and audiences are of course different, and it would be quite wrong to think of school geography as no more than a conveyor belt into further and higher education. But each has a measure of responsibility for the other, and we hope that the contributions of these volumes will help to promote a sustained dialogue between them.

For all that they have in common, however, these two books depart from the original volumes in a number of ways which we want to signpost in advance. In the first place, we have accepted that geography is a bipolar subject – like so many others – and we have therefore divided the contributions into human geography and physical geography. Some will no doubt regard this as a betrayal of the integrity of the subject, others as a mere convenience which reflects little more than the conventions of teaching and research. We see it, rather, as a way of drawing attention to the substantial differences between a human geography modelled on the humanities and the social sciences and a physical geography modelled on the natural sciences. This is not to say that there are no contacts or connections between the two, and we have attempted to chart some of the most important in both volumes. But we believe that the differences which remain – between a human geography which, as one of its central tasks, has to make sense of a 'preinterpreted' world which is intrinsically meaningful to the people who live within it, and a physical geography which seeks to explain a shifting, changing but none the less 'object' world – are of vital significance to the future development of both human and physical geographies. That some of the most exciting developments in geography lie now, as they have for the past century, at the point where these two worlds and their different intellectual traditions intersect strengthens rather than weakens the case for a bipolar approach. The integrities of each must be respected, not erased by the casual translation of one into the other.

In the second place, and in addition to these differences between the two volumes, there are differences within them. Neither has been conceived as a manifesto for some new orthodoxy. Each essay is of its author's making, and although we have drawn contributors' attention to cross-references and cross-connections, we have deliberately made no attempt to ensure uniformity of viewpoint. Common threads do emerge, but these have not been imposed by editorial design. One of the hallmarks of geography today, and a sign of its maturity, is its diversity. For this reason we have not aimed at an encyclopaedic coverage, but have preferred instead to identify a series of key topics and themes to be approached by different authors from different perspectives. These themes, and the structures that they create, are of course editorial artifacts, and should not be taken to represent a fixed or self-evident map of geography's intellectual landscape. It is, after all, a characteristic of a kaleidoscope that its component parts can build an infinite number of different but often equally satisfying patterns. The result, we believe, is thought-provoking testimony to the continuing power of that deep-rooted 'concern' for geography which Haggett and Chorley accentuated in the 1960s, and of their own reminder that 'to stand still is to retreat'.

Cambridge, Southampton and British Columbia

Michael Clark
Kenneth Gregory
Derek Gregory
Angela Gurnell
Rex Walford

Acknowledgements

The authors and publishers wish to thank the following who have kindly given permission for the use of copyright material:

Edward Arnold (Publishers) Ltd for figure 5.7 of *Locational Models* by P. Haggett, A. D. Cliff and A. Frey, 1977 (Figure 1.2.5).

Associated Book Publishers (UK) Ltd for figures 2.1 (p.13), 2.3 (p.23), 2.7 (p.32), 2.8 (p.36), 3.5 (p.81), 3.7 (p.95) from *Natural Resources: Allocation Economics and Policy* by Judith Rees, Blackwell Publishers Ltd (Figures 6.1.1, 6.1.2, 6.1.3, 6.1.5, 6.1.6).

Blackwell Publishers Ltd, Oxford, for a diagram from *The Limits to Capital* by D. Harvey (Figure 3.1.3).

W. H. Freeman & Company for illustration by Jerome Kuhl from 'The Carbon Dioxide Question' by George M. Woodwell, *Scientific American*, 238 (1) January 1978 (Figure 6.1.4).

International Energy Agency for diagram on changing trends of oil and gas imports, production and consumption, 1974–83, from *Quarterly Oil and Gas Statistics of OECD Countries*, IEA Paris, 1984 (Figure 6.1.7).

Museum of London for Plate 3.2.2, 'Peabody Square'.

Ohio State University Press for figures 5A, 5C and 10D from 'Dynamic models of agricultural location in a spatial interaction framework' by A. G. Wilson and M. Birkin, *Geographical Analysis*, vol. 19, no.1, January, 1987. Copyright © 1987 by the Ohio State University Press (Figures 1.2.6 and 1.2.7).

Regional Science Research Institute for figure 2 from 'Dynamics of Urban spatial structure: progress and problems' by M. Clarke and A. G. Wilson, *Journal of Regional Science*, 23, 1983 (Figure 1.2.8)

Rondor Music (London) Ltd for 'Telegraph Road' by Mark Knopfler, Rondor Music (London) Ltd Chariscourt Ltd (in Chapter 2.4).

Every effort has been made to trace all the copyright-holders, but if any have been inadvertently overlooked the publishers will be pleased to make the necessary arrangement at the first opportunity.

Notes on the Contributors

Bassett, Keith Lecturer in Geography, University of Bristol
Clark, Michael Lecturer in Geography, University of Southampton
Corbridge, Stuart Lecturer in Geography, University of Cambridge
Cosgrove, Denis Lecturer in Geography, Loughborough University of Technology
Dennis, Richard Lecturer in Geography, University College, London
Douglas, Ian Professor of Physical Geography, University of Manchester
Eyles, John Associate Professor of Geography, McMaster University, Ontario
Gregory, Derek Professor of Geography, University of British Columbia at Vancouver
Harriss, Barbara Lecturer in Agricultural Economics, University of Oxford
Harriss, John Senior Lecturer in Development Studies, University of East Anglia
Johnston, R. J. Professor of Geography, University of Sheffield
Lee, Roger Senior Lecturer in Geography, Queen Mary College, London
Massey, Doreen Professor of Geography, The Open University
McDowell, Linda Lecturer in Geography, The Open University
Mead, Bill Emeritus Professor of Geography, University College, London
Meegan, Richard CES Ltd.
O'Riordan, Timothy Professor of Environmental Studies, University of East Anglia
Rees, Judith Lecturer in Geography, London School of Economics
Short, John Lecturer in Geography, University of Reading
Smith, Graham Lecturer in Geography, University of Cambridge
Taylor, Michael Bureau of Transport and Communications Economics, Canberra
Taylor, Peter Senior Lecturer in Geography, University of Newcastle upon Tyne
Thrift, Nigel Reader in Geography, University of Bristol
Walford, Rex Lecturer in Education, University of Cambridge
Wilson, Alan Professor of Urban and Regional Geography, University of Leeds

Derek Gregory is Professor of Geography at the University of British Columbia and was formerly Lecturer in Geography at the University of Cambridge and a Fellow of Sidney Sussex College. His teaching and research interests are in social theory and human geography and in the historical geography of Britain and North America. He is the author of *Ideology, Science and Human Geography, Regional Transformation and Industrial Revolution* and *The Geographical Imagination*, and co-editor of *Social Relations and Spatial Structure* (with John Urry) and *The Dictionary of Human Geography* (with R. J. Johnston and David M. Smith).

Rex Walford was both a schoolteacher and a lecturer in a teacher education college before becoming University Lecturer in Geography and Education at the University of Cambridge. He is a Fellow of Wolfson College, Cambridge. When the Council of British Geography was formed in 1988, he became the first Chairman. He is a Vice-President of the Royal Geographical Society, Chairman of the RGS Education Committee, and a Past President of The Geographical Association. He edited both *New Directions in Geography Teaching* and *Signposts For Geography Teaching* and has written several books about the use of games and simulations as a teaching technique. He chaired the Geographical Association Working Party which produced the Report, *Geographical Education for a Multi-Cultural Society*.

Introduction: Making Geography

Derek Gregory and Rex Walford
University of British Columbia and University of Cambridge

Maps of the intellectual landscape are always awkward affairs. The boundaries between different subjects are not entirely contingent – reasons can always be found for the fences to run this way rather than that – but neither do they seem to correspond to any clearly defined, 'natural' divisions. And, as we know, maps are instruments of power: even (especially) maps of an intellectual landscape.

To locate geography on maps of this sort is even more difficult. It has never respected intellectual property rights. Perched on a triangulation point between the natural sciences, the social sciences and the humanities, its surveying expeditions have set off first to this frontier and then to that, and their reports have sparked off one intellectual gold-rush after another. In the 1960s, of course, the direction was unmistakable; for every doubting Thomas (or Harris) who warned about the lure of fool's gold, there were a hundred prospectors heading west, with calculators strapped to their thighs or (more plausibly, given the technology of the times) lashed to the chuck-waggon behind. The isotropic plain was staked out, the claims registered in countless central places and the prospectors began their search for spatial order.

Our metaphor may well be as cumbersome as those early calculators, but it does at least convey something of the excitement of post-war geography's Quantitative Revolution. To say that its episodes were neither uniquely quantitative nor especially revolutionary does nothing to diminish their collective importance. Once the dust had settled, of course, other appraisals were made, and these were (rightly) critical. But for all their power, the critiques of spatial science have not dimmed that sense of excitement. That the essays which follow are far removed from the old frontiers of spatial science – the rustbelt of human geography – will soon become clear, but they share in a movement whose excitement and enthusiasm is every bit as important as that which convulsed the discipline in the 1960s.

Our horizons are different from the old frontiers, however, and we want to erect two general sign-posts to them. First, it would not be difficult to show that the classical models of spatial science typically involved a movement *away* from the world, and that this was reflected in both the accounts of social life which they provided and the conception of science through which they were constructed. Human geography turned from the teeming complexity of the world in all its diversity towards an altogether simpler universe of point-patterns, concentric circles and nested hierarchies. If the world didn't fit, so much the worse for the world: its multiple voices were so much 'noise' to be filtered out, so many 'residuals' from the global trend, so many 'disturbances' to the pristine symmetries of equilibrium. It is scarcely surprising that so little of human geography was recognisable to the people it was supposed to be about, let alone sensitive to their own experiences and their own needs, and that the immensely difficult problem of geographical description – of *writing* geography – should have been dismissed as 'mere' description or something the discipline had grown out of. In contrast, most of the essays in this book take the problem of description very seriously indeed, and many of them seek to provide what Clifford Geertz once called 'thick descriptions' of the multiple layers of our human geographies. It should be said at once that this can be part of a properly 'scientific' programme – those writers who have broken with the philosophy of positivism to explore theoretical realism, for example, are engaged in providing descriptions of just this kind – but it can also speak directly to the humanities. Either way, it is a theoretically-informed enterprise, but one which directs us *back* towards the world we very nearly lost. Its purpose is not to reduce the complex to the simple (one of the catch-phrases of spatial science), but rather, as Lévi-Strauss once put it, to replace a complexity we don't understand with a complexity which we do. In other words, it seeks to make the world *intelligible*.

A number of commentators have urged that the problem of description – if we bother to think about it in theoretical terms (as we ought) – is symptomatic of a more general 'crisis of representation' throughout the human sciences. Put very simply, our texts are not mirrors which we hold up to the world, reflecting its shapes and structures immediately and without distortion. They are, instead, creatures of our own making, though their making is not entirely of our own choosing. If we treat texts as social constructions, then, on the part of both writer and reader, we are surely obliged to understand, much more rigorously than has been our custom in the past, what it is we do when we *read* and *write* – when we (literally) *make sense* of the world this way rather than that way.

Certainly, much of what is happening in human geography today is implicated in a reconfiguration of social and political thought. In one sense, of course, this has always been the case, for geography has never been an autonomous project, divorced from social pressures and social responsibilities. It is unhelpful to present its development as the free creation of the great minds of the past or as an inevitable progression towards the fashionable paradigms of the present. But what is of more moment, we think, and our second general sign-post, is the strategic role which human geography is now playing in the transformation of the wider intellectual landscape. It continues to be attentive to what is happening in other disciplinary enclosures, to be sure, but its concerns are now attracting eavesdroppers in their own right. The human sciences as a whole are coming to terms with concepts of place, space and landscape as never before. Their explanations – like their descriptions – are having to contend with the reality of a differentiated, distanciated world, and this has set in train a wholesale reformulation of their theoretical systems.

It would be absurd to draw up an account of the intellectual balance of payments. This would be beside the point, since the debates are being joined on equal (and exhilarating) terms. We are emphatically not suggesting, therefore, that human geography now exports concepts where in the past it imported them, wholesale and retail. Indeed, any map of today's intellectual trails would need to convey not only movements along them but the spectacular movements of the landscape itself. When Doreen Massey insists that *geography matters*, then, we do not want this to be mistaken for a special pleading. It is, rather, a central insight of the contemporary human sciences.

We hope that this collection of essays conveys something of this excitement, not least because we believe that the study of geography in schools and in higher education is a common enterprise. In particular periods and in particular forms it may not always seem so, but in our view there is a linking thread which ties together the different curiosities about the world of the primary-school child and the post-graduate researcher.

For most students in Britain, as we know only too well, full-time education stretches only from the ages of five to sixteen; even those who stay on into the sixth form or go on to further or higher education are not very likely to continue a study of geography. Nevertheless, the work done in universities and polytechnics has intense ramifications throughout the whole of education. Those who form the community of teachers will have had their views moulded by their own studies in higher education and by their in-service experience on courses. In the same way, advisers, Inspectors, editors of teaching journals and examiners are actively influenced by the current trends in the 'academic discipline'. The scare-quotes are there because, to return to our previous analogy for a moment, we want to keep the two-way trails open: higher education ought not to be a separate reservation, patrolled by a chisel-faced academic cavalry. To be sure, the frontier-scouts may not be traversing the same terrain as those who travel in the overcrowded (and often under-resourced) waggon-trains: but they send back signals, and the signals often cause changes in direction. (And, on occasion, the fires from the waggon-trains alert the scouts to developments which they had dismally failed to foresee.)

That said, the insights of higher education are not, of course, translated directly into the curriculum of the first form of the secondary school. There is a wholly proper re-evaluation of them, and they are subject to transformation through contact with a host of other influences too. Yet any school subject is the poorer without that vital, organic linkage. If school geography were to become a limited-objective, narrowly instrumental study, uninformed by the excitement and potential of contemporary research – which is now busily pushing *back* those very same constraints – then it would eventually lose its intellectual edge and its capacity to interest students. Those who accept separation or argue for divorce also, in our view, seek suicide.

This linkage, pulled tight, gave human geography a considerable stimulus in the 1970s. Whatever one thinks about the assumptions of positivism (and we do not now think too much of them), it would nevertheless be foolish to deny that the explorations conducted under its banner – studies which sought to model geography on the methodology of the natural sciences and to focus its energies on the discovery of spatial patterns and the search for principles of 'spatial organisation' – all of these things were, as we have said, a source of genuine excitement to young (and some not-so-young) schoolteachers struggling with the heavy burden of an information overload. What was more, the expansion of the school system at about the same time meant that the tide of this new movement had great effect, sweeping through teacher-education, the Inspectorate, textbook-publishing and, ultimately, the examination boards in a remarkably short space of time.

One key factor in this change was the publication of books directed towards school-teachers which deliberately tried to set out some of the most interesting work being done in universities and polytechnics. These books, buttressed by conferences and lectures, were not prescriptive in their approach to school work; they could not hope to be. Their intention – like ours – was to make current developments more accessible so that teachers could consider them carefully and critically.

This book, like its companion volume, is intended to follow in their foot-steps. But there are, even so, a number of more specific differences which we want to notice in advance. These relate not only to changes in the nature of geography since those pioneer writings, though these have been dramatic; they also connect, very directly, with the changed circumstances which everyone in schools (and outside them) must now confront – and which have been no less dramatic.

First, and most obviously, virtually all of the essays in the present collection are sharply critical of a geography based on (or aimed towards) the philosophy of positivism. The so-called 'New Geography' was not, we suspect, distinguished by any great philosophical awareness on the part of its proponents, but the intervening decades have seen a close scrutiny of its philosophical foundations. Other philosophies have been examined too – on occasion in a spirit of combat and (sadly) contempt – yet there is now, so it seems to us, a far greater awareness of the implications and entailments of different philosophical systems. All of this has made, perhaps paradoxically, for a surer understanding of the *limits* of philosophy. The old battles, with the heavy artilleries of 'positivism', 'humanism', 'structuralism', 'realism' and the rest sending brilliant salvoes to explode far above the heads of the poor bloody infantry (dug in to their own particular trenches) are drawing to a close.

This does not mean that the struggles were all for nothing, and neither does it herald a new age of co-operation and integration. What it does indicate is the end of the old absolutisms. There is indeed a plurality of traditions at play within geography today, but none of them can look with any confidence to philosophy as some sort of neutral arbiter, an independent court of appeal which can adjudicate their various claims *outside of the social practices in which they are necessarily (if often unconsciously) implicated*. The present collection is, therefore, a heterogeneous one: but none of the contributors is blind to the social and political implications of geographical work.

Second, then, the geographies which are described in the following pages are, for the most part, ones which have turned 'spatial analysis' into 'social analysis' *and vice–versa*. We use both of those terms in the widest of senses. These essays demonstrate, in different ways, that geography is not geometry: that it cannot be reduced to a fistful of techniques or an arsenal of hardware and software to bludgeon the *content* out of place, space and landscape. And these essays are attentive to particularities, specificities and differences not only over space but also through time. The functionalism which dominated so many versions of systems theory has no central place in these pages: it is replaced here by a concern with *transformation*. This is no abstract, academic problem; it is one with the liveliest of political implications. The book is in no sense a Marxist manifesto, but many of its contributors are, we think, seeking to illuminate one of Marx's most pregnant aphorisms: that people make history (and, let us add, geography), but not just as they please and not under conditions of their own choosing. Transformations do not 'just happen', still less do they just happen 'to' people; rather, they happen *through* human agency which, though dependent on and conditioned by a host of different structures, nevertheless cannot be separated from the capacities of human beings to *make* them happen: to *make* a difference. In some ways, as we have indicated, this is the focus of all the social sciences and the humanities. But many of the essays here seek to go still further, and to show that these transformations cannot be understood without a rich and rigorous reconstruction of their geographies. Marx's original claim was strategically incomplete, because people really *do* make their own geographies too. It is not only that 'spatial analysis' has become 'social analysis', therefore: it is also that any 'social analysis' which is to hold out a serious prospect of practical action must become, at the same time, 'spatial analysis'. The conduct of social life is not indifferent to the places, spaces and landscapes in which it (quite literally) *takes place*.

All of this bears directly on the emergence of a theoretically-informed and historically-sensitive regional geography which is announced, in different ways and with different emphases, in many of the chapters which follow. These remarks also help to show why calls for a new 'geographical literacy' and a new 'geographical awareness', with all the implications these have for the revival of traditional skills in reading maps, using atlases and understanding foreign languages, are not the stridently utilitarian, 'back to basics' bleatings of the backwoodsmen. Any genuinely critical geography depends on these skills: it is only ideologies masquerading as sciences that can afford to suppress them. Other skills are needed too, of course, but not as a substitute for them. Some of these skills are technical ones, but others are practical in the original sense of that word: they are, in other words, about the clarification of meaning, about interpretation, translation and understanding. They all help to make geography 'relevant' (an overworked word in any case) but, taken together, they make geography urgently, vitally 'relevant' in domains far beyond the narrowly instrumental.

In planning these two volumes we became acutely aware that proposals of this sort raise awkward questions about the relations between human geography and physical geography. Part of the problem is simply ignorance: human geographers often have strange ideas about what physical geography involves, and physical geographers entertain equally bizarre notions of what human geography is about. Even so, anyone who reads both books – and we hope that *will* happen, even though many teachers in schools seem to be as partisan in their interests as are their colleagues in universities and polytechnics – will surely recognise not only differences in content, but also differences in perspective, range and style. This does not mean, however, that human geography can somehow assume away the physical world: social life is not suspended in the air. (And even if it were, it would still not escape from physical geography!) Many of the essays in this volume, including some which are most centrally concerned with questions of ethics, meanings and values, are thus careful to accentuate the materiality of social life. They often do so in ways strikingly different from the conventions of physical geography, we realise, but a knowledge of and a concern for the physical world is, we believe, a vital component of any fully human geography.

The construction of the sort of critical geography we have in mind is a profoundly participatory project, and it is for this reason that (when planning this volume) we chose not to invite contributions from outside the United Kingdom. Teachers in other countries are working in different contexts, and they are not easily assimilated to our own (and nor should they be). But more important is our conviction that, in the contemporary reconstitution of human geography, teachers in schools are likely to be much more closely involved in its direction than they were in previous 'revolutions'. If this is a revolutionary book, then, it is not (particularly) because its ideas represent a radical break with old orthodoxies: some of them do not. But it may, perhaps, be revolutionary if teachers accept its invitation to join the conversation. Unlike *Frontiers in Geographical Teaching* and *Models in Geography*, the essays in this book have not emerged out of conference proceedings. We hope instead that they will be the springboard for subsequent meetings with teachers (and not merely meetings 'for' teachers). That is why we have confined ourselves in this way: to offer more opportunities for dialogue and discussion.

This decision has its costs as well as its benefits. We do not pretend that the present collection is a comprehensive or even a representative view of human geography. Everyone will be able to find ideas which they think should have been included – and some, no doubt, which they think should have been excluded – but it is an index of the vitality of the subject that it cannot be captured within the covers of a single book: even one twice the size. Two obvious omissions which we do want to single out, however, are geographical perspectives on race relations in multi-cultural societies (like our own) and geographical analyses of military and paramilitary power and violence. Both of these are immensely important questions, which cut right to the heart of human geography in every sense. Both of them will, we hope, be the subject of later volumes in their own right. If this first collection is unavoidably partisan, however, it is not altogether parochial. People living in other places will want to (and need to) construct their own geographies, but all of us will have to recognise (in our various ways) the wider world in which we now live. The essays in this book point towards the reconstruction of regional geography, then, but they do so in the knowledge that we are caught up in a truly global geography which is ours to make: or to destroy.

HOW TO USE THIS BOOK

There is a logic to the book, and we have prefaced each Section with an Introduction which shows why the chapters have been grouped in this particular way, which highlights the main points of each chapter, and which picks over some of their bones of contention as well as their points of agreement. The Guide to Further Reading at the end of each chapter should, we hope, provide some sign-points for further study.

The instinctive impulse of the dedicated reader might be to start at page 1 and work through to the end; but we have organised the book in such a way that other strategies are also possible (and, perhaps, preferable). Since each chapter has been written in broad knowledge of the others, it should be easy to dip in to any one of them on its own account and then to work 'outwards', following the cross-references through your own particular spiral of interests. If you want to begin with an overview, however, then read each of the Introductions before plunging in to individual chapters. There is also a detailed Index at the end to help stitch the arguments together still more completely.

PART I
BEYOND THE QUANTITATIVE REVOLUTION

Introduction

A number of commentators have noted that the 'Quantitative Revolution' was neither exclusively 'quantitative' nor especially 'revolutionary', but we use it here as an established short-hand for the cluster of changes which convulsed Anglo-American geography in the 1960s. To be sure, these involved more than the application of quantitative techniques to geographical problems, because the very *nature* of those problems was transformed by the use of theoretical languages which directed attention towards generalised models of spatial pattern and spatial structure. Equally, it is not very difficult to find antecedents of these developments: even Richard Hartshorne's *The Nature of Geography* – which is usually represented as the epitome of a supposedly reactionary regional geography – commended the writings of von Thünen and Weber and described an elementary trend surface model! Just as important, by no means everyone was swept along with the crowd; there were, even in the middle of all this, a number of vital advances in other traditions of geographical inquiry.

That all of these qualifications can now be made is the result of a continuing and critical appraisal of the exuberances (and the excesses) of those formative years. Distance has allowed a perspective to be drawn on the events surrounding the Quantitative Revolution, and we now know much more about both its philosophy and its history. But the chapters in this Section do not seek to pick over the entrails of those debates; rather, they chart some of the developments which have taken place since then.

It will be clear from **Michael Clark**'s chapter that the advances of the Quantitative Revolution have not lost their momentum. If anything, the technical changes which made so many of them possible (and, according to their protagonists, necessary) have now progressed to the point where the old problem – information overload – has been recreated at a new level through novel methods of data capture. Clark's view is that information technology has spectacularly increased 'both the spatial and temporal scope of data acquisition' to such an extent that this opens the door to 'new worlds'. The description of these worlds demands a series of conceptual innovations, but it also depends upon the extension of our traditional and intrinsically technical capabilities. The result, so Clark suggests, is that we will no longer have to see geographical change as 'a jerky moving film built out of a series of rapidly projected static frames'; we will, rather, be able to glimpse the continuous operation of processes and to explore their ramifications in dimensions 'otherwise inaccessible to the unaided human sense'.

One of Clark's central points is that 'simple number-crunching is now far behind us', and this is sharpened by **Alan Wilson** in his discussion of mathematical models and geographical theory. Like Clark, he is concerned that some of the ideas which he presents will be too readily assimilated to the philosophy of positivism and the methodology of the natural sciences: in his view, nothing could be further from the truth (or more damaging). His work has an insistently critical dimension and, in particular, transcends the *statistical* boundaries of the first-generation models of the Quantitative Revolution. His own concern, therefore, is with *mathematical* modelling. 'A purely statistical approach to theory and model-building is,' he insists, 'limited in scope and is also more directly connected to positivism.' What he seeks to do, in contrast, is to build from a simple model of spatial interaction and location – the two elements which he takes to be distinctive of geography – towards a more comprehensive theory of spatial structure and transformation. In the course of his reconstructions, he is able to show that the classical locational models of von Thünen, Weber and others are special cases of a more general formulation: and, significantly, one which explicitly considers structural change and so allows for 'a vast multiplicity of possible futures'.

Ron Johnston is just as sensitive to the importance of what he calls 'multiple outcomes', but he is also much more sceptical about the claims which surround these various advances. All of them, he argues, are confined to the sphere of the 'empirical-analytic' sciences and, as such, are driven by an essentially *technical* interest in the prediction and control of objectified systems. This deforms the discussion of fundamentally political questions, he believes, because the aggressive triumph of the empirical-analytical sciences threatens the integrity of an equally important *practical* interest in mutual understanding: in the meanings, intentions and values of human beings which are the concern of the 'hermeneutic' sciences. Any genuinely critical geography, Johnston contends, must seek to draw on both of these imperatives. One must not be promoted over the other. Johnston's argument is not, of course, peculiar to geography, and it finds echoes in many other fields which have also been influenced (like Johnston) by the critical theory of the German thinker Jürgen Habermas. But Johnston tries to show that these two traditions can be reconciled – 'reformulated' is perhaps a more accurate description – through the philosophy of (theoretical) realism. In doing so, he suggests, it is possible to speak in the *same* language about both the connections *and the contrasts* between human and physical geography.

All of this is rather too convenient for **Derek Gregory**. In a review of the implications of 'post-modernism' for human geography, he questions the priority which so many of these grand schemes ('Grand Theories') accord to totalisation – to the construction of systems of thought which claim to be comprehensive and complete – and explores instead the contemporary significance of fragmentation. This is a recurrent theme across the whole spectrum of the human and social sciences, and the humanities too, and Gregory seeks to show how the developing relations between geography and three other disciplines (political economy, sociology and anthropology) have reopened the traditional question of areal differentiation in a radically different language. It is a language which does not, so to speak, 'absolutize' spatial structure, freezing it in geometric frames of perpetual order, but rather explores, in terms at once nominally 'scientific' and nominally 'artistic', the flickering and fleeting geographies through which social life is conducted. Like Johnston, therefore, Gregory believes that 'geography matters', that concepts of place, space and landscape 'make a difference' to the constitution of social theory. Like Johnston, Gregory is keen to accentuate the radical consequences of these developments. But his discussion is concerned not only with their content but also with their form: not only with the politics of geography but also with the 'poetics' of geography.

Taken together, these four chapters provide a springboard for debate and discussion. They raise questions about the consequences of technical advances (good and bad); about the respective contributions of statistical and mathematical techniques; about the relations between philosophical reflection and the day-to-day practice of geography (inside the classroom and outside the lecture theatre); and about geography's changing location in the intellectual landscape of modernity. They clearly do not all speak with the same voice – which is precisely why we have grouped them together – but they do all consider, in different ways and with different inflections, the problem of transformation which we have already identified as one of the central questions of contemporary human geography.

1.1
Geography and Information Technology: Blueprint for a Revolution?

Michael J. Clark
University of Southampton

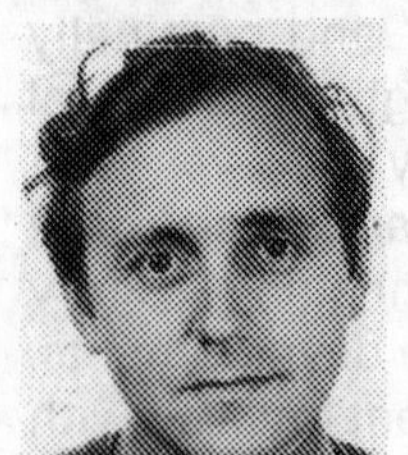

Michael Clark is Lecturer in Geography at the University of Southampton. A co-editor of *Horizons in Physical Geography*, his teaching and research interests focus on coasts and on information technology.

INFORMATION AND A CHANGING WORLD

The fervour with which the Information Technology (IT) 'revolution' has been launched and received reflects a widespread belief that knowledge is power, and that the IT path to increased knowledge is thus an assured route to increased power. This prompts us, of course, to ask what knowledge, what power – and at what price? Whilst the first inclination of some physical geographers might be to regard such questions as comfortably distant, they do in fact raise issues of considerable significance which have been addressed by a number of human geographers – amongst them Ron Johnston in Chapter 1.3 of this volume. A short-sighted view of their implications for the subject could be dangerous. The world is changing around us. To survive as a subject geography needs to change with it; to advance as a subject geography must change ahead of it. Simply to defend the present methodology and philosophy in the face of such change would inevitably lead to an irreversible divergence between geography and the real world that it aspires to understand and manage.

The changes thus required of geographers may well exceed in impact both the so-called quantitative revolution and even the more fundamental 'scientific' revolution of which quantification was a tangible symptom. Now, as then, the major problem is not simply to accept the opportunities presented by new approaches, but to learn to recognise just what the new approaches are and how they relate to geography. For what purposes these enhanced skills should then be used remains a question to be answered within the framework of whichever geographical philosophy we care to adopt. In particular, the use of IT will depend upon the degree to which it becomes associated with science, and the extent to which that association is attractive to geographers who might prefer other approaches.

Of course, information does not in itself equate with knowledge, and knowledge is markedly inferior to wisdom. Such a realisation encourages cautious handling of information, but is no excuse for rejecting the inherent value of IT as a pathway to knowledge or methodological innovation. Whether the individual geographer wishes to accelerate or reverse this trend must remain a personal choice, but in my view we ignore such fundamental processes at our joint professional peril.

'Technological and often computer-based systems for information gathering, storage, processing, transmission and retrieval' sounds a sufficiently non-geographical definition of IT to comfort those who want none of it, and sufficiently all-embracing to excite those who see this as a definition of the future. Whilst the resulting data may well be held in digital form, they may equally involve words or images, and even the digital data may represent maps or graphs. IT is tipped to dominate the employment market for those who are in work, the domestic and leisure scene for those who are not, and the academic world for those to whom knowledge is either an end or a means to an end. Still more fundamental, it can be suggested that since so many spatial patterns reflect the locations of interactions and transactions, IT may come to transform the basic concepts of both space and distance. Given the obsession of many geographers with the spatial dimension over the last two decades, it is difficult to over-emphasise the traumatic nature of the changes necessary if extensive social and economic transactions were released by IT from their current central locations. At the extreme, a complete reconceptualisation of location, zonation and spatial hierarchy might become necessary.

The real issue is not whether we should regard such prospects as a dream or a nightmare, but whether we have the courage and vision to accept them as an imminent reality. Once that hurdle has been crossed, geographers can decide whether to support or oppose the growing momentum of change, and whether to participate in the new opportunities that develop or reject them in favour of the proven traditional roles. Until they face this hurdle, however, they risk being swept aside by an externally-directed flood of change, ultimately to be stranded with no function other than to report on what other people have done to the world, and to discuss amongst themselves how much better things might have been if geographers had been in charge. The main danger, then, is not that we will make the wrong decision about the future, but that we will make no decision at all – partly because of indifference, but largely because we fail to appreciate just how very geographical are the implications of the forces now at work. The first stage in attempting a geographical evaluation of IT is thus to review some of the contexts within which it can be applied.

GEOGRAPHICAL KNOWLEDGE AND INFORMATION TECHNOLOGY

Data acquisition – more of the same?

It was deceptively easy in the 1960s to dismiss developments in statistical and computational power as yielding no more than an increased pace of analysis without altering the underlying direction of geographical investigation. Similarly, present-day IT developments could be denigrated as nothing other than 'a lot more of the same', forgetting that with time new trends have a habit of confounding their doubters. Nevertheless, we cannot regard IT as being self-evidently beneficial, and if it is to be welcomed as a potentially significant component of future geographies, then it must be able to justify that acceptance and survive informed criticism. Such evaluation takes as its starting point the assumption that information is essential to explanation and management. Of course, information alone is barren – but the case to be argued here is that, as geographical investigations become more *multivariate* (combining more attributes) and *multidate* (monitoring events or processes more frequently), IT allows hitherto unrecognised patterns to emerge. Indeed, as description becomes progressively more complete, even the distinction between description and explanation becomes blurred though once again we have to acknowledge the possible gulf between knowledge and understanding.

Since IT is centrally concerned with data acquisition, storage, manipulation and user-oriented retrieval, it is appropriate to start by considering how information is acquired in the first place. We are habituated to a world accessed by the human senses of sight and to an extent hearing (the other senses being subordinate), and are thus attuned to an awareness limited by the scope of these senses. To extend the information-base upon which our conceptualisation is founded, we have traditionally sought to gather data which make it possible to access other times (history) and places (geography) – but the viewpoint adopted in these temporal and spatial travels has always been human, transporting our eyes and ears to other times and places. An invaluable contribution of the sensing and recording technologies introduced over recent centuries and developed particularly over recent years has been to extend the spatial and temporal scope of data acquisition, thus allowing us to explore dimensions of the world that are otherwise inaccessible to the unaided human senses. Scale-related aspects of this new age of exploration are considered separately below, but first the possibility of sensing quite different types of information can be noted briefly.

So restricted is the range of the electro-magnetic spectrum which is capable of perception by our eyes that the whole social régime is geared to a phasing of activity by day and rest by night. All pattern is dominated by visual manifestations. The brain then takes this relatively crude input and builds from it complex models of the real world – models which far exceed in the completeness what the eye has actually registered, since the brain overlays meaning on to the nerve impulses. One of the primary advances offered by the branch of IT concerned with sensing and recording information about physical entities and events has been its role in extending our awareness to phenomena which are represented by *non-visible* parts of the spectrum. The effect is akin to that of the X-ray, revealing new patterns and opening the door on to new worlds. In non-military applications the potential is most easily seen in the science of remote sensing. Moving beyond 'visible light', the satellite or aircraft scanner sees first the near infra-red, with its greatly improved ability to achieve enhanced discrimination of such geographically-relevant phenomena as vegetation, soil and moisture, and then the further dimension of the thermal infra-red – adding still more information and transgressing for the first time the necessity for light in order to permit sight.

Equal potential lies elsewhere in the spectrum, previously limited to the hinted promise of the radar scanner. Each new sensor reveals a different aspect of the world. Each makes some sacrifice in order to do so, but in combination their products build up an ever more complete and complex picture of reality. To spurn this new vision would be as myopic as a blind person refusing the offer of sight on the grounds that he had always managed to get along quite well without it. A door has been unlocked by IT, and geographers have more to gain than most from pushing it open. What they find will not in itself solve any of their problems, but it will certainly fuel the possibility of such solutions. The barrier to accepting this challenge lies partly in the seemingly inevitable human resistance to change, but more tangibly it relates to the difficulty posed by the sheer volume of information provided. The next step must be, therefore, to tackle the problem of scale.

New scales, new worlds

Perhaps without knowing it, geographers are already thoroughly familiar with the relationship between scale, resolution and information. The limited capacity of eye and brain render it seemingly quite natural that 'global' problems should be studied in a generalised fashion, substituting overview for detail. At regional scales a compromise between detail and generalisation appears appropriate: crude or spatially ill-registered information is no longer satisfactory, but highly intricate detail which overwhelmed interpretation would be an embarrassment. Already it is clear that for many purposes complete accuracy is not only unnecessary, but often downright damaging. At the local level, however, the same total amount of information permits us quite naturally to perceive a smaller realm in greater detail.

Although this scale/resolution link seems so natural, it is merely a physiological and psychological artifact of the human neurological system. We have evolved to cope with the information volume that our senses can provide: touch within a meter, sounds within a hundred meters or so, sights within a few kilometers – all referring to the present and relying on a partial and rapidly-decaying memory for comparison or combination of past and present events. Thus, just as our consideration of new sensors revealed the drastic limitations of the eye-brain system in terms of the type of information accessed, so now we see the limits on the amount of information that the human system can handle unaided. Consequently, the intellectual rise of the human species has been related to the development of means of communication which permitted the individual experience to broaden into group consciousness, with consequent enormous increase in awareness and understanding. Whilst this evolution initially relied on speech and gesture, it was subsequently consolidated and accelerated by the technologies of recording (measurement, instrumentation, photography, etc.), handling (fingers, model, abacus, calculator, computer, etc.) and transmission (writing, printing, telegraph, radio, television, etc.).

The current emergence of IT could be regarded simply as the next step along this path, providing new means of acquiring, manipulating and transmitting information – its potential social and intellectual impact likened to that of the invention of printing. Yet the full implications go much further, for at both extremes the new scales of information open up entirely new realms of thought. Whilst geographers have long aspired to project a global viewpoint, their achievement (as Peter Taylor and other contributors note) has generally been lamentable, in part because the world-scale information has been either crude or outdated – or both. Even at this relatively early stage in their development, however, operational satellite environmental monitoring systems have started to break the scale/resolution link by providing frequent detailed regional and global coverage, whilst scanning electron microscopy has begun to access the fundamental microprocesses of physics, chemistry, physiology and (perhaps) psychology. Paradoxically, whilst local-scale and micro studies stand to benefit greatly from further improvements in the spatial resolution of these sensing systems, the real advantages of such detail for global purposes are much less apparent. Indeed, it is already clear that the volume of data produced by high resolution systems not only involves major data-handling problems, but can degrade our understanding by introducing spurious detail. At global scale it is up-to-date synchronous coverage that is important rather than detail.

This newly defined relationship between data need, provision and handling reflects a familiar underlying pattern – technology and technique have limitations in the volume of information that can be handled. The volume of data increases with the number of variables measured, the frequency and precision of measurement, and the number of points sampled (often meaning the area covered). Whilst this problem is particularly acute in the case of automated remote sensing (and is discussed by John Townshend in *Horizons in Physical Geography*), the concept could apply equally to any type of information-gathering system – like a census. Thus, if great detail is involved, it is likely that only a small area can be surveyed and the inter-survey period will be long. If frequent large area coverage is required (as with the inputs to daily weather forecasts), then the detail is likely to be sparse. Clearly as computing power increases, these restrictions on information handling will adjust so that an ever-greater proportion of the required tasks can actually be achieved. Thus the value of IT at a given time depends on:

- the nature of the information that is amenable to sensing,
- the spatial and temporal resolution of the sensor,
- the available computing power for storing and handling data,
- the existing skills of analysis and interpretation,
- the detail (resolution) required to make sense of the subject.

This latter point adds a further dimension to the delicate balancing act between what is needed to make IT genuinely useful, and what can actually be achieved by existing systems at acceptable cost. The information requirements for effective geographical analysis have, of course, long been appreciated, and a major contribution of IT has thus been to bring some of these requirements within the geographer's grasp for the first time. However, whilst this role can be regarded as essentially evolutionary, the impact of IT has been more revolutionary in the context of temporal resolution.

Temporal resolution and the prospect for real-time knowledge

Despite its historical pretensions, geography has often been dominated by a single-time static viewpoint. The primary framework has been 'now', with the past and the future being equally static snapshots of preceeding or post-dating states. From this viewpoint, change is regarded mainly as a transitory stage that has to be passed through in order to alter one state into another. The interest in processes that has emerged over the last two decades has helped to loosen this conceptual restriction, but the limitations of our observations (eye, census or instrument) and memory (brain, file or computer) still renders the resulting vision akin to a jerky moving film built out of a series of rapidly-projected static frames. The impression of movement (change) is an illusion whose realism increases as the gap between frames decreases. This analogy is realistic, since an early 'IT' success was the visual clarification of morphological change provided by high-speed cinephotography (slowing down very rapid change) and time-lapse photography (speeding up very slow change).

The temporal resolution with which change of form or process should ideally be viewed is related to the rate of change. In practice, however, the actual frequency and duration of observation are more likely to be constrained by cost, convenience and time. A single example can demonstrate the extent to which the attributes observed alter in nature as well as in detail when the observational frequency is varied. The amount of sediment carried by pro-glacial streams is both an indicator of the englacial drainage processes, and a contributor to the management of sedimentation in hydro-electric reservoirs and the mechanical wear of electricity-generating turbines. Annual observations of flow and sediment reveal little more than the gross pattern of inter-year variation, perhaps related to medium-term climate. Monthly measurements demonstrate the overall seasonal cycle in relation to annual weather pattern. An actual response of the water and sediment to individual weather events and to the gradual development of the englacial drainage channels emerges only when daily data are available.

More recently, it has been possible to deduce from hourly readings that a surprising proportion of total sediment transport relates to very short flow peaks which probably reflect changes within the glacier ice and flow rather than weather patterns. Even so, the full pattern is apparent only from a continuous trace of water and sediment, since superimposed on the occasional 'hourly' fluctuations are much more frequent sediment pulses often lasting no more than ten or twenty minutes and responding to very localised englacial effects.

Clearly the increase in sampling rate does not just reveal the same pattern in more detail, but actually reflects quite different patterns with quite different controls. Similar trends could be illustrated from other branches of human and physical geography. Since a major increase in sampling frequency is often dependent on automated instrumentation to collect the data and computation to analyse it, it follows that the ability of IT to increase both the spatial and temporal resolution of observation, and to handle the resulting data, is indeed opening up new worlds of geographical enquiry.

One of the most exciting recent advances in human geography has been in the recognition of the co-existence of different time perspectives – a form of multitemporality. Whilst in many senses this is a conceptual advance, it does have *technical* counterparts which allow IT to play an increasingly important 'multitemporal' role (though in the field of remote sensing the term 'multi-date' might be preferred). If we return to the example of satellite image processing, then it is possible to demonstrate completely new descriptive and explanatory dimensions developing when images are created which depict change rather than state. Thus it is possible to combine winter and summer images better to classify areas with a seasonal variation in land use or vegetation. Similarly, mathematical combination of night and day thermal images (usually gathered from aircraft) creates a composite image of heat lag (some areas warm up more rapidly during the day than others), and one potentially very valuable application of this lag is that it can be used to estimate the amount of soil moisture in the ground. In this way it is possible to depict notional patterns of non-visible phenomena – yet another example of IT opening up completely new worlds for exploration. It should be stressed that the implications of such technical innovation are by no means limited to remotely sensed images or to physical geography. Conceptually similar exercises are possible with spatially distributed social and economic information using the sophisticated analytical framework of a computerised 'Geographic Information System' (GIS), which is discussed further below.

Approaches to the creative handling of multivariate information

Information is only as useful as our ability to use it, so a major IT function is the design of systems to store data and allow it to be handled with the greatest possible ease and flexibility. When the main technology for storing words, numbers and images was on paper, the appropriate filing and retrieval systems were filing cabinets, card indices, punch cards, etc. The main aim was to make information readily accessible to the user, but the manipulation of that information (comparison, combination, sorting, analysis) was largely separate from the filing system. As information storage moved progressively into digital form (whether for words, numbers or images), priority switched to the database concept, and as a consequence the handling of information has become much more creative. Using computer control, a database can be upgraded to an information system which not only provides storage and retrieval, but also offers a host of associated facilities. The key is the design of software that permits users to formulate their enquiries in a way that can be satisfied by the system. Questions can be asked which involve many manipulations before the data are presented: thus with a planning information system, for example, we might ask for a listing of all those electoral wards within which there had been an increase of population greater than 10 per cent during the 1970s coupled with a decrease in average socio-economic status, and in which more than 50 per cent of housing had a below average rateable value for the area concerned.

In such a case, the data can be assembled because they are all filed according to electoral ward. Still greater flexibility is achieved in the Geographical Information System (GIS) in which the organisation of data is referred to spatial co-ordinates so that any spatial information can be displayed in combination on a screen or plotter. Coupled with digital cartography and data derivation from satellite or aircraft remote sensing systems, this approach offers all the advantages of maps together with the enormous enhancement of easy updating and user definition of the exact form of information to be displayed at a given time. The combined potential of digital cartography, remote sensing and GIS represent one of the most obvious contributions of IT to geography.

Some interim conclusions – what role for the geographer now?

Many of the trends discussed above have unavoidable overtones of the scientific ideals of the 1960s and 1970s, yet in their power and pragmatism pose something of a challenge to some subsequent non-scientific or anti-scientific shifts in philosophy. Whilst to some they may represent a dangerous regression from the values of the 1980s, they cannot be rejected simply on the grounds of intellectual poverty. In the first instance, the benefits may be most readily conceded by the physical geographer simply because at a facile level there seems to be a closer association between data, information handling and the positivist, rationalist or empiricist framework – but the advantages are not limited to the physical world, nor is that where their greatest potential lies.

As IT comes progressively to infiltrate the society, economy and politics of the western world, it can hardly fail to find a place (however uncomfortable) in the study of society, economy and politics. IT has obvious links with empiricism and positivism, but it is by no means unsuited to other philosophies such as realism. Once again we are brought face to face with the claim that much of the human realm may indeed be amenable to information-based study, but even if IT is not to be a technique of investigation or management, then at least its impact on society must be a fascinating object of geographical study.

The society-exploring potential of IT is excitingly pioneered in the BBC's 'Domesday Project', using a combination of software-controlled videodisc and microcomputer data handling to provide a fascinating exploration of British society in the 1980s through maps, photographs, images, text and digital data. It is not the mere availability of this information that renders 'Domesday' such a dazzling stepping stone, but rather the wealth of opportunities to sequence, combine and manipulate that information so as to create new worlds as well as merely recording an existing one. It follows that the availability of the Domesday videodiscs, and their many successors, will probably influence both education and lay perception, so that as well as exploring society IT will be influencing (or even manipulating) it. Manifestly, IT is a part of, not apart from, the world that we study – thus yielding a multidimensional relationship between study, studied and student that is reflected at a higher level in the function of geography itself.

In a still more pragmatic context, the analytical and communicative capabilities that are offered by IT may well provide such an irresistible temptation to the researcher at every level that the kinds of questions asked by geographers will again change to match the kinds of answers that have become accessible – as has happened in several recent 'revolutions'. This route to philosophy (defining means of producing answers, adopting questions appropriate to the answers, and then moulding a philosophy to encompass the questions) may seem to have a playful other-worldliness, but it is in fact a very real facet of the academic world more often than many would-be free-thinking intellectuals might care to admit. Whatever the motivation for change, its potential implications appear far-reaching even in terms of the simple enhancements of knowledge already discussed. Nevertheless, to further the evaluation it is clearly necessary to summarise both the power of IT and the price that must be paid for that power. Only then can a provisional balance sheet be drawn up.

POWER FROM INFORMATION

The potential power of IT in geography can be considered in the academic, management and planning contexts. It has been stressed that the combined information acquisition and data handling abilities of IT offer a real possibility of enhanced academic problem identification and explanation in all those fields of geography (qualitative or quantitative; subjective or objective; human or physical) in which these intellectual processes can be founded on the application of logic to a set of observations. Furthermore, the greatly improved modelling of many real-world phenomena offered by IT permits a considerable measure of scenario evaluation through which the impact of chosen values, goals or ethics might be effectively assessed, thereby extending its application well beyond the bounds of 'scientific' geography – whether human or physical. Thus far the primary practical limitations of IT could be seen as lying in the cost and volume of information, and its most significant theoretical limitation is probably an inability to contribute significantly to the examination of those phenomena which provide no observable manifestation or surrogate, either in themselves or in their impact on the world.

Some geographers have questioned empiricism on the grounds that important phenomena of human behaviour, motivation and aspiration are difficult to handle within such a framework. Such a viewpoint might represent a constraint on the scope of IT, though the opportunity for applying empirical methods and techniques even within a non-empiricist philosophy loosens this restriction. For many branches of geography, however, the prospect of improved description brought by IT carries with it a greatly increased possibility of explanation and prediction, and on this potential alone the academic importance of IT is self-evident. This merit is substantially reinforced by the power of IT to reveal previously inaccessible phenomena through new sensors, new spatial and temporal scales of observation, and new data recording systems and new opportunities for creative handling of information so as to reveal its inherent patterns.

The management and economic power of IT is easier to define in theory but more difficult to establish in practice. Management and planning decisions are based upon information concerning the present situation and its future status under the operation of given constraints, the whole context being adjusted for unpredictable fluctuations of any of the components. This combination of analysis and simulation is ideally suited to IT, and its merits are as great whether the final decision is to be a personal evaluation (the executive and planner processing information through their own powers of judgement), or an automated management system (for example, the horticulturalist's automatic environmental control system for a greenhouse, or the water manager's automated flood control system). In both contexts, IT is the framework through which the management information is gathered, accessed, analysed, interpreted and used as a basis for an informed decision. The more complex the situation faced, the greater is the role of IT in keeping the data up to date and in facilitating the combination of the widest range of information types within the most sophisticated model.

This clearly defined set of management needs provides an apparently obvious application for IT, but in practice the achievement of this potential is far from assured. In addition to personal conservatism, the manager brings to the problem the reality that success is a requirement, not a luxury. Whilst the academic can afford to experiment in order to test effectiveness, the manager can rarely afford to adopt methodologies that carry substantial risk additional to that already inherent in the decision-making system. At the same time, the new technique will be expected to move rapidly to become profitable, there being only very limited flexibility to improve the quality of decisions if the price is a disproportionate increase in the cost of decision-making. The point of change between businesses and services being unable to afford to adopt IT and their being unable to afford *not* to do so lay in most cases within the decade 1975–1985 in advanced western economies. In the Third World the same threshold may lie well in the future.

The political value of information cannot be over-emphasised, whether in terms of internal or international politics. At the most obvious level, the military backdrop to the development of IT is unavoidable. In part this reflects exclusively military/security applications of such techniques, but also transgresses into the hazy interface between military and civilian roles typified until recently by the mapping activities of the Ordnance Survey in Britain or the river and coastal management by the US Army Corps of Engineers. Civilian uses may ultimately dominate, but at present they are a spin-off. It would be misleading, however, to limit a political review of IT to the military sector, since the politico-economic implications are as far-reaching.

Satellite-based operational systems to predict global crop yields could be regarded as an altruistic mechanism for ensuring the readiness of necessary aid programmes, but could equally be seen as a foundation for less beneficial activities relating to price fixing or the political imposition of economic pressure on a country or institution in need. If both local and global politics draw closely on information sources, then both local and global geography must respond to the formats within which that information is acquired and processed. Should the geographer wish to participate in this process, then mastery of IT will be a prerequisite.

Although the point has repeatedly been made that information can only be used within a framework of social or political targets, some defined economically and others environmentally, even the above brief review of the power of IT is sufficient to confirm its potential importance. Thus, whilst it is possible to theorise that the heart of geography lies in the ethic that it generates, it can alternatively be suggested that a more practical target lies in the growing symbiosis of information and decision, with its tantalising prospect of an employable decision-making role for the geographer. It is here, if anywhere, that we will find the real power of IT, but however convincing that supposition might be, we are still entitled to question whether the price is justified.

WHAT PRICE POWER?

Whilst IT undoubtedly has much to offer the geographer, its benefits are neither free nor cheap. Indeed, even the economic cost alone may initially seem wholly unacceptable, since the digital data for a map or a remotely sensed image may cost a thousand times more than the corresponding printed map. The implication is simple: knowledge is a very valuable commodity. It is expensive and often difficult to produce, but highly profitable to the user, and therefore commands a high market price. Whilst the amateur geographer finds these prices intolerable, and the professional academic regards them as a significant barrier to use, it is increasingly the case that to major users such as governments, the military, services, public utilities and engineers they are highly cost-effective. The uses to which such data can be put now generate sufficient profit, or save sufficient expense, to justify the cost. An uncomfortable period of adjustment will be necessary before the education system can cope with these new demands, and it may well be that a clearer distinction will have to be drawn between the techniques appropriate at secondary and higher education levels – or even between institutions at a given level. Nevertheless, the increasing willingness of the user to pay for information can only benefit those geographers who seek a career in information provision and application.

Whilst it is attractive to regard information as a valuable new product and export, the related disadvantages should not be overlooked. I have already mentioned the data volume threshold, and it must be recognised that an increasing proportion of the huge quantity of data now being collected is destined never to be used. It may be that a measure of data redundancy is a necessary part of any information-based society and economy, but uncontrolled over-production is unlikely to be advantageous to either user or producer. The problem of unused information is not new to geographers (as any librarian or map curator will verify), but that offers no comfort. Most worrying, perhaps, is the fact that whilst little-used books and maps can in theory be accessed at any time in the future, digital data are stored in a format which not only decays physically more rapidly than properly-stored paper, but also becomes incompatible with the current hardware necessary to display or use it. Is the information race a mutant cuckoo in the technologist's nest, consuming an increasing proportion of the available resources but ordained to become extinct before it learns to fly?

Perhaps an even greater concern should be the extent to which a new global inequality is emerging between nations with ready access to information systems (and their associated advantages) and those without. It takes only the most rudimentary geographical awareness to appreciate that it is the currently under-privileged societies and sections of societies that stand least chance of exploiting IT's potential. The new industrial revolution is set to reinforce global hierarchies just as firmly as previous revolutions, and if less-developed groups seek to participate in IT use, then they become vulnerable to covert control by those few nations and companies that hold the keys to information and the computational hardware required in order to employ it. The technological dilemma is complete. Should the crew of a drifting boat accept the offer of an outboard motor, or reject it as making them too dependent on the suppliers of petrol and spare parts, or simply ask for a set of oars instead? There is a genuine possibility that IT could be used to solve global problems, but real effort and insight will be required to prevent solution turning into exploitation.

Nevertheless, to many geographers the greatest flaw in the IT promise lies neither in its economic cost nor in its socio-political inequalities. Technology suggests an over-reliance on empiricist approaches which appears to be fundamentally at variance with several philosophical trends of the 1970s and 1980s. This association is, of course, misleading – but it remains a powerful totem of resistance. It has been noted already, and will be reinforced later, that there is no inherent conflict between logic-based information systems and idealism. Neither is there any predetermined preference of IT to physical phenomena or instrumental data collection. Information remains but a stepping stone towards knowledge, which is itself an important precursor to understanding. As long as geographers are content with amateur status (with no derogatory overtones), they are free to reject any technique or methodology: indeed, they are free to prefer philosophising completely unbridled by the constraints of either methodology or information. However, if they aspire to professionalism (whether academic or not), they take a great risk in rejecting major trends in society and in the ways in which society may be studied and managed.

A PROVISIONAL BALANCE SHEET

Perhaps the most attractive conclusion is to dismiss the whole IT edifice as unfounded speculation and get back to the Third World, the inner city and the Environmental Impact Statement in the hope that these will accord us immunity from both information and technology. However, as we comfort ourselves that the geographer's life is quite complex enough without adding IT, we should perhaps pause to contemplate just how far-reaching are the proposed specifications for the fifth-generation computers. Simple number-crunching is now far behind us, and the micro-processor is seen as dominating logic and thus decision-making in an increasing proportion of fields. The design of computers is consciously mimicking brain processes, whilst growing familiarity with computers leads us to mimic them in structuring our thoughts and tasks. The convergence of people and machines can hardly fail to induce a rethinking of their inter-relationship as fundamental as that of the first industrial revolution. Whether or not actual artificial intelligence is a realistic prospect, the broad trends of IT are not science fiction themes but serious predictions, and developments as fundamental as these are unlikely to leave geography untouched.

The problem belongs to every facet of the educational spectrum. There is no reason why we should not welcome any resulting divergence between geography at school and in higher education. Even if schools in the immediate future play only a minor role in the technical adjustment to the IT revolution, they inevitably dominate the crucial formative role in developing attitudes and mental aptitudes. This type of future – heaven or hell according to personal taste – will certainly not replace all that we know and love in geography, but it may well lead in the 1990s to a substantial shift in emphasis. Even if a new philosophy fails to emerge, the pragmatic advantages of converging with trends in employment and research funding will not be lost on government and are likely to win converts amongst geographers.

This poses something of a challenge to those schools of thought which have pinned their faith on the suggestion that facts (an old term for information) should come very low down the list of philosophical and curricula priorities. Nevertheless, there is no intrinsic conflict between logic-based information systems and a concern for values (a new term for subjectivity and ethic) despite the fact that a superficial confrontation between these two interests seems likely. This need not worry us, since responsible conflict can be both academically and socially creative. As context and content change, so too must the relationship between the components of any subject. Thus, perhaps the greatest challenge now faced by many geographers is to convince themselves that it is worth going out actively to seek opportunities for change, rather than retreating behind the traditional defences of conservatism. New fields of study, understanding and application are being defined, and IT lies behind many of them. If they are not occupied by geographers in the very near future, then we may be sure that there will be other more adventurous spirits ready to step in and reap the benefits. Mere trend-following may suffocate true creativity, but when the trends are as strong and as richly varied as IT they offer greater freedom in acceptance than in rejection. We end, as we started, with the conviction that information within a framework of logic is the basis of knowledge, that knowledge blended with empathy yields understanding, and that through understanding comes power – to be used by the geographer for good or ill.

FURTHER READING

Several publications have started to address the issues raised by introducing new information-handling techniques into the classroom. See in particular Curran P. and Wardley N. (1985) 'Remote sensing in secondary school geography: the place of Landsat MSS.', *Geography*, 70, pp. 237–240 and Midgely H. with Walker D. (1985) *Microcomputers in Geography Teaching* (London: Hutchinson).

But it is important not to confuse the use of new techniques in teaching with their professional use in remote sensing, resource management and the like. John Townshend's review of remote sensing, 'Remote Sensing – Global and Local Views' in *Horizons in Physical Geography* (Macmillan 1988) pp.62–85 gives an indication of these possibilities, and David Rhind's monthly column in *The Geographical Magazine* provides a thoroughly up-to-date commentary on cartographic information systems.

Perhaps the best introduction to the subject is through regular reading of any quality newspaper – particularly one with a financial/business focus, which will usually encompass both economic and environmental implications. The techniques of study, the associated hardware, the service industries growing up to fulfil the IT demand and – above all – the many applications of IT will all be discovered through this route.

1.2
Mathematical Models and Geographical Theory

Alan Wilson
University of Leeds

Alan Wilson is Professor of Urban and Regional Geography at the University of Leeds. His teaching and research interests are in the fields of geographical modelling and related aspects of planning. He is the author of many papers in technical journals and a series of articles in *The Times Higher Educational Supplement*. His latest book is *Mathematical Methods in Human Geography* (with R. J. Bennett).

INTRODUCTION

A long-established tradition within human geography is concerned with the *location* of activities and their associated infrastructures and with the *interactions* between locations. The focus of such a geographical study may be some subsystem of interest such as an industry, or the set of subsystems which constitute a 'place'. Such foci are shared with other social sciences but it is, I suggest, the study of locational and interactional phenomena which largely distinguishes geography (though some overlap will always remain). When we ask, therefore, what constitutes 'geographical theory', we can expect location theory and interaction theory to play a prominent part. The aim of this chapter is to show some of the dramatic advances which have occurred in this aspect of geographical theory in recent years, and to demonstrate how these advances rest on the development of mathematical modelling as a method in geography. Although there are some obvious difficulties in expounding these ideas in a brief essay, the main concepts can be communicated with a minimum of mathematics and the results of applying them can be clearly demonstrated.

One useful way to proceed is to relate the new to the old: to show how the theory which is based on mathematical modelling provides a powerful substitute for what is traditionally thought of and taught as geographical theory – what might be called 'classical' theory which still figures, relatively uncritically, in most texts. If I can demonstrate this progression then at least I will have communicated the main ideas and might even provide an incentive for you to acquire sufficient mathematical technique – which does not amount to very much! – to take the subject further.

It is perhaps also useful at the outset to briefly relate the use of mathematical modelling methods to the philosophical discussion by Ron Johnston in Chapter 1.3. Perhaps the main point to emphasise here is that these methods should not be crudely identified with 'natural science' or 'positivism' *per se*, as is sometimes mistakenly done. They are available to help to handle complexity in a variety of situations. Having made this general point, however, it is important to recognise their limitations. They have relatively little to offer in relation to individual behaviour directly, so that, for example, the location and flow phenomena studied in this chapter are macro-scale rather than micro-scale. Furthermore, many examples can – and perhaps should – be criticised for their over-reliance on neo-classical economic theory: that is, for their representation of a world of perfect competition, rationality and equilibrium. But it is still possible to build models which can contribute to an exposition grounded in alternative theorems provided by (for example) historical materialism or critical theory. So, as geographical theory and its philosophical foundations are extended and developed, the methods of mathematical modelling will continue to be relevant – sometimes crucially.

My argument proceeds through six stages. First, I examine more formally the role and scope of location and interaction theory within geography. Secondly, I review briefly a range of 'classical' contributions in these areas. Thirdly, I explore the limitations of each of these cases. Fourthly, I examine what a mathematical methodology can offer and fifthly, I outline a range of results which can be achieved using these ideas. Finally, I review some of the implications of my argument for geographical teaching and research.

LOCATION AND INTERACTION IN GEOGRAPHICAL THEORY

In broad outline, the main subsystems of human geography might be taken as concerned with

- agriculture
- industry
- residential location and housing
- the provision and use of services
- transport flows and systems

and these can be combined together to form

- urban or regional systems

A 'region' here is taken as any areal unit at a scale larger than the 'urban'. Geographical studies may thus be intra-urban or inter-urban, intra-regional or inter-regional. The subsystems are strongly related to each other, both functionally and through the competition for land at different locations and, ultimately, a theory of the comprehensive urban or regional system must be the goal. Even so, considerable insight can be obtained from subsystem analyses, and each of the subsystems has a distinctive character.

In my view, the task of location theory for each of these subsystems is twofold: to be able to give an account of structures and patterns at each point in time, and to be able to explain change and so relate structures to the processes of change. In short, there is a static theory and a dynamic theory, the former, ideally, arising as a by-product of the latter. In each case also, different kinds of elements need to be identified and made explicit in the theory. Agricultural location theory is concerned with the patterns of different kinds of agricultural land use, residential location with different kinds of houses and the different kinds of people who live in them. For the industrial and service systems, further subsystems can be identified, but in all cases, the definitions of 'types' and 'categories' will be an important part of theory building.

The transport subsystem is a special case. Transport flows link the other subsystems: the journey to work linking residential and economic activity patterns; consumers connected to services; inter-industry linkages; and so on. Transport can be seen, therefore, as being determined by locational patterns. But there is a converse to this: it is often the nature of interaction which determines the structure of these patterns. There is, then, an interplay which should be at the heart of geographical theory.

THE CONTRIBUTION OF THE 'CLASSICAL' THEORISTS

It provides some interesting insights to ground the argument in terms of classical theory. There are two main reasons for this. First, these contributions are usually presented relatively uncritically in geographical texts and we need to develop a better understanding of them. Secondly, they provide one end of a bridge linking the old theory to the new. A task which has been neglected in the past is the building of this bridge, to show how theory based on mathematical modelling is not simply something new in geography, but that it can replace and be visibly more effective than the old statistical methods. As a first step to building this bridge, I want to review briefly but critically a selection of classical contributions which reflect the main subsystems I identified earlier. I will take in turn von Thünen, Weber,

Burgess and Hoyt and Reilly. In each case, only the barest outline will be given because the approaches are, by now, all well known. It should also be emphasised that I focus here on typical 'textbook' presentations of these authors. Deeper studies of the original texts repay the effort, not least because many of the authors anticipated the criticisms which are now often levelled at them.[1]

Agriculture Von Thünen's lasting contribution will turn out to be the introduction of 'bid rent' as a concept: the amount per unit of land a farmer is prepared to bid at a location for the production of a particular crop. Agricultural land use is then related to the sale of products at a single market and the maximisation of bid rents – essentially what can be recouped from selling at the market less the costs, including the cost of getting the product to the market – produces the familiar ring pattern indicated in Figure 1.2.1.

Industrial location Weber's work is usually exemplified by the task of optimally locating a single firm in relation to two sources of material inputs and, again, a single market. The optimum location is at the point which minimises transport costs and can be at one of the vertices of the triangle or at a point within the triangle (see Figure 1.2.2) depending on the relative weights and transport costs of the inputs and outputs.

Residential location Burgess worked with an ecological 'invasion and succession' hypothesis to produce a ring pattern of residential location, which was modified by Hoyt to introduce sectoral variation. Typical results are those shown in Figure 1.2.3. An alternative mode of generating ring patterns within the classical theoretical tradition is also provided by Alonso's use of von Thünen's bid rent concept.

Services As an example of the geographical analysis of service location, consider Reilly's use of gravity model hypothesis to distinguish between the market areas of centres at two places (see Figure 1.2.4). This is interesting in that it is a potentially 'modern' approach as I will show shortly, where concepts are deployed in a classical way.

Settlement patterns In principle, it should be possible to combine the different kinds of elements introduced above to generate an analytical portrait of settlement patterns. As an example of this, take Christaller's well-known central place theory (Figure 1.2.5). These settlement structures are based on the assumption of a uniform distribution of rural population and transport facilities, and assumptions about the hierarchical nature of service provision which leads to the nested pattern of villages and towns of different sizes.

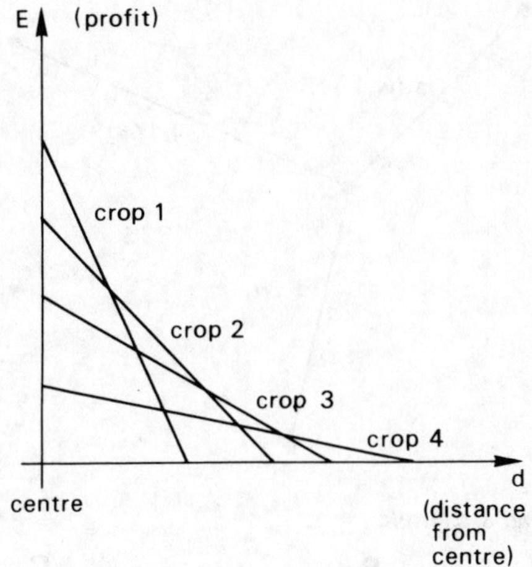

FIGURE 1.2.1 (a) *The argument for von Thünen's rings*

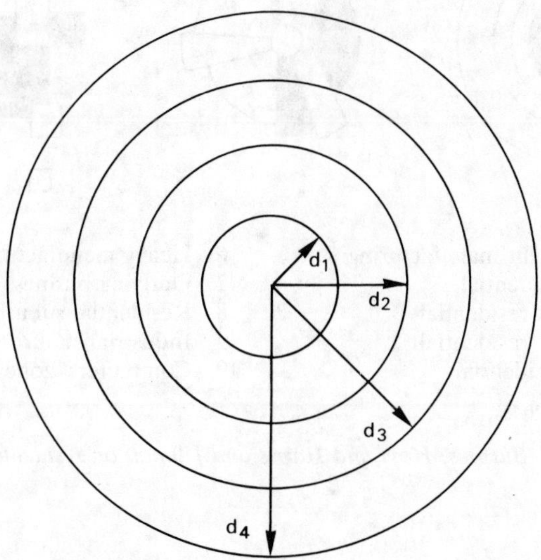

FIGURE 1.2.1 (b) *Von Thünen's rings*

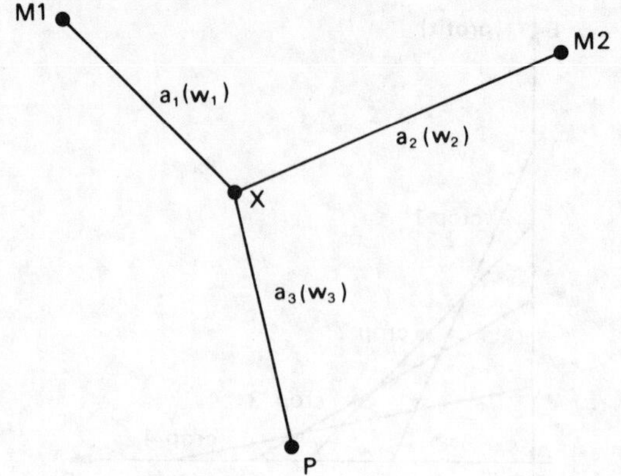

FIGURE 1.2.2 *Weber's triangle*

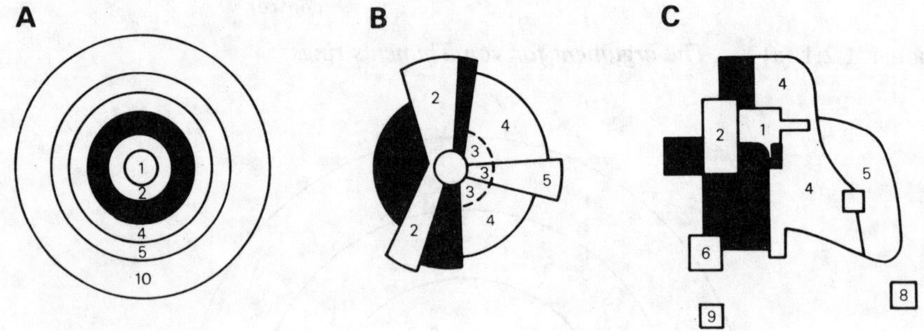

1 CBD
2 Wholesale Light manufacturing
Low-class residential
3 Medium-class residential
4 Medium-class residential
5 High-class residential
6 Heavy manufacturing
7 Outlying business
8 Residential suburb
9 Industrial suburb
10 Commuters' zone

SOURCE: Pred (1964)

FIGURE 1.2.3 *Burgess, Hoyt and Harris and Ullman on residential patterns*

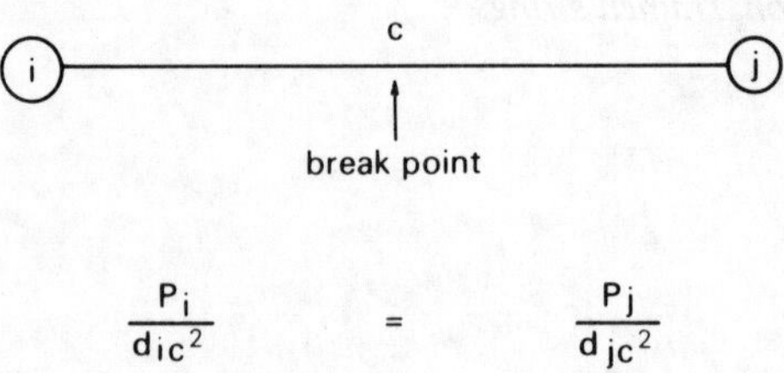

$$\frac{P_i}{d_{ic}^2} = \frac{P_j}{d_{jc}^2}$$

FIGURE 1.2.4 *Reilly and the break point between two markets*

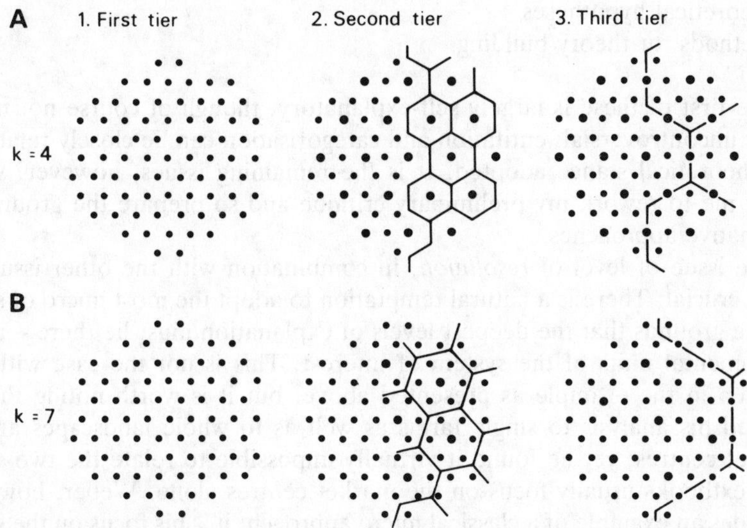

SOURCE: Haggett, Cliff and Frey (1977)

FIGURE 1.2.5 *Building up structure in Christaller's central place theory*

THE LIMITATIONS OF THE CLASSICAL THEORISTS

It is intuitively obvious that the examples I have considered are limited in their scope, but we need to be more explicit about the nature of these limitations. In the von Thünen case the main limitation is the restriction to a single market. A more realistic model would have to incorporate a spatial distribution of markets which would correspondingly complicate the land use pattern. Weber's argument is similarly limited by being restricted to a single firm. It could be argued that what is interesting is the effect of the competition of several firms both in relation to (larger numbers of) both materials sources and markets. The Burgess and Hoyt models are theoretically limited and essentially descriptive. Reilly suffers from only being able to demarcate market areas between pairs of service centres rather than a whole system (and also failing to recognise that, in reality, market areas overlap). The first of these problems is overcome by Christaller, but only at the price of developing an overly rigid system which it is difficult to 'relax' to represent reality.

I now want to set this critique in a more general context. In any attempt at analytical theory building, six kinds of issues have to be dealt with:

- identification of the elements of the object of study
- definition of a coherent *system* of interest ('entitation')
- level of resolution (or scale)
- spatial representation
- partial or comprehensive

- theoretical hypotheses
- methods for theory building

The first of these is largely self-explanatory, though of course not necessarily uncontroversial: entitation and categorisation can be closely related to the theoretical stance adopted. It is the remaining issues, however, which allow me to rework my preliminary critique and so prepare the ground for alternative approaches.

The issue of level of *resolution*, in combination with the other issues, is often crucial. There is a natural temptation to adopt the most micro of scales on the grounds that the deepest levels of explanation must lie there – in the fundamental units of the system of interest. This is not the case with von Thünen in the example as presented above, but it is worth noting that he applied his analysis to single farms as well as to whole landscapes around market centres; yet he found it virtually impossible to relate the two scales and textbooks usually focus on the market centres alone. Weber, however, provides an example of a classical micro approach: it is his focus on the single firm and the analytical difficulties of coping even with two firms in competition, let alone many (cf. Hotelling's two ice-cream sellers on a linear beach) which prevents progress towards more realistic problems. The rest of the examples operate at relatively coarse scales.

The issue of spatial *representation* also turns out to be crucial. In all the examples I have presented space is treated as continuous: that is, points or boundaries are located at exact coordinates in a Cartesian space. At first sight this also seems a natural assumption, offering maximum precision. But it turns out that the mathematical techniques involved in handling continuous space are more difficult than the alternative – and in many cases even intractable. The alternative is a discrete representation of location: that is, space is divided into zones, either through a grid system of appropriate scale or through the use of units for which data are available such as local authority wards. There is a loss of resolution in this, of course, because location is specified only up to a zone (and 'point' activities are probably assumed to be located at zone centroids); but powerful mathematical techniques are then available to solve problems which limit the classical examples. The deployment of these techniques probably involves a loss of resolution in another sense too: individual units of a type – people or firms, say – have to be lumped together as totals for each zone and processes of competition and the like are represented as processes between these elements rather than between the micro units. Even so, for many purposes, the benefits of analytical tractability outweigh the disadvantages.

Decisions on levels of resolution and spatial representation clear the decks for more ambitious approaches on the remaining three dimensions. It is possible to be more comprehensive; theory can be more ambitious – some of the more restrictive assumptions, such as all employment being at the centre of a city, can be avoided; appropriate methods can be found for the implementation of the theory for the building of more realistic models.

MATHEMATICAL MODELS AND BETTER THEORY

The range of methods

The following list provides illustrations of the kinds of methods which are available for geographical model building:

- spatial interaction models and associated location models
- account-based models
- optimisation and programming models
- network analysis
- dynamical locational analysis

Elements of these methods often have to be combined for a particular geographical problem. Here, however, I focus on the first and last items on the list because they provide the bases for improving the classical examples which I used for illustration.

Spatial interaction and location

Consider a spatial system in which zones are numbered consecutively 1, 2, 3, . . . and typical zones can be conveniently taken as i and j. Let T_{ij} then be a flow from i to j – say of people to work, money to shops or crops to markets. It is also convenient to define the total outflow from zone i, which I call O_i and the total inflow to each zone j which we call D_j.

One of the two crucial contributions of mathematical modelling to the analysis of the kinds of systems we have been discussing is in the estimation of spatial interaction flows, T_{ij}. Each flow is a (decreasing) function of distance or cost between i and j, written c_{ij}; and of properties associated with each 'end' of the flow, at i and j. In this last respect, there are choices. When one of the totals O_i and D_j is known, then it can be used in the model. When such a total is not available then another variable, appropriate to the theory for the particular subsystem, has to be substituted. In the case of retailing, for example, the O_i would be known, D_j unknown; at the j-end, I could then use (say) W_j as the amount of retail floorspace at j as a measure of the attractiveness of j. That model could then be written as

$$T_{ij} = A_i 0_i W_j^{\alpha_e - \beta c_{ij}} \quad \text{(Equation 1)}$$

and

$$A_i = 1/\sum_k W_k^{\alpha_e - \beta c_{ij}} \quad \text{(Equation 2)}$$

which has been calculated to ensure that

$$T_{i1} + T_{i2} + \ldots = \sum_j T_{ij} = 0_i \qquad \text{(Equation 3)}$$

The details of this are available elsewhere and are not central to the present argument. What is important is that this model can be used to predict the values of a *locational* variable from the postulated interaction variables:

$$D_j = T_{1j} + T_{2j} + T_{3j} + \ldots = \sum_i T_{ij} \qquad \text{(Equation 4)}$$

In the retailing example, for instance, if O_i is the amount of money being spent in a period by residents of zone i, then D_j is the set of total revenues attracted to each zone j *given* the floorspaces, W_j. Thus Equations 1, 2 and 4 constitute not only an interaction model, but also a locational model.

Application of spatial interaction concepts

An interaction model of some appropriate type is important for each of our examples. There is a locational prediction analogous to total retail sales in each case. Both flows and 'revenue' totals are predicted in relation to a set of *structural* variables analogous to the W_js. In all cases, it has to be assumed that a discrete-space representation is used, say a grid system for illustrative purposes. I can then consider for each example what the analogues of T_{ij}, O_i, D_j and W_j would be.

Agriculture I need a set of variables for each crop, k, say. Then O_i^k is the (assumed fixed) demand for crop k at market i; W_j^k is the amount of k produced at j; D_j^k is the revenue received at j for producing k; T_{ij}^k is the flow of k from each j to each i. Note as always with this formulation that there are no restrictions about numbers of markets or whatever.

Industry Let g be a superscript denoting a type of good and let m and n be the names of industrial sectors. Then let O_i^{mg} be the demand for g by sector m at i (that is, as an *input*) and let W_j^{ng} be the total produced in n at j (the *output*). D_j^{ng} is the revenue received for g in n at j. T_{ij}^{mng} is the flow.

Residential location and housing Let k now be an index denoting house type and w one denoting household type. The initial hypothesis here is that people are allocated to housing in relation to employment. Ultimately this needs to be modified and extended, though it will suffice for illustrative purposes. Then O_i^w will be the equivalent in household 'units' of the number of type-w-people working in i; W_j^k is the number of type k houses in j; D_j^k is the expenditure on type k housing at j; T_{ij}^{kw} is the 'flow'.

Services This was the example considered earlier, but I can usefully disaggregate by taking w again as household type and g as type of good to be bought (or service). Then O_i^w is the demand, W_j^g is a measure of supply and D_j^g the revenue attracted. T_{ij}^{wg} is the flow.

Transport flows Each of the interaction variables identified can be scaled into a number of trips for particular purposes: journey to work, journey to shop and so on. Hence, the interaction models can be used as the basis of transport flow models.

Comprehensive urban or regional system In each of the examples above, I have used, for immediate clarity, the notation used in the basic model – i.e. I have built on O_i, W_j, D_j and T_{ij}. In practice, a different set of letters is used to represent each subsystem and then it becomes possible to assemble the submodels into a comprehensive model. It can then easily be seen how such a system begins to represent the rich complexities of real systems. Postulate first a rudimentary settlement structure which is a system of agricultural markets. This will determine the pattern of agricultural land use and also the nature of the land use competition at the urban-rural fringe. Then postulate an initial job distribution within each city. This will determine the demand for goods and services by both people and organisations and will also generate 'new' households and housing. The 'shape' of the developing system will be determined in part by the form of the transport infrastructure.

It is clear even from a sketch that the comprehensive model is very complicated and that not only will resulting patterns depend on the theoretical components but also on the 'initial conditions' – in the above analysis, the initial postulates. The analytical task becomes one of predicting the *types* of structures which can result in a variety of different circumstances. It is to this second crucial model building task that I now turn.

Structure and dynamics

It turns out that the addition of a very simple hypothesis, together with some new mathematical methods for handling the complexities which result from it, provide a powerful *unified* theory, *applicable to each of the examples*. Let me illustrate the argument with the retail case. I took D_j as the revenue attracted to floorspace W_j at j. Now let C_j be the cost of supplying and running those facilities. The simplest notion of what C_j might be could be

$$C_j = k_j W_j \qquad \text{(Equation 5)}$$

for a set of constants, k_j; but much more realistic assumptions could be developed.

The key hypothesis can now be taken as: if D_j exceeds C_j, then W_j grows; if vice versa, W_j declines. At equilibrium, of course, this implies

$$D_j = C_j \qquad \text{(Equation 6)}$$

To follow the retail example through, recall Equation 4 for D_j and then Equation 7 for T_{ij}. I can also use Equation 5 for C_j. Substitutions then give:

$$\sum_i T_{ij} = k_j W_j \qquad \text{(Equation 7)}$$

which is (substituting for A_i from Equation 2 in the T_{ij} equation)

$$\sum \frac{0_i W_j^{\alpha_e} - \beta c_{ij}}{\sum_k W_k^{\alpha_e} - \beta c_{ik}} = k_j W_j \qquad \text{(Equation 8)}$$

This set of equations is presented here so that the principles of the methodology can be drawn out. Again, the details of the analysis are available elsewhere. A number of observations can be made. The set of equations numbered 8 are simultaneous equations in W_j, $j = 1, 2, \ldots N$, where N is the number of zones. This means that the hypothesis (Equation 6) together with the underlying spatial interaction models lead us to a model – the set of equations (8) – which represents the *structure* of the retailing system, the set of W_js. It can fairly be commented that the system is unlikely to be in equilibrium; but then we can return to the main hypothesis, preceding Equation 6, and construct a dynamic model from that. Here, we restrict ourselves to the equilibrium model – purely for illustrative purposes – and look at some more features of the model.

As a preliminary, we need to examine the roles of parameters like α and β. They stem from the spatial interaction model hypothesis. α gives an indication of the importance of facility size for the user: the larger it is, the larger should be the shopping centre size. β represents ease of travel: the larger it is, the more difficult travel is, and the shorter average trip lengths will be. There are useful 'behavioural' features to build into the model. It can now be seen that the equations numbered 8 are *non linear* simultaneous equations and in general cannot be solved analytically – only by numerical methods. It turns out that these features – nonlinearity and interdependence – guarantee the existence of bifurcation: in other words, there will be critical values of parameters like α and β at which the nature of the solution – for the W_js – changes in a dramatic way.

A real-life example would be the rapid transition from corner-shop to supermarket retailing in the 1960s. What this means, then, more generally, is that this model can begin to replicate important geographical *structural changes* which have occurred in the past and may give us clues – which would then be important for planning purposes – about the future. However, one of the striking features of this analysis is that it shows explicitly the *vast multiplicity* of possible futures.

Finally, we reiterate the point that this methodology is free of restrictive assumptions – the A_I term in Equation 1 [and the equivalent $\Sigma W_k^{\alpha} e^{-\beta c}ik$ term in (8)] handles competition between facilities in different zones, for example.

APPLICATIONS IN DIFFERENT FIELDS OF GEOGRAPHICAL THEORY

It is simple in principle, though often difficult in practice, to apply these ideas to the kinds of examples I reviewed from the classical literature. The flow models have to be spelled out. This will provide an estimate for the D_js. But then quite a lot of effort has to be devoted to articulating the cost functions, C_j. Then, for each case, a model of the same general form as Equation 8 can be generated – though they are each very different in their particulars. Here it is perhaps useful to show what can be produced; more detailed discussions will be found in the texts listed in the Bibliography.

Figures 1.2.6–1.2.9 show results for agriculture, industry, residential location and housing and retailing in turn. In the first two cases it is possible to set the assumptions to reproduce, in the discrete zone format, the cases of von Thünen and Weber respectively as generated by the new models. It can then be reasonably claimed that they are special cases within the new formulation. All can, of course, be combined into a comprehensive model. Figure 1.2.9 provides an initial guide, in its focus on services, to the nature of the replacement for central place theory.

IMPLICATIONS FOR GEOGRAPHICAL TEACHING AND RESEARCH

As I said earlier, classical location theory and its derivatives are often presented rather uncritically in text books. One conclusion to draw, therefore, is that they can be set in a more modern and powerful theoretical framework and that this provides the basis for a more critical assessment. Secondly, for adequate use of these developments to be achieved in teaching, rudimentary mathematical techniques are needed for both teachers and students. It is also worth emphasising here the importance of the *mathematical* approach relative to the *statistical*. Mathematical models offer greater power – as illustrated by their ability to reproduce classical theories as special cases. Statistics remain relevant for the calibration and testing of these models, but *a purely statistical approach to theory and model-building is limited in scope and is also more directly connected to positivism*.

On the research front, an exciting programme is created by these ideas. A great variety of particular systems can be identified for which the modelling principles outlined above are relevant, and this leads both to further theoretical research – articulating models for new examples – and to empirical research, particularly historical work involving the search for critical bifurcation points. With the new perspectives offered, such research comes within reach of student projects as well as offering larger-scale and more difficult possibilities.

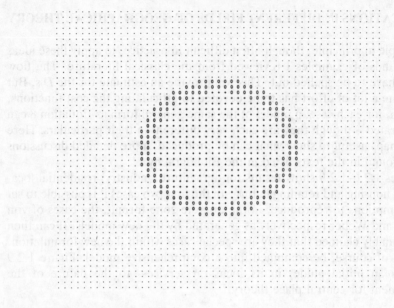

SOURCE: Wilson and Birkin (1984)

FIGURE 1.2.6 (a) *Von Thünen's rings produced with a discrete zone system*

SOURCE: ibid

FIGURE 1.2.6 (b) *Modification to show the effect of a transport corridor*

SOURCE: ibid

FIGURE 1.2.6 (c) *Land use with nine market centres and variable utility*

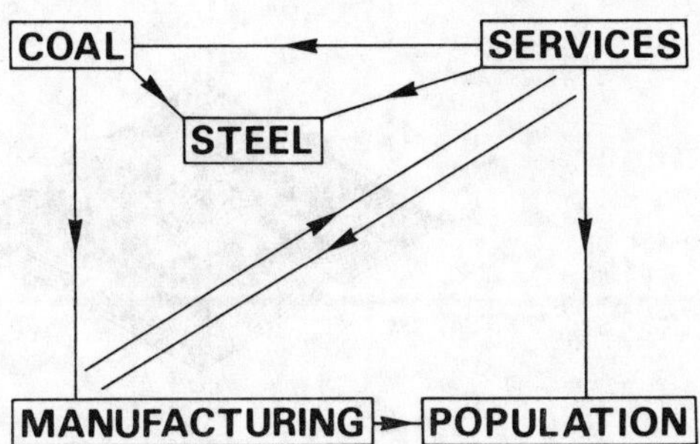

SOURCE: Birkin and Wilson (1983)

FIGURE 1.2.7 *Linkages in an illustrative five sector economy*

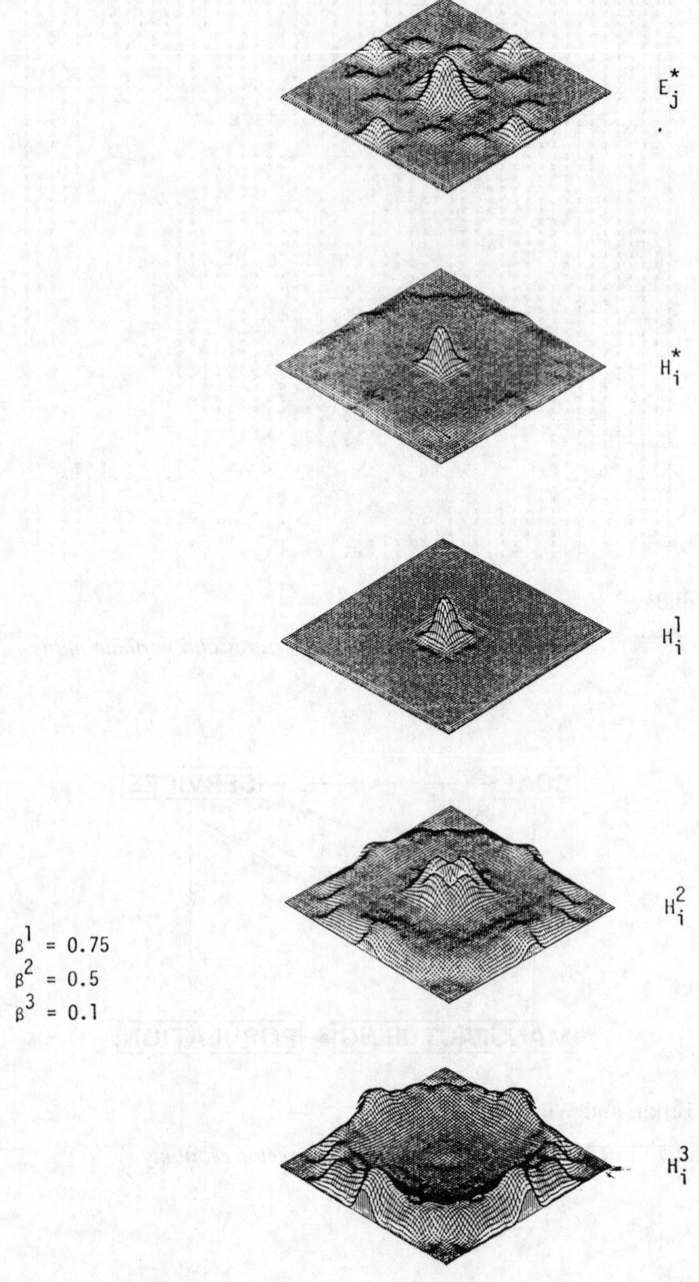

SOURCE: Clarke and Wilson (1983-A)

FIGURE 1.2.8 (a) *Housing patterns*

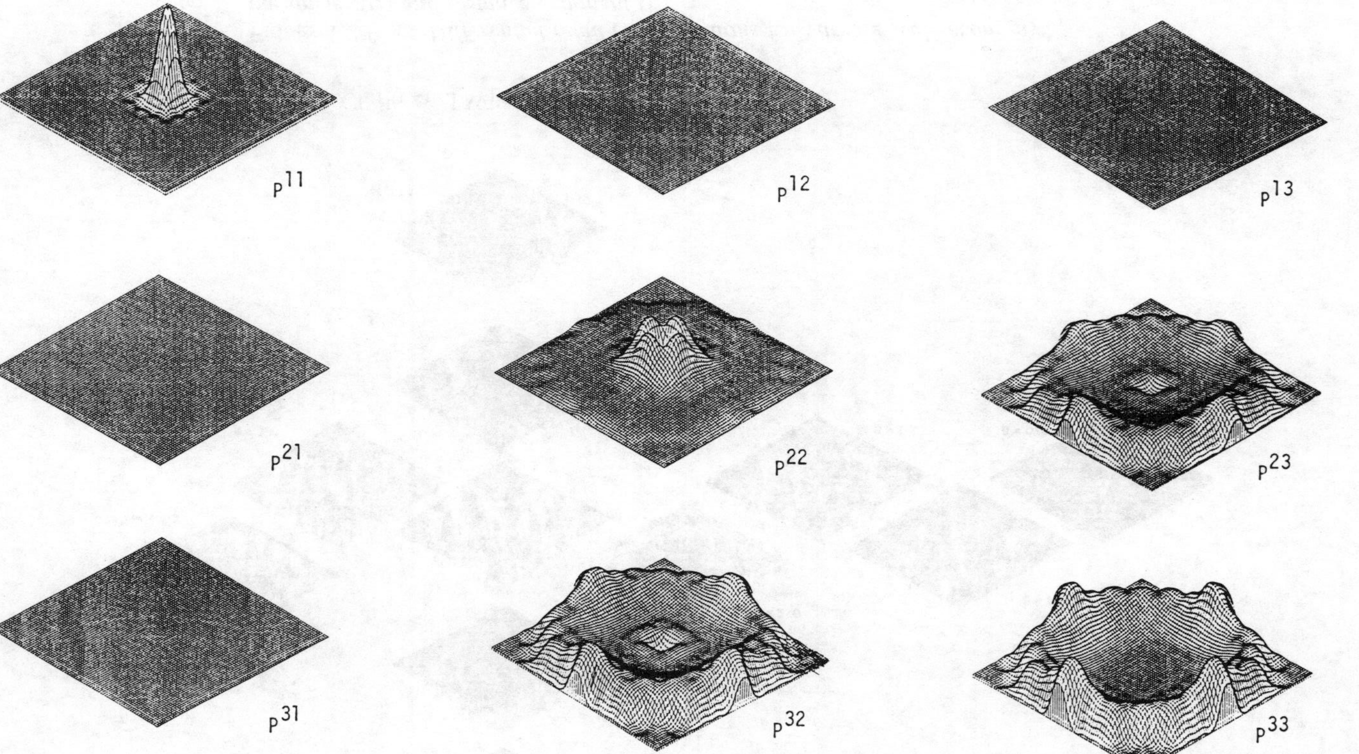

SOURCE: Clarke and Wilson (1983-A)

FIGURE 1.2.8 (b) *Residential location by income and house type*

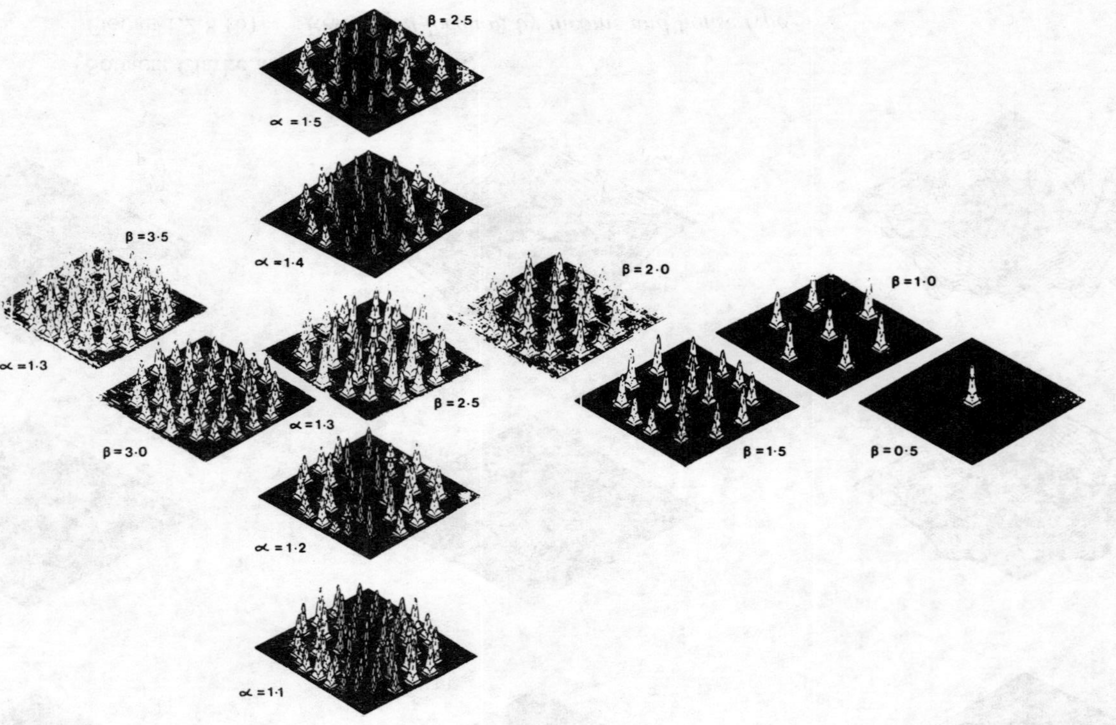

Source: Clarke and Wilson (1983-B)

Figure 1.2.9 *Differential retail configurations for varying scale economy parameter* (α) *and distance exponent* (β)

NOTES AND REFERENCES

1. For discussions of von Thünen, see Joern Barnbrock, 'Prolegomenon to a methodological debate on location theory: the case of von Thünen', *Antipode*, 6(1) (1974) pp.59–65; David Harvey, 'The spatial fix: Hegel, von Thünen and Marx', *Antipode* 13(3) (1981) pp.1–12. For an account of Weber, see Derek Gregory, 'Alfred Weber and location theory', in D. R. Stoddart (ed.) *Geography, Ideology and Social Concern* (Oxford: Basil Blackwell, 1981) pp.165–185. On the Chicago School, see J. N. Entrikin, 'Robert Park's human ecology and human geography', *Ann. Ass. Am. Geogr*, 70 (1980) pp.43–58; Peter Jackson and Susan Smith, *Exploring Social Geography* (London: George Allen & Unwin, 1984) pp.65–93.

FURTHER READING

For a more detailed account of the development of classical location theory into modern location theory, see Alan Wilson, 'The evolution of urban spatial structure: the evolution of theory' in R. J. Bennett (ed.) *European Progress in Spatial Analysis* (London: Pion, 1981) pp.201–215. An elementary introduction to the relevant mathematical techniques is provided by A. Wilson and M. Kirkby, *Mathematics for Geographers and Planners* (Oxford: Oxford University Press, 1980) (second edition). A fairly straightforward survey of applications is contained in A. Wilson, *Geography and the Environment: systems analytical methods* (Chichester: John Wiley, 1981), while a more advanced treatment is provided by A. Wilson and R. J. Bennett, *Mathematical Methods in Human Geography* (Chichester: John Wiley, 1985).

1.3
Philosophy, Ideology and Geography

R. J. Johnston
University of Sheffield

R. J. Johnston is Professor of Geography at the University of Sheffield. His main research interests are in electoral, political and urban geography: he is the author of *The Geography of English Politics: the 1983 General Election* and *Residential Segregation, the state and constitutional Conflict in American Urban Areas* He is a co-editor of *The Dictionary of Human Geography* and has also recently published *The Future of Geography* and *On Human Geography.*

KNOWLEDGE AND SOCIETY

Until the 1970s very few geographers would have paid any attention to philosophy and ideology in their academic education; nor would they have realised the importance of these areas of study to the practice of their discipline. Today few degree courses in geography are without a consideration of philosophy, although in most ideology probably still remains unconsidered. Yet without an appreciation of both, themselves the focus of much scholarly debate, an understanding of modern geography must be incomplete.

But why? *Philosophy* is the pursuit of wisdom and knowledge, terms which on the surface seem unproblematical. But what is knowledge? Geographers might answer – for example – that it is factual information about the earth as the home of humankind, structured so that we can account for the environment and how it is used. But is there only one way of structuring information or even consensus on what is information? Recent reflection and exploration have suggested to geographers that no single, unambiguous philosophy is available to them. There are several competing theories of knowledge, known as *epistemologies*. Associated with these are different definitions of what can be known (termed *ontologies*) and of means of acquiring information and knowledge (*methodologies*).

On what grounds do geographers evaluate and choose between philosophies? (Choice implies conscious decision-making, of course; many geographers have simply adopted a philosophy, perhaps implicit only, without prior evaluation.) According to many commentators, such choices are ideologically influenced. *Ideology* is defined in a variety of ways. As a positive term it expresses a world-view, a perspective on life and on the structure of society; negatively, it is used to describe a distorted view of reality, imposed upon some people in a society (usually a majority) because this leads them to accept the positive world-view of others (usually a minority). Within any society the prevailing ideology promotes the vested interests of the most powerful groups. No individual can be forced to accept it and some may personally, if not explicitly, oppose it. But a society is structured – through, for example, its educational institutions – to further that ideology, and attitudes, interests and goals are influenced accordingly. The positive world-view of the most powerful interests is thus promoted as the societal ideology, often phrased in nationalistic terms. In a capitalist society it is the ideology of those who benefit – the capitalists, or bourgeoisie – which is promoted thereby, according to some writers, obscuring the exploitative relationships between capital and labour which are fundamental to class societies. Such an ideology strongly influences the view – of society as a whole, of its powerful élites and of scholars themselves – of the desirable practice of an academic discipline such as geography.

It might be said that geography is the acquisition of knowledge about the world, and its application for the common good. (This, of course, is itself part of an ideology.) But, in the light of what I have just said, we must ask: what *kind* of knowledge? And what *is* the common good? The answer to the second question strongly influences that to the first. Your goals for society influence your definitions of knowledge and how it is to be used, and hence your philosophy as an academic, an educationalist, a trade unionist (the three are interdependent), or whatever. The remainder of this chapter outlines the philosophies which have attracted most attention from geographers in recent years, and illustrates their ideological origins.

A STARTING-POINT

In the nineteenth century geography developed as a descriptive discipline, providing accounts of the earth's environments and of the peoples who occupied them. It involved the collection (in the field and from secondary sources), the organisation and the dissemination of information. Its prime purpose was inventory and its implicit philosophy was *empiricism*, that is, all knowledge was based on experience, and so the correct methodology was observation and reportage. Accounts were accepted as factually correct (both those used by geographers and those produced by geographers) because of confidence in the reliability of the observer – a confidence which in many cases was bolstered because the observations could, if necessary, be independently checked.

Such a philosophy would appear problem-free; geographers were accurate, neutral observers, recorders and retailers of information. Or were they? Was their selection of the information to record, and the descriptive terms that they applied, entirely free of bias? With regard to the elements of the physical landscape the answer could, perhaps, be yes: the concepts applied, and the language used to present them, are universal – a beach is a beach and a river is a river – though there may be misinterpretations and phenomena may be encountered that are not readily classified according to existing concepts and criteria. But for elements of the societies the descriptive terms employed were rarely value-free and reflected – albeit unconsciously – the ideology of the observers/recorders. Thus geographers purveyed *particular types of information*, often according to the requirements of their sponsors: usually either to promote mercantile ambitions or to satisfy the curiosity of a society ideologically determined to prove itself superior to others.

Geographers chose a particular organising framework for the presentation of information. Unordered data are of little use and so a structure, based on popular scientific theories of the day (notably Darwinism), was used that seemingly identified a clear link between environment and culture. In its crudest form – environmental determinism – this was rapidly discredited, and so geographers retreated into a milder form – traditional regionalism. This did not explicitly portray people as governed by their environments, it presented the world as a set of distinct regions, characterised by their distinctive assemblages of physical and human features. Despite some debate, however, such regions were almost invariably defined by their physical features, and so even here the 'physical basis' of geography was tacitly accepted.[1]

FROM DESCRIPTION TO SCIENTIFIC EXPLANATION

Few people are satisfied with description alone; they want answers to the questions 'how?' and 'why?' as well as 'what?'. After World War Two many geographers found environmental determinist answers – whether explicit or implicit – profoundly unsatisfactory. And so began several decades of (still joint) involvement by human and physical geographers with another philosophy, *positivism* (which is in fact based on empiricism). Positivism assumes that the methods of the natural sciences can equally well be applied by the social sciences; the subject matter can be observed by the 'scientist', who stands outside the objects studied. The goal of observation is to describe, using a neutral and objective language, and hence to explain. The route to explanation involves two sorts of 'laws':

(a) To describe something to others it is necessary to use concepts that they accept. Terminology allocates the item being described to generally accepted classes – such as slope, town, precipitation and so on. (There is debate about the classes, of course, and whether a particular event meets the criteria for allocation to a certain class. Without agreement on the classification, however, explanation is impossible.) Thus positivism is based on classifications, or what we might call *membership laws*. Only when the membership laws are agreed can the search for explanations begin.

(b) Positivist science seeks explanations for the characteristics of the various classes of phenomena, defined in the membership laws, in terms of *functional laws*. These describe the invariant relationships among elements, either relational (if one property – x – is present, then another – y – will be also) or causal in the specific sense that if one condition – X – holds then a second – Y – will follow: i.e. Y is a function of X. The goal of positivist science is to identify these functional laws, thereby providing explanations of the observed world. For geographers, such an enterprise involved identifying co-locations in space (when X and Y are present in a place, then Z will follow; if C is present, it must have been preceded by B and A).

The scientific method associated with this search for functional laws combines theorising, model-construction and hypothesis-testing in a continuous looping procedure of organised speculation. It proceeds from what is known – a set of established laws embedded in a theory – through suggestions of what should be present by means of deduction, to tests of those suggestions. This may involve the construction of a model, a simplified presentation (usually mathematical, sometimes graphical, rarely verbal) of reality. A hypothesis is derived as a putative functional law. This hypothesis is then tested empirically, to establish the truth or falseness of the expected relationship.

Central to this procedure is the means for testing the hypothesis. Everything depends on application of a valid methodology, for acceptance by the scientific community of the results of a test is based on it being properly conducted. The test – not necessarily an experiment – must be replicable; to convince others of the validity of your results you must convice them that they were properly obtained.

Progress in this scientific procedure involves careful theorising, speculating and testing: it combines the rigours of logical deduction, careful experimentation and exact measurement with the occasional flash of insight. But what is an acceptable verification of a hypothesis? Can a hypothesis ever be verified? The answer to the latter question is, in fact, no, if the hypothesis refers to an unrestricted class of events – one can verify a restricted hypothesis (all the trees in this field are coniferous) but not an unrestricted one (all coniferous trees will die before they are 100 years old). The latter hypothesis can be falsified by a single observation: it can never be verified until the last tree dies. Thus any unrestricted functional law is tentative, and stands only until it is falsified. According to the followers of Sir Karl Popper, this means that scientific procedure should be directed towards critical tests of hypotheses: a perspective which is usually called *critical rationalism* (or 'falsificationism').

Even so, many geographers have adopted a philosophy of strict positivism ('verificationism') rather than critical rationalism and have organised their scientific work to verify hypotheses. For *physical geographers*, hypotheses are rationally-argued expectations regarding the explanations for their membership laws – their tentative accounts of the origins of hillslopes, for example, and of the nature of tropical cyclones. Testing those hypotheses has involved a great deal of measurement (some would claim too much measurement and too little theoretical preparation). Progress has been slow, albeit steady, for a variety of reasons.

The first reason for slow progress has been the great variety of processes – physical, chemical and biological – which operate in the environment and which must be appreciated, in combination as well as separately, if convincing explanations are to be produced.[2] The second reason is the difficulty of obtaining exact measurements. The third reason is the problem of evaluating the results. Both the verification and the falsification models are ideal types, suggesting that the test of the hypothesis produced a clear answer – it is either true or false. But correlations of 1.0 are extremely rare, for example, and 0.0 is not very common either. What does one make of a correlation of 0.3? Does it falsify the hypothesis?

The difficulties of answering this question are linked to a fourth problem, one which distinguishes environmental or field scientists (for example geologists, climatologists, geomorphologists) from laboratory or experimental scientists (for example physicists and chemists). Any field site comprises a large number of processes at work, not all of which can readily be held constant. Thus the physical geographer can rarely provide a complete empirical, as against a theoretical, explanation because the phenomena being examined are influenced by contingent factors, those neither under investigation nor held constant. Finally, the environment is ever-changing and not always slowly or (yet) predictably.[3] Thus any experiment may be unique in both space and time, making it difficult to integrate its results with those of others, conducted under slightly different circumstances.

A similar positivist-based approach to human geography was canvassed by some *human geographers* in the 1960s, arguing that the consistent operation of regular and repetitive processes should produce recognisable regularities in the spatial organisation and operation of societies. Although opposed by others, this approach came to dominate the research output of human geography by the early 1970s, and also replaced the more traditional offerings in many school sixth-form syllabuses, which focused in particular on several normative models of spatial organisation and behaviour, on the methodology of hypothesis-testing, and on the use of quantitative procedures.

The identification of membership and functional laws is central to this work. The former define the subject matter as classes of like phenomena – which may be places (fields, settlements, cities, regions, etc.) or types of people (defined by age, gender, wealth, occupation, race, etc.). The latter are either behavioural statements expressing regularities in the actions of individuals (for example about migration or shopping) or statements of the regular spatial forms that result from such actions (for example the von Thünen and Burgess models). Derivation of those laws combines deductive arguments from basic principles with inductive observations of behaviour patterns. The principle of least effort, for example, is an assumed behaviour pattern (people use the closest facility available, in order to minimise transport costs) from which models such as central place theory were deduced, providing hypotheses that, it was assumed, could be tested empirically.

As in physical geography, however, there are difficulties associated with the use of this approach in human geography because of the 'openness' of the systems being studied. It is almost impossible to devise 'experiments' that allow the testing of a hypothesis in a situation uncontaminated by the operation of many functional laws other than that being investigated, thereby making the results difficult to evaluate. It is difficult to distinguish the failure of an hypothesis from the failure of 'other things' to be 'equal' – the *ceteris paribus* clause which protects most models and which Hägerstrand mocks as the *ceteris absentibus* clause. Further, the interaction of the many assumed functional laws itself will generate complex behaviour patterns and spatial forms, creating problems for measurement and analysis (that is, the whole is more than the sum of the parts). The technical procedures employed have become extremely sophisticated as a result, as human geographers committed to this approach continue their search for the general functional laws of human behaviour (and the relevant membership laws underlying them) which specify regularities in spatial form, and which thereby provide both explanations for the past and present and predictions for the future.

ARE PHYSICAL AND HUMAN GEOGRAPHY COMMENSURATE?

According to the foregoing arguments, then, physical and human geography have a common philosophy. Their goals are the same: the statement of essential relationships which explain unique events as cases of general classes of such events. To do this, particular methods of reasoning and hypothesis-testing are applied, producing reliable results. Their success is measured by the ability of their functional relationships to predict – not necessary in the future, for a successful postdiction (an explanation of a pattern of the past) is also a mark of a scientific theory's validity; the goal is *explanation*, a rational account of how something came about through the operation of known laws.

Advocates of this approach recognise that this goal for scientific physical and human geography is a large one, and that approaching it is extremely difficult. Nevertheless, it is considered both viable and desirable, because by producing valid explanations geographers will also be producing useful knowledge. Against this, however, are arguments that challenge the validity of the positivist philosophy to human geography on two grounds.

THE PROBLEM OF MEMBERSHIP LAWS

The entire positivist approach is based on the belief that discrete classes of phenomena can be defined. For physical geography it is accepted that this is a reasonable starting-point; there may be debates about the boundaries of the classes, and the failure of some assumed functional laws to predict successfully will raise doubts as to the classifications used and the criteria for membership, but it is not usually doubted that, eventually, classes can be defined and functional laws identified. But whereas general features such as cuestas, temperate anti-cyclones and podsols may be definable, it has been argued that similar general features cannot be defined for human geography. The significant difference is that between *uniqueness* and *singularity*. A 'unique' phenomenon is something of which there is only one, but its characteristics can entirely be accounted for by general laws; it is a particular combination. A 'singular' phenomenon has features peculiar to it which cannot be accounted for by general laws. Thus, the Mississippi River is unique, but every aspect of it can be accounted for by general functional laws. I, on the other hand, am singular; there are aspects of me, it is contended, which cannot be accounted for by recourse to general laws.

Linked to this issue is a general debate within science between *reductionism* and *holism*. According to the 'reductionist' point of view, any phenomenon can be split into its component parts, the relevant functional laws identified, and the whole accounted for. Any scientific enterprise other than the most fundamental (atomic physics?) thus involves assembling the relevant laws to provide the needed explanation. According to the 'holistic' view, however, the assembly is insufficient to provide the full explanation; there are laws operating at the level of the whole which must be identified separately. (Some traditional regional geographers in fact adopted such a holistic view, arguing that the 'whole is greater than the sum of the parts' and that this whole is represented by the 'personality' of the region.) In many areas of science, including physical geography, the holistic view (as in the analysis of ecosystems) does not imply acceptance of the singularity position, because the wholes themselves are subject to both membership and functional laws. But to some human geographers it does.

The basis of the singularity argument in human geography is the assumed individuality of each person. I cannot be explained simply as a particular combination of living cells. I have independent powers of reason, and have emotional traits which set me apart from everybody else. I share many characteristics with others – sex, age, race, religion, occupation, etc. – some of which are inherited and others are adopted. These characterise me only in part because none of them determine what I am and what I do; I act as a thinking, feeling human being. Thus the only way to understand what I do is to understand me; to treat me as an exemplar of some category is to deny my individuality and to ignore my separate existence.

Because of my mental powers, I cannot be treated as akin to a machine that responds to particular stimuli in some ways, nor to part of a landscape which evolves in a predictable sequence. I govern my own actions, which I do within the environment that I create and not one that outside observers place me in. Thus what I deem a desirable residence may be an ugly building to others, what I identify as a pleasant way of spending my leisure time others may detest, and those with whom I chose to associate may be shunned by others. I exist in a phenomenal environment, a world of things and people, but I translate parts of it into a behavioural environment by giving those things and people meanings, and I ignore other parts. Since I *live* in the world that I create, my actions can only be understood in terms of that world; I cannot be represented as a case exemplar of some category of individuals, defined according to the meanings applied by the observer but not necessarily by me. Thus the positivist approach is entirely inappropriate, because my actions are singular and not unique. Physical geographers can apply the positivist philosophy, because they deal with a 'world of things'. Human geographers cannot, because they deal with a 'world of meanings'.

An approach which accepts the above argument for human geography is generally termed *humanistic geography*. It eschews explanation, and promotes instead the search for understanding. This involves an appreciation of the meanings that individuals give to the elements in their behavioural environments, and then conveying those meanings to a wider audience. The art and skill of interpretation, of conveying meanings, is known as *hermeneutics*, so that a double hermeneutic is involved in the humanistic geographer first deriving meanings from the subject being studied, and then transmitting those meanings to others. Meanings can be obtained directly from the individuals concerned: inter-personally, via *verstehen* (that is, obtained 'from within', empathetically); by presuppositionless observation (for example as a participant-observer); or by the sympathetic reading of texts. The last of these is the most widely used. For geographical work, the text need not be written; it could be another art form or the landscape itself, to the extent that the landscape is a repository of meanings reflecting the beliefs and feelings of its creators (see Cosgrove, in Chapter 2.2).

Humanistic work does not deny the possibility of individuals sharing behavioural environments, for the vast majority of people shape the worlds in which they live, in contact with, and as a consequence of their socialisation among others. Nor does it accept arguments that humanistic geography is 'merely' subjective: it deals with the subjectivity of others, but in an honest, open and objective manner. Further, it does not deny the possible use of quantitative procedures to describe aspects of the shared behavioural environment. But it does preclude theory, models, formal hypotheses and laws, all of which involve the imposition of categories and procedures determined by the observer rather than recovered from the observed. Whereas positivistic work involves analysis *of society*, therefore, humanistic work is analysis *in society*. Its purpose is to appreciate the meanings that underpin actions so that the latter might be understood. Humanistic geography does not describe a place from the outside but portrays what it is like to be a part of that place (see Eyles, Chapter 2.1).

THE PROBLEM OF FUNCTIONAL LAWS

The humanistic critique of positivist work focuses on its ahuman treatment of the individual actor, presenting her or him as an exemplar of a category. It proposes placing the individual centre stage. But some argue that the case is carried too far, because the humanistic approach separates the individual from the context in which personal theories and laws are developed, thereby giving the individual an autonomy which he or she does not possess.

We are able to think, to argue, to rationalise, to feel emotions and to assign meanings because we are provided genetically with the neural facilities for this. As structuralist psychologists such as Piaget have shown, however, our genetic inheritance provides us with those facilities, but the information that we process, and the context in which we process it, comes from our environment. Thus our mode of intellectual functioning provides us with the ability to assimilate material and to accomodate this with our experience of the world, but it doesn't experience and evaluate the world for us.

We experience the world, especially in our earlier years, through the guidance of others. We are socialised, in most cases by parents, kin, neighbours and schools, into accepting certain concepts and reacting to particular situations in given ways. In other words we assimilate a culture, components of which – such as language and religion – have a strong influence on us. We go on assimilating it as we grow older and as our range of contacts widens, though the rate of assimilation slows and we are more likely to close our minds to new material in later life. But culture is not something 'out there', separate from us. It is part of us and we are part of that culture; by practising a religion, for example, we contribute to its continuation as part of the socialisation environment; by using a language, we reproduce it and, maybe, alter it slightly by the creation of new words, new meanings for old words, and by making others obsolete. (Again see the chapters by Eyles in Chapter, 2.1 and Cosgrove in Chapter 2.2 for more detailed discussions).

But what if there are influences on the individual that cannot be observed, but which are nonetheless real – even though they may not be appreciated? The law of gravity influences us, but we cannot observe it, only its effects – which we may or may not interpret as the law of gravity. There is then a 'hidden' mechanism in the physical environment. Are there similar mechanisms that are human creations? Some theories of society, such as Marxism, claim that there are in the sense that they are not part of our everyday, taken-for-granted thinking (that is, they are obscured by *ideology*). These are the imperatives of a mode of production, the driving forces which propel it and which, if not properly fuelled by human actions, can malfunction and create social problems. In the capitalist mode of production, those forces are supposed to be essentially materialist: the dynamo of capitalism is the accumulation of wealth. If the imperatives of the dynamo are not met, it will slow down and social reproduction will be affected including, eventually, the ability of the system to survive (see also Lee, Chapter 2.4).

Neither the 'natural' law of gravity nor the human-made imperatives of a mode of production can be isolated and immediately observed, yet each – and many other such mechanisms – is influencing us daily. We interpret these mechanisms without necessarily knowing what they are, and those interpretations create and recreate our empirical world. So how might geographers study such influences? They can analyse the empirical world and find the outcomes; they can analyse the interpretations; and they can convey these analyses to others. But how might they analyse the hidden mechanisms (assuming that they accept their 'existence')?

THE EMPIRICAL, THE ACTUAL, AND THE REAL

A philosophy which offers insights into causal mechanism is *realism*, as developed by Bhaskar and others.[4] It is based on a three-tiered ontology which seeks to describe what Bhaskar calls 'the stratification of reality'. This is not as forbidding as it sounds. As Table 1.3.1 shows, the three tiers are:

- the *mechanisms* – the 'causal powers' of specific structures;
- the *events* – particular realisations of the mechanisms;
- the *experiences* – individual appreciations of the outcomes of the events.

The mechanisms cannot be directly apprehended or observed, since they exist in what is called, technically, the *real* domain or the 'underlying structure'; just as we cannot observe the law of gravity so we cannot observe the basic laws of capitalism. We can observe the events in the *actual* domain, however – whether they be the law of gravity operating in some way or individuals making decisions in the light of their interpretations of the laws of capitalism. Finally, we can experience the outcomes of the events in the *empirical* domain – just as Isaac Newton experienced a realisation (a falling apple) of the law of gravity and an unemployed miner in Durham experienced a realisation (closing an 'uneconomic' pit) of the National Coal Board's interpretation of the basic 'laws' of capitalism. The three domains are, of course, linked, in that any empirical experience can be traced through the actual to the real.

Realism is presented as a philosophy of both natural and social science, and so is relevant to both physical and human geography. Differences between

TABLE 1.3.1 *The ontologies and domains of realism**

	Domain		
Ontology	*Real*	*Actual*	*Empirical*
Mechanism	X		
Event	X	X	
Experience	X	X	X

* an X in the table indicates a valid area of study

SOURCE R. Bhaskar, *A Realist Theory of Science* (Brighton: Harvester Press, 1975) p.13.

the two reflect fundamental differences in the subject matter, but can, in principle, be embraced within the same philosophy. For physical geography, the mechanisms are described by the fundamental laws of physics and chemistry which govern all activity other than human (as far as we know only humans have large memories, the power of reasoning and the ability to transmit information other than via direct contact). These mechanisms cannot be observed directly. They exist as theoretical statements that are consistent with observations. The mechanisms are realised – put into operation – in environmental situations where they produce empirical outcomes.

So far, this portrayal of a realist science seems to differ but little from the positivist view: the main difference is that, according to the realist, empirical work – whether experimental or in the field – does not of itself provide explanations: observation must be integrated with theory. A body falling to earth at a predicted rate does not explain itself: the explanation lies in the theory used to make the prediction, with which the observation is consistent. If those predictions can be tested on many occasions, however, it appears that they are confirmed by a major body of evidence. But if the theory is correct, a single experiment is sufficient to validate it and, as critical rationalists argue, a single failure is sufficient to prove it wrong.

The problem for many sciences, and certainly the environmental sciences such as those embraced by physical geography, is that they deal with an apparently infinite number of observations, none of which is exactly the same as any other because of variations in the contingent environment. Thus in climatology very many mechanisms are realised in an even larger number of combinations (environmental situations). Experiments holding many of the mechanisms constant are neither possible nor valuable, the former because of the scale problem and the latter because it is the interactions of the mechanisms at the actual level which produce the empirical outcomes. Hence prediction is difficult. It may not be impossible, but the task of successfully integrating all of the needed information is immense. We can describe the outcomes, we know many of the mechanisms, and we know how some of the outcomes are produced in particular circumstances (warm air rising over a mountain range, for example). Hence we can link outcomes to mechanisms via the realisations, but only as probability statements because we are as yet unable to model successfully all of the interactions that take place.

The words 'as yet' are crucial in the last sentence; they imply that eventually successful prediction is possible even in such a complex, non-experimental environmental science as climatology – every event will be fully accounted for. For physical geographers, the widely-accepted goal of the scientist – successful prediction – is there to be achieved.

Is it the same with human geography? Perhaps so. Take, for example, spatial variations in the nature and intensity of productive activity and of the links between the many components of this. Attempts are being made to build models of how regional and national economies operate, as well as global models, and as they improve so we should be better able to explain spatial variations in, say, employment levels and rates of inflation, to predict future variations and to engineer changes in those variations by manipulating key components of the system. The systems are complex, more so perhaps than those studied by the environmental scientists, and our knowledge of them is currently very poor – hence the difficulties with national economic policies which are based on the manipulation of a few parameters of the system only, such as money supply. But the size of the problem should not prevent us from seeking the solution. Indeed, it should speed us to greater efforts, because of both the intrinsic nature of the challenge and the potential pay-offs.

But is the analogy between climatological and economic systems a valid one? According to realists it is not, for two major reasons. The first concerns the actual level. In the climatological system this involves the bringing together of two or more mechanisms in a particular combination, the production and consequences of which should be explainable in terms of general laws of composition (that is, holistic laws at the actual level). But in the economic system no such general laws are possible, because the realisation is undertaken by individual human agents who, as the humanistic perspective indicates, cannot be treated as if they were components in a machine. They are using their capabilities and powers to interpret the mechanisms and the context (the empirical world) in which they are to be activated; their own reasons are, in part, the causes. Such interpretations can be understood and appreciated, but not predicted. (The agents, or a large number of them, may respond similarly for a time, but this is not an inevitable reaction, and reflects particular circumstances. A particular outcome should not be interpreted, it is argued, as an inevitable outcome.)

The second reason concerns the domain of the real. In the climatological system the mechanisms are fixed in nature and, we believe, are unchangeable by human action. (We can counter the law of gravity, for example, but never remove it.) The basic mechanisms of any mode of production (feudalism, capitalism, socialism, etc.) are human creations, however, and as such are changeable by human action. Indeed, those mechanisms are continually being created and changed by human action. Every time we sell our labour power, purchase a commodity, make a profit on a product or whatever we are reproducing the mechanisms. But we may be changing them too, because the bargains that we drive, the institutions that we establish and the relationships that we develop with others can alter the basic mechanisms themselves. Under industrial capitalism in the nineteenth century, for example, a large number of independent entrepreneurs competed to make profits. The relative success of some led to the twentieth-century development of monopoly capitalism, in which a few large, linked enterprises (not entrepreneurs) collude over the distribution of market shares, aided by an increasingly interventionist state. This is a development that can be appreciated as a rational outcome – one which makes 'sense' – but it was not inevitable and hence not predictable. Furthermore, the developments have differed from place to place, indicating not only that they are not inevitable but also that the processes of capitalist reproduction are place-particular. Geography matters, for the world that we interpret is spatially and temporally circumscribed into regions.

Putting these two reasons together, the practice of social science then seems, from the realist perspective, a very different enterprise from that of a physical science despite the similarities between them. In both, the epistemology defines knowledge as an explanation of the empirical through comprehension of how mechanisms are put into operation; the success of an explanation is judged by the logic of the links, not by the number of times the expected result is observed. In both, too, a three-tiered ontology is defined, but only an epistemology that combines all three levels of knowing is judged valuable. *But whereas natural scientific realism deals with fixed mechanisms and events, in social scientific realism both are human creations and hence changeable.*

The differences are illustrated in Figure 1.3.1. In physical geography there is a unidirectional link between the real and the actual. The link between the actual and the empirical is bi-directional, because the agents can also influence the mechanisms. In addition, there are two further links – interpretations. Agents are not influenced directly by the mechanisms and by the empirical world (that is, the phenomenal environment) but by their interpretations of the empirical and of the real. It is those interpretation links that make realist social science a separate enterprise – we are not influenced by the imperatives of capitalism but by our interpretation of those imperatives and our interpretations of the consequences, now in the empirical world, of earlier interpretations. Our decision environment is structured for us, but our decisions are not determined; we, through our own agency, chart a path through that environment, as we understand it.

What of the links between human and physical geography, which are presented by some as the core and *raison d'être* of the discipline? Figure 1.3.1

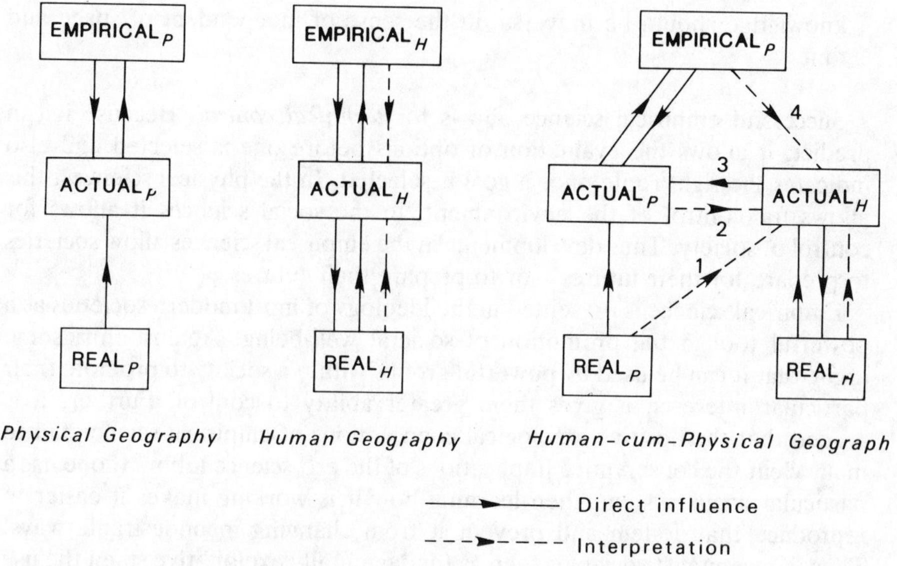

FIGURE 1.3.1 *Differences between physical and human geography*

suggests a realist model for these, too. The key bridging links are: 1) our interpretations of the physical mechanisms; 2) our interpretations of what happens when these mechanisms are realised; 3) our direct influence on the realisation of the mechanisms; and 4) our interpretations of the empirical world. We influence the physical environment by actions which take place in the context of our understanding – or, as Ian Douglas (Chapter 3.3) shows, sometimes *mis*understanding – what it is and how it works.

AND IDEOLOGY?

This discussion has identified three separate types of scientific enterprise. These have different philosophies, and are linked to different ideologies.

1. The *empirical* (or analytical) sciences operate in the empirical domain only of the realist trilogy. Their presentation to others in research reports and textbooks, however, evidently involves hermeneutics. Most adopt a positivist philosophy and employ a definition of science such as

> knowledge of the real world ascertained by observation, critically examined and classified systematically under general principles . . . knowledge should provide an explanation of what is of value in past discoveries and it should also make some prediction of future events . . . Scientific

knowledge should be universal in the sense of independent of space and time.[5]

Successful empirical science allows for *technical control*. Because it can predict, it allows the evaluation of options before one is selected and also indicates the right route once a goal is selected. In the physical sciences, this allows for control of the environment; in the social sciences it allows for control of society. Thus developments in the empirical sciences allow societies to prepare for their futures – or to prepare their futures.

Empirical science is presented in the ideology of most modern societies as a powerful tool in the promotion of societal well-being. Against this, some argue that it can be used by powerful groups within a society to promote their particular interests; it gives them greater ability to control. Further, it is argued that the positive ideological connotations of empirical science fail to make clear the conservative implications of the pro-science lobby. If one has a particular social system, then learning how it is working makes it easier to reproduce that system and prevent it from changing in undesirable ways. Thus, if a capitalist society is seen as fundamentally exploitative, then the use of scientific findings to further that society's goals will, according to its critics, extend the exploitation.

2. The *hermeneutic* sciences are those which focus on the agents, the individuals in society, their actions and the meanings that underpin them. As sciences, their goal is to appreciate people and what they do. They advance *mutual understanding* and inter-personal accommodation, enriching society by making individuals better aware of both each other and themselves.

3. Finally, there are the *critical* sciences, which combine study of the real with investigations of the actual and the empirical. Their goal is to explain the empirical world in terms of the mechanisms involved and of the events that set them in operation. This requires not only empirical anlysis and hermeneutic understanding, but also theoretical accounts of the mechanisms; to most critical scientists, it is the development of valid theories of the 'abstract real' and their use in explaining concrete realisation which are the fundamental tasks: empirical information alone cannot provide the material for explanation and too much attention to the agents suggests that they have greater freedom of action than they really have.

The goal of critical science is *emancipation*, freeing people from the ideological (and material) constraints to their understanding. For the full development of human powers, individuals must be able to assess all of the options available to them, and not only those that conform to society's ideology. Thus self-determination requires knowledge, not only of the empirical and hermeneutic kind alone – valuable though this is – but also of the critical sciences. These aim to expose people to exactly how and why their society operates, thereby allowing them to become fully involved in its transformation to the sort of society that they want. They can then produce *their* futures.

These three types of science are linked to three very different ideologies. The empirical sciences, especially the empirical social sciences, are associated with a conservative ideology which takes the current structure and functioning of society as given, and seeks to manipulate and engineer its trends. The hermeneutic sciences are conservative too, in the sense that they are not necessarily linked to any programme for change, but they are also liberal in that they canvass individual freedom, in full appreciation of all others exercising their freedoms. The critical sciences are fundamentally radical, however; they oppose the domination of the empirical sciences in a capitalist society, for example, because these do not tackle, and so implicitly promote, the basic inequalities on which societies are built, and they fault the hermeneutic sciences because they present a false ideology of human self-determination.

In a capitalist social formation such as our own, the empirical sciences are much favoured, because they offer the prospect of technical control over environment and society. (They thereby present a particular theory of nature.)[6] For the environmental and natural sciences including medicine, a realist philosophy is acceptable because it emancipates people from false beliefs – in the power of the witch doctors, for example. But in the social sciences realist/critical science is potentially 'dangerous', the emancipation would unmask society's ideology and expose its role in the promotion of the vested interests of powerful groups (associated with capital) in the exploitation of the majority (labour). Critical social science is subversive and potentially even revolutionary. (Note that it need not be Marxist. Some versions of Marxism are undoubtedly realist, but all realist social science is not Marxist). The hermeneutic sciences are neither useful nor potentially dangerous. To the extent that they support an uncontentious cultural element within society they are acceptable (though note that much of what is considered culturally good – in art, for example, and in literature and architecture – is that sponsored by society's powerful élites).

In Britain (and North America) there has been an increased emphasis on the empirical sciences in general: within the social sciences the favoured disciplines are those which seem to offer most in the reconstruction of the British economy – economics is acceptable, business and management studies are better still, and accountancy is very good; sociology and politics are denigrated, history and literature are tolerated; within the humanities only (certain) languages are desirable. Geographers have reacted by seeking reputations for relevance, for contributing to programmes of technical control. In physical geography this has focused on the need for environmental understanding and impact assessment, and in human geography on data manipulation and analysis with a view to prediction. Perhaps most important of all, geographers have promoted technical developments and training in data acquisition (remote sensing), collation (geographic information systems) and portrayal (automated cartography) as major disciplinary growth – and selling-points (see Clark, Chapter 1.1).

The conduct of a social science like human geography is not value-free. Methodological decisions (how to do research) come relatively low in what Harrison and Livingstone call the presuppositional hierarchy.[7] Before they can be made, individual geographers must decide which is the relevant epistemology and ontology and this decision will be externally influenced (negatively or positively) by the dominant ideology in their milieux. Since an ideology is a world-view, then the academic decisions are closely linked to the human geographer's perspective on life in general – whereas the strongest external influences are those linked to the dominant ideology.

For the social scientist the choice between ideologies as they relate to academic work is linked very closely to the choice between various models of human agency. Harrison and Livingstone have suggested that this choice is between three sets of metaphors: for the positivist social sciences the relevant metaphors are machine and organism, with human agency reduced to mechanistic stimulus-response systems; for the humanistic approaches text and language game are the appropriate metaphors, focusing on meanings and intentions; whereas in the realist approaches construction and domination express the role of the hidden structure and of powerful classes within it.[8]

Choice of metaphors reflects one's ideology, one's view of the significance of human agency in the creation of spatial forms and hence one's belief about the possibilities for change.

GEOGRAPHERS IN DEBATE

Geographers, like many other teachers and researchers, are now looking very hard at the future of their discipline (and themselves). To some, the philosophical debates outlined here are seen as dangerous, because they fragment the discipline and make it difficult to present a coherent picture to those with power over the purse. But those debates will continue because, as I have argued here, although at face value they are about philosophical questions they are really about ideology. And for as long as ideological debate is feasible, a 'party line' is almost impossible.

This does not imply, however, that most academic geographers are spending a lot of time in philosophical debates rather than 'doing geography'. Quite the opposite. Most avoid the debates, and when confronted by them respond by suggesting that pluralism is good for the discipline, that diversity enriches it and that orthodoxy is dangerous. (These responses are themselves ideological, of course.) Others are prepared to question, and there is indeed much still to question. Important items on the agenda include:

1. Must empirical science necessarily be positivist?
2. Can one be rigorously quantitative and yet not ideologically conservative?
3. Is it possible to structure research programmes on the assumption that similar situations will reappear?
4. How do we know that a realist theory of mechanisms is valid, if it is not subject to direct empirical testing?
5. If we cannot predict the future, what is the value of social science?
6. If we can predict the future, can we change it?
7. Is it possible to integrate physical and human geography?

The present chapter has indicated the context within which these, and many other, questions are being asked. *Our* task is to explore, debate and structure the answers – according to what *our* views of the purpose of science are. In that way, we will be making the geography of the future – geography *is* what geographers do.

Acknowledgement

I am grateful to Alan Hay, Derek Gregory and Rex Walford for their critical readings of a first draft of this chapter.

NOTES AND REFERENCES

1. R. J. Johnston, 'The region in twentieth-century British geography', *History of Geography Newsletter*, 4 (1984) pp.26–35.
2. A. M. Hay and R. J. Johnston, 'The study of process in quantitative human geography', *L'Espace Géographique*, 12 (1983) pp.69–76.
3. D. Brunsden, 'The future of geomorphology', In R. King (ed.), *Geographical Futures* (Sheffield: Geographical Association, 1984) pp.30–55.
4. R. Bhaskar, *A Realist Theory of Science* (Brighton: Harvester, 1975).
5. S. Richards, *Philosophy and sociology of science: an introduction* (Oxford: Oxford University Press, 1983).
6. T. O'Riordan, 'Environmental ideologies', *Environ. Plann. A*, 9 (1977) pp.3–14.
7. R. T. Harrison and D. N. Livingstone, 'Philosophy and problems in human geography: a presuppositional approach', *Area*, 12 (1980) pp.25–31.
8. R. T. Harrison and D. N. Livingstone, 'Understanding in geography: structuring the subjective', In D. T. Herbert and R. J. Johnston (eds) *Geography and the Urban Environment* vol. 5 (Chichester: John Wiley, 1982) pp.1–40.

FURTHER READING

This discussion draws upon and builds from two recent books of mine: *Geography and Geographers: Anglo-American Human Geography since 1945* (London: Edward Arnold, 1983) (2nd edn) and *Philosophy and Human Geography: an introduction to contemporary approaches* (London: Edward Arnold, 1986) (2nd edn). These ideas are developed further in my *On Human Geography* (Oxford: Basil Blackwell, 1986).

The fullest discussions of many of the issues raised here are Derek Gregory, *Ideology, Science and Human Geography* (London: Hutchinson, 1978) and Andrew Sayer, *Method in Social Science: a realist approach* (London: Hutchinson, 1984).

The application of these ideas in teaching is developed in John Huckle (ed.) *Geographical Education: reflection and action* (Oxford: Oxford University Press, 1983) and Russell King (ed.) *Geographical Futures* (Sheffield: Geographical Association, 1985).

1.4
Areal Differentiation and Post-Modern Human Geography

Derek Gregory
University of British Columbia

Derek Gregory is Professor of Geography at the University of British Columbia and was formerly Lecturer in Geography at the University of Cambridge and a Fellow of Sidney Sussex College. His teaching and research interests are in social theory and human geography and in the historical geography of Britain and North America. He is the author of *Ideology, Science and Human Geography, Regional Transformation and Industrial Revolution* and *The Geographical Imagination*, and co-editor of *Social Relations and Spatial Structures* (with John Urry) and *The Dictionary of Human Geography* (with R. J. Johnston and David M. Smith).

Searching for an epigraph to his *Philosophical Investigations*, Ludwig Wittgenstein considered using a quotation from *King Lear*: 'I'll teach you differences.' 'Hegel,' he once told a friend, 'always seems to me to be wanting to say that things which look different are really the same. Whereas my interest is in showing that things which look the same are really different.' — Terry Eagleton, *Against the Grain*.

POST-MODERNISM

If my title seems strange, so much the better. In this essay I want to explore some fragments of the contemporary intellectual landscape and to suggest some of the ways in which they bear upon modern human geography: and all of this will, I suspect, be unsettling. (Or, at any rate, if I can convey what is happening successfully then it ought to be unsettling.)

I use 'post-modernism' as a short-hand for a heterogeneous movement which had its origins in architecture and literary theory. The relevance of the first of these for human geography must seem comparatively straightforward – especially if the interpretative arch is widened to span the production of the built environment or, wider still, the production of space[1] – but the second is, as I will seek to show, every bit as important for the future of geographical inquiry. The converse may also be true: Frederic Jameson, one of the most exhilarating literary critics writing today, claims that 'a model of political culture appropriate to our own situation will necessarily have to raise spatial issues as its fundamental organizing concern'.[2]

Post-modernism is, of course, much more than these two moments. It has spiralled way beyond architecture and literary theory until it now confronts the terrain of the humanities and social sciences *tout court*. But whatever its location, I shall argue that post-modernism raises urgent questions about place, space and landscape in the production of social life.

Post-modernism is, in its fundamentals, a critique of what is usually called 'the Enlightenment project'. The European Enlightenment of the eighteenth century provided one of the essential frameworks for the development of the modern humanities and social sciences. It was, above all, a celebration of the power of reason and the progress of rationality, of the ways in which their twin engines propelled modernity into the cobwebbed corners of the traditional world. Both 'reason' and 'rationality' were given highly specific meanings, however, and a number of thinkers have been disturbed by the triumph of the particular vision of knowledge which those terms entailed. The more radical of them have sought to overthrow its closures and its supposed certainties altogether. Their critique has, for the most part, been conducted at high levels of abstraction – the exchanges between Habermas and Lyotard are of just such an order[3] – but one of the most concrete illustrations of what is at stake has been provided by David Ley in a remarkable essay on the politico-cultural landscapes of inner Vancouver.

Ley contrasts two redevelopment projects on either side of False Creek. To the north, 'an instrumental landscape of neo-conservatism': high-density, high-rise buildings whose minimalist geometric forms provide the backdrop for the spectacular structures of a sports stadium, conference centre, elevated freeway and rapid transit system and the towering pavilions of Expo '86. To the south, an 'expressive landscape of liberal reform': low-density groupings of buildings, diverse in design and construction, incorporating local motifs and local associations and allowing for a plurality of tenures, clustured around a lake which opens up vistas across the waterfront to the downtown skyline and the mountain rim beyond. The north shore is a monument to modern technology, to the internationalisation of 'rational' planning and corporate engineering: one of Relph's 'placeless' landscapes. The south shore, by contrast, is redolent of what Frampton calls a critical regionalism, a post-modern landscape attentive to the needs of people rather than the demands of machines and (above all) sensitive to the specificities of particular places.[4]

This contrast is, of course, emblematic of others, not least between different styles of human geography. But, as I must now show (and as the term itself suggests), post-modernism is no traditionalist's dream of recovering a world we have lost. It is a movement *beyond* the modern and, simultaneously, an invitation to construct our *own* human geographies. I will build my argument on three of its basic features.

Firstly, post-modernism is, in a very real sense, 'post-paradigm': that is to say, post-modern writers are immensely suspicious of any attempt to construct a system of thought which claims to be complete and comprehensive. In geography, of course, there have been no end of attempts of this kind, and many of those who have – in my view, mistakenly – made use of Kuhn's notion of a paradigm have done so *prescriptively*. They have claimed the authority of 'positivism', 'structuralism', 'humanism' or whatever as a means of legislating for the proper conduct of geographical inquiry and of excluding work which lies beyond the competence of these various systems. Others have preferred to transcend these, to them partial, perspectives and to offer some more general ('meta-theoretical') framework in which all these competing claims are supposed to be reconciled.

For over a decade this was usually assumed to be some kind of systems approach and now, apparently, it is the philosophy of realism (perhaps coupled with some version of Habermas's critical theory) which holds out a similar promise. But post-modernism rejects all of these manoeuvres. All of these systems of thought are – of necessity – incomplete, and if there is then no alternative but to pluck different elements from different systems for different purposes this is not a licence for an uncritical eclecticism: patching them together must, rather, display a sensitivity towards the differences and disjunctures between them.[5] And 'sensitivity' implies that those different integrities must be respected and retained: not fudged. The certainties which were once offered by epistemology – by theories of knowledge which assumed that it was possible to 'put a floor under' or 'ground' intellectual inquiry in some safe and secure way – are no longer credible in a post-modern world.[6]

Secondly, this implies, in turn, that post-modern writers are hostile to the 'totalizing' ambitions of the conventional social sciences (and, for that matter, those of the humanities). Their critique points in two directions. First, they reject the notion that social life displays what could be called a 'global coherence': that our day-to-day social practices are moments in the reproduction of a self-maintaining social system whose fundamental, so to speak 'structural' imperatives necessarily regulate our everyday lives in some automatic, pre-set fashion. These writers do not, of course, deny the importance of the interdependencies which have become such a commonplace of the late twentieth-century world, and neither do they minimise the routine character of social reproduction nor the various powers which enclose our day-to-day routines. (These are, on the contrary, some of the most salient foci of their work). But they do object to the concept of totality which informs much of modern social theory, because it tacitly assumes that social life somehow adds up to (or 'makes sense in terms of') a coherent system with its own superordinate logic.

Second, and closely connected to this, these writers reject the notion that social life can be explained in terms of some 'deeper' structure. This was one of the premisses of structuralism, of course, and it still surfaces in some of the cruder versions of realism. It is largely through this opposition that post-modernism is sometimes identified with 'post-structuralism' and, put like this, I imagine that the post-modern critique will seem to echo the complaints of those who saw in structuralism a displacement of the human subject. In human geography as elsewhere, many commentators were dismayed by the way in which various versions of structuralism replaced the concrete complexities of human agency by the disembodied transformations of abstract structures.[7] But post-modernism is not another humanism. It objects to structuralism because its sharpened concept of structure points towards a 'centre' around which social life revolves, rather like a kaleidoscope or a child's mobile; but it objects to humanism for the very same reason. Most forms of humanism appeal to the human subject or to human agency as the self-evident centre of social life. And yet we are now beginning to discover just how problematic those terms are. Concepts of 'the person', for example, differ widely over space and through time and so, paradoxically, it is their very importance which ensures that they cannot provide a constant foundation for the human sciences. They are the *explanandum* not the *explanans*.

Thirdly, the accent on 'difference' which dominates the preceding paragraphs is a *leitmotiv* of post-modernism. One of the distinguishing features of post-modern culture is its sensitivity to heterogeneity, particularity and uniqueness. To some readers this insistence on 'difference' will raise the spectre of the idiographic, which is supposed to have been laid once and for all (in geography at any rate) by the Hartshorne–Schaefer debate in the 1950s and by the consolidation of a generalising spatial science during the 1960s. To be sure, the caricature of Hartshorne as a crusty empiricist, indifferent to the search for spatial order, blind to location theory and ignorant of quantitative methods could never survive any serious reading of *The Nature of Geography*. There were, as several commentators have emphasised, deep-seated continuities between the Hartshornian orthodoxy and the prospectus of the so-called 'New Geography'. But Schaefer's clarion call for geography as a nomothetic science, compelled to produce morphological laws and to disclose the fundamental geometries of spatial patterns, undoubtedly sounded a retreat from areal differentiation which was heard (and welcomed) in many quarters. Specificity became eccentricity, and the new conceptual apparatus made no secret of its confinement: it was, variously, a 'residual'; background 'noise' to be 'filtered out'; a 'deviation' from the 'normal'. And yet in the 1980s other writers in other fields have given specificity a wider resonance. In philosophy, Lyotard claims that 'post-modern knowledge . . . refines our sensitivity to differences'; in social theory de Certeau wants to fashion 'a science of singularity . . . that links everyday pursuits to particular circumstances'; and in anthropology Geertz parades 'the diversity of things' and seeks illumination from 'the light of local knowledge'.[8]

In geography too there has been a remarkable return to areal differentiation. But it is a return with a difference. When Harvey speaks of the 'uneven development' of capitalism, for example, or when (in a radically different vocabulary) Hägerstrand talks about 'pockets of local order' (I shall have more to say about both of these in due course) they – and now countless others like them – are attempting much more than the recovery of geography's traditional project. For they herald not so much the reconstruction of modern geography as its *deconstruction*. I mean this to be understood in an entirely positive and specifically technical sense: not as a new nihilism, still less as the enthronement of some new orthodoxy, but as the transformation of the modern intellectual landscape as a whole. I should admit at once that it is still barely possible to map that new landscape – not least because it is radically unstable – but in what follows I will try to put some preliminary markers around what Soja calls the 'post-modernization' of geography.[9]

Two disclaimers are immediately necessary. First, to work within disciplinary boundaries is obviously open to objection – and I am as uneasy about doing so as anyone else – but I have retained the conventional enclosures because I want to show that 'geography' has as much to contribute to post-modernism as it has to learn from it. In so far as social life cannot be theorised on the point of a pin, then, so it seems to me, the introduction of concepts of place, space and landscape must radically transform the nature of modern social theory. Second, to say that geography has re-opened the question of areal differentiation is to invite the response that, for many, it was never closed. I accept that it would be wrong to minimise the continuing power of traditional regional geographies which, at their very best, have always provided remarkably sensitive evocations of the particular relations between people and the places in which they live. And I insist on this not as a politeness to be pushed to one side as soon as possible. On the contrary, the 'problem of geographical description' with which so many of these writers struggle is, as I will show, part of a more general 'crisis of representation' throughout the contemporary human sciences. This realisation, pregnant with consequences at once theoretical and practical, has also played its part in changing the modern intellectual landscape: so much so that we need new, theoretically-informed ways of conveying the complexities of areal differentiation if we are to make sense of the post-modern world.

I realise that many readers will be uncomfortable at my emphasis on theory, and some of them will object to yet more intellectual baggage being strapped to the heads of the credulous. But hostility to theory, as Eagleton remarks in another context, 'usually means an opposition to other people's theories and an oblivion to one's own'.[10] Even so, I can understand how anyone, assaulted by the abstract technologies of spatial science and then bloodied by the philosophical critique of positivism, can yearn for an end to geography's alienation from – well, *geography*. Let me make it plain, therefore, that I have no interest in theory for its own sake. To be sure, one can derive genuine pleasure from theoretical work: and why not? But exercises of this sort cannot be justified by intellectual hedonism alone, and the theories that I propose to discuss demand, by their very nature, an engagement with the world rather than an estrangement from it: they are, in other words, profoundly critical, political constructions.

It will make things much clearer, I hope, if I sketch out the emerging relations between geography and three other disciplines: political economy, sociology and anthropology. This is, very roughly, the order in which cross-fertilisation has occurred in the post-war decades, but it also corresponds to a movement in the direction of post-modernism.

GEOGRAPHY AND POLITICAL ECONOMY

Post-war geography had a close but curious relationship with mainstream neo-classical economics. I say 'close' because so many of the early models of spatial science assumed a neo-classical world of perfect competition, in which producers and consumers freely entered into price-fixing markets as sovereign individuals. Their exchanges were regulated by the frictionless intersection of supply and demand schedules, so as to sustain a partial or general equilibrium. And I say 'curious' because this was a world without history or geography, and once those 'imperfections' or 'distortions' were introduced the assumptions of neo-classical economics became untenable. As late twentieth-century capitalism was plunged into a profound crisis whose restructurings reverberated through local, national and international space-economies, so the *historical geography* of capitalism became ever more visible and the credibility of the neo-classical calculus ever more precarious. It was then, in the early 1970s, that a new relationship started to be forged between geography and political economy.

Political economy could properly claim to deal with social relations rather than hypothetical individuals, with the sphere of production as well as the sphere of exchange, and with crisis and conflict rather than equilibrium. It was historically sensitive too. Both Ricardo and Marx recognised the dramatic transformations wrought by the Industrial Revolution at the turn of the eighteenth and nineteenth centuries, and those who followed in their footsteps continued to insist on the importance of subsequent transformations in the basal structures of capitalism.

But neither Ricardo nor Marx had much to say about geography. A number of writers have sought to develop a broadly neo-Ricardian perspective on location theory, but the most thorough-going geographical reconstruction of political economy has undoubtedly been neo-Marxian. Marx certainly drew attention to the 'annihilation of space by time', but this had little impact on the main currents of Marxism. The phrase proved to be unusually prophetic: *historical* materialism had little room for the historical *geography* of capitalism. Although Marx offered some remarkably suggestive theses about the spatial structures of capital circulation, in David Harvey's view 'one of the extraordinary and outstanding failures of an otherwise powerful

Marxist tradition' has been the way in which it appeared 'to license the study of historical transformations while ignoring how capitalism produces its own geography'. His careful delineation of *The Limits to Capital* must thus be read in a double sense, marking both the bounding contours of capitalist development and an important silence in Marx's master work.[11]

The limits to capital

It is impossible to do justice to the richness of Harvey's argument here; let me instead open just one window on his work. There are, so he claims, a number of fundamental tensions in the landscape of contemporary capitalism (see Figure 1.4.1).

One of the most basic is between processes working towards agglomeration in place and processes working towards dispersal over space. Harvey argues that the rationalisation of capitalist production pulls clusters of economic activities into a 'structured coherence' *within* particular regions. In so far as capitalism is inherently expansionary, however, capital circulation is obviously not confined to those regions, and this means that capital accumulation must also depend upon time-space co-ordination *between* regions. The tension between the two can only be reconciled, so Harvey claims, through the 'urbanization of capital'. In effect, the circulation of capital through an urbanised space-economy brings different labour processes at different locations into a general social relation. Put like this, of course, the old oppositions between the particular and the general disappear; but, more than that, *concrete* labour processes acquire *abstract* qualities tied to value as socially necessary labour time. This is of immense importance because the notion of 'socially necessary labour time' is absolutely essential to Marx's labour theory of value. Without it, the whole structure of class exploitation through the appropriation of surplus value collapses. What Harvey is able to show, therefore, is that the mainspring of Marx's political economy, in contradistinction to the aspatial calculus of neo-classical economics, *depends upon* the production of a differentiated and integrated space-economy.

Even so, that framework is chronically unstable, because the constant drive to reduce the turnover time of capital produces exactly that 'annihilation of space by time' which Marx accentuated. Changes in transportation and communication systems, credit networks and the like have all contributed to a remarkable increase in the speed of the global economy, and its accelerating rotations have progressively transformed the relative locations of existing production configurations. The deflation of old locational values has impelled changes in the geography of multinational investment, shifts in the international division of labour and the emergence of new zonal and regional cities. These processes are far from straightforward, Harvey points out, because a knife-edge has to be negotiated 'between preserving the values of past commitments made at a particular place and time, or devaluing them to open up fresh room for accumulation'. The tension between the immobility of

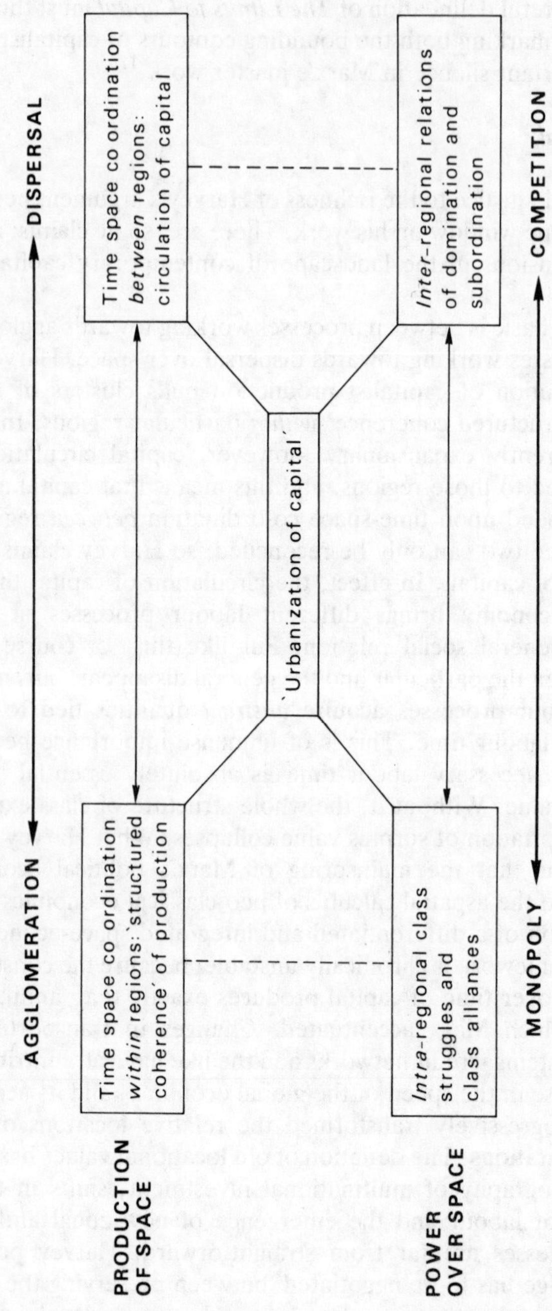

FIGURE 1.4 *Fundamental tensions in the landscape of contemporary capitalism*

spatial structures and their capacity to stretch across ever wider spans of time and space is almost palpable. To Harvey: 'the produced geographical landscape constituted by fixed and immobile capital is both the crowning glory of past capitalist development and a prison that inhibits the further progress of accumulation precisely because it creates spatial barriers where there were none before.'

The transcendence of these barriers to continued accumulation depends not only on the production *of* space, Harvey insists, but also on power *over* space. It is, in other words, a matter of geopolitics. The production of clusters of economic activities within regions is paralleled by the formation of equally unstable and place-specific 'class alliances'. These coalitions are territorially-based social movements which seek to intervene in the competitive struggle between different regions within what is an increasingly complex and constantly changing hierarchy of domination and subordination. Class alliances are obviously forged out of a mix of different interests, but their instability is heightened by their double function. On the one hand, they have to protect those immobile regional infrastructures which provide for continued production and reproduction; yet on the other hand, they must secure their own upward spiral of accumulation by capturing new rounds of investment. Class alliances thus become caught between 'the stagnant swamp of monopoly controls fashioned out of the geopolitics of domination' and the 'the fires of open and escalating competition with others'.

These theses are obviously pitched at a high level of abstraction, and although Harvey has provided a number of empirical vignettes it is in Doreen Massey's work that one finds some of the most concrete studies of the historical geography of contemporary capitalism. 'While an abstract model of capitalism, by providing the necessary concepts, is an aid to analysis,' she writes, 'it cannot substitute for the analysis itself.' Her *Spatial Divisions of Labour* is thus intended to provide the basis for a much more specific project: 'a new regional geography' of the United Kingdom.[12]

Spatial divisions of labour

Massey's model is simpler than Harvey's and, in a purely formal sense, bears some of the marks of much older notions like Derwent Whittlesey's sequent occupance or H. C. Darby's juxtaposition of cross-sections and vertical themes. But it has a much sharper bite.

Massey begins with the formation of spatial structures of production. Each phase of capital accumulation – each 'round of investment' – is supposed to involve the allocation of different functions within the social relations of production to different regions within the national and international space-economy. I have tried to make this clearer by translating it into a game of cards (Figure 1.4.2). In the first round a single suit is dealt (representing a phase of capital accumulation), and each player (representing a different region) receives a different card (representing a different function). In the second and third rounds, other single suits are dealt. As one phase is succeeded by another, so 'the structure of local economies can be seen as a product of the combination of "layers", of the successive imposition over the years of new rounds of investment [and] new forms of activity'. Similarly, at the end of three rounds of our game, each player has a different hand: but in each case this is connected 'horizontally' to the hands held by other players and 'vertically' to the cards dealt in the previous rounds.

In much the same way a local economy may, through the mix of its activities, be embedded in a multitude of 'horizontal' spatial structures, each of which entails different relations of domination and subordination within the space-economy, and in a multitude of 'vertical' spatial structures containing the traces of the relations of domination and subordination put into place during previous rounds of investment. If you think about this for a moment, you will see that this means that the same round of investment can produce 'very different effects in different areas as a result of its combination with a different pre-existing structures'.

But Massey is quick to point out that localities do not merely *reflect* processes determined at national and international scales. On the contrary, the vast variety of conditions at the local scale materially affects the operation and outcome of those very processes. The combination of layers signifies a form of mutual determination, therefore, with each side of the process affecting the other. 'The uniqueness of place and the constantly evolving and shifting systems of interdependence [that is, relations of domination and subordination] are two sides of the same coin.'

Massey then broadens the base. 'The layers of history which are sedimented over time are not just economic', she says, because there are also cultural, political and ideological strata which also have their local specificities and which must also be brought into the analysis. Their importance for Massey is, in part, that they affect the investment strategies selected during each round – in Harvey's terms, the way in which 'space is produced by capital' – and, in part, that they shape the political strategies pursued by the social groups involved (including Harvey's 'class alliances'). Different layers have created the conditions for different social movements, Massey concludes, and if the last decade has seen 'a reassertion of defensive [working class] solidarity' in the declining manufacturing regions of the United Kingdom, the cities have become important 'foci for resistance' where 'new alliances are being constructed out of the wreckage'.

The contours of political economy

For all the differences, there are a number of parallels between Harvey and Massey. Both of them emphasise the primacy of production; both of them see the ceaseless formation and re-formation of geographical landscapes as vital moments in the reproduction and transformation of contemporary capitalism;

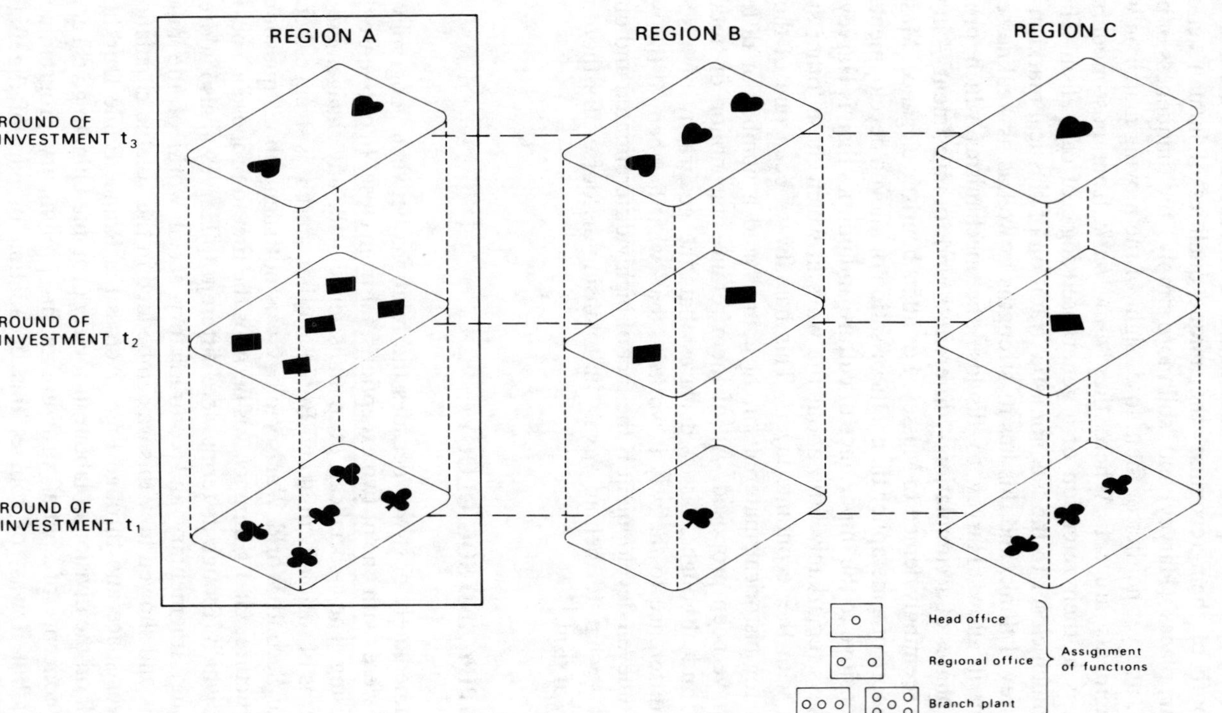

FIGURE 1.4.2 *Phases of capital accumulation – translated into a game of cards*

and both of them draw out the implications of their arguments for political action.

Where they *approach* post-modernism is in their recovery of areal differentiation: both of them recognise 'the unique qualities of human action in [particular] places' (Harvey) and, still more simply, 'the uniqueness of place' (Massey), and yet neither of them loses sight of the moving matrix in which those fragments are set. Where they *draw back* from post-modernism, however, is in their retention of a generalised logic of capitalism. Harvey remains much closer to the 'economistic' tradition of classical marxism than does Massey, I think, and this has its strengths as well as its weaknesses. In particular, it allows Harvey to disclose the mechanisms which produce different phases of accumulation – different 'rounds of investment' – in ways which are seemingly denied to Massey. For all its heuristic elegance, Massey's model is more of a metaphor than a theorisation of uneven development. She is more sensitive to the importance of culture and politics than is Harvey, but she still says remarkably little about the ways in which these 'other strata' articulate with the 'economic layer'. This has always been one of the key questions for historical materialism, of course, and a number of different answers have been proposed. All of them retain some notion of 'totality', however, and although Massey declares that 'the geography of a society makes a difference to the way it works' – that 'what lies behind the whole notion of uneven development is the fact of highly differentiated and unique outcomes' – what lies behind *this* is the totalising discourse of a thoroughly modern Marxism.[13]

GEOGRAPHY AND SOCIOLOGY

In the immediately post-war decades the relations between geography and sociology were, with one or two exceptions, far from close. In one sense this is not surprising. The a-social cast of spatial science made any engagement with the concerns of sociology unlikely. But in another sense it is strange, because before the Second World War sociology was not silent about questions of spatial structure. Georg Simmel was perhaps the first to propose a 'sociology of space', which (though its terms were different to Harvey's) also addressed the fleeting, fragmentary and contradictory social world of the modern metropolis and showed how this was embedded in the volatile circulation of money over space and through time. Across the Rhine, Emile Durkheim's early work on the division of labour in society prompted him to give a central place to concepts of spatial structure in his preliminary programme for sociology: but it was, of course, this occupation of part of the field of *géographie humaine* which prompted many champions of Vidal de la Blache to insist on the integrity of the pre-existing intellectual division of labour. The barricades went up. The story was much the same on the other side of the Atlantic. The doyen of the Chicago School of urban sociology, Robert Park, drew a sharp distinction between a supposedly 'idiographic' human geography and his own avowedly 'nomothetic' human ecology.[14]

Towards the end of the 1970s, however, a new dialogue was opened between geography and sociology. Like the continuing conversation between geography and political economy, this was distinguished by its historical sensitivity. Indeed, one of the most obvious features of late twentieth-century sociology has been the revival of historical sociology. But, just as significant, this has (in many cases) been accompanied by the rediscovery of concepts of spatial structure. Although this too echoes the geographical reconstruction of political economy, some of the most exciting work has in fact been stimulated by the *shortcomings* of historico-geographical materialism. Much the most important has been its failure to overcome the tension between what is sometimes called the 'two Marxisms': one celebrating the power of conscious and collective human agency, the other preoccupied with the structural logic of the mode of production. 'On this score,' Perry Anderson once concluded, 'classical Marxism, even at the height of its powers, provided no coherent answer.' And, as other commentators have noted, these two basic orientations have reappeared throughout the subsequent history of modern Marxism.[15] Historico-geographical materialism has proved to be no exception: or at any rate not much of one.[16]

To be sure, the same oppositions surface throughout non-Marxist social theory as well, and it is perfectly possible to speak of 'two sociologies' or 'two geographies' in broadly similar terms. But it is undoubtedly the Marxist tradition which has been the single most important source for the development of a critique seeking to transcend the dualism between human agency and social structure. And, as I now want to show, the incorporation of time-space relations has proved to be a strategic moment in the development of this 'post-Marxist' theory of structuration. For its principal author, Anthony Giddens, insists that '[the] spatial configurations of social life are just as much a matter of basic importance to social theory as are the dimensions of temporality' and that 'there are no logical or methodological differences between human geography and sociology'.[17]

The time–space constitution of social life

The compass of Giddens's writings is extraordinarily wide, but Figure 1.4.3 is a simple sketch of one of the basic frameworks of his theory of structuration.[18]

In Giddens's view, societal integration – however precarious and partial it might be – depends upon the 'binding' of time and space into the conduct of social life. To say more than this entails an analytical distinction between social integration and system integration.

Social integration The continuity of day-to-day life depends, in large measure, on routinised interactions between people who are *co-present* in time and space. This is what 'society' meant before the eighteenth century:

simply the company of others. Giddens suggests that Hägerstrand's time-geography provides a notation through which the characteristic shapes of *time–space routinisation* can be captured (Figure 1.4.4). Thus each day we meet other people and part from them at particular times and at particular places ('stations') in order to fulfill particular purposes ('projects'). In doing so, we necessarily trace out 'paths' in time and space. From this perspective, therefore, time and space are, in effect, resources which have to be drawn upon in the conduct of everyday life. It is for this reason that Hägerstrand sometimes describes his work as a time-space ecology. But this is much more than a metaphor: one of Hägerstrand's central concerns is the competitive struggle between people and projects for open paths. It is this 'jockeying for position' which is implied by the very concept of space he uses – in Swedish *rum* – for which the closest English equivalent is perhaps 'room'. The pattern of paths can then be seen as a time-space template of *power*.

For a population, of course, those patterns would seem bewilderingly complicated: imagine what the paths for just ten people would like, let alone a hundred or a thousand! And then try to visualise them not just for a single day but for a whole year. Even so, Hägerstrand believes that if one looks closer (and thinks harder) then a fleeting and flickering time–space coherence can be discerned.

This arises partly because the social practices which are carried forward along those paths are, as I've said, typically routinised; their intersections repeatedly form knots of social activity in time and space ('bundles') which are tied and retied over and over again. But it also arises because those social practices are shaped by – and in turn themselves shape – wider structural features of the social systems in which they are implicated. Those structures can be glimpsed in concrete form in the various institutions which regulate access to constellations of stations and stipulate modes of conduct within them. Hägerstrand calls these constellations 'domains' – and there you can surely hear the distant echoes of the geopolitics of *domination* which so exercised Harvey. Although Giddens is critical of several of Hägerstrand's theoretical claims, and in my view rightly so, the time–space relations between power and domination constitute one of the main axes of structuration theory.[19]

System integration In so far as routinised social practices are recognisably the same over varying spans of time and space, then Giddens argues that they flow from and fold back into structural relations which reach beyond the 'here and now' to define interactions with others who are *absent* in time or space. This is what 'society' came to mean after the eighteenth century: the larger world stretching away from the human body and the human being. Giddens suggests that a basic task of structuration theory is therefore to show how 'the limitations of individual "presence" are transcended by the stretching of social relations across time and space'. This sounds metaphysical, even mystical, but it turns out to be much more ordinary. What Giddens is talking

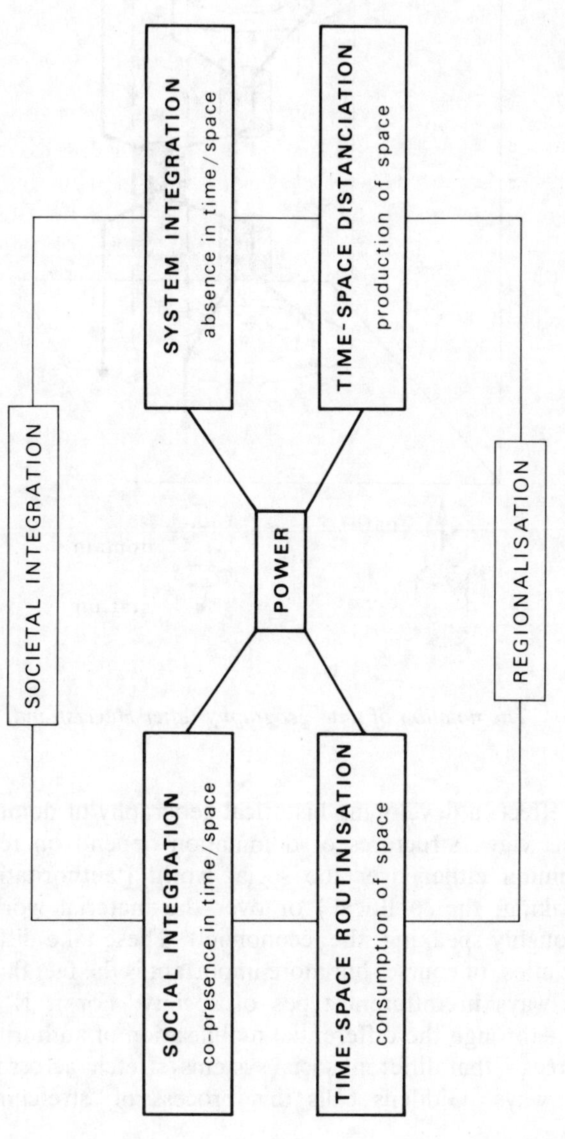

FIGURE 1.4.3 *Giddens's theory of structuration*

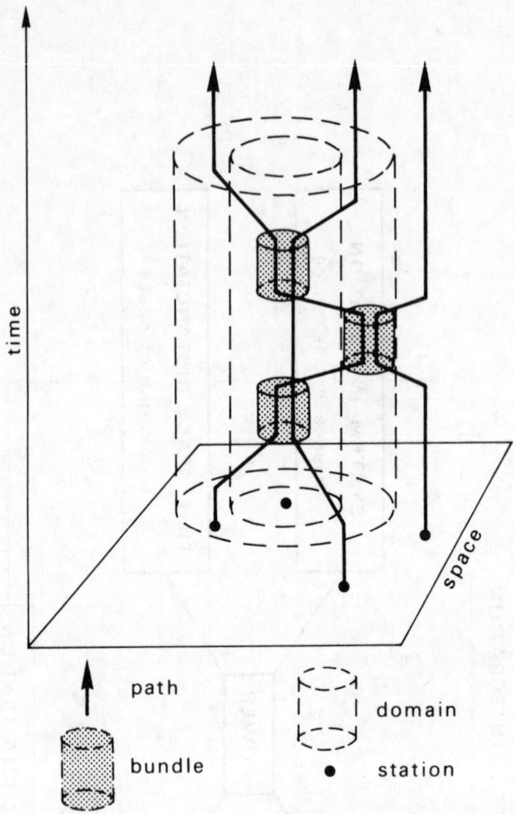

FIGURE 1.4.4 *The notation of time–geography (after Hägerstrand)*

about is, in effect, a developing historical geography of domination (Figure 1.4.5). In his view, structures of domination depend on resources which sustain dominion either over the social world ('authoritative' resources: roughly speaking, the 'political') or over the material world ('allocative' resources: roughly speaking, the 'economic'). These take different forms in different societies, of course, but more important is the fact that they connect in different ways in different types of society. For it is through these connections – through the differential mobilisation of authoritative and allocative resources – that different social systems 'stretch' across time and space in different ways. Giddens calls this process of 'stretching' *time–space distanciation*.

Giddens sorts some of the most powerful media of time–space distanciation into two sets (though there are undoubtedly others). The first set includes the emergence of writing, which was almost everywhere closely identified with the origins of the state and the formation of class societies, and which opened up spheres of interaction far beyond the spoken circles of oral cultures and traditional tribal societies and the diffusion of printing and other communications technologies, which dramatically enhanced the surveillance capabilities of the state and allowed it to penetrate much more deeply into the day-to-day lives of its subject populations. These various changes correspond to the mobilisation of authoritative resources.

The second set includes the emergence of money – Simmel repeatedly drew attention to 'the power of money to bridge distances' – and the subsequent universalisation of a convulsive money economy, which Giddens (like Marx) regards as the cutting edge of the so-called 'commodification' of everyday life in class-divided capitalist societies. These various changes correspond to the mobilisation of allocative resources. In the late twentieth century these two sets intersect in innumerable ways, perhaps most obviously in the way in which, as Harvey notes, credit transfers 'can move around the world as quickly as information and instructions concerning their use will allow'.[20]

The dissolution of the social

Gidden's work advances beyond Hägerstrand's in a number of directions. Where Hägerstrand puts the accent on the *consumption* of space, in which time and space are conceived as resources drawn upon in the realisation of

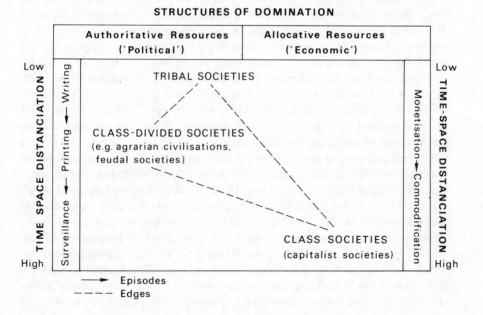

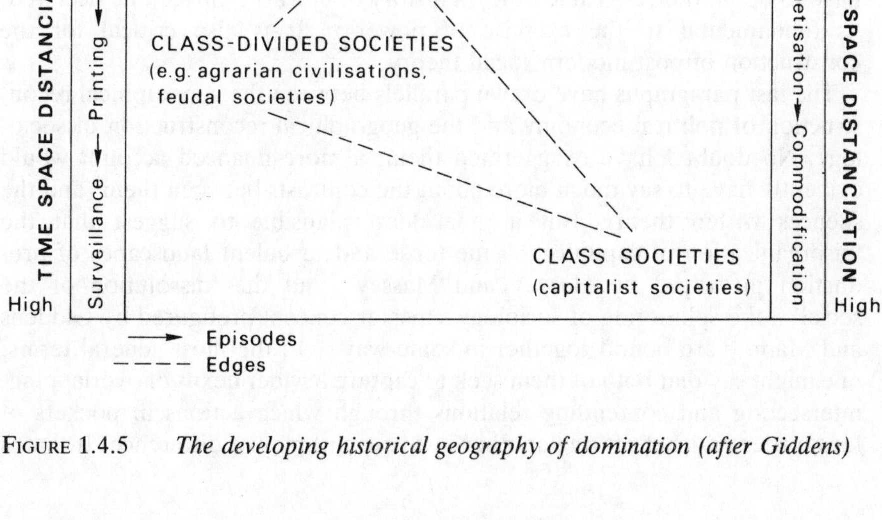

FIGURE 1.4.5 *The developing historical geography of domination (after Giddens)*

individual and collective projects, structuration theory is equally concerned with what Harvey would call the *production* of space – the 'annihilation of space by time' – through changing modes of time–space distanciation. And where Hägerstrand emphasises the creation of 'pockets of local order', structuration theory is equally attentive to what Massey would call the changing systems of interdependence in which they are embedded. These couplets both find common ground in *regionalisation*. Giddens regards this as a phenomenon of decisive importance for social theory. 'No single concept helps more to redress the misleading divisions between "micro-[scale]" and "macro-[scale]" research,' he argues, and 'no single concept helps more to counter the assumption that a "society" is always a clear-cut unity with precisely defined boundaries to it.'[21]

The last point is put most sharply by Michael Mann. Against the grain of conventional sociology, he writes:

> Societies are not unitary. They are not social systems (closed or open); they are not totalities . . . Because there is no whole, social relations cannot be reduced 'ultimately', 'in the last instance' to some systemic property of it – like the [mode of production] . . . Because there is no bounded totality, it is not helpful to divide social change or conflict into 'endogenous' and 'exogenous' varieties . . . Societies are much *messier* than our theories of them.[22]

Like Giddens (though *unlike* him in other respects), Mann conceives the constitution of social life in terms of multiple sociospatial networks of power. This is not to say that social life can be fully accounted for in these terms, of course, but they are nevertheless of strategic importance to any post-modern social theory. 'A whole history remains to be written of *spaces*,' Michel Foucault once wrote, 'from the great strategies of geopolitics to the little tactics of the habitat.' And he made it plain that a project of this sort would have to be, at the very same time, 'a history of *powers*', 'Space,' he declared, 'is fundamental to the exercise of power'.[23] It is also critical for the construction of post-modern social theory.

The last paragraphs have drawn parallels between the geographical reconstruction of political economy and the geographical reconstruction of sociology. No doubt I have exaggerated them; a more nuanced account would evidently have to say much more about the contrasts between them (and the silences within them). But it is at least plausible to suggest that the 'disorganization of capitalism' – the tense and turbulent landscapes of production portrayed by Harvey and Massey – and the 'dissolution of the social' – the splintering of sociology's master-concept prefigured by Giddens and Mann – are bound together in some way.[24] In the most general terms, one might say that both of them seek to capture a wider nexus of overlapping, intersecting and contending relations through which actions in pockets of local order ricochet off one another in a constant play of difference. If that is indeed the case, then one of the most exacting problems in post-modern social theory turns on what a previous generation called 'the problem of geographical description'. For how can we convey all this *in our writing*? Some preliminary answers can be found in the developing relations between geography and anthropology.

GEOGRAPHY AND ANTHROPOLOGY

Post-war geography in Britain was strangely indifferent to the achievements of anthropology, and yet the two could claim a common lineage reaching back to the eighteenth and nineteenth centuries. Geography emerged, so Stoddart claims, 'as Europe encountered the rest of the world, and indeed itself, with the tools of the new objective science, and all other geographical traditions are necessarily derivative and indeed imitative of it'. What 'made our own subject possible,' in his view, was 'the extension of scientific methods of observation, classification and comparison to peoples and societies'. Among these extensions Stoddart numbers 'a new concern for realism in illustration and description', through which 'places came to be seen as objects which could be recorded and related to each other in an objective manner, rather than simply as triggers to mood and to expression'.[25] Anthropology can claim much the same history (though one usually written in less triumphal terms). Yet – with the exception of Daryll Forde, H. J. Fleure and a handful of other geographers – the relations between anthropology and geography have, for most of the twentieth century, been much closer on the other side of the Atlantic. Cultural geography is still a much more prominent feature of the North American intellectual landscape, where it has even been suggested that one of Carl Sauer's most far-reaching achievements was the 'amalgamation' of the two.[26]

Ethnography and writing cultures

I mention Sauer not only because of his central role in the development of cultural geography. His writings are especially illuminating because they were animated by two traditions. The first derived from the work of Alfred Kroeber and Robert Lowie. These two Berkeley anthropologists saw culture as a coherent totality: as what Kroeber called a 'superorganic' collectivity which transcended the actions of individual human beings. This was a powerful and, as it turned out, an influential talisman: hence, presumably, Sauer's belief that human geography 'is a science that has nothing to do with individuals but only with . . . cultures'. It continued to be an article of faith in cultural geography (and elsewhere) for many decades. At the beginning of the 1980s, however, this totalising vision was subjected to a critique which, though it was scarcely confined to Sauer's particular formulations, nevertheless did much to re-direct some of the most interesting work in cultural geography towards a more 'interpretative' (which is not to say an individualistic) anthropology.[27]

The writings of Clifford Geertz have been of particular importance in this movement (and, in my judgement, are likely to become more so). 'The force of our interpretations,' Geertz insisted in one of his most famous essays, 'cannot rest, as they are now so often made to do, on the tightness with which they hold together'. For 'nothing has done more to discredit cultural analysis than the impeccable depictions of formal order in whose actual existence nobody can quite believe'. This could stand as an indictment of geography as easily as anthropology; but there is more.

> If anthropological interpretation is constructing a reading of what happens, then to divorce it from what happens – from what, in this time or that place, specific people say, what they do, what is done to them, from the whole vast business of the world – is to divorce it from its implications and render it vacant.

It is largely for this reason that Geertz commends *ethnography*, a research process in which one seeks to describe the day-to-day lives of people in other, particular cultures through a sustained encounter with them and the multiplicity of contexts in which they live. Its purpose is 'thick description': rendering the layers of meaning in which their social actions are embedded less opaque, less refractory to our own (no less particular) sensibilities, yet without destroying altogether the 'strangeness' which drew us to them in the first place.[28]

This is the impulse which now informs many descriptions of the geography of everyday life and, by extension, many de-codings of the cultural landscape. These developments have done much to blunt the prescriptions which Stoddart derived from the natural sciences, and they have, I suggest, extended the boundaries of 'realism' far beyond the confines of objects and objectivities. But they have not, in any substantial sense, challenged its *textual conventions*. And this matters more than you might think. For what do ethnographers do? *They write*, says Geertz. And ethnography is now not confined to anthropology (if it ever was): we all write. Yet we don't seem to have a developed understanding of the modes of representation which we deploy, let alone a willingness to experiment with them.[29]

This brings me to the second tradition which surfaces through Sauer's cultural geography. For this was suffused with the idealism of the Romantics who contested the unqualified naturalism of the Enlightenment. Foremost among them was Goethe. 'The foundation of Sauer's metatheory [about the morphology of the cultural landscape] rests,' so Speth argues, 'on Goethe's conception of morphological change'.[30] Goethe sought to reconcile the scientific and the artistic imaginations through the study of morphology, the ceaseless transformation of living forms, and to convey, in the same moment, 'both . . . the form produced and . . . the process of formation'. Sauer's morphology was perfectly consistent with this, of course; so too, for that matter, were elements of locational analysis. But what is of special interest is that, according to two commentators, Goethe's conception of form 'pervades all his writings, verse as well as prose, not only in the sense that conceptual statements of it are incorporated into his philosophical poems; *it is implicit in the structural relations of the language itself*.' There was thus in Goethe (but not, I think, in Sauer) a self-conscious attention to linguistic forms and textual conventions. One finds there, in part in consequence, a tension between order and chaos. Hence Goethe's anguished presentiment of 'a world bereft of forms, when time and place shivered to atoms and the normal congruence between self and surroundings snapped, found its precipitate . . . in his poetry'.[31]

I am not, of course, claiming that Goethe prefigures post-modernism: but the importance of linguistic forms and textual conventions is surely clear enough. It is this which Geertz accentuated; and it is this which is being explored, in a different register, by various experiments in post-modern ethnography.

Experiments in ethnography

I have already referred to the problem of geographical description.[32] 'Elevated to a central concern of theoretical reflection,' George Marcus and Michael Fischer propose, 'problems of description become problems of representation'. There is now, in their view, a crisis of representation throughout the human sciences. It is one which has demanded serious theoretical reflection about particular textual strategies (whose consequences, it so happens, reach far beyond the text), but it has also occasioned a series of practical experiments in writing ethnographies. Marcus and Fischer accentuate that what is important in all this 'is not experimentation for its own sake, but the theoretical insight that the play with writing technique brings to consciousness'.[33] This needs emphasis, I think, because in geography there have been rather too many calls for 'plain writing' by commentators who signally fail to understand the consequences of conventional genres and modes of representation. Those who dismiss the work of Gunnar Olsson, for example, need to see that the giving of descriptions is never a purely empirical exercise. It is not only that all observations are inescapably 'theory-laden' (a leading theorem of virtually all post-positivist philosophies of science) but that the very act of stringing them together – of structuring the accounts in which they are placed – is *itself* an irredeemably theoretical practice. Olsson has in fact made this point in the most telling way possible: his theoretical reflections *on* discourse are themselves deliberate experiments *in* discourse.[34]

For all that, however, there have been pitifully few experiments in writing contemporary geography. There have been countless injunctions to exercise the geographical imagination, but these have usually been disciplined by the established conventions of (literary) realism. It may well be true that we are not trained to be painters or poets but, like Pierce Lewis, I don't think we should boast about it. For if we cannot evoke landscapes, if we cannot provide descriptions of the relations between people and places 'so vivid that they move our emotions', then – to adapt a phrase from Geertz – we radically 'thin' our geographies.[35] Consider the following:

> My love affair with those Michigan dunes . . . had everything to do with violent immediate sensations: the smell of October wind sweeping in from Lake Michigan, sun-hot sand that turned deliciously cool when your foot sank in, the sharp sting of sand blown hard against bare legs, the pale blur of sand pluming off the dune crest against a porcelain-blue sky. Lake Michigan a muffled roar beyond the distant beach, a hazy froth of jade and white. As I try to shape words to evoke my feelings about that far-off place and time, I know why the Impressionists painted landscapes as they did – not literally, but as fragments of colour, splashes of pigment, bits of shattered prismatic light.

Is that geography? Or is it an extract from a novel?[36] If you can give a straight answer to the question, then I must suppose you can draw a clear distinction between the two. But on what basis? And *why*?

In fact, one of the most important elements in the movement towards a post-modern ethnography has been a serious consideration of the textual strategies of contemporary fiction. For ethnographies *are* fictions, in the literal sense of *fictio* – 'something made'. And there are no end of ways in which they can be 'made'. What is more, some of the most interesting experiments in ethnographic writing derive from the Impressionism (and post-Impressionism) registered in the passage I have just cited; from the multiple voices and multiple perspectives which shatter the convention of a single author, outside the text and surveying, with a single gaze, all that happens inside its frame.[37] For it is this blurring of inside and outside which is one of the most arresting developments in post-modern fiction (think of John Fowles's *The French Lieutenant's Woman* or Christopher Priest's *The Glamour*): and it also distinguishes some of the very best experimental ethnography. As James Clifford sees it, the 'ground' from which conventional representations of the world have issued has been transformed.

> A conceptual shift, 'tectonic' in its implications, has taken place. We ground things, now, on a moving earth. There is no longer any place of overview (mountaintop) from which to map human ways of life, no Archimedean point from which to represent the world. Mountains are in constant motion. So are islands: for one cannot occupy, unambiguously, a bounded cultural world from which to journey out and analyze other cultures. Human ways of life increasingly influence, dominate, parody, translate and subvert one another. Cultural analysis is always enmeshed in global movements of difference and power.[38]

That was the *real* lesson of Europe's encounter with the rest of the world, but we have been astonishingly slow to grasp its implications. Eric Wolf makes things a good deal clearer when he censures traditional ethnographies for clinging leech-like to the myth of the pristine primitive, closed off from a wider nexus of political and economic relationships stretching across time and space. 'Europeans and Americans would never have encountered these supposed bearers of a pristine past,' he writes, 'if they had not encountered one another, in bloody fact, as Europe reached out to seize the resources and populations of the other continents.' And not only Europe (and America). 'Has there ever been a time,' he wonders, 'when human populations have existed in independence of larger encompassing relationships, unaffected by larger fields of force?' Wolf doubts it. Hence his conclusion:

> Once we locate the reality of society in historically changing, imperfectly bounded, multiple and branching social alignments . . . the concept of a fixed, unitary and bounded culture must give way to a sense of the fluidity and permeability of cultural sets. In the rough-and-tumble of social interaction, groups are known to exploit the ambiguities of inherited forms, to impart new evaluations or valences to them, to borrow forms more expressive of their interests, or to create wholly new forms to answer changed circumstances. Furthermore, if we think of such interaction not [only] as causative in its own terms but as responsive to larger economic and political forces, the explanation of cultural forms must take account of the larger context, that wider field of force.[39]

It is not just that, as Marcus and Fischer insist, 'experience has always been more complex than the representation of it that is permitted by traditional techniques of description and analysis'. Of course that is true, and experimental writing can properly be regarded as 'a radicalization of concern with how cultural difference is to be represented in ethnography'. But it is also the case that we need, somehow, to show how that very complexity derives from the way in which the day-to-day lives of particular people in particular places are in part shaped through their involvement in larger systems which stretch beyond the immediacies of the 'here and now' (or the 'there and then'): that 'the "outside" . . . [is] an integral part of the construction and constitution of the "inside"'. Recognising this, Marcus and Fischer continue, experimental ethnographies are concerned

> to capture more accurately the [historico-geographical] context of [their] subjects, and to register the constitutive workings of impersonal international political and economic systems on the local level where fieldwork usually takes place. These workings can no longer be accounted for as merely external impacts upon local, self-contained cultures. Rather, external systems have their thoroughly local definition and penetration, and are formative of the symbols and shared meanings within the most intimate life-worlds of ethnographic subjects.[40]

These are, so it seems to me, substantially the same concerns which exercised Harvey and Giddens. But they are also the concerns which animate Fowles and Priest.

And yet, when set alongside the variety of textual strategies encompassed by the contemporary novel – changes in perspective, jump-cuts and cross-cuts between scenes, dislocations of chronology and composition, commentaries on the construction of the text by author and reader, and so on – the conservative character of many of the most radical geographies is truly astonishing.[41] Let me repeat: this is not an argument for experimentation for the sake of experimentation. It is instead a recognition that the form which we give to our texts materially affects what we say through them. Narrative, to take just one example, is not an innocent genre. It makes a series of strategic assumptions, usually unremarked, about closure and coherence. Stories are supposed to 'hang together', to make sense in a particular way; loose ends have to be tied up and a sense of finitude achieved. But what entitles us to represent the world – to 'make' sense of it – in this *particular* way? And, make no mistake, it is a particular way; other textual strategies are possible and, to some critics, even preferable.

Frederic Jameson contends that narrative is a 'socially symbolic act' which belongs to everyday life 'as lived on the social surface'. His thesis, as I understand it, is that the 'comprehensible order' of the conventional narrative conceals a much more tense and fundamentally contradictory social reality. Similarly, Hayden White suggests that the value we usually ascribe to narrative in the representation of 'what happened' arises 'out of a desire to have real events display the coherence, integrity, fullness and closure of an image of life that is and can only be imaginary'. For both writers, therefore, conventional narratives are structurally implicated in the construction of highly *specific* ideologies.[42] Post-modernism is, in part, a challenge to those conventions and an exploration of other possibilities.

It is not my purpose to debate these claims here: but they *ought* to be debated if we are to be vigilant about our work. One of the reasons Harvey's *Limits to Capital* is so different – so much more schematic, so much more systematised – than his later *Consciousness and the Urban Experience*, for example, is to do with the formal differences between the two texts: the one a sustained theoretical critique with, as I have shown, a central object and a master-narrative directed towards the urbanisation of capital, the other a collection of essays with a looser structure and an episodic, almost fragmentary evocation of the urbanisation of consciousness. This is to overstate the contrast, I know: Harvey has still not broken with the totalising vision of modern Marxism. But the change in textual strategy evident in his extraordinary essay on the historical geography of Paris is, I think, indicative of a growing tension in his work. Theory construction, he says, 'does not proceed in isolation from reflection, speculation and historical-geographical experience. But it does proceed rather differently.' And he admits that his thinking 'has been as much influenced by Dickens, Balzac, Zola, Gissing,

Dreiser, Pynchon, and a host of others' as it has been by 'dry-as-dust science'.[43] And that influence, I suggest, extends beyond their evocations of urban experience to the modes of representation which they deploy.

In sum, I believe we might profitably attend to the poetics of our descriptions as much as to their poetry: to the textual strategies which shape what we say as much as the words which we use.[44] Put like that, then for those who worry about these things geography is an 'art' (it is a 'science' too); *but the 'arts' are every bit as 'theoretical' in their sensibilities as the 'sciences'*. Poetics is about the theoretical scrutiny of textual strategies in whatever medium and in whatever field they are used, and the modes of representation which we deploy in our texts surely deserve our most careful theoretical reflection. There *is* a poetics of geography, for geography *is* a kind of writing – and writing, along with reading, is still the most difficult of all the skills we have to learn.

POST-MODERNISM?

There is an irony in all this. I said at the very start that post-modernism was suspicious of master-narratives, of systems with centres, of stories that claimed coherence and completeness. And yet my own account has been shaped by a conventional chronology, in which the successive cross-fertilisations of geography and political economy, sociology and anthropology have moved towards a post-modernism haunted by a central theme. There is probably comedy too: not only post-modernism but post-positivism, post-structuralism, post-Marxism, post-Impressionism . . . Where will it all end?

But the tragedy would be to treat the developments I have described here as symptomatic of yet another 'revolution', one more sea-change to roll with or roll back. These are, instead, ideas to think about and to work with – critically, vigilantly, constructively. One way of measuring the distance between them and modern human geography is, perhaps, to reverse one of the catch-phrases of spatial science: that there is more *disorder* in the world than appears at first sight is not discovered until that disorder is looked for.[45] That is more than mere word-play; it may be that one of the most ideological impulses of all – the 'commonsense' response to the complexity of the world – is to impose a coherence and a simplicity which is, at bottom, illusory.

Even so, I would not wish this essay to be taken as an unqualified manifesto for post-modernism. I am well aware that post-modernism can be read in a number of different ways, some of them acutely conservative as well as insistently radical; that there are all sorts of difficulties in its formulations which I have had no space to consider here; and that some of its own criticisms (of Habermas, for example) are wide of the mark. That said, the various themes which I have pulled together raise questions which, in my view, cannot be ignored. For, like Eagleton, I suspect that we are presently strung out between notions of social totality which are plainly discreditable and a 'politics of the fragment or conjuncture' which is largely ineffectual.[46] And to go *beyond* these limitations, I suspect, we need, in part, to go *back* to the question of areal differentiation: but armed with a new theoretical sensitivity towards the world in which we live and to the ways in which we represent it. Whether we focus on 'order' or 'disorder' or on the tension between the two – and no matter how we choose to define those terms – we still have to 'look'. We are still making geography.

Acknowledgements

I am grateful to Michael Dear, Felix Driver, Peter Jackson, David Ley, Chris Philo, Ed Soja, Nigel Thrift and Rex Walford for discussing the themes of this essay with me and for their comments on an early draft. I am also indebted to Denis Blackburn and Stella Gutteridge for preparing the illustrations.

NOTES AND REFERENCES

1. See Michael Dear, 'Postmodernism and planning' *Environment and Planning D: Society and Space*, 4 (1986) pp.367–384.
2. Frederic Jameson, 'Postmodernism, or the cultural logic of late capitalism', *New Left Review*, 146 (1984) pp.53–92.
3. See Richard Rorty, 'Habermas and Lyotard on Postmodernity', in Richard J. Bernstein (ed.) *Habermas and Modernity* (Cambridge: Polity Press, 1985) pp.161–175; Peter Dews, 'From post-structuralism to postmodernity: Habermas's counter-perspective', *ICA Documents* 4 (1986) pp.12–16.
4. David Ley, 'Styles of the times: liberal and neo-conservative landscapes in inner Vancouver, 1968–1986', *J. Hist. Geogr.*, 13 (1987) pp.40–56; see also Edward Relph, *Place and Placelessness* (London: Pion, 1976) and Kenneth Frampton, 'Towards a critical regionalism: six points for an architecture of resistance', in Hal Foster (ed.) *The Anti-aesthetic: Essays on Postmodern Culture* (Port Townsend: Bay Press, 1983) pp.16–30.
5. It is to the disclosure of these differences and disjunctures that 'deconstruction' is directed. I have found the following introductions particularly helpful: Terry Eagleton, *Literary Theory: An Introduction* (Oxford: Basil Blackwell, 1983) pp.127–50; Christopher Norris, *Deconstruction: Theory and Practice* (London: Methuen, 1982); Michael Ryan, *Marxism and Deconstruction: A Critical Articulation* (Baltimore: Johns Hopkins University Press, 1982) Chapter 1.
6. This thesis is argued with a special clarity in Richard Rorty, *Philosophy and the Mirror of Nature* (Oxford: Basil Blackwell, 1980); see also

Richard J. Bernstein, *Beyond Objectivism and Relativism: Science, Hermeneutics and Praxis* (Oxford: Basil Blackwell, 1983).

7. James Duncan and David Ley, 'Structural Marxism and human geography: a critical assessment', *Ann. Ass. Am. Geogr.*, 72 (1982) pp.30–59.
8. Jean-François Lyotard, *The Postmodern Condition: A Report on Knowledge* (Manchester: Manchester University Press, 1984); Michel de Certeau, *The Practice of Everyday Life* (Berkeley: University of California Press, 1984); Clifford Geertz, *Local Knowledge: Further Essays in Interpretative Anthropology* (New York: Basic Books, 1983). I cite these three texts as examples, not because I accept their particular theses.
9. Edward Soja, 'What's new? A review essay on the postmodernization of geography', *Ann. Ass. Am. Geogr.*, 77 (1987) pp.289–293. Cf. Michael E. Eliot Hurst, 'Geography has neither existence nor future.' In R. J. Johnston (ed.) *The Future of Geography* (London and New York: Methuen, 1985) pp.59–91.
10. Eagleton, *op. cit.*, p.vii.
11. These remarks, and those in the section which follows, are derived from David Harvey, *The Limits to Capital* (Oxford: Basil Blackwell, 1982); idem, *The Urbanization of Capital* (Oxford: Basil Blackwell, 1985); idem, 'The geopolitics of capitalism', in Derek Gregory and John Urry (eds) *Social Relations and Spatial Structures* (London: Macmillan, 1985) pp.128–163.
12. Doreen Massey, *Spatial Divisions of Labour: Social Structures and the Geography of Production* (London: Macmillan, 1984); the section which follows is derived largely from a reading of this text.
13. Massey, *op. cit.* For a connected but contrasting view of the geography of 'disorganized capitalism' – one which departs radically from the totalizing ambitions of modern Marxism – see Scott Lash and John Urry, *The End of Organized Capitalism* (Cambridge: Polity Press, 1987). Cf. Martin Jay, *Marxism and Totality* (Cambridge: Polity Press, 1984).
14. See Peter Jackson and Susan Smith, *Exploring Social Geography* (London: Allen & Unwin, 1984).
15. Perry Anderson, *In the Tracks of Historical Materialism* (London: Verso, 1983) p.34; Rick Roderick, *Habermas and the Foundations of Critical Theory* (London: Macmillan, 1986) pp.142–3. Habermas's writings are particularly instructive on these questions, though he is sharply critical of both post-structuralism and post-modernism: see Note 3.
16. Nigel Thrift, 'On the determination of social action in space and time', *Environment and Planning D: Society and Space,* 1 (1983) pp.23–57; Edward Soja, 'The spatiality of social life: towards a transformative retheorisation', in Derek Gregory and John Urry (eds) *Social Relations and Spatial Structures* (London: Macmillan, 1985) pp.90–127.
17. Derek Gregory, 'Space, time and politics in social theory: an interview with Anthony Giddens.' *Environment and Planning D: Society and Space,* 2 (1984) pp.123–32; Anthony Giddens, *The Constitution of Society:*

Outline of the Theory of Structuration (Cambridge: Polity Press, 1984) p.368.

18. The discussion which follows is largely based on Giddens, *op. cit.;* idem, *A Contemporary Critique of Historical Materialism* Volume 1: *Power, Property and the State* (London: Macmillan, 1981) Chapters 4–7; Derek Gregory, *The Geographical Imagination: Social Theory and Human Geography* (London: Hutchinson, forthcoming).
19. For a critique of time-geography, see Derek Gregory, 'Suspended animation: the stasis of diffusion theory', in Derek Gregory and John Urry (eds) *Social Relations and Spatial Structures* (London: Macmillan, 1985) pp.296–336.
20. Harvey, Limits *op. cit.,* Chapter 9.
21. Giddens, Constitution *op. cit.,* p.365.
22. Michael Mann, *The Sources of Social Power* Volume 1: *A History of Power from the Beginning to A.D. 1760* (Cambridge: Cambridge University Press, 1986) pp.1–4.
23. Michel Foucault, *Power/Knowledge: Selected Interviews and Other Writings* (edited by Colin Gordon) (Brighton: Harvester, 1980) p.149. I have provided a detailed discussion of Foucault's analytics of space in *Imagination, op. cit.*
24. Cf. Scott Lash and John Urry, 'The dissolution of the social?', in Mark Wardell and Stephen Turner (eds) *Sociological Theory in Transition* (Boston: Allen & Unwin, 1986) pp.95–109.
25. D. R. Stoddart, *On Geography and its History* (Oxford: Basil Blackwell, 1986) pp.35, 39.
26. W. W. Speth, 'Berkeley geography 1923–33', in Brian W. Blouet (ed.), *The Origins of Academic Geography in the United States* (Hamden: Archon, 1981) p.231.
27. See James Duncan, 'The superorganic in American cultural geography', *Ann. Ass. Am. Geogr.,* 70 (1980) pp.181–98; cf. Note 7.
28. Clifford Geertz, *The Interpretation of Cultures: Selected Essays* (New York: Basic Books, 1973) p.18.
29. These days we don't only write, of course, and the importance of film and video should be kept constantly in mind. Even so, the discussion which follows is confined to written texts, and although Geertz has noted the various ways in which the text can serve as a model for many other means of cultural expression, including landscapes, I do not mean to suggest that graphic images do not present their own, distinctive potentials (and problems).
30. Speth, *op. cit.,* pp.233–4.
31. E. M. Wilkinson and L. A. Willoughby, *Goethe: Poet and Thinker* (London: Edward Arnold, 1962) pp.182–3.
32. The classic paper is H. C. Darby, 'The problem of geographical description', *Trans. Inst. Br. Geogr.,* 30 (1962) pp.1–14.
33. George Marcus and Michael Fischer, *Anthropology as Cultural Critique:*

The Experimental Moment in the Human Sciences (Chicago: University of Chicago Press, 1986) pp.9, 42.
34. See Gunnar Olsson, *Birds in Egg/Eggs in Bird* (London: Pion, 1980) for an early example.
35. Geertz, *Interpretation op. cit.*
36. It does in fact come from Pierce Lewis's Presidential Address to the Association of American Geographers: 'Beyond Description', *Ann. Ass. Am. Geogr.*, 75 (1985) pp.465–77.
37. Cf. Stephen Kern, *The Culture of Time and Space 1880-1918* (Cambridge, Mass: Harvard University Press, 1983) pp.140–43.
38. James Clifford, 'Introduction: partial truths', in James Clifford and George Marcus (eds) *Writing Cultures: The Poetics and Politics of Ethnography* (Berkeley: University of California Press, 1986) p.22.
39. Eric Wolf, *Europe and the People without History* (Berkeley: University of California Press, 1982) pp.18, 387.
40. Marcus and Fischer, *op. cit.*, 39, 43.
41. Exceptions are now beginning to appear, though few of them have the freshness or immediacy of the best contemporary travel writing: and in my view they *ought* to.
42. Frederic Jameson, *The Political Unconscious: Narrative as a Socially Symbolic Act* (Ithaca: Cornell University Press, London; Methuen, 1980); Hayden White, 'The value of narrativity', in W. J. T. Mitchell (ed.) *On Narrative* (Chicago: University of Chicago Press, 1981) pp.1–23. See also Wallace Martin, *Recent Theories of Narrative* (Ithaca and London: Cornell University Press, 1986). An important geographical essay which is sensitive to these questions (though not as critical of conventional narrative as I would want to be) is Stephen Daniels, 'Arguments for a humanistic geography', in R. J. Johnston (ed.) *The Future of Geography* (London and New York: Methuen, 1985) pp.143–58.
43. David Harvey, *Consciousness and the Urban Experience* (Oxford: Basil Blackwell, 1985) pp.xv–xvi.
44. For a brilliant demonstration of what I have in mind, which shows just how constrained Darby's conception of the problem of geographical description really was, see John Barrell, 'Geographies of Hardy's Wessex', *J. Hist. Geogr.*, 8 (1982) pp.347–61.
45. The original phrase was Sigwart's, cited in P. Haggett and R. J. Chorley, 'Models, paradigms and the New Geography', in R. J. Chorley and P. Haggett (eds) *Models in Geography* (London: Methuen, 1967) p.20.
46. Terry Eagleton, *Against the Grain: Selected Essays* (London: Verso, 1986) p.5.

FURTHER READING

The clearest summary of Harvey's work will be found in his 'The Geopolitics of Capitalism', in Derek Gregory and John Urry (eds) *Social Relations and*

Spatial Structures (London: Macmillan, 1985) pp.128–163. (Many of the essays in this book are directly relevant to the themes addressed in the present chapter). For more detail, sample the essays collected together in Harvey's *Consciousness and the Urban Experience* and *The Urbanization of Capital* (Oxford: Basil Blackwell, 1985). For Doreen Massey, see her chapter with Richard Meegan in this volume and the references given there.

The best introduction to Giddens's ideas is still, in my view, his *A Contemporary Critique of Historical Materialism* Volume 1: *Power, Property and the State* (London: Macmillan, 1981). New readers should begin at Chapter 3!

George Marcus and Michael Fischer, *Anthropology as Cultural Critique: an experimental moment in the human sciences* (Chicago: University of Chicago Press, 1986) is essential reading for anyone interested in the problem of description and representation.

I have developed these ideas further in my *The Geographical Imagination* (London: Hutchinson, forthcoming).

PART II
PEOPLE AND PLACES, SOCIETIES AND SPACES

Introduction

These next four essays build from the local to the global, and a number of common themes run through them.

A central claim is that a genuinely human geography needs to explore the relations between what **John Eyles** calls the 'biographies of individuals' and the 'structures of society'. If for the most part our day-to-day lives seem ordinary and commonplace, this is simply because we take so much for granted. Eyles insists that if we stop to reflect on the seemingly mundane aspects of everyday life, we can begin to see how even the most repetitive and routinised of our actions is bound in to the reproduction of much wider and deeper social structures. Like Linda McDowell, he suggests that time-geography might – with some modifications – sensitise us to the ways in which we are shaped by, *and in turn ourselves shape*, the frameworks which contain our day-to-day lives.

On this reading, the future is not something which happens to us: it is, rather, something which we have a hand in making. This is a profoundly political vision, of course, and one which will undoubtedly disturb some readers. But it follows directly from the critical programme proposed by Ron Johnston in Chapter 1.3.1, and one of the most challenging developments in modern human geography is precisely this recovery of people as *knowledgeable* and *capable* human subjects. These emphases differ from those of conventional behavioural geography, because they are not concerned with revealing some fundamental (and usually strictly utilitarian) 'rationality' which shapes human actions into geometric patterns. They are, rather, about recovering the various ways in which people not only know a great deal about the worlds in which they live but can also create for themselves, through their own actions, the conditions for a meaningful existence. And they are obviously different from the models of spatial science, in which people were reduced to dots on maps or symbols in equation systems. Modern geography, then, is as much about the social organisation of space as it is about the spatial organisation of society.

But this does not mean that human geography is free to ransack anthropology, sociology and the other social sciences and humanities. As Derek Gregory argued in Chapter 1.4, it is impossible to make sense of the relations between human agency and social structure without *at the same time* examining place, space and landscape. Most of the formulations of the other social sciences (and even the humanities) turn out to be strategically incomplete because they assume that social life is somehow conducted on the head of a pin. These essays challenge that view. For Eyles, place is a 'profound centre of human existence'. And this is no abstract philosophy (though it can be connected to some writings in existentialism and phenomenology). Eyles shows that, for all the apparent 'sameness' of everyday life in the modern world – the bland homogeneity of the consumer society of advanced capitalism – the relations between people and places are negotiated through a multiplicity of different time-space routines which vary over time and space.

It should come as no surprise, then, to find **Denis Cosgrove** declaring that 'geography is everywhere': even in the commonplace encounters on a Saturday morning shopping trip. In his essay Cosgrove illustrates, through a series of vignettes, the ways in which visible landscapes reproduce cultural norms and effectively (if often surreptitiously) establish the values of dominant groups within societies as legitimate and even, on occasion, 'natural'.

The same lesson can be drawn from McDowell's feminist critique of urban geography and urban planning, which has produced (quite literally) a '*man*-made environment' dominated by the assumptions of men and often at odds with the needs of women. Cosgrove is thus surely right to remind us of the need to 'de-code' the apparently familiar worlds in which we live and to expose the social relations of power which are embedded in them. To be sure, those relations are not confined to the local or to the landscape.

In the next essay, therefore, following in some part the trail blazed by David Harvey in *The Limits to Capital*, **Roger Lee** sketches out the social relations which structure contemporary capitalism and shows how the day-to-day routines in the home, on the shop-floor or at the office mesh with the larger rotations of the world economy. His analysis similarly depends upon an understanding of spatial structure since, as he says, 'social relations are inseparable from geographical relations'.

If human geography is to pull together elements which are so often artificially separated – and the 'social' and the 'spatial' is only the most general example – it must also overcome its own sub-divisions. Lee's skeletal diagrams reveal, with an extraordinary clarity, the ways in which the various circuits through which capital moves around the modern world are all connected to a distinctive set of social relations. And yet, at the same time, those circuits (and even particular moments within them) are usually severed one from another and the structure dismembered for purposes of teaching or research: 'economic geography', 'social geography', 'urban geography', 'regional geography' and so on. It is no wonder that traditional human geography sometimes seems so lifeless.

Linda McDowell goes still further. Her essay argues not only that separate economic, social and political geographies (and the rest) make it virtually impossible to grasp their interconnections: those divisions also erase the significance of gender differences in the constitution of social life. 'The challenge that feminism poses to geography,' so she concludes, 'is to deconstruct accepted categories and to establish new ways of thinking about conventional divisions within geography'.

One division which *is* transcended in all of these essays is that between 'historical' and 'human' geography. All four authors are sensitive to historical depth, to the historical specificity of their arguments and to the importance of examining the geography of major social transformations. When Lee announces that 'there can be no universal geography or history based upon the working out of some invariant process', therefore, he speaks for all of them. From Eyles's changing communities to Cosgrove's changing landscapes, from McDowell's changing cities to Lee's changing economies, the message is the same: a changing world demands a changing geography.

For all their common ground, however, there are also a number of differences between the essays. These differences are, we think, constructive; they indicate some of the debates which are likely to take centre-stage in the next decade. So, for example, Lee's description of the modern world is much closer to the mainstream of modern Marxist thought than McDowell's: in her view, most Marxist analyses in geography still pay too much attention to class and too little to gender. Even so, McDowell's own account is more concerned with the bluntly material dimensions of day-to-day life – like waged and unwaged work – than with the cultural questions addressed by Eyles and Cosgrove. And whereas Lee, McDowell and Eyles treat geography as a social science, Cosgrove draws out the threads which have traditionally linked geography with the humanities and which still offer a remarkable opportunity to enlarge our own sensibilities and those of our students.

2.1
The Geography of Everyday Life

John Eyles
Queen Mary College, London

John Eyles is Associate Professor of Geography at McMaster University, Ontario. His teaching and research interests are in social geography, social theory and social policy. He is the co-editor (with David Smith) of *Qualitative Methods in Geography* and the author of several papers and *Senses of Place.*

THE NATURE OF EVERYDAY LIFE

At first sight, everyday life may not appear to be a subject worthy of academic investigation. When we think about what we do in everyday life, we tend to think of mundane, routine activities (often seen as chores) which we all appear to do. Indeed, because of its routine nature not many of us think about our everyday lives very much at all. Of course, we do ponder about segments of our lives – a family event, problems at work, making a journey – but as soon as we bring these activities into our consciousness they tend to be taken from everyday life and given their own distinctive and special meaning and status. But what we should recognise is that these distinctions are only seen as distinctions in the *context* of our everyday lives and concerns. We thus treat everyday life as unproblematic and unimportant at our peril.

What, then, is everyday life? It is simply the fundamental reality which creates, maintains and transforms everyone of us as self-aware and self-conscious individuals. It is therefore the world of experience which, through our self-awareness, we see as being both under our own control and shaped and even determined by forces and events outside of that control. Further, everyday life is not a static phenomenon, but is rather a dynamic process which is continually unfolding and emergent. It may appear to be merely an unchanging something that is there, but it only has this appearance because it is the unquestioned background to our lives. To constantly interrogate everyday life and experience would, of course, make our lives virtually unbearable. But not to reflect at all leaves the impression of everyday life as an immutable, 'natural' force to which we have to bow. It is important, therefore, for all of us to reflect upon the nature of our everyday lives in our families, homes and localities. I want to suggest that this can, in part, be carried out through studies of our own lives and those of others in our own localities.

It is in this need for reflecting on everyday life that we may discern the significance of everyday life itself. In seeing the individual in relation to the context and structure of everyday life one of the central questions of social science and philosophy emerges, namely the relationship between the individual and society (cf Derek Gregory's ideas in Chapter 1.4). Or to put it a little less succinctly, what is the relationship between the *structures of society* and the *biographies of individuals*? Those structures and biographies are enmeshed in everyday life and experience. Everyday life is, therefore, a taken-for-granted reality which provides the unquestioned background of meaning for the individual. It is a social construction which becomes a 'structure' itself. Thus through our actions in everyday life we build, maintain and reconstruct the very definitions, roles and motivations that shape our actions. We continuously maintain the culture and society which are the unquestioned background to our experience. But our actions do not occur within a vacuum. The patterns and meanings of, and reasons for, human actions are structured into and by the societies into which we are born. We both create and are created by society and these processes are played out within the context of everyday life.

Everyday life is, therefore, the *plausible social context* and *believable personal world* within which we reside. From it, we derive a sense of self, of identity, as living a real and meaningful biography. Everyday life is thus crucial for understanding human life and society. But that understanding must not just be a passive one, and while an examination of everyday life in its own terms is vital and important, we must also look at it interpretatively and critically. In other words, it is unlikely that we can obtain complete understanding by investigating the world of experience *per se*. Such an investigation is likely to emphasise our own control and individual agency, and it may not be so easy to discern the 'structures of society', the societal contexts of everyday life, which may significantly shape and constrain our experiences. To attempt to establish the salience of such structures and contexts requires the employment of theoretical constructs. It involves recognising that life is not necessarily coincidental with our immediate, taken-for-granted perceptions of it and that the facts (the experience of everyday life, for example) do not always speak for themselves.

To locate an analysis of everyday life in its contexts demands, therefore, recognition of the limitations of natural scientific procedures and of the power of the critique of positivism. This is not the place to rework that debate (but see Johnston, Chapter 1.3). Suffice it to say that the central assumption of conventional natural science – that analysts, their data and categories are context-independent – is untenable in the human and social sciences. There (here) analysts are members of a society and their materials emanate from its social fabric. Their (our) theories are not, therefore, context-independent. This can be used to advantage – theories ought to be informed evaluations of social life, albeit from specific viewpoints – and it is in this sense that theoretical constructs can be employed to interpret everyday life critically.

THE PARAMETERS OF EVERYDAY LIFE

While there are several different theoretical constructions concerning the nature of everyday life, perhaps the dominant themes are those of *routine* and *mundaneness*. But as Sinclair Lewis succinctly put it: 'The greatest mystery about a human being is not [their] reaction to sex or praise, but the manner in which [they] contrive to put in twenty-four hours a day.'[1] His own heroine, Carol Kennicott, in the town of Gopher Prairie, acted thus:

> In Carol's twenty-four hours a day she got up, dressed the baby, had breakfast, talked to Oscarina about the day's shopping, put the baby on the porch to play, went to the butcher's to choose between steak and pork chops, bathed the baby, nailed up a shelf, had dinner, put the baby to bed for a nap, paid the iceman, read for an hour, took the baby for a walk, called on Vida, had supper, put the baby to bed, darned socks, listened to Kennicott's yawned comment on what a fool Dr. McGanum was to try to use that cheap X-ray outfit of his on an epithelioma, repaired a frock, drowsily heard Kennicott stoke the furnace, tried to read a page of Thorstein Veblen – and the day was gone.[2]

Such a day appears perhaps commonplace and dull. But this example does demonstrate the rhythm of the day and its localisation and so reveals two of the most important parameters of everyday life: time and space. The rhythm of everyday life may also be seen in the structure of the agricultural year and its impact on the everyday lives of farming communities, and its localisation can readily be traced in our own customary activities which revolve around the spatial coordinates of home, work, shops, family, neighbourhood and so on.

It is necessary to counter the view that everyday life is simply dull. There is certainly a *familiarity* which we, as individuals, experience. And, of course, it is that familiarity that makes for the taken-for-granted, unquestioned nature of everyday life. Carol Kennicott sees this familiarity and contentment in the residents of Gopher Prairie. For its everyday life, the town provides the following: 'An unimaginatively standardised background, a sluggishness of speech and manners, a rigid ruling of the spirit by the desire to appear respectable. It is contentment . . . of the quiet dead . . . it is dullness made God.'[3] Lewis overstates the case but puts the 'dullness' into context by referring to the standardised background. Everyday life thus appears mundane not because it is dull but because it has become homogenised. Its *homogeneity* between places stems from two apparently contradictory but interrelated forces, and it is in these forces that we may begin to discern the importance of a geography of everyday life.

First, the homogeneity of everyday life comes from the need to get on with family and neighbours, to conform, to some extent, in styles of everyday behaviour and thought. While the increasing privacy given to individual and family life by the characteristics of dwellings and the use of discretionary time makes such conformity less straitened than in Lewis's day, localism – the localisation of activities – still exerts a conservative pressure. Place becomes a central focus of everyday life, although this is not to say that this pressure has only negative connotations for individuals. Conforming or, rather, simply being a fully participating member of a locality by sharing its dominant ways of thinking and acting, may bring considerable benefits. The warmth, solidarity, caring and sharing of traditional working-class communities in Britain helped their residents overcome or deflect the pressures and exploitations of the labour process. Indeed, their actions helped create such a milieu, although enmity as well as friendship could on occasion be produced in circumstances which were as straitened as they were localised. But in any case this is an environment which is fast disappearing, as the individualisation of life through the construction of single-family dwellings, the privatisation of leisure through the advent of the car and the television and the loss of self-help and communal-help through the growth of contribution-funded welfare schemes, continue apace. The necessary improvements in the material standards of life of the working class have, therefore, been bought at the price of a loss of a sense of community.

Secondly, the homogeneity of everyday life stems from societal forces emanating from industrialisation and resulting in the production of a mass culture and consciousness. The concentration and centralisation of the industrial process in advanced capitalism has led to the homogeneity of products and of life-styles. This homogeneity has an important geographical expression:

> The universal similarity – that is the physical expression of dull safety. Nine-tenths of the American towns are so alike that it is the completest boredom to wander from one to another. Always west of Pittsburgh, and often east of it, there is the same lumberyard, the same railroad station, the same Ford garage, the same creamery, the same box-like houses and two-storey shops. The new, more conscious houses are alike in their very attempts at diversity: the same bungalows, the same square houses of stucco or tapestry brick. The shops show the same standardised nationally advertised wares; the newspapers of sections three thousand miles apart

> have the same 'syndicated features'; the boy in Arkansas displays just such a flamboyant ready-made suit as is found on just such a boy in Delaware, both of them iterate the same slang phrases from the same sporting-pages, and if one of them is in College and the other is a barber, no one may surmise which is which.[4]

While the features change over time and between places, this description of the homogeneity of everyday life seems to ring true. Further, it points up the structures and constraints that impinge on our everyday lives. But are they like that? Are they so familiar and homogeneous that we simply live them whatever the consequences?

At one level, this argument seems to have great power, relating as it does societal forces to the sphere of everyday living. At another level, however, everyday life is not experienced as a unity. It consists of a mass of typical but unrelated routines, each of which is taken for granted by the participants. There are, then, many everyday realities – work, family life, leisure pursuits and so on – and these may be constructed, defined and legitimated in quite discrepant ways. This '*pluralisation of life-worlds*'[5] means that the construction of and adherence to one world view becomes difficult. We follow not routine but rather routines. Thus the apparent homogenisation of everyday life and of public issues in general can affect us in quite different ways. The homogenising tendency is real enough, but our responses, at the level of what it means for us and how we react to it, are not predetermined. A geography of everyday life must thus investigate the *specific* responses of people in *concrete* social and spatial settings. Cross-cultural comparisons suggest that the detail of everyday life varies significantly between places. Do similar variations occur within cultures?

Further, while routines are both typical and ordinary, they are part of a world that does not stand still. Of course, if nothing interrupts the flow of mundane activities, there is no apparent need to think about the world and our consciousness about everyday life recognises this possibility of infringement.

> The ebb and flow of everyday life involves more than routine, it involves consciousness of differences between the boring present and the threatening future, the possibility of pain and suffering, and, more appositely, consciousness of the actuality of personal troubles.[6]

CHANGE IN EVERYDAY LIFE

We are, then, conscious, self-aware beings who recognise the potential for disruption to everyday life. And when people have to confront their personal troubles and concerns in relation to public issues in particular, it is possible to obtain powerful insights not only into the nature of everyday life but also into the forces that impinge on everyday life. In a geographical context, confrontations of this sort have occurred over housing, environmental quality and the destruction of neighbourhoods and localities through factory closure and economic restructuring.

Although many studies of this kind have focused attention on the structural conditions necessary for the development of urban social movements, of the collective responses to the penetrations of the state and business on everyday life, only a few have examined the nature of social experience in such changing circumstances. Such analyses focus, of necessity, on the *politicisation of everyday life*, whether that involves middle-class residents fighting against a particular road route proposal or working-class people creating self-help organisations to combat the ravages of insecure employment and welfare cutbacks. In Croydon, near London, for example, the relatively affluent inhabitants of the southern part of the Borough have withstood attempts to introduce high density housing and reorganise educational services and facilities so as to preserve their established way of life in pleasant surroundings. In Greenpoint-Williamsburg, New York, poor residents formed block associations to make their everyday lives more bearable in precarious economic and welfare-provision conditions. Welfare bureaucratic intransigence coupled with variable landlord-tenant relations and poor employment opportunities led to residents mustering their slender resources to develop networks of households, that is to restructure parts of everyday life.

These networks, based on domestic and child-rearing assistance, cannot be seen in isolation; their restructuring attempts were more likely to succeed where programmes had already been established by the state. In general, not only are successful local movements likely to be accommodative to the existing order of things, but their perspectives are unlikely to be shared by all inhabitants. Again, there is a pluralisation of life-worlds so that particular people may see improvements to their everyday lives in different ways. Thus, in St Ann's, a poor district in Nottingham, there were significant differences in attitudes towards different types of urban renewal, with tenants seeing comprehensive redevelopment as a way to the more favoured public housing and landlords and owner occupiers preferring rehabilitation. In any event, in all these examples we may note that it is the disruption of routine through the threat or reality of urban renewal, welfare problems and so on – through, therefore, the intermeshing of private worries with public issues – that we can identify most readily the forces that are normally taken for granted in routine everyday life, the *economic* and the *political*.

There is another such force, the *ideological*, which shapes the *consciousness* of everyday life. It is this force that may be seen in the homogenisation of everyday life. It refers particularly to certain pervasive ideas, values and meanings which shape the ways we think and act. It has been suggested that there is a dominant meaning-system (or 'hegemony'), a world view which through its emphases tends to help reproduce existing social relations. In capitalist society, it is argued, the dominant values are those of individualism, competitiveness, avarice, acquisitiveness and, by extension, consumerism. These values inform our consciousness of a privatised and fragmented world. This mass consciousness is the basis of the homogenisation of everyday life and it is the store of the meanings which are applied to social settings. Everyday life becomes an adjunct to consumer capitalism and all human relationships are seen as extensions of the market, that is they are commodified and objectified.[7]

Such a view assumes, of course, that hegemony is monolithic and that individuals are simply passive recipients of its ideology. But I have already suggested that individuals construct their own social realities, albeit not with materials of their own choosing, and their constructions are based on socialisation and experience. It is extremely unlikely that all experiences are fully consonant one with one another, and so different values are likely to emerge whose meanings derive from particular sets of experience. Thus while the constraints of economy and polity cannot be ignored at the level of consciousness, we must also recognise that individuals actively create and creatively transform themselves, and that these constructions and reconstructions are located firmly in an experience of everyday life which may result in *different* ways of seeing, and acting in, the world. Such a position, I think, enables us to recognise the importance of place in the context of everyday life.

PLACE IN EVERYDAY LIFE

The significance of place, along with that of age, gender, ethnicity and family, is usually hidden by the overarching homogenisation of everyday life. To put it differently, there are several principles which can shape the nature of individual lives and the nature of the social structure. Everyday life is, therefore, shaped by what are sometimes called 'dimensions of structuration'. *Structuration* focuses attention on the relations between the conduct of life and its containing structures. These relations are often seen in terms of 'agency and structure', where 'agency' refers to the essence of experience found in everyday life and 'structure' to the rules and resources of social systems. For our present purposes we are not interested in how these various dimensions come together to form particular social groupings. We must not forget, of course, that such a coming together is likely and that none of the dimensions is truly independent. But to say that a dimension lacks independence is not to say that it lacks significance and it is in this regard that I want to examine *place*.

Although 'place' has not been explicitly investigated from the viewpoint of concrete everyday experiences, place as a meaningful existential category has been most successfully treated by humanistic geography. Borrowing from existential and phenomenological philosophy, it sees place as being of intrinsic importance. Place is seen as a centre of felt value, incarnating the experience and aspirations of people. Thus it is not only an arena for everyday life – its geographical or spatial co-ordinates – it, in itself, provides *meaning* to that life. To be attached to a place is seen as a fundamental human need and, particularly as home, as the foundation of our selves and our identities. Places are thus conceived as profound centres of human existence. As such, they can provide not only a sense of well-being but also one of entrapment and drudgery. To be tied to one place may well enmesh a person in the familiar and routine from which no escape seems possible. This may affect the relatively immobile most of all.

While perhaps the greatest sources of immobility are poverty, disability and infirmity, age may also be important in its own right. Place does not seem to loom large in the everyday lives or consciousness of the poor. The shabbiness and squalor of living conditions may be there but it is the entrapment, produced by the lack of resources and of communal assistance, that causes their pain and rage. By their very nature the places of the poor affect their everyday lives, but they live where they do because they are poor and not as a result of an attachment to a particular place. The elderly may be poor too, but place for them does seem meaningful. Their present locations are often the foci of their constrained social lives and they also reminisce about past places. Such reminiscence – nostalgia for past places – may militate against the immobility of their present everyday lives.

But there is a confusion in humanistic geography. On the one hand, it is argued that place is the centre of felt value and that it is a fundamental human need, vital for the establishment of personal identity. On the other, it is suggested that the homogenising tendencies in the modern world result, for the mass of people, in an 'inauthentic' attitude to place and a state of 'placelessness'. There is then no awareness of the deep and symbolic significance of places and no appreciation of their identities. People live in sprawling non-places (suburbs or subtopias) and holiday in specially created tourist environments, all of which are seen as being without existential meaning. Such a view is surely élitist, because it regards particular places and 'high culture' as the embodiments of true meaning. It seems to me that such a perspective gives neither credence nor consideration to the abilities of people to – for example – create meaningful places and identities in their everyday lives in the suburbs or to the needs for recuperative and diverting leisure pursuits and locations. Such a view also assumes that place is an independent dimension of everyday life rather than just a significant one. Despite its reliance on the homogenisation argument, it fails to consider the contest of everyday life and particularly its *material parameters*. People do shape their own lives and create their own identities, but not necessarily or overwhelmingly in conditions of their choosing. For most people in Britain, the 'choice' is between different suburban locations or housing estates and between the beach resorts of Britain and the Mediterranean.

The importance of putting place in the context of the material conditions that shape everyday life is exemplified by those communities for whom such conditions are of most immediate import: the poor, the ethnic minorities and the working class in general. I have already referred to the significance of place (localism) in the construction and reproduction of certain working-class values and life styles. As one of Jeremy Seabrook's respondents put it:

> I can remember the street on an afternoon; all the women'd be standing round the doors, talking to each other. One would say 'Ah've got nowt for tea, what have you got?' The next one would say 'Ah've got nowt either, I don't know what Ah'm going to do.' Then one would say 'Why don't we make up a parcel and take it down to the pawnshop?' One would say 'Ah've got a pair of pillowcases'; another would have a pair of sheets, another some curtains. So they'd make up a parcel and take it to the pawnshop, and whatever they got, they'd share it out between them, get something for tea . . . The hardships of life didn't bother us like they bother people now . . .[8]

We must be aware of romanticising the past because such localities contained disagreements and conflicts as well as comfort, and this sense of sociability, solidarity, sharing and 'making do' is, of course, fast disappearing with urban redevelopment and the privatisation of social life. But the example does demonstrate the importance of place in relation to material conditions in everyday life. Today even working-class localities are fragmented with a multiplicity of realities. Significant divisions include those based on age, gender and 'respectability'. In Leytonstone, London, for example, the elderly look back longingly to the everyday life of the past in which things (and people) seemed more fixed and certain. The young men are concerned with now and with the pleasures of drink, girls and gambling. What does unite the generations is a belief in fate, or more positively luck, which conspires to ensure good or indifferent family life or work prospects. In fate, of course, we may see the operations of those forces over which the individuals feel they have no control but which significantly affect their everyday lives.

The significance of place in everyday life in not, however, the preserve of the working class. Investigation of the whole range of the population in Towcester, a small English town, revealed that most people have a sense of place which is *a* foundation of identity but which is constrained by the necessities of material existence. In the main, it was everyday activities and notions which gave shape to this sense of place. Everyday social interactions with family, neighbours and friends influenced attitudes to place in a variety of ways. Some saw place as being defined almost entirely in terms of intense social relations, while others saw it as the arena or stage for conventional social ties. Place was also regarded as a means to an end, seen in terms of the opportunities (work, shopping, leisure) it provided for everyday activities. And finally a significant number saw place as unimportant in their everyday lives. They either felt powerless to shape the courses of their lives or demonstrated little interest in place or life in general. The following is a selection of extracts from my unpublished field notes:

> It don't matter where you live: you still get fucked. It's either them bosses or managers or supervisors. Or if not, it's the council. They tell you what to do. Sweep the floor; no, you can't have a break; you can't smoke here . . . . And they won't listen. I've complained and moaned about them broken bannisters. But they won't come till someone breaks his neck . . .

> I don't know. I don't think anything about where I live really. You've got to live somewhere. Stands to reason, of course. If I didn't live here, I'd have to live somewhere else, wouldn't I? . . . It's like you've got to work somewhere. It doesn't matter where long as you've got enough money . . .

Thus far, I have looked at the meaning and significance of everyday life and have tried, through examples, to demonstrate the necessity of a geography of everyday life. As is probably apparent, there have been few contemporary studies of everyday life in advanced capitalist society so we are left searching for clues to its nature by examining studies which were carried out for other purposes. It is not surprising, therefore, that we have a compartmentalised view of everyday life, with different sets of investigations focusing on behaviour, meanings and constraints in everyday life.

TIME AND SPACE IN EVERYDAY LIFE

Behaviour and time–space routines

It is not the intention of this chapter to review the legion of studies in behavioural geography, viz shopping behaviour, leisure activities, voting behaviour, residential mobility and so on. Of course, such studies provide clues to the nature of everyday life, but they do not conceive of life in its wholeness or for that matter of individuals in their wholeness. Such studies tend to present a segmented view of people and their activities and it is difficult to envisage how the views may be joined together.

But one line of enquiry worthy of some consideration is *time-geography*,[9] largely based on the work of Torsten Hägerstrand and the Lund School, because it does take an holistic view: and it also adds the dimension of time. This approach recognises that the indivisibility of human beings places certain *capability constraints* on their actions. Not only is the time-span of existence limited, but individuals have a limited ability to participate in more than one task at any one time. All tasks use time, whereas space has a limited capacity to accommodate events. And most tasks require individuals to 'connect up' for particular periods of time at particular places. These realities act as *coupling constraints*, defining what 'connections' are made where, when and for how long. There are also *steering constraints* which limit access to particular locations in time and space – opening-hours and bus timetables for example – and regulate conduct within them. Time-geographic methods have been used to chart individual projects and biographies through time and space, and thereby to discern which activities are possible and which are not as a result of the intersection of these basic, 'structural' constraints. Time-geography has been particularly useful in examining the way in which such structures are affected by age, class and gender (see, for example, McDowell in Chapter 2.3).

Time-geography thus charts the possibilities of everyday life, and can be used to increase and improve them through the spatial rearrangement and temporal rescheduling of events. From time-geography too we glean the idea of 'packing', and realise that there is a finite capacity to the activities and events which may be packed into everyday life. It is, of course, possible to increase this packing capacity by creating more space (for example, high rise building and reclamation schemes as in Hong Kong) or by 'colonising' different times for activities as the active day is extended into the night for entertainment, socialising and even business. Of course, there must be a pool of labour to service these activities and the perceptions of advantage must outweigh those of risk. Further, one person's infrequent colonisation of the night is another's routine existence. The reconstruction of the active day depends, therefore, on the mundane activities of others, which depend in turn on the economics of provision. This is an essential insight because, in focusing on the individual, time-geography has tended to underemphasise the significance of such material, societal contexts. It has also neglected, of necessity, meanings and the social construction of social life in its concentration on universal dimensions of existence and on formal structures of constraints.

Meanings and symbolic landscapes

The meanings that people employ in their everyday lives have been examined in an implicit way by studies in perception geography, architecture and planning and environmental psychology, which have focused on images of places and environments. It has been demonstrated, for example, that different social and ethnic groups have different images of the city, with higher status and white groups possessing more detailed and extensive images than lower status and black groups. These images may be regarded as representations of the ways in which individuals and groups define their everyday living environments. These images or definitions are important parts of the learning process. In fact, they may be regarded as 'inner representations' of the world which shape, define and give meaning to our activities and lives. These meanings are, of course, socially and culturally differentiated, and their configurations will depend on the particular circumstances of our upbringings and socialisations. Thus working-class images tend to be the products of more crowded spaces than those of the middle class, while, for Europeans privacy and the inviolability of personal space are of greater importance than, say, for Arabs. Up-down, front-back, left-right, centre-periphery, near-far – all have culturally-determined meanings which we use unselfconsciously in everyday life. Not all cultures define these phenomena in exactly the same way. There are, for example, different meanings attaching to proximity and therefore population density and 'crowding', with concomitant effects on the nature and conduct of everyday life.

These studies are all indirect, however, in that they focus mainly on the environment rather than on the person and his or her everyday life. This is particularly, but understandably, the case with perception geography in which meaning is identified through the landscape. It is important, however, to see the landscape as *constituting* (and reconstituting) a particular social order so that the identified meaning shapes and structures everyday experience (see also Cosgrove, Chapter 2.2). Thus in the Sudan, flimsy wood and grass houses are symbolic of the lowest economic and social classes, while in Australia and the United States a house with a peripheral location and natural vegetation identifies high status. Landscape symbolises meaning which in turn shapes the social relations and activities of particular locales and groups – the poverty and drudgery of the Sudanese village and the mobile, interest-based experience of the Australian and American suburb.

To focus on the group and its everyday life may be a more fruitful starting point, however, though its locale would undoubtedly remain a significant defining characteristic. Indeed, some recent work within humanistic geography has such an emphasis. Everyday experience and its environing conditions can affect psychological well-being. Where everyday life is dominated by drudgery and exploitation and where symbols of identity – wealth, prestige, honour – are lacking, a group may enhance its identity and solidarity by expressing strong attachments to neighbourhoods, as for example with the Cape Coloureds of South Africa and District Six. This particular research is interesting in another respect too, because it demonstrates the significance of context and constraint for the production of meanings and the shape of everyday life: in this case, the apartheid state.

Context and constraints in everyday life

The constraints operating in and on everyday life may be seen as social and/or systemic. Social constraints arise from the fact that our meanings and behaviour do not occur in a vacuum. Everyday life is a series of social interactions between ourselves and others. Indeed our very selves are constructed in relation to others – individuals, institutions, ideas. The recognition of these constraints leads to the view of everyday life as a 'drama' in which expressions are sent and presented by ourselves and impressions are received from and reflected back by others. These others shape everyday life, as exemplified by some tenants on the Shetland Islands, who let the outward appearance of their cottages decay so that their landlords thought they were relatively poor and could not afford higher rents. Such a 'management' of ourselves in the presence of others demonstrates not only the social construction of reality but also its *negotiation*. Such negotiation is not a once-and-for-all matter. Reality is many-sided and we inhabit a 'pluralisation of life-worlds', some of which are mundane and taken for granted, while others demand recognition of the power and competence of others.

The *power* of others is in fact one of the systemic constraints that can also significantly shape everyday life. Such power largely determines the life patterns of black people in the group areas, townships and 'homelands' of South Africa. This may be an extreme example of the way in which everyday life can be determined by forces outside our control, but some writers have sought to generalise the power of such constraints. For them, everyday life is seen as alienating, with little or no immediate or existential meaning. It is shaped and distorted by market and state mechanisms, and conditioned by the rhetoric and ideology of consumer capitalism. Everyday life becomes filled with repressive contradictions such as the glorification of the individual to bureaucratic and marketing logic. Thus suburban living and owner occupation are seen as being modes particularly conducive to the enhancement of capitalist accumulation and capitalist social relations. We deceive ourselves that we have choices in our lives, while everyday life itself becomes a 'concentration camp' in which we are passive spectators to our own subjection, with only individual resistances and 'escape-attempts' possible. Even the escape to leisure is no escape, because such activities occur within spaces and facilities created by similar forces that entrap us in our workaday lives.

Such views deny virtually all human creativity, seeing people as victims and automatons with no power to construct their own identities and lives. As such, they overstate their case. Like studies emphasising behaviour and meanings, this perspective provides a necessary but limited account of everyday life, the investigation of which requires the interactive treatment of *all* the dimensions involved.

Has this ever been carried out? It is possible, perhaps, to cite the much criticised 'community studies' as examples. They sought to investigate the totality of social life in specific locales, but were condemned for their implicit suggestion that ways of life coincided with settlement: indeed, such coincidence was demonstrated to be increasingly unlikely and even untenable. Recently, however, there have been examinations of everyday life that genuinely grasp the totality of everyday life. Such studies bring methodological issues to the fore because they rely on a small number of cases rather than on representative samples. Such *ethnographic* analyses, emphasisng case-studies and analytic induction, represent a rediscovery of anthropological methods. These methods involve the overt or covert participation in the lives of those investigated to ask questions, to listen to what is said and to watch what happens. Their great strength is that they are the bases of in-depth descriptions set in a theoretical context. They also represent perhaps the most likely route to a profound understanding of the complexity of everyday life, which is seen to involve social activities and the social construction and negotiation of meaning in circumstances which not only enable the creation of self and identity but also significantly constrain the range of possible activities, constructions and creations.

Thus in a study of perceptions of health and illness, in Bethnal Green in East London, it was found that the nature and experience of work and professional health care shaped these perceptions.[10] But these perceptions were also governed by commonsense ideas and values which were grounded in the people's way of life, which was itself shaped by the nature of the local housing and labour markets. In a study of eight household, in Battersea in South London, individual options and expectations within households were assessed through 'resource systems' which included not only money and property but time, experience, information and social interactions.[11] These resources shape the nature of everyday life and influence the ability of individuals and households to manage. They affect and are affected by the way the households see and define themselves, their presents and their futures.

CONCLUSIONS

I have tried to show that the study of everyday life raises both methodological *and* philosophical-cum-theoretical questions. In answer to the first – how is everyday life to be investigated? – the need for detail on so many interrelated facets of life points to the efficacy of ethnographic methods. But since these also entail interpretation, classification and ultimately explanation of social constructions, the study of everyday life – commonplace as it might seem – is not a theory-neutral enterprise.

But how else may we conclude? What in fact does a *geography* of everyday life entail? It must recognise, I suggested, that time and space are fundamental, organisational categories of human life. Everyday life has a temporal mobility; it is a project with a past, a fleeting present and (we hope) a future. It also exists in the reality of space. It is localised; at the most basic level in the relation of self to others, but also in that propinquity and 'packing' are necessary (but not sufficient) conditions for many features of everyday life. There does exist a friction or a tyranny of distance, albeit one modified by personal attributes and definitions and by class and cultural parameters, and within these spatial templates lies the rationale for a geography of everyday life.

The study of everyday life must also recognise self as the being which conceptualises and acts in everyday life. Self is reflexively aware, but a significant part of identity is based on the presence of others. We experience ourselves simultaneously as subjective sources of projects and as objective reflections and reactions of others. We must mutually construct each others' lives and this unquestioned construction is the basis of sociality, which itself occurs as social interaction. Indeed we may define ourselves in terms of the accumulated history and anticipated future of interactions that make up our lives. These interactions, along with our interpretations, imaginations and constructions make up our biographies. Further, these interactions may be based on intimate face-to-face contact (we-relationships) or contradictory, depersonalised ones (I-it relationships) or they may be characterised by varying degrees of anonymity.

Interaction thus takes place within concrete situations or environments which shape the encounters. These situations may be defined or made by ourselves, but most are predetermined to some extent by culture and social usages and regularities. Situations act as a context of constraint for the pursuit of everyday life. And while the effects of situations may be negotiated, we must recognise the importance of forces almost beyond our control, particularly power and structure. I say 'almost' because individuals produce and are the product of society. A geography of everyday life must address this central contention. Everyday life is a constrained social construction, consisting of behaviour, meanings and context. No one dimension is necessarily of greater importance than the others. And while I began with the core features of everyday life and ended with its core categories (time, space, self, other, interaction, biography, situation, power and structure), both beginning and end forcefully state and restate the key theme: in the context of everyday life can be seen the dialectical relationship between 'individual' and 'society'.

NOTES AND REFERENCES

1. Sinclair Lewis, *Main Street* (New York: Signet, 1961 edition) p.254.
2. Ibid., p.255.
3. Ibid., p.257.
4. Ibid., pp.260–1.
5. See Peter Berger, Brigitte Berger and Hansfried Kellner, *The Homeless Mind* (New York: Random House, 1973).
6. Arthur Brittain, *The Privatised World* (London: Routledge & Kegan Paul, 1977).
7. See Henri Lefebvre, *Everyday Life in the Modern World* (New York: Harper and Row, 1971).
8. Jeremy Seabrook, *Unemployment* (St Albans: Paladin, 1982).
9. For an introduction to time-geography, see Tommy Carlstein, *Time Resources, Society and Ecology* (London and Boston: George Allen & Unwin, 1982).
10. Jocelyn Cornwall, *Hard-earned Lives* (London: Tavistock, 1984).
11. Sandra Wallman, *Eight London Households* (London: Tavistock, 1984).

FURTHER READING

An important account of everyday life as a routine, taken-for-granted construction is Peter Berger and Thomas Luckmann, *The Social Construction of Reality* (Harmondsworth: Penguin, 1967), while illuminating descriptions of how individuals present and manage their identities will be found in Erving Goffman, *The Presentation of Self in Everyday Life* (Harmondsworth: Penguin, 1971).

I have reviewed studies in humanistic geography in John Eyles, *Senses of Place* (Warrington: Silverbrook Press, 1985). Some of the philosophical and methodological issues which I raise here are addressed by Anthony Giddens, *New Rules of Sociological Method* (London: Hutchinson, 1976), while more practical questions are discussed in Martyn Hammersley and Paul Atkinson, *Ethnography: Principles in Practice* (London: Tavistock, 1984).

2.2
Geography is Everywhere: Culture and Symbolism in Human Landscapes

Denis Cosgrove
Loughborough University of Technology

Denis Cosgrove is Senior Lecturer in Geography at Loughborough University of Technology. His teaching and research interests include landscape and environmental art, particularly in Renaissance Italy and Victorian England, the built environment and geographical thought. His publications include *Social Formation and Symbolic Landscape* and several articles on cultural geography and the idea of landscape.

MEANINGS AND LANDSCAPES

On Saturday mornings I am not, consciously, a geographer. I am, like so many other people of my age and lifestyle, to be found shopping with my family in my local town-centre precinct. It is not a very special place, artificially illuminated under the multi-storey car park, containing an entirely predictable collection of chain stores – W.H. Smith, Top Shop, Baxters, Boots, Safeway and others – fairly crowded with well-dressed, comfortable family consumers. The same scene could be found almost anywhere in England. Change the names of the stores and then the scene would be typical of much of western Europe and North America. Geographers might take an interest in the place because it occupies the peak rent location of the town, they might study the frontage widths or goods on offer as part of a retail study, or they might assess its impact on the pre-existing urban morphology. But I'm shopping.

Then I realise other things are also happening: I'm asked to contribute to a cause I don't approve of; I turn a corner and there is an ageing, evangelical Christian distributing tracts. The main open space is occupied by a display of window panels to improve house insulation – or rather, in my opinion, to destroy the visual harmony of my street. Around the concrete base of the precinct's decorative tree a group of teenagers with vividly coloured Mohican haircuts and studded armbands cast the occasional scornful glance at middle-aged consumers. I realise that, unemployed as they almost certainly are and of an age when home is the least comfortable environment, they will 'hang around' here until this space is closed off by the steel barriers that enclose it at night.

The precinct, then, is a highly textured place, with multiple layers of meaning. Designed for the consumer, to be sure, and thus easily amenable to my retail geography study, nevertheless its geography stretches way beyond that narrow and restrictive perspective. The precinct is a symbolic place where a number of cultures meet and perhaps clash. Even on Saturday morning I am still a geographer. Geography is everywhere.

Culture and symbolism are words that today do not slip easily or frequently off the tongues of most human geographers in Britain. By and large we rather pride ourselves on our down-to-earth practicality and relevance. We prefer to handle tangible, empirical materials, to interpret the world in the precise and measurable terms of practical necessity. Since the 1960s British human geographers have tended to work with certain unstated assumptions about how they should set about explaining patterns of human occupance and activity, assumptions which tend to exclude from consideration culture and symbol. These assumptions are:

(i) that the physical world, the natural environment, is the domain of scientific physical geography. It may set bounds to human conduct, but such bounds are so broad as to render dangerous any appeal to them in human geographical explanation. Ecologists rather than geographers have pre-empted questions of environmental relations. However, both space and population serve as legitimate starting points for explanation in human geography.

(ii) that humans behave in a rational, fairly predictable manner, when viewed in aggregate, to achieve personal and social goals that are overwhelmingly practical. Rationality is tacitly agreed to mean economic maximisation or satisfaction. Other motivations are treated as 'irrational' and geographically interesting only as deviations from the model form.

(iii) that geographers should seek a practical or utilitarian outcome from their studies. Human geography should be 'relevant', its results applied to some 'real world situation'. Human geographers display a strong moral commitment to bettering their world, one reason why human geography remains popular in schools and colleges. This relevance must, apparently, be immediate and direct. Therefore human geographers, certainly in the last decade, have warmly embraced as issues for study socially laudable causes like inner urban redevelopment, conservation of past landscapes, regional equality and third world development.

(iv) that human geography despite, or perhaps because of, its elevated moral purpose should as far as possible avoid overt and contentious political, ideological and even philosophical questions. It should strive for objectivity by analysing facts and ensuring that its statements are anchored securely to empirical warranty.

These assumptions are in no sense dishonourable. But they do result in excluding from our agenda much that human geography could potentially study in the realms of human spatial activity and its environmental expressions. Further, they produce a deep contradiction within the subject. If our intentions are morally founded and the outcome of our work supposedly of value to humankind, while our materials remain exclusively empirical and our interpretations of human motivation resolutely utilitarian, we deny ourselves a language for framing the very goals we seek: the making of a better human world. Some of the varied consequences of this dilemma are dealt with in other essays of the book. My intention here is to highlight two of them.

Firstly, lost on the tide of earnest practicality and among the shingles of demonstrable fact is the real magic of geography – the sense of wonderment at the human world, the joy of seeing and reflecting upon the richly variegated mosaic of human life and of understanding the elegance of its expressions in the human landscape. This is the experience that still makes the *National Geographic* one of the most popular journals in the world. Geography, after all, is everywhere. John Eyles shows how it is there in everyday life (see Chapter 2.1). One of the tasks of geographers is to show that geography is there to be enjoyed. Too often we have been more successful in dulling rather than enhancing that pleasure.

Secondly, what we also lose in the utilitarian functionalism of so much geographical explanation is the recognition of human motivation other than the narrowly practical. Banished from geography are those awkward, sometimes frighteningly powerful motivating passions of human action, among them moral, patriotic, religious, sexual and political. We all know how fundamentally these motivations influence our own daily behaviour, how much they inform our response to places and scenes, even the shopping precinct. Yet in human geography we seem to wilfully ignore or deny them, refusing to explore how such passions find expressions in the worlds we create and transform. Consequently our geography misses much of the meaning embedded in the human landscape, tending to reduce it to an impersonal expression of demographic and economic forces. The idea of applying to the human landscape some of the interpretative skills we deploy in studying a novel, a poem, a film or a painting, of treating it as an intentional human expression composed of many layers of meaning, is fairly alien to us. Yet this is what I propose to explore, and to suggest ways of treating geography as a *humanity* as much as a social science.

Such an approach has begun to emerge among a small number of human geographers since the early 1970s.[1] A brief guide to their work is offered at the end of the chapter. As with all shifts in the direction of geographical research, this change is related to broader social movements: protests against environmental exploitation and pollution, unease with megascale planning and the anonymous landscapes of urban redevelopment, the growing voice of organised women challenging the dominance of male culture and the failure of the post-war social and political consensus have all played their part in nudging human geography towards *humanistic* geography. But the idea of human geography as a *humanity* is scarcely a mature or fully developed one. So what follows must be a personal assessment of possibilities. I will approach this through a discussion of three terms – landscape, culture and symbolism – and lead on to some examples of interpreting the symbolism of cultural landscapes.

LANDSCAPE

Landscape has always been closely connected in human geography with culture, the idea of *visible* forms on the earth's surface and their composition. Landscape is in fact a 'way of seeing', a way of composing and harmonising the external world into a 'scene', a visual unity. The word landscape emerged in the Renaissance to denote a new relationship between humans and their environment.[2] At the same time cartography, astronomy, architecture, land surveying, painting and many other arts and sciences were being revolutionised by the application of formal mathematical and geometrical rules derived from Euclid. Such rules, it was believed, would return the arts and sciences to their classical perfection. Perhaps the most striking of all these 'mechanical arts' from the point of view of space relations was the invention of linear perspective. Perspective allows us to reproduce in two dimensions the realistic illusion of a rationally composed three-dimensional space. A consistent order and form can be imposed intellectually and practically across the external world. Little wonder that in the same period landscape painting appeared for the first time in Europe as a popular style, paralleled by a blossoming art of landscape in poetry, drama, garden and park design. This was also the age when terrestrial space was being mapped rationally onto the graticules of sophisticated map projections, while rational human landscapes were being constructed in capital cities like Rome, Petersburg and Paris, and written across newly-reclaimed lands in northern Italy, Holland and East Anglia, or on the enclosed estates of progressive landowners and over the vastnesses of overseas colonial territories.

Landscape is thus intimately linked with a new way of seeing the world as a rationally-ordered, designed and harmonious creation whose structure and mechanism are accessible to the human mind as well as to the eye, and act as guides to humans in their alteration and improvement of the environment. In this sense landscape is a complex concept of whose implications I want to specify three: (i) a focus on the *visible* forms of our world, their composition and spatial structure; (ii) unity, coherence and rational order or design in the environment; (iii) the idea of human intervention and control of the forces that shape and reshape our world. Such intervention, it should be stressed, is not a mindless, exploitive or destructive relationship but one which should harmonise human life with the inherent order or pattern of nature itself. This point is crucial, for as we can see from even the merest acquaintance with landscape representation in painting, poetry or drama, the most powerful themes are those which comment on the ties between human life, love and feeling and the invariant rhythms of the natural world: the passage of the seasons, the cycle of birth, growth, reproduction, age, death, decay and rebirth; and the imagined reflection of human moods and emotions in the aspect of natural forms.

For these reasons landscape is a uniquely valuable concept for a humane geography. Unlike *place* it reminds us of our position in the scheme of nature. Unlike *environment* or *space* it reminds us that only through human consciousness and reason is that scheme known to us, and only through technique can we participate as humans in it. At the same time landscape reminds us that geography *is* everywhere, that it is a constant source of beauty and ugliness, of right and wrong and joy and suffering, as much as it is of profit and loss.

CULTURE

I claimed above that landscape in human geography has long been associated with culture. This is particularly so in American human geography, where Carl Sauer's teaching and writings gave birth to a school of landscape geography focusing on humans' role in transforming the face of the earth.[3] The emphasis was mainly on technologies: for example the use of fire, the domestication of plants and animals, hydraulics, but also to some extent on non-material culture (that is religious belief, legal and political systems and so on). Attention centred on pre-modern societies or their evidence in the contemporary landscape, for example the evidence in the American scene of the various Indian, African and European cultures that have shaped it.

Cultural geography in this tradition concentrated on the visible forms of landscape – farmhouses, barns, field patterns and town squares – although in Britain a similar tradition examined such non-visible phenomena as place names for evidence of past cultural influences. Culture itself was regarded as a relatively unproblematic concept: a set of shared practices common to a particular human group, practices that were learned and passed down the generations. Culture seemed to work *through* people to achieve ends of which they seemed but dimly aware. Critics have called this 'cultural determinism', and have stressed the need for a more nuanced cultural theory in geography, particularly if we are to treat contemporary landscapes and sophisticated modern culture.[4]

A revived cultural geography seeks to overcome some of these weaknesses with a stronger cultural theory. It would still read the landscape as a cultural text, but recognises that texts are multi-layered, offering the possibility of simultaneous and equally valid different readings. There follows an outline of three main ways in which modern cultural geography moves theoretically beyond former approaches.

Culture and consciousness

Culture is not something that works through human beings, rather it has to be constantly reproduced by them in their actions, most of these being the routine unreflexive actions of daily life examined in Eyles's chapter. A religion, for example, or a political creed can only survive if people practice them. Most of us will speak in a low, respectful voice on entering a church without thinking consciously why we are doing so. We do the same in an art gallery and would be hard put to say why. A suburban householder may well be equally unaware when mowing the lawn of maintaining a cultural sign of propriety in a proprietory landscape, so mundane has the practice become. If asked to examine what we are doing most of us find the meaning of our activities difficult to articulate. But without such practices cultural expressions like church, gallery and lawn would disappear from our landscapes. Change in cultures comes from changes, rapid or slow, in their practice, in the act of cultural reproduction. But culture is always *potentially* able to be brought to the level of conscious reflection and communication. This is in fact what we do when we examine cultural expression in studying the humanities. So culture is at once determined by and determinative of human consciousness and human practices.

Culture and nature

Any human intervention in nature involves its transformation to culture, although that transformation may not always be visible, especially to an outsider. The different constructional materials and techniques of farmhouses may be obvious landscape indicators. Such things have been much studied by geographers. But often the most meaningful cultural events are less obvious. The tomato, a natural object, is removed from the vine, it is cut and 'dressed' and presented as human food. The natural object has become a cultural object, it has been layered with meaning. Cultural meaning is locked into the object and may also lock the object to others apparently unrelated to it in nature. That the tomato is a cultural product does not mean that its natural properties are lost. Its colour and weight are unaltered, a chemical analysis would yield the same results before or after the cultural event. But to these properties have been added cultural attributes which we may identify and discuss.

To do so requires that we enter the cultural consciousness of others. In the landscape, the sacred grove or holy spring, the site of the battle that founded or saved a nation are locations of intense cultural significance which the uninitiated pass by. To reveal the meanings in the cultural landscape requires the imaginative skill to enter the world of others in a self-conscious way and then *re*-present that landscape at a level where its meanings can be exposed and reflected upon. One advantage we have in treating landscape in this way is that many of its meanings are 'naturally' found in the sense that their point of departure is something common to our experience as ourselves part of nature – for example when associating the spring meadow with the surge of new life, or the autumn orchard with melancholy.

Culture and power

Most humans live in societies that are divided – by class, caste, gender, age or ethnicity. Such divisions generally correspond to the division of labour (see Massey and Meegan, Chapter 4.1). Obviously a different position in society implies a different experience and consciousness, a different culture to some extent. The degree of such difference varies enormously. A society may include cultures so radically different that they appear incompatible, as do Catholic and Protestant cultures in Northern Ireland. Here power is contested between groups of relatively equal strength, reproducing their cultures at a high level of consciousness. In such cases the visible evidence in the landscape of each is considerable, although even here the graffiti, churches, lodge halls and flags are but the most superficial expressions of a world of different meanings in daily life. Semblance of social unity is maintained only through the threat and exercise of external military force. More frequently we are dealing with subcultures within a dominant culture. The games, language and symbols of a school playground in a Durham mining village are different in terms of class and region from those of a similar playground in Esher, as is the age of those of the local working mens' club and of conduct from those of the cathedral close in Durham City. The State, however, as representative of a 'national interest', seeks to introduce at least the rudiments of a common culture across every schoolroom.

The study of culture is thus closely connected with the study of power. A dominant group will seek to establish its own experience of the world, its own taken-for-granted assumptions, as the objective and valid culture of all people. Power is expressed and sustained in the reproduction of culture. This is most successful when least apparent, when the cultural assumptions of the dominant group appear simply as common sense. This is sometimes referred to as cultural *hegemony*. There are therefore dominant and subdominant, or alternative, cultures, not merely in the political sense (although I will concentrate on that) but also in such terms as gender, age and ethnicity.

British culture is dominantly English in region, bourgeois in class, male in gender, white in colour, middle-aged and Anglican in religion. It has a characteristic landscape, observable at all scales from house interiors to the arrangement of whole regions. It is typified daily in TV advertising. Subdominant cultures may be divided not only in the terms already listed but also historically, as residual (which remain from the past), emergent (which anticipate the future) and excluded (which are actively or passively suppressed) like the cultures of crime, drugs or fringe religious groups. Each of these subcultures finds some landscape expression, even if only in a fantasy landscape.

SYMBOL

To understand the expressions written by a culture into its landscape we require a knowledge of the 'language' employed: the symbols and their meaning within that culture. All landscapes are symbolic,[5] although the link between the symbol and what it stands for (its referrent) may appear very tenuous. A dominating slab of white marble inscribed with names, surmounted by a cross and decorated with wreaths and flags standing at the heart of a city is a powerful symbol of national mourning for fallen soldiers, although there is no link between the two phenomena outside the particular code of military remembrance. The birthplace of a great national figure may be an ordinary house, yet it bears enormous symbolic meaning for the initiated.

Much of the symbolism of landscape is far less apparent than either of these examples. But it still serves the purpose of reproducing cultural norms and establishing the values of dominant groups across all of a society. Take for example the municipal park of an English provincial town. Normally it occupies ten to fifteen acres in the Victorian inner suburbs, accessible on foot from the town centre. Surrounded by green or black painted railings, it still maintains its nineteenth-century design of mown lawns, carefully edged, serpentine paths winding past herbaceous borders, chromatic summer beds and shrub plantations with perhaps a small lake and scattered deciduous trees. In one corner is a childrens' playground, carefully fenced off.

Anyone entering the park knows instinctively the boundaries of behaviour, the appropriate codes of conduct. In general one should walk or rather stroll along the paths. Running is only for children and the grass for sitting on or picnics. Ducks may be fed, but the pool neither paddled nor fished in. Trees should not be climbed, nor should music be played except by the uniformed brass band on the wrought iron bandstand. In sum, behaviour should be decorous and restrained. When these codes are transgressed, and they are, by music centres, BMX bikers, over-amorous couples or bottle-toting tramps, then the fact is observed, and disapproval clearly registered by those who, although perhaps numerically a minority, nevertheless have the moral symbolism of the whole designed landscape on their side. There is little need for signs, although the unread printed park regulations peeling at the entrance would confirm the interpretation of the righteous guarantors of propriety.

Despite the enormous social changes that have occurred since its Victorian origins, the codes of behaviour still have legitimacy in the park because the landscape itself, the organisation of space, the selection of plants, the use of colour and the mode of maintenance will remain largely unchanged. They communicate a specific set of values. If we trace the history of such parks we find that the declared aim of their founders was moral and social control. With the intention of improving the physical and spiritual welfare of the labouring classes (whose dissolution cut into profits) the Victorian middle class actively discouraged traditional pastimes: tavern drinking, cockfighting and common-land festivals or fairs. They substituted the public park, writing the rules of conduct within it most precisely. Despite the passage of time, these characteristic slices of English urban landscape still symbolise ideals of decency and propriety held by the Victorian bourgeoisie.

All landscapes carry symbolic meaning because all are products of the human appropriation and transformation of the environment. Symbolism is most easily read in the most highly-designed landscapes – the city, the park and the garden – and through the representation of landscape in painting, poetry and other arts. But it is there to be read in rural landscapes and even in the most apparently unhumanised of natural environments. These last are often powerful symbols in themselves. Take for example the polar landscape, whose cultural significance derives precisely from its apparent savage unconquerability by humans. During the period of the great polar expeditions at the turn of the century the landscape of ice, crevice, snowstorm, polar bear and green seas became the very paradigm of a *Boys' Own* world, the setting for a British upper-class male cultural fantasy. Scott's death in 1912 made a corner of Antarctica 'forever England'. Imperial themes of military heroism taking strength from a barren and hostile environmental setting were revived in 1982, as British troops 'yomped' across the South Atlantic islands during the Falklands–Malvinas war.

READING SYMBOLIC LANDSCAPES

The many-layered meanings of symbolic landscapes await geographical decoding. The methods available for this task are rigorous and demanding, but not fundamentally esoteric or difficult to grasp. Essentially they are those employed in all the humanities. A prerequisite is the close, detailed reading of the text, for us the landscape itself in all its expressions. Geographers have always recognised, at least by lip service, the centrality of a deep and intimate knowledge of the area under study. The two principal routes to this are via fieldwork, map-making and interpretation. In developing such personal knowledge a highly individual response is inevitably generated. This is a response, or responses, of which we need to be conscious, not in order to discount them in the search for 'objectivity', but rather so that they may be reflected upon and honestly acknowledged in the writing of our geography.

At the same time we seek 'critical distance', a disinterested search for evidence and a presentation of that evidence free from conscious distortion. By evidence I mean any source that can inform us of the meanings contained in the landscape, for those who made it, altered it, sustain it, visit it and so on, and evidence that may challenge our predelictions and theories just as its very collection will be informed by those predelictions and theories. It is important to realise that what is proposed here does not presuppose profound or specialised knowledge, only a willingness to look, to ask the unexpected question and be open to challenges to taken-for-granted assumptions. Very often it is children, so much less acculturated into conventional meanings, who can be the best stimulus to recovering the meanings encoded into landscape.

The kind of evidence that geographers now use for interpreting the symbolism of cultural landscapes is much broader than it has been in the past. Material evidence in the field and cartographic, oral, archival and other documentary sources all remain valuable. But often we find the evidence of cultural products themselves – paintings, poems, novels, folk tales, music, film and song can provide as firm a handle on the meanings that places and landscapes possess, express and evoke as do more conventional 'factual' sources.[6] All such sources present their own advantages and limitations, each requires techniques to be learned if it is to be handled proficiently. Above all, a historical and contextual sensitivity on the part of the geographer is essential. We must resist the temptation to wrench the landscape out of its context of time and space, while yet cultivating our imaginative ability to get 'under its skin' to see it, as it were, from the inside. Finally, in such a geography *language* is crucial. The results of our study are communicated primarily through the texts that we ourselves produce. The text of a geographical landscape interpretation is the means through which we convey its symbolic meaning, through which we *re-present* those meanings. Inevitably our understanding is informed by our own values, beliefs and theories, but it is grounded in the pursuit of evidence according to the acknowledged rules of disinterested scholarship. In the act of representing a landscape written words and maps, themselves symbolic codes, are the principal tools of our trade.

DECODING SYMBOLIC LANDSCAPES: SOME EXAMPLES

I suggested earlier that from the perspective of culture as power we could speak of dominant, residual, emergent and excluded cultures, each of which will have a different impact on the human landscape. I will use that threefold typology as the framework for exemplifying the approach to landscape that a 'humane' geography might adopt. I make no claim for the inclusiveness or objective validity of the classification. It serves as a useful organising device, no more.

Landscapes of dominant culture

By definition dominant culture is that of a group with power over others. By power I do not mean only the limited sense of a particular executive or governing body, rather the group or class whose dominance over others is grounded objectively in control of the means of life: land, capital, raw materials and labour power. In the final analysis it is they who determine, according to their own values, the allocation of the social surplus produced by the whole community. Their power is sustained and reproduced to a considerable extent by their ability to project and communicate, by whatever media are available and across all other social levels and divisions, an image of the world consonant with their own experience, and to have that image accepted as a true reflection of everyone's reality. This is the meaning of ideology.

To take a specific example: during the years immediately following the French Revolution there was considerable fear among the English ruling class, still dominated by landed interests, that English agricultural labourers, the largest single group of workers, might become 'infected' by the revolutionary spirit of liberty, equality and fraternity. From the perspective of an English squire such an outcome would be disastrous for the whole social order, because the harmonious balance which it suited him to believe existed between all classes in his justly-governed realm would be shattered and anarchy would take its place. All sorts of appeals to patriotism and the ancient liberties of freeborn, well-fed English yeomen appeared, together with caricatures of emaciated French peasants starving in their liberty.

Another, probably only dimly conscious, response was the popularity among connoisseurs of painting – themselves landowners and ruling class members – of painted landscapes showing peaceful rural scenes with contented labourers gathering abundant harvests or resting with their families at the cottage door. Such scenes, however distant from rural realities, were recognisably English in topography and reassuringly peaceful socially. Only by looking at such landscape images in their context can we begin to uncover one of their key cultural meanings: that for the English squirearchy God was in his heaven and all was well with the world. They also give us a purchase on one of the most enduring images of English landscape, an image still reproduced today in the landscapes we seek to conserve in picturesque villages and well-regulated fields of hay and corn, as well as on our postscards and tourist posters.

In terms of existing landscapes, of course, we are most likely to see the clearest expression of dominant culture at the geographical centre of power. In class societies, just as the surplus is concentrated socially so it is concentrated spatially, in country houses and their parks for example,[7] but above all in the city. It is instructive to observe how historically consistent has been the use of rational, geometrical forms in the design of cities: the circle, square and axial orthogonal or grid-iron road system all recur. Such geometry is radically different from the curves and undulations of natural landscape. It represents human reason, the *power* of intellect. Euclidian geometry as the foundation of urban form is to be found in ancient Greek, Roman, Renaissance, Baroque and Victorian city plans, even in the apparently benevolent landscape of Ebenezer Howard's garden city design, as well as in Chinese, Indian and Mayan urban form. Modernist city landscapes are equally exercises in applied geometry, whether we are considering Le Corbusier's Radiant City or the cubes of Manhattan or Dallas skylines.

To take on specific example of this theme of power and geometrical landscape, consider the capital city of the USA. Built upon 'virgin land' handed to the federal government by Virginia and Maryland and named after the first President, Washington DC was to be the seat of power for the first new nation of modern times and the centre of a territory larger than all of Europe. In its Declaration of Independence and Constitution the white, Europeanised, patrician founders of the United States had declared their vision of a new and perfect society and democracy. It was their cultural ideals that were celebrated in the designed landscape of Washington DC. The French architect L'Enfant composed the plan (Figure 2.2.1) of two simple geometrical designs: the orthogonal radiating pattern traditionally favoured by European monarchs exercising an absolute power which radiated from their persons and their courts, and the infinitely repeatable grid pattern which had become the basis for every colonial town, a democratic and egalitarian form that gives no single location a privileged status.

Here, inscribed in the very street pattern of the nation's capital, is the American resolution of European centralism and colonial localism, of federalism and states' rights. Observe the plan more closely and we see how it produces fifteen nodes, one for each existing state of the Union (thirteen former colonies plus Kentucky and Tennessee), and how the central symbolic buildings are located. The White House and Capitol, the two balanced powers of executive and legislature under the American Constitution, stand at the ends of a great L at whose corner rises the Washington Monument commemorating the founding hero of the revolution, located on the bank of the Potomac river where nature and culture meet. White House and Capitol are joined directly by the line of Pennsylvania Avenue, named after the 'keystone state'. Washington's urban landscape can thus be 'read' as a declaration of American political culture written in space.

Such symbolic landscapes are not merely static, formal statements. The cultural values they celebrate need to be actively reproduced if they are to continue to have meaning. In large measure this is achieved in daily life by the simple recognition of buildings, place names and the like. But frequently the values inscribed in the landscape are reinforced by public ritual during major or minor ceremonies. Each year the British monarch 'opens' Parliament, an occasion of elaborate ritual at the Palace of Westminster. Much of the ritual is highly public and employs London's landscape. The monarch in a state coach accompanied by a retinue of the military and civil establishment processes

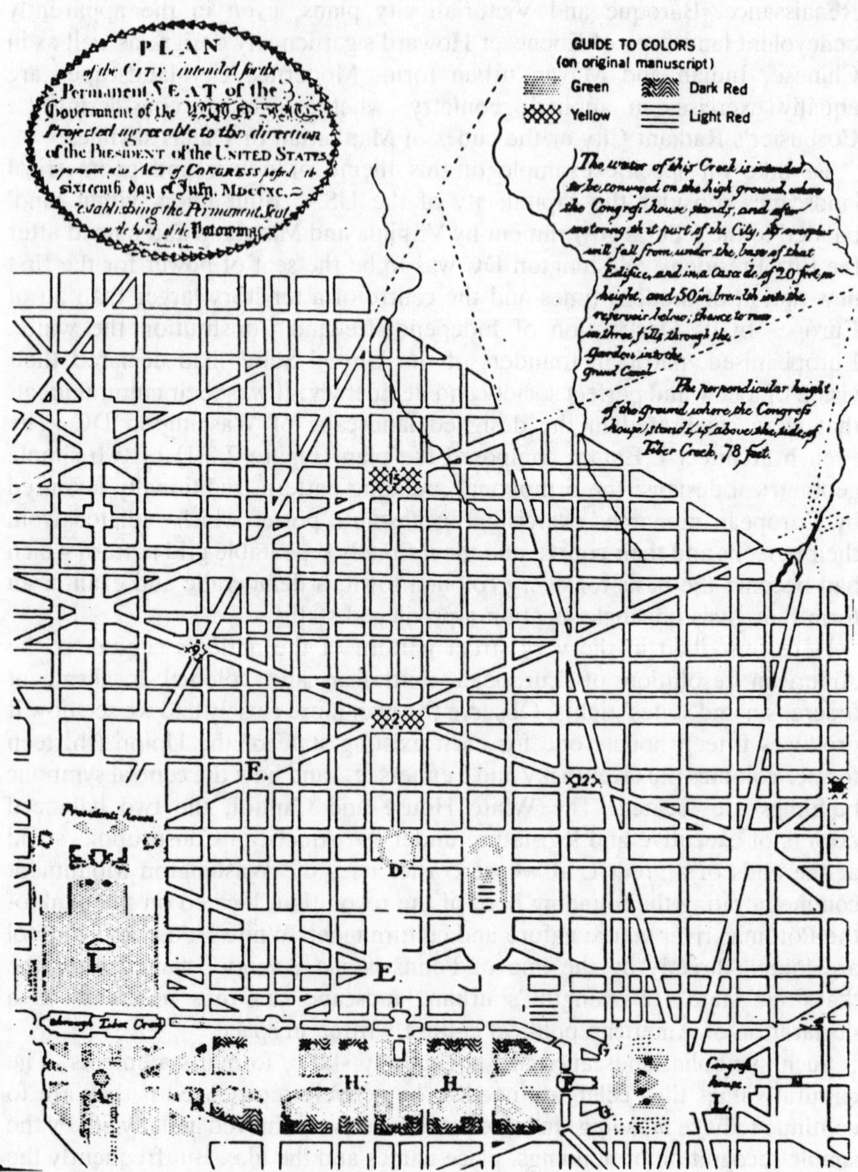

FIGURE 2.2.1 *The design of Washington DC composed by P. C. L'Enfant*

from Buckingham Palace down the Mall and through Admiralty Arch – through a gate opened only for the passage of the Crown – passing Trafalgar Square with its monuments to British military victories and down Whitehall to Parliament. Crown and Parliament are thus conjoined via a ceremonial route and the passage marked by elaborate and impressive public ritual. Here, and at other such rituals, such as Trooping the Colour, State visits, royal weddings and victory parades, urban space combines with (often invented) tradition and patriotic references in order to celebrate 'national' values and present them as the common heritage of all citizens. It is instructive to compare the routes taken by such official cultural events with those followed by other ceremonial users of the urban landscape: trades union processions, nuclear protesters or West Indian carnivals for example. A similar analysis could be applied at different scales to the design and use of space in any community from the largest city to the smallest village with its symbolic locations of war memorial, church, square, British Legion Hall of working men's club. Each of these landscapes has its ritual uses as well as its symbolic design. To examine and decode them allows us to reflect upon our own roles in reproducing the culture and human geography of our daily world.

Alternative landscapes

By their nature alternative cultures are less visible in the landscape than dominant ones, although with a change in the scale of observation a subordinate or alternative culture may appear dominant. Thus most English cities today have areas which are dominated by ethnic groups whose culture differs markedly from the prevailing white culture. This can produce a disjuncture between the formal built environment of inner city residential areas, constructed before the post-war wave of immigration from former imperial territories and still bearing the symbols appropriate to that time, and the informal uses and new meanings and attachments now introduced in a plural society. The former tram depot may be a mosque, bright paintwork, reggae rhythms and evangelical posters may be layered over a street of Victorian bye-law terraces. But however locally dominant an alternative culture may be it remains subdominant to the official national culture. At this latter scale I divide alternative cultures into residual, emergent and excluded.

Residual Many landscape elements have little of their original meaning left. Some may be devoid of any meaning whatsoever to large numbers, as for example the concrete pyramids that can still be found near British coasts scattered over flat terrain and half overgrown – relics of symbolic wartime protection against invading German tanks. Geographers have long taken an interest in relict landscapes, generally using them as clues for the reconstruction of former geographies. But as with all historical documents, the meaning of such features for those who produced them is difficult to recover, and indeed the interpretations we make of them tell us as much about ourselves and our cultural assumptions as about their original significance.

A case in point is Stonehenge. Set starkly on the Wiltshire downs it is a dominating symbol, not merely because of its size and age but because its original cultural meaning lies beyond reasonable hope of recovery. Inigo Jones, the seventeenth-century architect, believed it was the ruin of a Roman theatre, discounting existing theories that it had been a Druid temple or the magic setting for Arthurian deeds created by Merlin's wand. Later theorists have claimed it as a giant observatory, a calendar device and the focal point of a sacred ley-line system whose influence still exists. Each of these interpretations indicates the role of residual landscape symbols in revealing contemporary alternative cultures.

The most ubiquitous residual landscape element in Britain is the medieval church building. From great gothic cathedral to village steeple, nearly every settlement has its ancient church, however altered by later accretions and renovations. In location, architecture and scale these are still powerful symbolic statements in our landscape, and their surrounding graveyards trace the cultural history of their community in layout, headstone design, lettering and funerary inscription. A gothic pointed arch is still recognised by the least religious of us as a sacred symbol. Yet the role of the church in contemporary English life cannot in any sense be called dominant. Indeed, one indication of its residual status is the difficulty architects have in finding a style appropriate to the cultural role of the church in modern life. Ancient church buildings *become* discotheques and cheap supermarkets while new church buildings *look* like discos and cheap supermarkets! There is much interesting work to be undertaken on landscapes of the past and their contemporary meanings, and their apparent re-creation in museums and theme parks is a good point of departure.

Emergent Emergent cultures are of many kinds, some being very transient and having relatively little permanent impact on the landscape as, for example, the hippie culture of the late 1960s with its associated communes, alternative foodshops and organic smallholdings. Yet they all have their own geography and their own symbolic systems. It is in the nature of an emergent culture to offer a challenge to the existing dominant culture, a vision of alternative possible futures. Thus their landscapes often have a futuristic and utopian aspect to them, as for example the geodesic domes so favoured by commune dwellers in America during the 1970s.[8] But precisely because of this utopian strain emergent cultures very often deal in blueprints – paper landscapes. They are no less interesting or relevant to geographical study for that, because every utopia is as much an environmental as a social vision. There *is* a geography of 1984, of Brave New World and of Things To Come, as well as of every science fiction book, comic or film.[9] To study that geography tells us much about the links between human society and environment.

We should not scorn the study of imaginative geographies, nor the use of real landscapes to anticipate future cultures and social relations. The New York skyline, for example, has been used since the days of King Kong and Superman to present an image of future urban society and its sophisticated yet precarious culture, tottering always on the edge of destruction by overwhelming forces of evil. There is also the landscape of sport, particularly international and Olympic sport, which remains a utopian vision of human concord even though its landscape expression has consistently been subverted by nationalistic culture, from Nuremburg in 1936 to Los Angeles in 1984. Contrasting landscape symbols of the future are rarely as poignantly juxtaposed as they are in the few hundred yards that separate the grey, regimented nuclear silos and the sprawling domestic anarchy of the Peace Camp at Greenham Common.

Excluded By the time this essay appears in print one of those two emergent landscapes may well have disappeared. The particular culture promoted in the womens' Peace Camp may have been officially excluded. In general women represent the largest single excluded culture, at least as far as impact on the public landscape is concerned. Female culture is evident in the home, perhaps in the domestic garden. But the domestic landscape is one that geographers, significantly, have avoided studying. The organisation and use of space by women presupposes a very different set of symbolic meanings than by men, and in the past decade some important beginnings have been made in revealing the significance of gender in the attribution and reproduction of landscape symbolism.[10] This has largely been the work of anthropologists. The maleness and femaleness of public landscape remains largely an excluded subject for geographical investigation, for no other reason than that the questions have never been put (see McDowell, Chapter 2.3).

The same is very largely true for other excluded cultures, apart from the occasional study, itself usually treated as either of marginal interest or mildly suspicious. But the human landscape is replete with the symbols of, and symbolic meaning for, excluded groups. The symbolic space of childrens' games and their imaginative use of everyday places to create fantasy landscapes, the gypsy caravan site,[11] the marks left by tramps to indicate the character of a neighbourhood as a source of charity, the graffiti of street gangs, the discreet notices and landscape indicators of such varied groups as gays or freemasons or prostitutes, are all coded into the landscape of daily life and await geographical study. It is fascinating to compare the official landscape meanings of the public park discussed earlier with its symbolic geography for various excluded cultures.

The taken-for-granted landscapes of our daily lives are full of meaning. Much of the most interesting geography lies in decoding them. It is a task that can be undertaken by anyone at the level of sophistication appropriate to them. Because geography *is* everywhere, reproduced daily by each one of us, the recovery of meaning in our ordinary landscapes tells us much about ourselves. A humane geography is a critical and relevant human geography, one that can contribute to the very heart of a humanist education: a better knowledge and understanding of ourselves, others and the world we share.

Acknowledgements

I would like to thank the following people for comments on this paper during its writing: Isobel Cosgrove, Stephen Daniels, Joanne Magee, Jane Bateman, Janet Atkin, Michael O'Leary, Penny Smith, Carolynne Specht, and David Trotter.

NOTES AND REFERENCES

1. See Denis Cosgrove (ed.) *Geography and the Humanities*, Loughborough University of Technology, Department of Geography, Occasional Paper 5, 1982.
2. D. Cosgrove, 'Prospect, perspective and the evolution of the landscape idea', *Trans. Inst. Br. Geogr.*, 10 (1985) pp.45–62.
3. C. O. Sauer, *Agricultural Origins and Dispersals* (New York: American Geographical Society, 1952).
4. P. Jackson, 'A plea for cultural geography', *Area*, 12 (1980) pp.110–113; D. Cosgrove, 'Towards a radical cultural geography: problems of theory', *Antipode*, 15(1)(1983) pp.1–11.
5. A. Rapoport, *The Meaning of the Built Environment* (London: Sage, 1982).
6. D. Meinig (ed.) *The Interpretation of Ordinary Landscapes* (Oxford: Oxford University Press, 1979); Hugh Prince, 'Landscape through painting', *Geography*, 69(1984) pp.3–18.
7. S. Daniels, 'Humphrey Repton and the morality of landscape', in J. R. Gold and J. Burgess (eds) *Valued Environments* (London: George Allen & Unwin, 1982) pp.124–44.
8. J. E. Vance, 'California and the search for the ideal', *Ann. Assoc. Am. Geogr.*, 62 (1972) pp.185–210.
9. P. W. Porter and F. E. Lukermann, 'The Geography of Utopia', in D. Lowenthal and M. Bowden (eds) *Geographies of the Mind* (Oxford: Oxford University Press, 1976) pp.197–223.
10. Shirley Ardener (ed.) *Women and Space: Ground Rules and Social Maps* (London: Croom Helm, 1981); Women and Geography Study Group of the I.B.G., *Geography and Gender: An Introduction to Feminist Geography* (London: Hutchinson, 1984)
11. David Sibley, *Outsiders in an Urban Society* (Oxford: Basil Blackwell, 1981).

FURTHER READING

Two important collections of essays are John R. Gold and Jacqueline Burgess (eds) *Valued Environments* (London and Boston: George Allen & Unwin, 1982) and D. Meinig (ed.) *The Interpretation of Ordinary Landscapes* (Oxford: Oxford University Press, 1979).

I have provided a theoretical discussion and a series of detailed studies at odds with some of the orthodoxes of humanistic geography in Denis Cosgrove, *Social Formation and Symbolic Landscape* (London: Croom Helm, 1984). A spirited critique of humanism from a somewhat different perspective will be found in Edward Relph, *Rational Landscapes and Humanistic Geography* (London: Croom Helm, 1981), and S. Daniels 'Arguments for a humanist geography', in R. J. Johnston (ed.) *The Future of Geography* (London: Methuen, 1985).

2.3
Women, Gender and the Organisation of Space

Linda McDowell
The Open University

Linda McDowell is a Lecturer in Geography at the Open University. Her teaching and research interests include feminism and human geography, property relations and the urban housing market. She has prepared a number of publications for Open University courses and is also the author of several papers and (with John Allen) of *Landlords and Capital*.

HIDDEN FROM GEOGRAPHY?

Geographers have never had much to say about women. A glance along the shelves of any library or bookshop, at lists of courses on offer in schools, colleges, polytechnics and universities, or at the contents lists of new books immediately reveals that only half the human race seems to be important: *man* and environment, *man*'s role in the developing world, the city as the home of *man* . . . A more charitable interpretation of this emphasis is that the term 'man' is used to include women. This may be so, but in itself it implies that gender differences are not significant, that it is unimportant for geography teachers and students to distinguish and differentiate between women's and men's beliefs, behaviour and activities in space. It is remarkable how 'sexless' geographical analysis is. In studies of retailing, migration, residential choice and journey-to-work patterns, for example, there has seldom been an explicit recognition of the gender of the individuals concerned, or any acknowledgement that women and men may have different interests and behaviour patterns. Differences are concealed beneath the general concern for establishing a spatial geometry and search for spatial patterns and regularities.

Even in studies where gender obviously is significant, in marriage migration patterns or the investigation of fertility differences between and within regions, the analysis is usually conducted and reported in an impersonal, unproblematic way with little recognition of the special interests of women and men. In other areas, the relevant subject matter for study has been so defined as to exclude the vast majority of women's lives from the outset. In mainstream economic geography, for example, 'work' tends to be synonymous with waged labour, or in studies of the Third World it is structured to include the informal economy. Domestic labour, that is work undertaken without wages in the home, is habitually excluded.

The purpose of this chapter is to demonstrate that women do matter to geography, and to argue that the failure to take gender differences into account impoverishes both geographical scholarship and teaching. By taking examples from different areas of human geography – from urban, economic and 'welfare' geography – I will first show how 'sex-blind' most work in these areas has been and then look at recent attempts to counter this bias. I then want to argue that it is not enough just to add women in as an additional category. Feminist geography, as opposed to a geography or geographies of women, entails a new look at our discipline. It poses several awkward questions about how we currently divide the subject matter into convenient academic parcels and also challenges current practice in teaching and research.

Why now?

In the last few years, in a few isolated places, some geographers have begun to include women in their work and, further, to demonstrate the significance of feminism and feminist analyses for geography. Most of this work is still in an early stage of development; it is exploratory and often difficult to get hold of, possibly not published at all or in ephemeral or non-geographical journals. In 1984, however, the first teaching text in this area, *Geography and Gender*, was published in Britain, so the time appears to be right, at least as measured by the economic criteria of a major publishing firm, to establish women firmly on the geographical agenda.

There are a number of reasons why women are becoming increasingly visible on the geographical landscape. Part of the explanation is to be found in changes within geography itself and part in wider social changes. Geography, like any other discipline, is a product of its times. All knowledge is a social creation and as such reflects the conditions under which it is produced and transmitted. The type of geography that is currently taught in schools and elsewhere is to a large extent determined by the hold which higher education institutions, and the universities in particular, have over defining what constitutes geographic knowledge.

Academic geography has a particular history. The ideal of an unfettered search for knowledge and wisdom, of the steady progress towards scientific truth, has had a powerful influence on the content of geography and on geographic method. The idea of objectivity and unbiased method gripped geography in a stranglehold until the end of the 1960s and, indeed, is still important in some areas of the discipline. For many the purpose of their work is a search for spatial processes, using positivist methods (see Johnston, Chapter 1.3) that tend to exclude issues of social relevance and questions about social change. The dominance of this view is quite clear in the still influential *Models in Geography*, published in 1967.

However, the social changes of the last two decades have made their mark on geography as well as on society at large. The rediscovery of poverty in the midst of affluence in Britain and the United States in the 1960s, the increasingly significant questions of class inequality, the student protest movement, a growing general awareness of international issues and then, later, the deepening recession and rising rates of unemployment in advanced capitalist societies raised issues that geographers found increasingly difficult to ignore. Humanist, structuralist and Marxist critiques of 'spatial fetishism' and of positivism placed these new issues on the geographical agenda, particularly in human and social geography, and new methods have been developed to explore the links between social processes and spatial patterns. However, both humanists and Marxists have tended to ignore questions of gender inequality, Marxists in particular focusing almost exclusively on class differences.

Geography, unlike some of the other social science disciplines, has remained remarkably untouched by the rise of the Women's Movement over the last twenty years and the expansion of a body of feminist theory and empirical research. It is difficult to be sure why, but it is partly a question of scale: geographers, unlike sociologists, usually exclude the small-scale and the 'private' from consideration, ignoring the interior world, the social and spatial relationships that take place within buildings. Concern is for patterns and processes that take place outside, or in the 'public' world of institutions, places, areas and regions. So, in industrial geography we analyse spatial differences in the type and nature of work and in pay rates, or we look at journey-to-work patterns but do not go inside the factory gates or office doors with the workers. In urban geography we look at the production of the built environment, its distribution in urban space, how households gain access to certain types of housing in particular parts of towns and cities, but again we stop at the front door and ignore questions about the division of responsibility for work within the home or the structure of power relations within households. As John Eyles argued in an earlier Chapter in this section, everyday life is often ignored as an area for academic investigation (see Chapter 2.1).

Another part of the explanation may lie in the overwhelming predominance of men in positions of power within geography. Geography departments, particularly in the universities, are very much bastions of male power. Half the university departments in the country, for example, had no women on their full-time teaching staff at the end of the 1970s. The major journals tend to be edited and controlled by men, and the Institute of British Geographers has only had one woman President in its 100 years of existence: Alice Garnett in 1966. But there are women in geography departments. Indeed, half of the undergraduate students are women and as many girls as boys do geography at school, up to and including 'A' level standard. And in schools, students are much more likely to be taught by women than in higher and further education; certainly the Geographical Association, the teachers' professional body, has a better record in electing women Presidents than the Institute of British Geographers. Teachers at all levels are now beginning to take into account the work of a new generation of scholars who have been influenced by the Women's Movement and the general resurgence in feminist writing since the 1960s.

Wider social changes are also adding to the pressures to include women on geographical syllabuses. Probably the most important change has been the growth of women's participation in the labour market. Since the 1950s an increasing number of women have undertaken waged work, so that the vast majority of women 'go out to work' at some time in their lives. In Britain single women are now as likely to have jobs as single men, half of all married women 'work' and so do a quarter of all women with children under five. In total, just over 40 per cent of all waged workers were women in 1984. There are two reasons why these increases have important implications for geographical analysis. First, the changing shape of the economy and the regional patterns of employment decline and growth – that is the conventional subject matter of the geography of employment – are inextricably bound up with changes in the gender composition of the work force. Manufacturing employment, especially traditional, heavy manufacturing jobs in steel, coal and ship building – which are jobs for *men* – is on the decline. What new jobs there are in manufacturing are in areas such as electronics assembly and instrument engineering, and many of these are 'for women'. But the greatest increase in jobs has been in the service sector – a quarter of a million jobs between 1977 and 1981 – and the vast majority of these were for women too.

The second reason why women's entry into the labour market has brought 'women's issues' to the fore in geography is because it reveals inherent contradictions in the spatial distribution of urban land use, and raises new questions about the integration of time and space. Many women live on the margins of two worlds, where the demands of children, husband and home constantly compete with the demands of the labour market. One of the key problems for working women is the relationship – both in space and through time – between waged work and child care, shopping, schools and other necessary domestic work. Women somehow have to fit together a range of activities arranged in different places in space. I will expand on these points and suggest how they might be integrated into geography in the next section.

ADD WOMEN AND STIR?

One of the first tasks of a new geography that recognises the importance of gender differences is simply to look at the gender of actors and to establish whether there are significant differences in the spatial behaviour of women and men. In studies ranging from the more local to the international, women are now being added to the analysis. In the next sections I want to look at some examples in the fields of 'welfare', urban and economic geography.

Welfare geography: access to facilities

Spatial distribution, distance and accessibility are key concepts in geography, and studies of unequal access to both publicly and privately provided resources and facilities and of the 'optimal' distribution of services have a long history. In what has become known as welfare geography, analysts tend to focus on access to that range of goods and resources which are predominantly provided by the state but also, and increasingly since the election of 'radical' right-wing Conservative governments in Britain in 1979, 1983 and 1987, by the market. These include, among others, health services, education, child care and recreational facilities.

The impetus to studying the social and spatial distribution of these services in the 1970s was a growing concern among geographers to study socially relevant issues. An early exponent of such a focus was David Smith who devised the phrase 'spatial variations in social well-being' to sum up the subject matter under consideration. In 1977 he published a text book designed to reinterpret the whole of human geography within a welfare framework.[1] David Harvey, too, who has inspired a whole generation of geographers with his work, argued that unequal access to spatially distributed resources reinforces social inequalities primarily generated through the labour market to produce enormous inequalities in what he termed 'real incomes'.[2] The major emphasis of most studies in this tradition, however, is on *class* inequality, and the particular problems of women tend to be ignored by most researchers. But there are some exceptions. The work of Risa Palm and Alan Pred provides one example.[3] They used Hägerstrand's time-geography to reveal the particular constraints that affect women (see also Eyles, Chapter 2.1 and Gregory, Chapter 1.4). The approach is based on identifying the sources of constraint over human activities, given the physical or time–space context in which activity occurs. The volume of time–space available to any particular individual in a day is a 'prism' defined by the constraints that affect whether and how particular projects and activities can be carried out.

Figure 2.3.1 shows the prism for 'Jane', an unmarried mother. She cannot leave home for work before a certain hour of the day, because of her child's dependence on her for feeding and other needs and because the only accessible nursery is not yet open. Jane has no car, like most women, and hence is faced with severe restrictions in reaching the nursery (N_1) and her place of work (W_1). She is dependent on the availability and timetable of public transport. Her choice of jobs is, therefore, restricted by the constraints imposed by combining childcare, waged work and by the operation of the public transport system. These constraints also restrict her chances of acquiring and holding down a better-paid job that would relax the constraints and widen her prism. She has to collect her child in mid-afternoon as the nursery closes then and is thus effectively restricted to part-time work. Suppose she had a choice of two jobs, one better-paid and offering her the chance to run a car (W2), making it possible to take her child to a nursery further away. On taking the better-paid job, she finds that the time taken in driving to the nursery, to and from work and then back home (H) again does not allow her time to do other necessary tasks such as shopping, cooking and housework. She may therefore feel 'forced' to leave the job for a low paid, part-time alternative nearer home (W_1).

This example reveals very clearly the limitations of conventional geographical approaches to accessibility, based solely on distance minimisation. Jane's day is based on a careful combination of tasks through time and space. Her shopping trips, for example, are probably fitted in during the lunch hour and so originate from her workplace rather than her home. In most studies in retail geography, however, it is assumed that shopping is undertaken by women and that women are based in the home, so that trips from residential areas to shops are usually used to calibrate shopping models. So the double assumption here that *only* women shop and that all shopping trips originate from the home has important implications for retail planning. Shops are seldom built on industrial estates to enable waged workers to shop in their breaks, nor is waged work organised to make it easy to integrate paid work and domestic responsibilities. In fact, it may be argued that the organisation of waged work, of the transport network and of overall urban land use, are all based on the assumption that each worker has a wife at home.

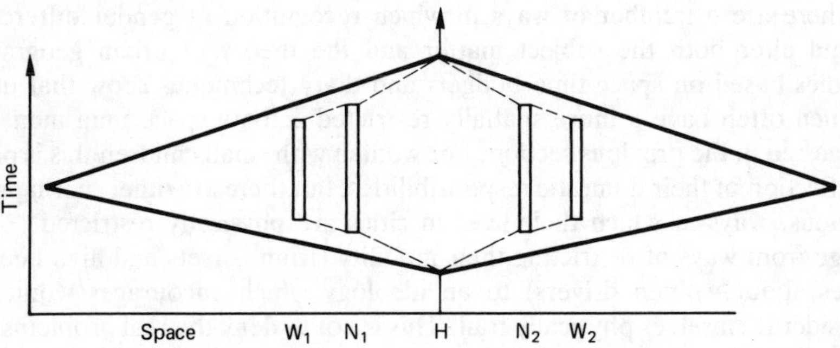

SOURCE: Palm R and Pred A. 'The status of American women: a time-geographic view' in D. A. Lanegran and R. Palm — *'An Invitation to Geography'* (N.York, McGraw Hill, 1978)

FIGURE 2.3.1 *The space-time prism of Jane*

Think, for example, of how paid jobs are organised. The hours seldom fit with school hours, so who picks up the children? The gas man will call 'sometime' on a certain day to change the meter, or a child needs to visit the dentist. Waged work is not organised so that time can easily be taken off to deal with these 'emergencies'. And the separation of land uses in cities and towns means that the child's school or dentist is seldom in the same area as paid employment – or at least of the father's work. When women work for wages they are often restricted in their choice of job by the need to be close to home so that they can fit in all these conflicting demands. Further, because women are expected to deal with such domestic emergencies, they gain a reputation of being unreliable at work which reinforces their segregation into low wage and low status and often part-time jobs. I will expand these points in the next two sections on urban land use and employment.

Women and urban land use

Urban geographers are among the most gender blind of all. There is a voluminous literature dealing with the revolutionary transformation of land use that took place in industrialising capitalist cities in the nineteenth and twentieth centuries, as well as with pre-industrial cities and urbanisation in the contemporary Third World. The rapid growth of the urban population, the development of particular land use patterns, of class-based residential differentiation, the growth of the suburbs, and the development of specialised shopping and service centres – all these form part of most courses on the urban geography of capitalist cities. And yet one of the most important aspects of industrial urbanisation – the separation of home life from waged employment and its impact on the lives of women and men – has been ignored by most urban geographers. Indeed, the relegation of the 'private' sphere of the home from urban geography and the conventional disciplinary divisions between urban and economic geography make it difficult to study some of the most important implications of this growing spatial division.

There are a number of ways in which recognition of gender differences would alter both the subject matter and the theory of urban geography. Studies based on space-time budgets and diary techniques show that urban women often have a more spatially restricted activity space than men, as I suggested in the previous section. For women with small children this is partly a reflection of their domestic responsibilities, but there are other, perhaps less obvious, ways in which their lives in cities are physically restricted. These range from ways of restricting their mobility (from corsets and high heels to jokes about women drivers) to an ideology which encourages women to consider themselves physically frail. This is not to deny the real problems that arise from the fear of male violence and the assaults and attacks on women that influence how they use space. Studies have recently been undertaken on whether women and men students use the university campus in different ways through space and time. Such studies might be repeated in schools with students of each sex, discussing from their own experience and from surveys of their peers, whether or not they feel equally free to visit different areas within their own locality at particular times of the day. There are other ways in which women are being made more visible in the urban landscape. Discrimination against women in urban housing markets and through state policies is a focus for contemporary research. Related to this is a strand of work showing how 'atypical' families, that is any form of household that does not conform to the conventional dual-headed nuclear family with children, is discriminated against because of the biases in building form and allocation policies. In Britain, for example, the vast majority of homes and flats have two or three bedrooms, and so both large and small households, whether headed by women or not, tend to find it more difficult to gain access to decent accommodation than do traditional families.

Another strand of work picks up the theme of urban design and planning and looks at the disjunction between women's needs and behaviour and the local environment in which they spend much of their time. Many of these studies focus on the suburbs or on planned communities such as new towns. Related to this are a small number of studies investigating the impact (or, rather, lack of impact) of women in the design professions. Some authors seem to be suggesting that an increasing number of women would result in a more female-oriented environment. This is open to debate given the overall structure of society and the wider factors leading to women's oppression, but there are a few fascinating speculative books and articles now published on the form of a non-sexist city: Dolores Hayden's book is an excellent example, as is the work of the 'Matrix' group of feminist architects (both of these are listed in the Bibliography).

Finally, research on the home, on the functions of the interior of houses and on women's domestic roles, is beginning to find a place in urban geography. Some geographers are using less conventional materials such as advertisements to examine the spatial frame of reference typically associated with women and men – and a glance at any glossy magazine or TV advert is usually sufficient to reveal the overwhelming dominance of the common stereotype that 'women's place is in the home'. In some urban, and some historical, geography courses the relationship between socially sanctioned ideas of gender roles and domesticity, how these change over time and in different places, how they affect who does what work in the home, is now part of the curriculum.

This type of 'unpacking' of the previously unexplored world of the home is a challenge to the conventional urban theories we are accustomed to teach in urban geography. Think, for example, of the models of the Chicago School (Burgess's rings and Hoyt's sectors) and those of the neo-classical economists (Alonso and Muth) which are included in most courses. The unit of analysis is either the household or an individual, and in either case this unit or person is sexless – or rather it seems clear that it is in fact an employed man whose goal in life appears to be to combine his work in the city centre with relaxing in his suburban home at the least possible cost to himself. The models spare not a thought for wives and children who have different priorities and locations to 'trade-off'.

In the 1970s urban theory was reconstructed around the concept of collective consumption, which appeared for a time to offer both a definition of what to include in 'the urban' and a method of analysis (see Bassett and Short, Chapter 3.1). It remained for feminists to point out how yet again this (male?) definition of the subject matter excluded women. The term 'collective consumption' primarily includes state provided services such as housing, transport and the health services, which aid the social reproduction of individuals *and not those goods and services provided in the home by domestic labour*. Consequently, the role of the family and of patriarchy is excluded. Indeed, so gender-blind were the majority of urban theorists in the 1970s that they seemed unaware that a critical question for ordinary households was the decline in collective provision and increasing reliance on the family and the community to provide essential 'social' services. The recession and increasing cuts in state expenditure have made these issues harder to ignore in the 1980s.

The contributions that I have just outlined – integrating women and 'women's issues' into a previously male-dominated urban geography – are obviously important; but ultimately they continue to perpetuate the division between the 'private' sphere of the home and the 'public' sphere of work. I shall argue that this division is an inappropriate one and that what are currently defined as 'urban' issues and 'economic' issues by geographers should be analysed together. To do so, I need to complete this critical survey by looking at economic geography.

Women and the changing shape of the labour market

The increasing visibility of women in economic geography parallels the developments in urban geography. Women have been added into the analysis as an additional category, but seldom have the conventional theories used to explain regional and sectoral changes in the labour market been challenged. Stereotypical attributes of 'femininity' such as 'docility' or 'dexterity' continue to be relied on as explanatory factors, with little consideration of how these attributes are constructed within society at large and within the labour market itself.

The main reason why women have at last come to be recognised in economic geography lies in their growing participation in waged labour and in the related changes in the structure and location of jobs. In Britain in 1982 over 10 million women worked for wages, accounting for just over 40 per cent of the workforce. Married women, in particular, are now in the labour market in large numbers. They now make up 26 per cent of the total workforce compared with only 4 per cent before World War Two. This growth in the number of women 'workers' has been associated with changes in the structure and location of industry. The shift towards the service sector in Britain is well documented and it is here that women are overwhelmingly concentrated – 75 per cent of all women workers are in service occupations, mainly segregated into routine or clerical jobs or in personal services such as hairdressing, childminding or retail jobs. The growth of women's employment opportunities, and the decline in manufacturing, has taken a particular spatial form and here traditional analysts, almost without realising it, have worked on the geography of women's employment, mapping the emerging pattern of regional variations.

The areas where there has been the greatest growth in female participation rates are those where few women worked before the war. These are areas such as the older industrial regions where male employment in ship building, heavy engineering and mining once predominated as in Scotland, in the rural areas of the South West and East Anglia, or in Wales and the North where both agriculture and heavy manufacturing were important. The regions in which the rate of increase was relatively small were the prosperous areas of the South East and West Midlands, both with a history of a high demand for labour and the North West, with a long tradition of female employment in the textile industry. So, as Figure 2.3.2 shows, there has been a convergence between regions in female participation rates. But this distinctive regional pattern has not resulted solely from an absolute decline in the number of men in work. A fall in male employment has occurred but this new geography of female employment has been influenced both by pre-war patterns of men's and women's work and by post-war changes in industrial production.

How have these changes been explained by economic geographers? In general there has been little attempt to look at the specific reasons for, and the implications of, the expanding numbers of women in the labour market. Four types of studies may be distinguished. First, those which examine changing patterns of regional inequality by using measurements of aggregate or male employment and unemployment patterns. This has been common in analyses of the impact of state regional policy on employment in the Assisted Areas. The use of aggregate or male employment statistics in such studies has meant that the substantial changes which have taken place in the gender, occupation and wage composition of employment in the Assisted Areas have been overlooked.

Secondly, there are studies which offer explanations of the regional variations in women's economic activity by measuring correlations between regional differences in female activity rates and other assumed determinants of women's participation in the labour force. For example, variations in female activity rates have been explained as functions of regional differences in the degree to which mothers with dependent children leave the labour market, in the extent to which there is a tradition of women's work or the amount of part-time work for women.

The third body of work is conceptually close to the second type. Analyses of the spatial decentralisation of manufacturing activity point to the importance of female labour as a location factor. The geographical decentralisation

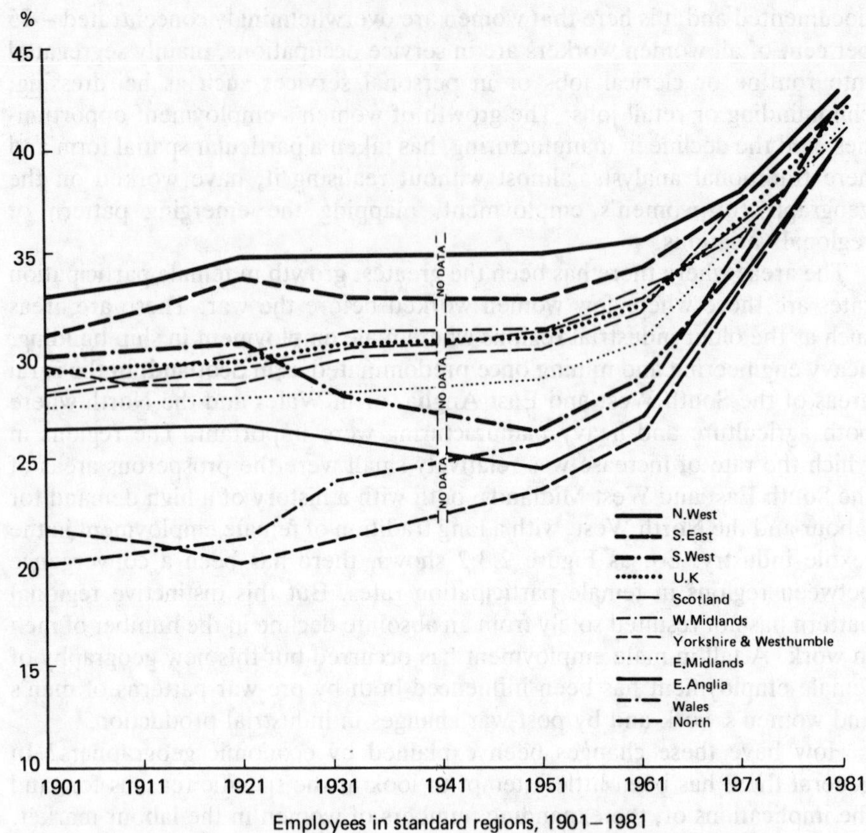

SOURCE: Women in Geography Study Group of IBG, *Geography and Gender* (London: Hutchinson, 1984).

FIGURE 2.3.2 *Women workers as a percentage of total employees in standard regions, 1901–1981*

of manufacturing activity has been perceived as a response to the rise of 'agglomeration diseconomies' in metropolitan areas. Metropolitan diseconomies include high rents and rates, deteriorating infrastructure, traffic congestion and the age and unsuitability of premises. Conversely, economies to be reaped in non-metropolitan areas include the availability of cheaper land, rents and rates, cheaper labour and government grants, and other similar incentives. Keeble, for example, uses indices such as the density of manufacturing employment, residential preference and female activity rates as correlates of the geographical decentralization of manufacturing industry.[4] But in these studies 'explanations' of the spatial decentralisation of manufacturing capacity are provided by describing the characteristics, and not by explaining the processes of decentralisation or the changes taking place in the organisation of the production process.

Finally, a critique of the types of studies outlined above has been developed in Marxist analysis and radical political economy, where the *mechanisms* underlying recent changes in the labour process, in the organisation of production and in the location requirements of industry have been the focus of analysis. However, in this literature too, the specific role of gender divisions in the changes has seldom been considered. Questions about why a demand for *female* labour was generated, about why women are considered 'docile' or 'dextrous', why they are concentrated in low paid, low skilled occupations, why the majority of women work part-time and questions about the effect of waged labour on domestic labour and vice-versa are not (yet) common in regional analysis. It is exactly these questions which are being raised in feminist theory and analysis, and so I now want to look at the implications of this work for developing a feminist geography rather than a geography of women.

FEMINIST GEOGRAPHY

The challenge that feminism poses to geography is to deconstruct accepted categories and to establish new ways of thinking about conventional divisions within geography. Although the work outlined in the preceding pages makes a valuable step forward in recognising that women's lives are an important part of geographical study, the work is united by its acceptance of 'common sense' definitions and divisions. In welfare geography, for example, the differences between men and women's lives are examined, but little attention is paid to why these differences occur, whether they are common in all parts of the country, whether they vary over time. In urban geography the 'private' sphere has become an accepted area of study, but the segregation of female and male roles and women's isolation in this private sphere is taken for granted rather than explained. Similarly in economic geography, the construction of 'femininity' in the home and in the workplace and how this is linked to women's occupational status is not explained. Links between waged and unwaged work are not drawn. There is a growing body of work, however, undertaken predominantly from a socialist-feminist perspective, that is developing an historical analysis of the origins of women's current oppression and the privatisation of family life in capitalist industrialisation.

During the nineteenth century in Britain the segregation of production and reproduction and the allocation of gender specific roles in industrial production and domestic work was virtually completed. Industrial production became a male-dominated sector, and from the late nineteenth century a belief in the home as the centre of social, not working life, became predominant. Historians, economists and geographers are beginning to untangle the progress and consequences of this process in different parts of Britain at different periods of time, showing how the organisation of production and specific ideologies of femininity intersect to produce particular forms of women's oppression that find their expression in gender divisions within the labour market, at home and in the form of the built environment. Thus the overall social processes that produce women's subordinate position are the focus of analysis rather than the differences that occur between women and men's behaviour in particular areas of life. Feminist economists, for example, are challenging the disciplinary division of labour between economics and sociology, arguing that women's position in the labour market cannot be understood without taking into account women's domestic responsibilities. If economists focus solely on the labour market and sociologists on 'the family', explanation in both disciplines is impoverished. Another look at the example of regional variations in women's participation rates will illustrate how an understanding of the social construction of femininity, of gender division and an awareness of the inter-relationship of waged work and domestic labour improves an explanation of these patterns.

The introduction of new routine assembly techniques and labour intensive service activities demanded new sources of labour: labour that was cheap, not militant and capable of putting up with monotonous, fiddly work. Women qualified on all grounds. Female labour is cheap as 'women's work' has traditionally be regarded as secondary, as a source of 'pin money'. Trade union wage bargaining has been based on the concept of a 'family wage' for male breadwinners, regardless of the actual situation. In Britain today, for example, only 18 per cent of male workers are financially solely responsible for their dependants. Women also qualified on other grounds. Docility, dexterity and an ability to do boring repetitive tasks uncomplainingly are female attributes learnt at school and in the nuclear family – think of what doing housework entails! In fact, many of the tasks women perform in light manufacturing or service industries are no less unskilled than those performed by many skilled male manual workers. It may be the case that certain jobs are classified as unskilled because women do them, rather than because of the intrinsic nature of the work.

Why were women in particular regions drawn into the labour market? The areas where jobs for 'women' expanded most quickly in the 1960s and 1970s were those where women previously had not 'worked' or had worked on a casual and seasonal basis. The explanation here lies in a large part in past gender divisions of labour and in women's previous domestic responsibilities. In the areas of heavy manufacturing or agricultural work the conditions of male work imposed heavy demands on women. In the coal mining areas of the North East, for example, men did dirty, dangerous work on a shift basis. Women's labour in the home was an essential part of men's work in the pits. The employers and employees alike relied on women washing clothes and making meals at all times of the day and night. Women themselves were restricted to the home both by this burden and by a lack of alternative opportunities. A similar situation arose in agricultural areas such as East Anglia, where the nature of men's paid employment and the division of responsibilities between the sexes within the home also led to a heavy domestic load for women. After the war, in both these areas, jobs for women expanded, whereas in Lancashire, where women traditionally had worked for money, their very experience and history of unionisation worked against them in the search for inexperienced, 'green' labour by the new footloose industries. (These points are discussed in more detail in the essay by McDowell and Massey and the book by Massey listed in the Bibliography.)

The effects of women entering the labour market are also important for geographers. The gains for women in the North East, for example, have been seen as second-best and at the expense of 'real' jobs for men. Part of this hostility stems from the threats imposed by women's greater independence to traditional, 'macho' images of men's roles in this area. To some extent, though, the fears are real. Women's jobs are lower paid than men's, and this has important implications for overall living standards in these regions. The jobs also tend to be insecure, both for individual women as most are employed on a part-time basis, but also for women as a whole. In the North East, for example, many of the light manufacturing branch plants that came to the area in the 1950s and 1960s have now closed. The entry of women into the labour market also raises questions about the spatial integration of their 'dual' roles, about the location of home and factories, child care facilities and shops and so again challenges conventional distinctions within the discipline.

Doing feminist geography

The key question that faces feminist geographers is how to integrate perspectives directed from feminist theory into geographical teaching and research. I have already argued that adding women as another category into conventional analyses is insufficient. The problem still remains, however, of whether feminist research and teaching should be added as one thread among many within human geography, or whether a feminist perspective might be developed within all the subdivisions of human geography. The first option entails the risk of ghettoisation and makes it easier for feminism to be ignored, ridiculed or marginalised. In a time of cuts in school resources and in further and higher education, too, it is difficult to secure resources for mounting an additional course, even were it possible within the constraints of existing examination syllabuses might seem preferable, but my main argument in this chapter has been that feminism *challenges* current divisions in human geography and that issues now conveniently divided between the 'urban' and the 'economic' need to be considered *in combination*. Material from non-geographical sources, too, needs to be included.

Here the argument for a separate feminist geography, at least at post-school level, seems stronger. Staff and students would share a common body of knowledge and theory derived from debates in the wider feminist literature. In addition, a commitment to feminism often results in a challenge to conventional methods of working within geography and within educational institutions more generally. Feminists are trying to evolve a style of working that is non-hierarchal and less individualistic than is common in most schools and virtually all further and higher education departments, to challenge the myth of value-free scientific objectivity and to take account of the gender of the teacher and the taught, the researcher and the researched, in a thoughtful and significant way.[5] To be realistic, however, it is clear that, in the present climate, changes will be gradual and marginal. School syllabuses are unlikely to include a paper or even several questions on feminist theory and research in the near future. But if teachers take every opportunity to correct the explicit and implicit sexist biases in the material they teach and the texts they use, changes will come about. Try for a day to say 'she' every time 'he' comes naturally; it's a surprisingly difficult thing to do at first, but even such a simple step increases the awareness of gender-biases among students. In teaching, in marking or in setting projects, an awareness of the differences between men's and women's experiences and behaviour will raise many new issues for discussion and new areas for exploration. Feminism poses an exciting challenge to geography, and geography in its turn has much to offer to feminists who all too often have ignored spatial divisions and differences.

Acknowledgement

I am grateful to the Women and Geography Group of the Institute of British Geographers, without whom the ideas outlined here would not have been developed so far.

NOTES AND REFERENCES

1. David Smith, *Human Geography: A Welfare Approach* (London: Edward Arnold, 1977).
2. David Harvey, *Social Justice and the City* (London: Edward Arnold, 1973).
3. R. Palm and A. Pred, 'The status of American women: a time-geographic view', in D. Lanegran and R. Palm (eds) *An Invitation to Geography* (New York: McGraw-Hill, 1978) pp.99–109.
4. D. Keeble, 'Manufacturing dispersion and government policy in a declining industrial system: the UK case 1971–1976', in J. Rees et al (eds) *Industrial Location and Regional Systems* (New York: Bergin, 1981).
5. See J. Bale, 'Sexism in geographic education', in A. Kent (ed.) *Bias in Geographical Education* (London: University of London Institute of Education, 1984) pp.3–11; B. Larsen, 'Geography', in J. Whyld (ed.) *Sexism in the Secondary Curriculum* (London: Harper and Row, 1983); P. Wiegand, 'Geography, gender and justice.' *Times Education Supplement*, 1 April 1983.

FURTHER READING

Although not a geography text in the accepted sense, Bea Campbell's *Wigan Pier Revisited* (London: Virago 1984) is an eye-opening look at women's lives in different parts of Britain; it is, in part, a corrective to George Orwell's male view of the world in the original *Road to Wigan Pier*. Dolores Hayden's *The Grand Domestic Revolution: A History of Feminist Designs for American Homes, Neighbourhoods and Cities* (Cambridge, Mass.: MIT Press, 1980) is an exciting story of nineteenth-century campaigns whose arguments are sadly still relevant today.

Doreen Massey, *Spatial Divisions of Labour* (London: Macmillan, 1984) is a new approach to the regional geography of Britain which shows how social and spatial changes are integral to each other; Chapter 5 is particularly relevant to the arguments developed in this essay. So is Linda McDowell and Doreen Massey, 'A woman's place', in Doreen Massey and John Allen (eds) *Geography Matters!* (Cambridge: Cambridge University Press, 1984) pp.128–147.

An introductory text, written in a concise and jargon-free style, has been produced by the Women and Geography Study Group of the Institute of British Geographers under the title *Geography and Gender* (London: Hutchinson, 1984). Also useful is a very readable collection of short essays by a group of architects, designers and teachers called Matrix, *Making Space: Women and the Man-made Environment* (London: Pluto, 1984).

2.4 Social Relations and the Geography of Material Life

Roger Lee
Queen Mary College, London

Roger Lee is Senior Lecturer in Geography at Queen Mary College, London. His teaching and research interests include the relations between economic and urban geography and the urbanization of Britain in the early twentieth century. He is the author of numerous papers and (with B. W. Hodder) of *Economic Geography*. He is editor of *Change and Tradition: Geography's New Frontiers* and (with P. E. Ogden) of *Economy and Society in the EEC*. It comforts his conscience to believe that his academic output would be so much greater without the distractions of politics, sailing and cricket.

To be traditionally geographical for a moment, it is remarkable that people manage to live on the equator and in settlements located beyond 78°N and 55°S; in areas with population densities ranging from 17 000 people per square kilometre to those with only one person per 39 square kilometres; in conditions of torrential rain and in burning aridity; on the coast and as far as 2250 kilometres from the sea; below sea-level and at 5100 metres above the sea; and that they live on stable platforms and perch, more or less neurotically, upon unstable fault lines.

From such diversity, visible to anyone who cares to browse through an atlas, derives the fascination of much of geography. And yet, fascinating as they are, a preoccupation with such patterns of human occupance may seduce us into a limited, limiting and theoretically bankrupt view of the kaleidoscope of human geography. The very remarkability of the diversity of natural conditions in which people have made and continue to make the geographies and histories of their lives, and the somewhat less fascinating spatial logic that appears to bind them together, may blind us to the involvement of social relations in enabling and constraining the actions of people in nature. It is the character of such social relations and their significance for the complex processes of the development of human societies that forms the subject matter of this essay.

DOWN THE TELEGRAPH ROAD: A NAIVE HISTORICAL GEOGRAPHY

An examination of the role of social relations in shaping the geography of societal development is not merely an academic indulgence, nor is it reducible to the rather more defensible concern to push out the frontiers of knowledge. Rather, a consideration of social relations reflects aspects of human being that are central not only to the very existence of society both now and in the future, but to our day-to-day experience of and participation in it. The network of social relations into which we are born – familial, legal, racial, sexual, industrial – reflects the place and time of our birth and exerts a profound influence upon our lives. These relations may be transformed only with great difficulty and so they become commonplace: we can but work with them for today, no matter how hard we may strive to transform them for tomorrow. It is this mix of the profound and the habitual which endows social relationships with such material power.

The character and significance of social relationships – what they are and what they do – are expressed simply and directly in the following song, which was written by Mark Knopfler and is called *Telegraph Road*:

A long time ago came a man on a track walking thirty
miles with a sack on his back and he put down his load
where he thought it was the best
he made a home in the wilderness
he built a cabin and a winter store
and he ploughed up the ground by the cold lake shore
and the other travellers came riding down the track
and they never went further and they never went back
then came the churches then came the schools
then came the lawyers then came the rules
then came the trains and the trucks with their loads
and the dirty old track was the telegraph road

Then came the mines – then came the ore
then there was the hard times then there was a war
telegraph sang a song about the world outside
telegraph road got so deep and so wide
like a rolling river

These words – taken, it will be apparent, not from a philosophical tome but, to emphasize the immediate and day-to-day significance of social relations, from a rock song – provide a straightforward account of the influences that deny the hypothesis of the 'noble savage' postulated in the first few lines of the song. Contacts carried forward from a world left behind, distance, locational choice, the notion of home, the material practices involved in production and in providing shelter, chain migration, religion, education, the law, economic and military connections with a wider world and, later in the song, the social conditioning of affective emotion and the loss of innocence: all point to the diverse and complex ways in which we are bound to a wider society and which exert a dominant but not necessarily determinant influence upon our lives. We cannot, it seems, simply insert people directly into nature. But it is equally apparent that social relations are complex, both in their character and in their effects. In attempting to make sense of them, we must begin to untangle and order the complex of connections within social existence.

Three features of human being are vital in beginning to make sense of this complexity. First, human life is *social* and it is so at the most elemental level. The long period during which the infant human being is dependent upon others for survival ensures an extensive process of socialisation which can never be completely erased, no matter how much its effects may be modified with the passage of time. Nothing that we do as humans is done purely as individuals: we always carry society from the past into the present and we are virtually unable to avoid communication with others in our daily lives. The properties of social systems form an inseparable and integral part of human life. Social behaviour does not consist of the kind of action and reaction observable between balls on a snooker table; it involves understanding, but not necessarily agreement, between the individuals and groups concerned. Thus human life necessarily involves a network of social relations – they are a condition of our existence. The character of such relations is not simply given; they are constructed by human beings in society and they take many forms. The struggle to establish acceptable social conditions of existence against both the constraints of the natural environment and the established social order provides one of the great driving forces of history.

Secondly, human life is *material*. As human beings we do not simply live in nature, we are of nature and so are subject to certain of its laws. Human beings must, by the material exploitation of the natural environment, satisfy certain needs in order to survive. We must eat, drink and find shelter from the natural environment by working upon it and producing from it. We must also recognise that the physiological make-up of human beings itself changes in time and space. Nevertheless, and this is the third point, the human species is not merely a passive product of natural forces but is, rather, *active*. Humanity is a part of nature, but it is a part that has acquired the ability actively and thoughtfully to transform nature to its own use. By a process of thought, planning and directed labour, people may become increasingly at one with their own internal nature as well as with the external natural world. The most obvious example of this kind of action is the mental and physical process involved in the training of an athlete. Education and the process of production achieve the same objectives, but on a much broader front. Similarly, religion may not merely be a relief from social pain ('the opium of the people') but a reflection upon and a social reaction to intimations of mortality.

The three major implications of these features of human being for an understanding of social development are a) that human life is both directed and governed by socially-understood and socially-produced arrangements; b) that is it materially based; and c) that it is dynamic. This dynamism has its roots in what is sometimes called the recursive quality of the transformation of internal and external nature. In other words, the conscious transformation of either necessarily redefines the relationship between them and so redefines the basis of human action. In this sense human activity is constantly restless. Nevertheless, the extent to which this restlessness is also developmental is determined, at least in part, by the precise nature of the existing social relations within which human activity takes place. It is with the active and formative role of these social relations that the rest of this essay is concerned.

BEYOND THE TELEGRAPH ROAD

Social relations and societal development

The materialist principle that people must first be able to live – to produce and sustain the material conditions for their existence – before they can begin to make their geographies and histories in any other sense, does not imply that the principle somehow 'predates' either systems of social meaning and significance or specific sets of social relations. Human actions cannot take place outside a set of social relations and even in the most desperate circumstances of material deprivation, people try to make sense of their material needs by reflecting upon what has brought them to desperation and how they might transcend it or become reconciled to it. Material production is always a social and reflective as well as a material, environmental and technical process. As such it may be understood only if its social and material aspects are defined and examined together.

Material production involves the application of human labour to external nature with the objective of transforming natural or only crudely-formed objects into a condition in which they may satisfy human needs. It necessitates prior thought and planning (how may the work best be done and for what purpose?), and also social organisation (how should the productive tasks be organised and the resultant product be shared out or distributed?) Thus, when people engage in production they not only involve themselves with nature but also with each other. They create and recreate specific forms of social organisation. Not only do they produce commodities from nature, they produce and reproduce the social relations of production. It is in this *social definition of production* that the materialist principle derives its primacy.

But, just as production is a social process so, too, is it historical. It takes place in different ways under different social relations and norms which are themselves distinctive historic products of social action. This means that there can be no universal geography or history based upon the working out of some invariant processes. Universal schemes of development, such as that implied by Walt Rostow's stages of growth, are both misleading and inaccurate (see Taylor, Chapter 5.1). Different configurations of social and material relationships produce *different* geographies and histories, each having a manifold of *distinct* social, material and cultural processes at work within them. Social relations of production are both expressed in and condition the ways in which individual producers and those with whom they work have rights over the use of their own labour, over the means and forces of production (tools, machines, factories, transport facilities and so on) and over what they produce.

The social relations of production are not pre-given to history. They are a human construct and so may take on a multitude of possible forms. However, a limited (if disputed) number of distinct *sets of social relations* have been identified as having widespread significance. So-called 'primitive communism' is characterised by the common ownership of the means of production and egalitarian distributive principles which may be based upon biologically-defined or culturally-defined notions of kinship. In slavery, the labourer does not own even his or her own labour. Under feudal relations of production characteristic of much of pre-industrial Europe, some of the means of production may be owned by individual serfs. However, the lordly ownership and control of land endows political and military power and exacts a proportion both of the product of the labour and of the labour power (for military and agricultural service) of the serf who is legally bound to the lord's domain.

The characteristic relations of capitalist production involve the dependent 'freedom' of labour to sell its labour power as a commodity, and the private ownership of the means of production by capital. Although labour and capital are thus separate from each other they are, at the same time, vital to each other's existence. This separation and mutual dependence has some highly significant effects. It avoids the rigidities characteristic of feudal relations in which ties, based upon the ownership of and access to land, greatly limited the scope of both the quantitative and geographical possibilities for economic expansion and social development. The separation of capital and labour reduces the productive contact between them to that of the wage contract, and so endows the productive process with great flexibility. The possibilities for constant change in the labour process and the facility to organise the production and circulation of commodities at any geographical scale are not only unfettered but positively encouraged by the social relations of capitalist production.

Only when labour is both separated from (is 'free' of) the means of production, and when it is 'free' of direct relations of domination such as slavery or serfdom, can it become a commodity, free to be bought and sold in the marketplace. Under these circumstances in which capital has no prior obligation to labour, they are both 'free' to combine at the highest possible level of available productive technology. More to the point, however, under capitalism capital and labour are not only 'free' to combine in this way, it is necessary that they should do so. This is because capital consists of separate productive units, the competitive relations between which are controlled by relative levels of profitability. Capital is forced to sell commodities in order to buy labour power and the means of production, and to innovate in order to maintain its competitive position. This process of innovation generates a tendency to a sustained increase in the productivity of the labour process, and so generates systematic increases in the productive power of capitalist society. However, because capital has few obligations to labour outside the wage contract, labour is forced to struggle in order to improve its own conditions of existence in what could become a completely dehumanised environment. Thus, the apparently beneficial flexibility of capitalist social relations is, at the same time, the source of the most fundamental conflict in capitalist society.

By contrast, socialist relations of production involve both the collective ownership of the means of production and a (more or less) democratically-controlled system governing the use and distribution of the social surplus. The contradiction between the immediate consumption of the surplus and its use for further development of the productive forces is the more problematic when and where production is characterised by low levels of output and productivity. Under such conditions, the furtherance of social development depends, to a considerable extent, upon improvements in the forces of production. Such improvements are themselves dependent upon the allocation of labour to the output of production goods and, by implication, upon a reduction in the proportion of total output available for immediate consumption.

The significance of social relations of production for an understanding of the geography of social development does not lie merely in the provision of a basis for social classification, helpful thought that may be. Rather, an emphasis upon social relations exposes the diversity of the strategic relationships involved in the organisation of production, and of the material and ideational ties of human sociality. It should, perhaps, be re-emphasised that such relationships are sustained and changed by social struggle. Thus, the contemporary socio-geographical differentiation between eastern and western Europe, for example, has its roots in the divergence of the sixteenth century, when feudal relations began to be transcended by progressive forces in the west, whilst the possibilities for change were suppressed by the still powerful feudal forces in the east.

Social relations and geography

The separation and mutual freedom of labour and capital under capitalist relations of production necessitates a circuit of interaction between them. The capitalist must advance money capital in order to purchase labour power. In this way capital is transformed into labour power which has the potential ability (not unique to human labour) to produce a greater value of commodities than it itself needs for comfortable survival. Labour power is combined with the means of production, also purchased as a commodity by capital, to work on the object of labour in order to produce further commodities having a greater value than the combination of labour power and the means of production used to produce them. Extra value may thus be created by labour in the process of production, and the capitalist must realise this 'surplus value' in money form by selling the newly-produced commodities on the market. This process of the circulation of capital both requires and creates a geography of the supply and movement of labour power, of capital (in both money and commodity forms), and of production.

We may represent this circuit of productive capital as follows:

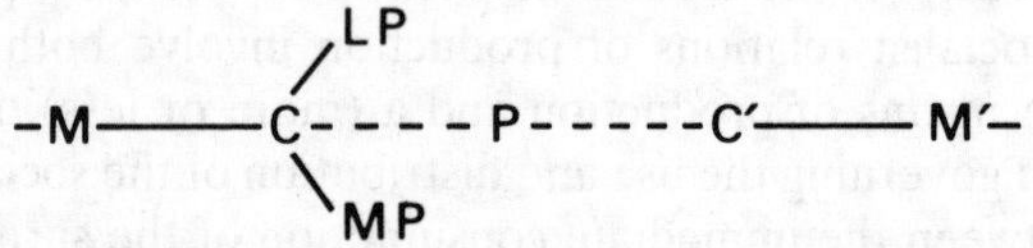

$$-M\text{———}C\begin{smallmatrix}\nearrow LP\\ \searrow MP\end{smallmatrix}\text{- - - - }P\text{ - - - - }C'\text{———}M'-$$

FIGURE 2.4.1 *The circuit of productive capital*

where M = value of money capital advanced in the first round of investment

C = value of labour power (LP) and means of production (MP) bought as commodities in the market place

P = process of production

C′ = value of commodities produced

M′ = enlarged amount of money capital advanced in the second round of investment (i.e. M plus surplus value).

Successful realisation of surplus value enables a second round of circulation and production to proceed. This second round may be on a quantitatively larger scale, as the realised surplus value may be added to the original money capital advanced; it may also take place at a geographically enlarged scale and with a changed geography of circulation, production and consumption. This geographical reorganisation may result from a technologically-transformed relationship between labour and the means of production, or from other aspects of the conditions of production and circulation. If capital is to remain as capital, it must always be thrown back into such enlarged and modified circuits.

The circuit of productive capital is subject to two major sets of transformations as material life proceeds. First, the systematic tendency to increase productive power results in a progressive and, at times, dramatic geographical, quantitative and technical transformation of the social system as a whole. As the circuit expands in a quantitative sense, the means of communication between its various elements, the process of production, the supply of labour power and of the means of production, and the sale of commodities must also expand. A concomitant of this quantitative expansion is that the circuit may also expand geographically. Geographical expansion may also be induced by the qualitative characteristics of the relations of production. As labour and capital are formally connected to each other only through the wage contract, they are both potentially highly mobile and the geography of the circuit may reflect this both in its scale and in its propensity to change.

The second major set of transformations concerns the internal structure of the circuit which becomes progressively more complex as the division of labour proceeds. Whilst larger units of capital may be able to finance a large proportion of their investments from their own resources, the financial markets provide access to the resources of finance capital which specialises in the collection and lending of capital for investment. Productive firms may, for example, borrow from banks or other more specialised finance companies at agreed rates of interest in order to facilitate an expanded or technically transformed round of investment. Interest payments must then be subtracted from the surplus value produced by the investment. Similarly, by specialising in the distribution of the finished product, merchant capital may be employed by productive capital to market its commodities. This strategy may be particularly important if the time-lapse between the production of the commodities and the receipt of their money value is likely to be extensive or subject to long delays. Telegraphic and electronic means of communications have served to reduce time lapses due to distance but other delays may occur as a result, for example, of national barriers to the free movements of commodities in trade, or because credit assistance is required in order to manage the consumption of large items and to spread the cost over time. The employment of merchant capital enables productive capital to eliminate time and to receive the value of the commodities produced, less the cost and profits of merchant capital, immediately.

We can now make our original diagram more realistic by inserting these complications.

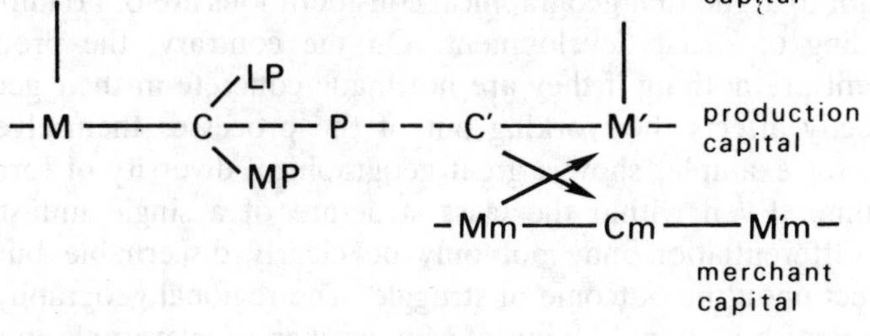

–Mf ———————— M′f – finance capital

LP

–M —— C – – – P – – – C′ —— M′ – production capital

MP

–Mm —— Cm —— M′m – merchant capital

FIGURE 2.4.2 *Circuits of capital*

These complexities in the circuit are introduced in the sphere of circulation, but they each imply a process of production: financial and merchanting services have themselves to be produced in circuits similar to that of productive capital. Production and circulation thus interpenetrate in a highly complex fashion, and involve not only conflicts between capital and labour but between different fractions of capital (for example capital versus productive capital). The diagram, summarising as it does some of the central components and crucial interactions within capitalist society, provides a summary of the processes involved in the creation of its human geography. The interactions described by the diagram cannot exist in a vacuum, they must take on concrete form: they must have a *geography* if they are to work in practice. And, just as the circuit is dynamic and riddled with conflict, so too is its geography which both constrains and enables the circuit.

Characteristically, the geography of the circuit of capital is described and analysed in fragmented and uneven terms. The study of the geography of headquarters and offices for example is largely devoid of a consideration of the structure of productive or finance capital, whilst the location of labour power is subsumed under a geography of population or a geography of housing (cf. McDowell, Chapter 2.3). The study of industrial location has, in the main, been undertaken separately from that of other aspects of production, whilst a geography of wholesaling and retailing – the former rare, the latter highly evident – tends to be thought of in terms of central place theory. Similarly, the geographies of transport and trade are regarded as purely spatial, while studies of the structure of the space-economy as a whole tend to be phrased in exclusively spatial terms, rather than in terms suggested by the social processes involved in the circuit of capital.

As a result of these tendencies, the relationship of the spatial structure of development to the process of development has tended to be defined in technical and universal terms, involving concepts like distance minimisation. This has had the effect that, in geographical study, purely spatial concepts came to dominate what are essentially social and historical processes of development. The particular nature of the social relations of production, which underlie social development and which help to define the parameters of the geography of development, are often ignored in the construction of spatial models resting upon the false assumptions of the universality and autonomy of economic processes.

This is not to argue that geographical considerations are of no import in an understanding of social development. On the contrary, the processes of development are nothing if they are not made concrete in their geography, which directly affects the working out of the processes themselves. Class structures, for example, show a great geographical diversity of form at any point in time. Even within the class structure of a single industry, geographical differentiation may not only be clearly discernable but have a crucial effect upon the outcome of struggle. The regional geography of class within the British National Union of Mineworkers, for example, played just such a role in the miners' year-long struggle (1984/5) to resist the closure of mines.

Not only is the process of development itself diversified by such geographically-differentiated class structures, but they also help to create geographically-distinctive forms of social life which interpret and shape processes of change in a geographically diverse manner. This argument suggests that the nature of social relations actually helps to define both the nature of spatial relations (the geography of day-to-day life in feudal Europe was very different from that characteristic of capitalist Europe largely because of the geographical differences induced by the different social relationships) and, as we have seen, the process of development itself. In other words, *social relations are inseparable from geographical relations*.

The form taken by the social relations of production may be highly influential not only in regulating the immediate process and geography of production, but also in establishing the social frontiers of what is thought to be possible or impossible. These frontiers may be impervious to mere technical advance. This point may be demonstrated more fully by a consideration of socialist relations of production, in which the flexible but contradictory relations between capital and labour under capitalism are replaced by the collective ownership of the means of production and a comprehensive system of economic planning. One consequence of such a system is that the social basis of production is immediately obvious. In capitalism, by contrast, the separation between labour and capital makes it appear that the individual, operating freely and independently, is the basic motor of the system; as a result the underlying need for capital accumulation is obscured. Thus, attempts in capitalist society to move towards a comprehensive system of planning for industrial development have foundered, not just because such planning is technically difficult (although it is certainly that) but because it would be impossible in a social system in which capital is privately owned and may be disposed of in a way acceptable to the capitalist rather than to the wider society. The attempt to plan industrial development in a comprehensive fashion requires a centrally-planned, democratically-controlled economy, operating within socialist relations of production.

Any technical similarities between, for example, major industrial regions within capitalist societies and the territorial production complexes (TPCs) within the Soviet Union, mask more fundamental differences deriving from the social relations in which each becomes possible. Industrial linkages abound in both, but the capitalist industrial region is made up of individual capitals pursuing their own corporate self-interest and profitability, whereas in the TPC the whole is designed (more or less successfully) to contribute to particular developmental objectives established by the central planning agency. And geography matters in the development of Soviet TPCs, not only because they represent a particular geographical solution to a technical problem of production (especially the problem of effective linkages), but also because they represent an attempt to integrate a vast geographical region – Siberia – into the national economy and to exploit the national resources contained within it.

Social relations and the state

Social relations of production emerge in a more or less impure and unstable form by a process of *social struggle*, in which the objective, explicit or not, is to attempt to improve the conditions of existence of the proponents of struggle. The emergence of a specific set of social relations of production must involve its widespread acceptance or imposition. The productive effectiveness of particular social relations is a necessary but insufficient condition for acceptance or successful imposition. It is insufficient because any potentially subordinate groups in the new social arrangements may resist their advance. The struggle involved in the emergence of a set of social relations means that its characteristics cannot be known in advance.

The widespread acceptance or imposition of a set of social relations of production implies not only an acceptable level of economic success, materially demonstrated, but the establishment of legal, political and cultural conditions in which the emergent relations of production may be sustained in the wider society. However, such conditions will themselves be affected by the relations of production, which exert a central influence upon the shape of human society at large.

The force which brings labour and capital together within capitalist society is the private interest that each of them has in obtaining what the other possesses. The concomitant of this self-interest is conflict, and the resultant need for the two classes each to attempt to control the actions of the other. This tendency towards work-based class conflict is exacerbated in capitalist society by the tendency for incessant innovative changes in the production process. Thus, although capitalist relations of production enable the potential development of material production by removing obstacles to productive efficiency and by ensuring that such an objective will be actively sought, they also induce social conflict.

Given the unplanned and competitive relations of profitability between individual units of capital, each is compelled to reduce its costs and extract the maximum value from labour. If this process is over-extended, it reaches a natural limitation, when labour power is destroyed faster than it is produced. The principal reason why labour power is not so destroyed is that labour itself has something to say and do about the process. Labour is not a passive recipient of conditions laid down by capital; it, too, struggles to improve the conditions of its own existence. The most direct institutional product of this struggle is the trade union but, more generally, the state must also respond.

Only the state has the power to establish the conditions to prevent the tendency of capital to destroy the basis of its own existence, both within and beyond production. The state imposes laws, rules, conditions, procedures and taxation which influence the operation of capital. These interventions result, in part, from the struggle of the working class to secure the conditions for their own reproduction. The development of the state in capitalist society is, to a significant extent therefore, the result of the struggle of workers to sustain and improve their own conditions of existence within the sphere of circulation. This conclusion also implies that the state is itself a part of the struggle between capital and labour and between competing capitals; it is not a separate or an independent entity.

The state is also a crucial element in contemporary socialist society. But here its basis is rather different. As a result of the heightened awareness of production as a social process under socialism, there is an explicit recognition that social development involves the extension and reproduction in time and space of the productive system as a whole. Such a recognition cannot be so nearly apparent in capitalism, dominated as it is by the ideology of individualism. Three aspects of extension and reproduction appear to be crucial in socialist societies. They include the socialist relations themselves, without which collectively-organised planning would be impossible; the size of the social product and of the surplus to be used for the further development of the productive forces; and the labour force, which must be extended in terms of skill and productivity.

Nevertheless, as long as it remains necessary for productive activity within socialist societies to generate the means of the further development of the productive forces, and as long as people differ in their views of the relative importance of further investment as opposed to immediate consumption, some form of state mechanism will remain a prerequisite of social order. Within the Soviet Union, for example, the central planning agency, Gosplan, is the formal decision-making body responsible for regulating prices, purchasing policy and the allocation of productive resources. Attempts to integrate these decisions with the long-term objectives of socialist development in the USSR are made in the programme of five-year plans, formulated in consultation with the Central Committee of the Communist Party and passed on as directives to state enterprises and agricultural collectives.

However, such a mechanism of economic control is far from being a smooth or merely technical process. The socialist state must attempt to impose its plans upon the labour force, although not necessarily in a more repressive manner than that involved in the imposition of new methods of production, or products by capital upon labour in capitalist society. Nevertheless, socialist states are not devoid of class struggle: the enforced limitations on the migration of Chinese peasants to the cities and the ill-fated Cultural Revolution are forms of class struggle which replace unemployment and wage bargaining in capitalist society. The recent freeing of central controls within the Chinese economy marks an attempt to use competitive struggles more directly to stimulate productivity and growth.

Alternative interpretations of the relationship between state and society under socialism give rise to alternative characterisations of the nature of contemporary socialist societies. These interpretations range from state socialism at one extreme, in which the central planning of production is directed at social use with the influence of the working-class operating indirectly through the Party, to state capitalism at the other, in which state power is used to exploit the working class in competing for economic and political power within the international system of nation states. Other categorisations tend to stress the exploitative role of the socialist bureaucracy, with some interpretations going as far as to suggest that the existence of a dominant bureaucratic class is the most distinctive feature of socialist societies.

THE GEOGRAPHICAL SHAPE OF CONTEMPORARY SOCIETY

The creation of the modern world has its roots in two fundamental social revolutions, scarcely two centuries old. The French Revolution of 1789 and its precursor the American Revolution of 1776 involved, for the first time in human history, an attempt to restructure an entire social order from below on the truly revolutionary basis of universal liberty and equality. Whatever the subsequent achievements of the social order that ensued, political democracy is now, in formal terms at least, an inescapable item on the social agenda. Certainly, the political transformations that followed the French Revolution – slow, uneven and incomplete as they were and are – have helped to substantiate the separation of capital and labour within capitalist society. The emergence of the latter has been variously dated, but it is clear that what we now call the Industrial Revolution, beginning in Britain in the late eighteenth century, involved more than the temporal concentration of technical change. Indeed, as Karl Marx's narrative of the transformation makes clear, the Industrial Revolution was a complex process involving the constructive interaction between the development of social relations of production and processes of technical change. In this account the Industrial Revolution may be understood as the material consequence of the geographically – and sectorally – uneven spread of capitalist relations throughout productive life. These developments set in motion in a number of novel and fundamental geographical transformations, in which the modern world is still embroiled.

Industrialisation and urbanisation

As we have seen already, the 'freedom' of capital and labour induced productive flexibility and insisted upon productive efficiency. But these changes involved – and continue to involve – complex geographical, rather than merely economic, processes. On the one hand, the growth in manufacturing took the form, well into the nineteenth century, of proto-industrialisation – a multiplication of small producing units in rural areas, often surrounding industrial cities like Manchester, Lille, Rouen, Barcelona, Zurich, Basel, Geneva and Moscow. The continued connection of the proto-industrial workforce with the land ensured a continued, if only partial, control over their means of production. On the other hand, the sectorally-uneven concentration of the workforce into a growing but only slowly dominant factory system, and the associated expansion of activities necessary to service and sustain the growing level of output, led to a thorough proletarianisation of labour within an unprecedented process of urbanisation. Meanwhile, as an awareness of the social, political and environmental consequences of the concentration of the working population into totally inadequate living spaces was thrust into political consciousness, the state, both local and national, began to regulate and control the conditions within and without the work place.

These transformations were effected not only by the mass migration of labour from the land and the de-industrialisation of the countryside, but also by the geographical demands of the new productive processes for spatial concentration and geographically-centralised coordination. The geographical distribution of population and economic activity was transformed as cities grew in number and size and, for the first time in European history, urbanisation dominated the day-to-day lives of the mass of society. In pre-industrial Europe the city was exceptional, not in the sense that it was marginal to economic life – it was, in fact, central to the activities of merchants and to the organisation and administration of certain critical elements of society like the church. But it was marginal to the daily lives of the mass of the people whose livelihood was made in, if not determined by, rural – but by no means purely agricultural – conditions.

The present century has seen a gradual reversal of the process of mass physical urbanisation within capitalist societies. This has been the result not merely of the greater spatial flexibility stemming from the growing sophistication of communications, mass and personal transport systems and of ever-more spatially tolerant sources of energy and their systems of delivery, but from a change in the social relationships within capitalism. The continuing concentration (the competitive elimination of the weak by the strong) and centralisation (the absorption of the weak by the strong) of capital have now passed the point at which the narrow spatial coincidence of an individual unit of capital and its source of labour is the norm. Individual capitalist enterprises are now, like capitalism has always been, geographically unconstrained. Labour is increasingly exploited by non-local firms operating at a world scale. As a result, the reproductive conditions of a local circuit of capital are much less significant in advanced capitalism than they were in the era of competitive capitalism. In the nineteenth century physical urbanisation was a major control on the circuit of industrial capital; in the present century corporate structure has become a major influence upon urbanisation.

The organisation of capitalist production now resembles a gigantic version of the old putting-out system. A small number of centres of finance and industrial capital, located within a handful of world cities, are responsible for directing the spatial structure of the circuit of world-wide capital just as merchant capital controlled production in the hinterlands of the pre- and proto-industrial city. As a result, the autonomy of the pre-industrial city is being recreated in the contemporary world city, but the basis of that autonomy is fundamentally different. It now rests upon the integration of the city with the world-wide economy, rather than upon the separation of the pre-industrial city from the daily activities of predominantly locally-organised economies. But this integration itself implies separation. Even within the world cities, local conditions of production may be affected more by the influence of the international network of the production and circulation of surplus value than they are by the local geography of their immediate location. The urban consequence of the centralisation and concentration of capital is momentous. The city as the manifestation of industrial capital is undergoing fundamental change. No longer necessary as the spatial mainstay of capital, the big industrial city is increasingly redundant as a site for production.

By contrast, urbanisation and geographically-concentrated industrial development remains a marked feature of socialist societies and, in some established industrial areas – Upper Silesia, for example – the share of national industrial output and employment continues to rise. Similar emphases throughout Eastern Europe point to the continued priority attached to industrial growth and improvements in productivity, in a region with an uneven but relatively low-level of development of the forces of production. Equally, the concentrated spatial structure of economic development reflects the importance attached to heavy industry in industrial development, and the relatively recent development of integrated energy supply and transport systems which have long been instrumental in facilitating geographical decentralisation within developed capitalist societies. However, collective decision-making, and the management of economic linkages also tends towards geographical concentration in socialist societies, although the increasing importance of light industry presents both demands and opportunities for geographical decentralisation.

Such circumstances are also conducive to the concentration of population in cities, although extensive commuting appears to be an important feature of socialist urbanisation. This is due partly to the failure to provide sufficient living spaces within the major city-based centres of employment. Nevertheless, in Eastern Europe for example, most countries continue to experience rural depopulation at a time when counter-urbanisation is a pronounced feature of the settlement system in the west. Furthermore, urban growth in Eastern Europe tends to be concentrated at the top of the urban hierarchy and in and around the national capitals, whilst the planned linking of the settlement system to the economic system is a continuing concern of planners in the more highly-developed socialist societies.

Nevertheless, the influence of the world-economy is increasingly insistent within both capitalist and socialist societies. Whether the emergence of a single world-economy is related to the effects of the Industrial Revolution, or whether it came into existence, at least in terms of trading links, in the fifteenth or sixteenth centuries, the role of capitalist relations of production was central in both facilitating and stimulating its emergence as an internally differentiated, but essentially global economy, organised and operative at a world scale.

The world-economy

Three phases in the development of the world-economy may be recognised, each reflecting the productive and geographical flexibility of the circuit of capital. The world-wide trading and sourcing of raw materials was accompanied towards the end of the nineteenth century by the world-wide flow of money capital in search of profitable investment. Today, the operation of the world-economy is dominated by global production and the so-called *new international division of labour*, based upon the operations of multi-national capital. As capitalist development has proceeded, the competitive relations between the singular units of capital has resulted in their growth, via the processes of concentration and centralisation. The sophisticated internal organisation of these corporations and the facility of electronic communications allows the global organisation of production, whereby global capital may not seek out its preferred conditions of existence throughout the world, but also take profitable advantage of economic inequalities and political discontinuities.

The contemporary world-economy is characterised by a single but highly dynamic division of labour, operating over the world's complex mosaic of cultural systems and environments. None of these may, therefore, be understood simply in their own, purely local, terms or considered to be autonomous and completely self-contained. The geography of any particular part of the world must take full account of its relationships with the operation and organisation of the world economy. Perhaps the most obvious example here is that of the underdeveloped world. The *condition* or *state* of underdevelopment may be understood (and, ultimately, rectified) only if the *processes* of underdevelopment (for example, the extraction of surplus value) are seen as a complex set of economic, social and political relationships between the underdeveloped world and the world-economy. Equally, the de-industrialisation of an advanced economy, like Britain, is closely related to increasingly dominant and hypermobile multinational capital, which is able to take the world as its locale and to seek out and create cheap labour and favourable political régimes to ensure its continued profitability. In the process it helps to create the so-called newly industrialising countries which are, in truth, little more than the latest manifestation of the geographically-uneven operation of global capital.

The place of the socialist states within the global economy is a subject of some controversy. Whilst it is possible to differentiate between the social relations of production in socialism and capitalism, it is not so easy to separate them in practice within the contemporary world-economy. It is clear that most socialist states are affected, directly or indirectly, by the operation of the world-economy within or around them. Even the most powerful – the Soviet Union – is indirectly involved in the world-economy through its participation as a global superpower in the political and material relationships within the international network of nation states. Furthermore, although Soviet involvement in world trade amounts to less than 10 per cent of the value of its annual production, it has recently begun to re-emphasise production for a world market, to participate in the transfer of technology and to deal with multinational corporations for both production and trade. Thus, despite its territorial size, rich resources and potentially large internal market, the costs of developing socialism from a weak industrial base, appear to necessitate Soviet participation in the world system. Nevertheless, the integration of the socialist states into the world-economy is unevenly developed from sector to sector, as well as from country to country.

The creation of a world-economy has momentous implications for our understanding of the world in which we live. Development and underdevelopment are global processes, and it is to them that we must look if we are to begin to understand the human condition and to act to improve it:

> Drawn by these forces into convergent activities, people of diverse origins and social makeup were driven to take part in the construction of a common world. They included the European sea merchants and soldiery of various nationalities, but also native Americans, Africans, and Asians. In the process, the societies and cultures of all these people underwent major changes. These changes affected not only the peoples singled out as the carriers of 'real' history but also what the populations anthropologists have called 'primitives' and have often studied as pristine survivals from a timeless past. The global processes set in motion by European expansion constitute their history as well. There are thus no 'contemporary ancestors', no people without history, no peoples – to use Lévi-Strauss's phrase – whose histories have remained 'cold'.[1]

Here, in a sense, we are back full circle with a diverse world which is more than merely fascinating. It is a world constructed by a global set of social relations, developed and underdeveloped by the same processes – the precise mechanisms of which cause controversy in theory as well as in practice – and divided by ideologies sustained by the terrifying control of the means of violence in the system of nation states. It is a world which we fail to strive to understand at our own, very real, peril.

NOTES AND REFERENCES

1. Eric R. Wolf, *Europe and the People without History* (Berkeley and London: California University Press, 1982) p.385.

FURTHER READING

An introductory account of the double involvement of individual and society – of the ways in which we create society at the same time as we are created by it – is provided by Anthony Giddens, *Sociology: a brief but critical introduction* (London: Macmillan, second edition 1987); more difficult is John Urry, *The anatomy of capitalist society* (London: Macmillan, 1981).

Analyses of the relationships between the social relations of production and the geography of social development are provided by David Harvey, *The Limits to Capital* (Oxford: Basil Blackwell, 1982), especially Chapters 12 and 13; Neil Smith, *Uneven Development* (Oxford: Basil Blackwell, 1984); Doreen Massey, *Spatial Divisions of Labour* (London: Macmillan, 1984); and Michael Dunford and Diane Perrons, *The Arena of Capital* (London: Macmillan, 1983).

For the world system perspective, see Peter Taylor's chapter in this volume. A brilliant substantive account of the development of the world is Eric R. Wolf, *Europe and the People Without History* (Berkeley and London: California University Press, 1982). The contemporary capitalist world economy is discussed by Nigel Thrift, 'The Geography of International Economic Disorder' in R. J. Johnston and P. J. Taylor (eds) *A World in Crisis*? (Oxford: Basil Blackwell, 1986).

PART III
EXPLORATIONS IN THE CITY

Introduction

The essays in this section are concerned with different aspects of "urban geography". **Keith Bassett** and **John Short** draw attention to the rapid growth of urban geography: indeed, some commentators see its development as being so explosive that it promises to disintegrate into a myriad fragments. Certainly, it has proved remarkably difficult to put analytical boundaries around the city in advanced capitalism, and even those who still accept the possibility of a distinctively 'urban' focus for their studies (however that might be defined) are now likely to have to integrate their inquiries into wider and deeper investigations of the constitution of society as a whole. Not surprisingly, therefore, urban geography has itself been drawn into the mainstream of the social sciences.

But it is possible to glimpse a precarious order in this fast-changing intellectual landscape, and Bassett and Short identify two waves which have surged through urban geography in the last twenty years. The first of these was part of the sea-change brought about by spatial science in the 1960s and early 1970s; the second has drawn its strength from political economy, sociology and anthropology. The second wave was not, of course, confined to urban geography: virtually every branch of human geography has been shaken by its force. It has had a number of consequences. Studies are now more 'human', less preoccupied with abstract patterns or atomistic individuals and more likely to probe – to take only the most obvious examples – the social relations which structure (and are structured by) the housing and property markets, the different day-to-day experiences of different groups of people in the city, and the formation of local communities and urban social movements concerned to defend a particular 'sense of place' and a particular set of values and aspirations. In direct consequence, studies in urban geography have also become more alert to the politics (rather than simply the policies) of contemporary urbanism: they are not – and cannot hope to be – detached reports from the sidelines.

In so far as many of these newer approaches have tapped into modern extensions of Marx and (Max) Weber, then another of their vital themes is the importance of historical depth. This was particularly clear in Marx's writings, of course – his was an *historical* materialism after all – but it was also central to Weber's work. The reopening of historical perspectives across the social sciences as a whole certainly owes as much to Weber as it does to Marx, and **Richard Dennis** can call on a plurality of distinguished traditions to demonstrate that the past is pivotal to any critical understanding of the present. His essay can be read as a series of exemplifications of the ideas reviewed in more general terms by Bassett and Short, but in tracing several continuities between the urban geographies of the past and the present Dennis also emphasises that 'as we learn about the past, so we see our own condition through freshly-opened eyes'. This stands in stark contrast to the functionalism of the simple models of spatial science, of course, though Dennis is as attentive to the strengths of quantitative analysis as he is to the sensitivities of more humanistic approaches.

Similar themes are taken up by **Ian Douglas** in his programmatic geography of the urban environment. If our understanding of the urban environment is not to be confined to a reduced version of the earth sciences, Douglas declares, 'allied with environmental geology and sanitary engineering', then we need to adopt an historical approach capable of capturing the ever-changing intersections between physical and social systems. And Douglas's view of human geography is not – unlike that of so many physical geographers – an outdated vision of spatial scientists ranged against misty-eyed romantics. His cities are 'pulsating, vibrant, evolving, changing expressions of people's achievements, ambitions, hopes, fears and failures'. And, once again, any comprehensive geography of their physical environment must address questions of politics as well as policy: Douglas's vision of physical geography is much more than a narrowly technical, instrumentalist one. All of this intersects neatly with the views of Bassett, Short and Dennis, but what Douglas demonstrates in addition is that, although Marx's approach may have been an historical *materialism*, it never said much about the physical world: and that it is as important to fill that gap in urban geography as anywhere else. Douglas also directs our attention away from 'the declining inner cities of the old industrial conurbations of the Western world' and towards a future urban geography centrally concerned with 'the hectic tumult of growth, overcrowding and environmental deterioration of the cities of low latitudes'.

These three essays help to establish an exhilarating agenda for urban geography. They underscore the salience of its *social* dimension; they insist on the importance of an *historical* perspective; they sharpen its *materialist* edge through an examination of the physical environment. And in doing so, they cut through the traditional boundaries which separate cities from societies, past from present, built environment from physical environment, and North from South.

3.1
Development and Diversity in Urban Geography

Keith Bassett and John Short
University of Bristol and University of Reading

Keith Bassett is Lecturer in Geography at the University of Bristol and **John Short** is Lecturer in Geography at the University of Reading. They are the joint authors of *Housing and Residential Structure*; John Short has also written *An Introduction to Political Geography*.

CONTEXTS OF CHANGE

Since the publication of *Models in Geography*, the whole context of work in urban geography has dramatically changed. In the mid-1960s economic growth still seemed assured in most advanced capitalist countries, there was an expectation of continuously rising living standards, and a large measure of social consensus prevailed. Although a handful of writers in Britain and America were in the process of 'rediscovering' poverty, many of what were perceived to be urban problems were related to growth and its consequences. By the 1980s, however, economic growth had faltered or come to a halt in all but a few favoured economies, unemployment had increased alarmingly and in many cities deprivation had deepened in the inner areas and begun to spread to more and more suburban estates. New sources of social tension and new lines of political cleavage emerged, culminating in Britain in several waves of urban riots.

Urban geography was at first slow to respond to this changing context. Writing in 1973 in *Social Justice and the city*, Harvey bemoaned the apparent inability of geographers to say anything of depth or profundity about the urban problems that were emerging. 'The objective social conditions', he argued, 'demand that we say something sensible and coherent or else forever . . . remain silent' (p.129). Geographers have not remained silent since then; in fact a veritable babble of voices has been raised, putting forward a wide range of new approaches to the study of urban problems. In the process the voices of urban geographers have become intermingled with those of sociologists, economists and political scientists, to an extent that has brought into question the very status of a separate urban geography. Whether, along the way, something 'sensible and coherent' has been said is a matter for the reader to judge.

THEORETICAL APPROACHES, 1965–1985

We cannot hope to cover the vast volume of work undertaken in the last twenty years in urban geography. We prefer instead to identify what we see as the principal *theoretical* frameworks that have emerged over this period. This will enable us to present a resumé of key themes and to locate the contributions of representative authors. We will largely limit our remarks to work on cities in advanced capitalist countries, with particular reference to the UK.

The relative importance of the main frameworks is summarised in Figure 3.1.1. Such a classification is necessarily crude and some of the theoretical boundaries are much sharper than others. Although we prefer to avoid the much abused terminology of 'paradigms', these frameworks are similar to paradigms in the sense that they involve different sets of research questions, assumptions and concepts. Broadly speaking, the first part of the period tended to be dominated by the approaches we have labelled 'ecological', 'new urban economic' and 'behavioural', and while these approaches are still in evidence today, the latter part of the period has witnessed the increasing dominance of 'neo-Marxist', 'neo-Weberian' and 'humanist' approaches.

We will explain these terms in the sections which follow, but it should be said that this list of theoretical frameworks does not completely capture the range of urban studies generated during this period. We can note two important strands of research which have been more concerned with classification and prediction than with theoretical explanation as such. Firstly, a strong *empiricist* current has been evident, in the sense that a large volume of intra-urban research has been simply concerned with the collection and classification of data about urban areas. Causal explanation has been a secondary concern. This empiricist current has been dominant in research concerned with mapping census data and delimiting urban sub-areas, in studies of urban manufacturing which have been concerned with the classification of 'components of change', and in many impact studies of the effects of particular central and local government policies. It is not our intention to attempt to summarise this vast mass of material here.

THEORETICAL ROOTS	THEORETICAL APPROACHES 1965	1975	1985
Chicago school Social area analysis Human ecology	ECOLOGICAL	Ecological	Ecological
Neo-classical economics Land use economics	URBAN ECONOMIC	NEW URBAN ECONOMIC	New Urban Economic
Environmental psychology Organisation theory Behavioural psychology	Behavioural	BEHAVIOURAL	Behavioural
Marxism		Neo-Marxist	NEO-MARXIST
Weberian sociology Community power studies		Neo-Weberian	NEO-WEBERIAN
Phenomenology Existentialism Idealism		Humanist	HUMANIST

FIGURE 3.1.1 *Approaches in urban geography*

Secondly, a strongly *instrumentalist* approach has been evident in much of this literature on urban planning models. These models have been developed in response to the policy demands of the physical planning process in urban areas. They have mainly been used for plan generation and plan evaluation, and as such they describe the effects of deeper causal mechanisms rather than seeking to explain the mechanisms themselves. Empiricist and instrumentalist approaches encompass a large literature, but they are peripheral to our central concern with more explicitly theoretical approaches where the concern with *explanation* predominates (see also Johnston, Chapter 1.3).

THE FIRST WAVE

The ecological approach

Elements of this approach can be traced back through the work of the Chicago school of human ecology in the 1920s, to certain themes in the work of Darwin and Durkheim. The Chicago school developed a distinctive approach to the city incorporating ecological principles such as competition, selection, succession and dominance. Early debates with a geographical flavour revolved around the relative merits of Burgess's concentric zone model of the city and the sector model subsequently proposed by the land economist Hoyt.

In the 1960s ecological themes were fused with the theory of 'social area analysis', which promised a means of classifying urban areas in terms of certain underlying 'dimensions'. The subsequent expansion of computer facilities and the development of factor analysis as a statistical tool encouraged a more and more inductive approach to establishing the dimensions of urban structure. The theoretical content became steadily diluted in a flood of factorial ecologies of different towns and cities.

These studies did at least establish that the Burgess and Hoyt models were in many respects complementary: the class and status dimension was likely to show a sectoral pattern, whilst family status was likely to show a zonal pattern. However, after a decade of over-indulgence, this line of research was generating diminishing returns, and by the early 1970s interest was beginning to fade in the face of the difficulty of penetrating beyond descriptive, aggregate generalisations of urban patterns to underlying generating mechanisms.

The new urban economics (NUE)

This approach is, in effect, a spatial counterpart to mainstream neo-classical economics. A standard NUE model is usually based upon a number of assumptions. It is usual to assume a concentric, homogeneous city with a single centre in which is concentrated the production of a composite consumption good. Housing demand relates only to plot size and location. Externalities and public sector policies are ignored. Activities are allocated in space by land rent variations which reflect competitive market processes. On the basis of these assumptions, a typical NUE model can then be used to determine a long-run equilibrium pattern of land uses. In a residential location model, for example, families are assumed to attempt to maximise utility, which is supposed to be a function of amount of housing space consumed, distance from CBD and consumption of a composite consumption good. Maximisation is subject to a budget constraint. Such utility maximising behaviour generates a rent and residential density gradient that declines from the centre.

The standard NUE model is obviously highly restrictive, and much of the work carried out in the 1970s has been concerned with relaxing various assumptions and extending the model. Thus more recent models have incorporated multiple centres, different transport modes, externalities such as pollution, and public goods. Residential location models have incorporated income variations, differences in household preferences, variations in environmental quality and racial discrimination in housing markets.

Criticisms of the restrictive assumptions, however telling, miss the more important point that this whole approach has been subject to fundamental criticisms from behavioural approaches and, more recently, from neo-Marxist, neo-Weberian and humanist approaches. Following the behavioural lead, humanists have criticised the dehumanisation implicit in reducing individuals to simple, rational, decision-making units operating in an abstract market environment. Neo-Marxists have perhaps gone furthest in attacking the ideological aspects inherent in the neo-classical foundations of the models. They have argued that they preserve the fiction that the city is a reflection of consumer choice and so serves to justify the restriction of state intervention to the correction of externalities, in order to enable competitive market processes to work more efficiently. Their focus on consumer sovereignty and market processes conceals underlying class and property relations and the deeper mechanisms of capitalist accumulation.

The behavioural approach

This approach is much more diverse and so much more difficult to define precisely than the previous two. It grew out of criticisms of the oversimplified concepts of human behaviour implicit in neo-classical and ecological models and, more generally, in the quantitative models that gained ground in geography in the 1960s. The behavioural approach sought to bring greater realism into model building by drawing upon sources as diverse as environmental psychology, anthropology and theories of organisational behaviour. A fundamental distinction was drawn between the 'objective' environment and the cognitive image of that environment by an individual or group. This led to a general shift from macroscale studies to microscale studies of individual and small group behaviour, and to a greater emphasis upon processes rather than aggregate patterns. So, for example, some writers sought to model residential mobility in terms of decision-making processes using concepts such as place utility, household needs and expectations and housing environmental stress. Other authors explored the contrasting urban images of residents in different parts of the city, and demonstrated the complexity of the perceived images of shopping centres that underlay seemingly simple consumer shopping behaviour.

By the late 1970s the behavioural approach itself rapidly became a target for attack from a variety of directions. It was generally criticised for its over-emphasis on individual rather than group behaviour, and its over-simplistic views on the relation between cognition and behaviour. Both neo-Weberians and neo-Marxists criticised it more for its over-emphasis on individual choice, as well as its under-emphasis on the constraints which social structures imposed on choice. Even sympathetic critics concluded that although the behavioural approach had introduced more realism into urban research, 'its approach to subjectivity and experience was overly structured, suppressing too severely the dynamism and ambiguities of everyday life'.[1] To those who subsequently made the shift to 'humanist' approaches, behavioural geography had been subverted by spatial analysis and had become little more than an appendage to location theory.

These criticisms have provoked a re-thinking by those who still wish to defend the basic thrust of the behavioural approach. Attempts have been made to strengthen the initially crude behavioural assumptions in fields such as innovation diffusion and residential mobility, and more effort has gone into building links between models of individual behaviour and wider societal constraints. A particularly important line of development in this respect has been the reformulation of Hägerstrand's original work on time-geography, by writers such as Allan Pred, in order to explore the interface between individual time paths, institutional structures and different forms of time-space constraint (see Eyles, Chapter 2.1 and McDowell, Chapter 2.3).

THE SECOND WAVE

Neo-Marxist approaches

There has been a major upsurge of studies within a broadly Marxist framework in the last decade. This has not been peculiar to geography: most of the social sciences have experienced similar developments. This is perhaps not surprising. As advanced capitalist countries have experienced deepening economic and social problems, so more social scientists have become interested in an intellectual tradition that offers perhaps the most famous and comprehensive theory of capitalist crisis.

Neo-Marxist studies obviously draw their inspiration directly or indirectly from Marx's writings. Marx presented a theory of history in terms of successive modes of production, whose internal development is governed by the conflict between the developing productive forces of society and the more rigid social relations of production within which they are embedded (see Lee, Chapter 2.4). Changes in the social relations of production are interrelated with changes in class structure and conflict. The transformation of the economic base of study generates changes in the social superstructures of law, the state and ideology.

The influence of Marx's writings has not, however, been simple or direct. Marx's writings contain many ambiguities and key areas of his theoretical structure were left unfinished. This particularly applies to the labour theory of value, central to the economic analysis of capitalism, and also to theories of class and the capitalist state. Some writers have even identified contradictory tendencies *within* the central core of Marx's work. It is not surprising, therefore, that a complex Marxist tradition has developed over the past 100 years, in which different 'schools' have drawn upon and emphasised different aspects of Marx's original work.

Urban geography was perhaps the first area of geography to feel the impact of neo-Marxist approaches. In general terms, such approaches emphasise that the form and development of the capitalist city is governed by the laws of development of the capitalist mode of production of which it is an integral part. In this context major contributions have been made by Manuel Castells and David Harvey, both of whom have offered general theories of capitalist urbanisation. A comparison of these two writers will indicate something of the diversity and development within the Marxist tradition.

Castells' work drew heavily upon the French 'structuralist' school of Marxism. In *The Urban Question* (1972, translated 1977) Castells offered an elaborate theoretical framework for the analysis of social systems. He distinguished different 'levels' (subsystems) of the social system – the economic, the political and the ideological – with the economic level ultimately determining the structure of the whole in complex and indirect ways. Spatial structure was then presented as a reflection of the interacting effects of the contradictory tendences within and between these levels (see Figure 3.1.2). As Castells put it: 'To analyse space as an expression of the social structure amounts, therefore, to studying its shaping by the elements of the economic system, the political system and the ideological system, and by their combinations and the social practices that derive from them.'[2]

According to Castells, these levels are combined in particular ways in urban systems. The ideological level is represented by symbolic space – by the various ways in which the built environment symbolises particular social meanings and social values. The political level is represented by institutional space – by the political geography of local government and urban administration. Neither of these levels is limited to the city, of course, and Castells is equally clear that cities are not distinctive units of production either: production is increasingly organised on a regional or even an international

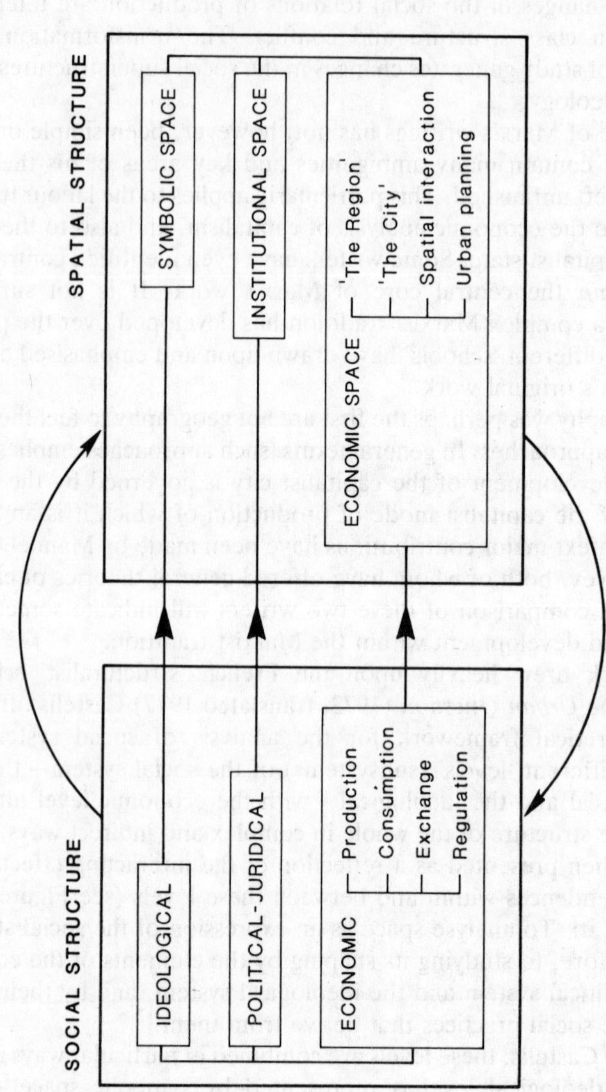

FIGURE 3.1.2 *Castells' framework for the analysis of urban structure*

scale (cf. Thrift and Taylor, Chapter 4.3). The distinctiveness of cities, so Castells argues, lies increasingly in their functions in the sphere of consumption. Cities are 'units of collective consumption', where the state is increasingly involved in the daily and generational reproduction of labour power through the provision of collectively consumed goods and services (education, health care, public transport, etc.). However, the urban system, like the wider capitalist system of which it is a part, is riddled with contradictions which manifest themselves in urban crises. 'Urban planning' refers to the various means by which the state intervenes to try and regulate these system contradictions.

The approach laid out in *The Urban Question* is pitched at a highly abstract level and, in the face of criticism from both Marxists and non-Marxists, Castells has subsequently moved some way from this original position and has condemned his early work for its excessive abstraction and unnecessary obscurity. His later works represent important theoretical revisions and contain a subtler and more complex analysis of the inter-relationships between class, politics and urban conflict.

The City and the Grassroots (1983) focuses upon urban social movements, defined as collective actions that consciously aim at the transformation of the social interests and values embedded in the forms and functions of historically given cities. Here Castells is critical not only of the 'theoretical formalism' of his earlier work, but also of previous Marxist perspectives in so far as they have attempted to reduce the city and space to expressions (or 'reflections') of an underlying logic of capital. Castells' new approach, partly arrived at 'through the glorious ruins of the Marxist tradition', now seeks to integrate the analysis of structure with that of human agency. Spatial forms are now shaped by the interests of the dominant class operating through specific 'modes of production' and 'modes of development', by the power relations of the state, and by patterns of gender domination. At the same time, however, these forces interact with various forms of resistance and challenge. Within this framework, Castells conducts a detailed series of theoretically-informed empirical studies of urban social movements in different cities at different time periods. In each case he seeks to identify their relations to wider social structures and social conflicts, the nature of their goals, the determinants of their success and failure, and their impacts on urban meaning and urban form. In summary, 'social conflict and change' has emerged as the dominant theme in Castells' work, displacing the earlier focus on 'structure and social reproduction'.

By contrast, Harvey's work has drawn upon other sources within the Marxist tradition and followed a different trajectory. *Social Justice and the City*, published in 1973, was something of a transitional work, the 'liberal formulations' of the first part giving way to the 'socialist formulations' of the second part. Less influenced by the formalistic urges of structuralist Marxism, Harvey concentrated more on a reworking of some of Marx's central economic theories, applying Marx's concept of economic surplus to an analysis of the changing role of cities in history, and Marx's categories of rent to the analysis of urban land use patterns. Subsequent work extended the analysis of urban rent and explored the inter-relations of finance capital, class and state policy in the moulding of American urban systems. By 1977 Harvey had developed the outline of a general framework for the analysis of capitalist urban systems, based upon the notion of inter-related 'circuits of capital' as seen in Figure 3.1.3 (cf. Lee, Chapter 2.4). Capital, or surplus value, is created in the production process. If there is a surplus of capital in the primary, production circuit, then capital may flow into the secondary circuit where it may be invested in fixed capital or the 'consumption fund', both of which have physical expressions in the built form of the city. Finally, the flow of capital into the tertiary circuit, where it is used for investment in science and technology and for social expenditure, is particularly dependent on state intervention. Harvey uses this framework to explore the dynamics of urban crises and cycles of development and redevelopment.

Although Harvey now refers to the 'tentative' and even 'erroneous' formulations of *Social Justice and the City*, there is more continuity in his subsequent work than in Castells'. *The Limits to Capital* in particular incorporates many of the themes of the latter part of *Social Justice*, but reworks them in the context of a comprehensive review and reconstruction of Marx's *Capital*. A 'first cut' theory of crisis is built up from Marx's most basic economic categories, abstracting from many of the complex features of the economic system. A 'second cut' theory is then developed, incorporating money, credit and finance and the role of fixed capital. The 'third cut' theory begins to incorporate space in a systematic way, building from rent theory, through to the spatial mobilities of capital and labour and on to the analysis of regional and international uneven development and global crises. The 'circuits of capital' approach to urban analysis is now incorporated in a much broader framework, bringing together processes operating simultaneously at different spatial scales.

The dominating influence of Castells and Harvey should not obscure the important contributions by other authors, who presented theories of capitalist urbanisation of varying degrees of generality. Alongside them, a large number of more specialist studies have also been published, which have applied Marxist concepts to specific problem areas such as housing and residential structure and urban property development. Increasing attention has also been paid to the role of the state in urban government, planning and service provision. Whereas earlier approaches tended to apply theories of the central state to the local state in an unproblematic way, more recent studies have explored the specificity of the local state and the sources of tension between central and local policies.

Although neo-Marxist approaches have gained ground they have been the subject of extensive criticism from contending neo-Weberian and humanist approaches. From the humanist perspective, for example, Marxists have been accused of reducing individual decision-makers to puppets whose actions are

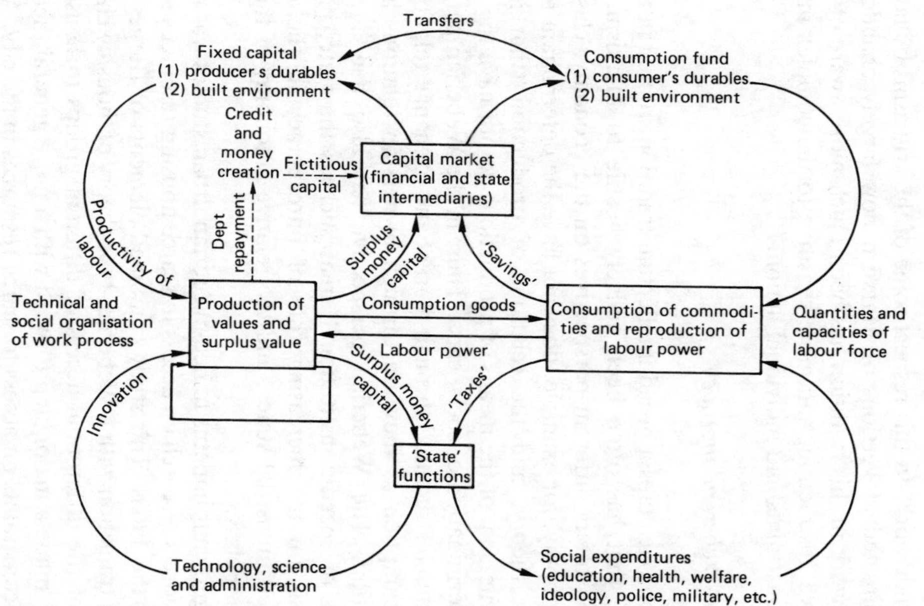

SOURCE: Harvey, D. *The Limits to Capital* (Blackwell, Oxford, 1982) p. 408.

FIGURE 3.1.3 *The circuits of capital*

determined by deeper structures, thereby impoverishing social experience. Marxists are thus accused of constructing highly abstract macrostructures which are then assumed to have a life and purpose of their own. Similar criticisms have been made from neo-Weberian perspectives although, as we shall see, their approach differs in important respects from the humanist one.

Neo-Marxists have not been unresponsive to some of these criticisms, as we have seen, and some have acknowledged the structuralist excesses of some of the earlier work. In this respect some of the criticisms by non-Marxists have been directed at versions of Marxism now largely abandoned. The more recent work in this tradition has been much more aware of the problems of excessive abstraction, and more sensitive to the complex interplay of structural constraints and individual action.

The neo-Weberian approach

This approach taps a broad intellectual tradition, rooted in the work of Max Weber, that has often been actively hostile to Marxism. The Weberian tradition offers different perspectives on the economy, class and the state. The economy, for example, does not have the determinant role that it has in Marxist theory, and the relations of production (that is ownership or non-ownership of the means of production) do not have the same saliency in the determination of social class. Thus, in the Weberian perspective, classes are as much structured through market and exchange relations in the sphere of consumption as they are through ownership relations in the sphere of production. The Weberian perspective has also had a more developed analysis of specific institutional areas such as the state, placing particular emphasis on the increasing role of bureaucracy in the development of advanced industrial states, and the relative autonomy of the state from the dominant class.

A significant impetus to neo-Weberian urban studies was provided by Rex and Moore's research on access to scarce housing resources in inner Birmingham in the 1960s. This study combined elements of Burgess's theory of the zone of transition with a Weberian-type theory of 'housing classes', defined in terms of the differential access of different groups to housing. Pahl subsequently made a major step forward with a more general theory of social and spatial constraints on access to scarce resources in the city. A prominent role was accorded to urban managers who acted as 'gatekeepers', to control access to scarce resources through a variety of rules and procedures. Pahl's work led to a spate of studies into the role of 'private' agents such as estate agents, landlords, developers, building societies and financial institutions. However, increasing attention was paid to the role of local authorities as key suppliers of housing and housing finance. Studies in this area covered slum clearance policies, allocation and transfer policies, improvement grant policies and council house sales. Such studies provided a great deal of information on the processes at work in the housing system and, by emphasising supply side constraints, provided a valuable corrective to the earlier neo-classical and behavioural models which focused on individual decision-making and choice. Many, though by no means all, of these studies had a geographical flavour, tracing decision-making processes through to an examination of spatial outcomes.

This early version of the 'urban managerialist' approach came under increasing attack, however, for a number of alleged deficiencies. Critics claimed that the theory as it stood failed to specify who or what should be included in the category of significant urban managers, and failed to specify the nature of the constraints that imposed limits on their autonomy. Such criticisms provoked some substantial revisions by Pahl and others, generally directed at incorporating the original insights of urban managerialism into a more coherent and broader theoretical framework. Thus Pahl redefined the role of his managers in terms of a mediating function between the public and private sectors, in the context of a social system that Pahl considered to be increasingly dominated by a 'corporatist state' operating relatively independently of capitalist interests. By the early 1980s other authors had begun to apply this corporatist model to the analysis of themes such as urban land use change and its distributional impacts.[3]

Over the past few years a number of more ambitious, broadly neo-Weberian approaches to the analysis of urban systems have been pursued, which have often been critical of earlier work in this tradition. In many respects Saunders offers the most comprehensive critique and revision, and in *Social Theory and the Urban Question* (1986) he outlines an ambitious framework for the study of urban conflict, politics and policy-making. He draws a series of distinctions between social consumption and social investment expenditures by the state, between central and local government, and between pluralist and corporatist state structures. His 'dual state' thesis then suggests that social investment decisions (investment in economic infrastructure which directly affects capitalist profitability, for example) tend to be associated with corporatist policy-making at the national and regional levels of government. This is while social consumption decisions (social welfare expenditure, for example) tend to be associated with competitive political struggles focusing on local government at the urban level.

The political groupings which form around social consumption issues such as housing, education and the welfare services, are, at the urban level, not class based: they are constituted on the basis of 'consumption sectors' (council tenants, the elderly, public transport users, etc). These consumption sectors, so Saunders argues, are becoming the major form of social cleavage in contemporary society. This perspective on class, politics and the city leads on to a re-conceptualisation of urban managerialism. 'Urban managers' are now those whose functions straddle the divisions between corporate and competitive politics, central and local government, and investment and consumption policies. They are 'personifications' of the contradictory relations between these different dimensions.

These latest neo-Weberian approaches represent a considerable development over the earlier tentative explorations of particular problem areas. Nevertheless, these developments and revisions have not satisfied Marxist critics, who have objected to the concepts of class and the state that are employed and, fundamentally, to their failure to relate both to the deeper, underlying dynamics of capital accumulation and crisis in the contemporary capitalist economy. To Marxists, the Weberian approach lacks roots in a deeper analysis of the structural constraints and imperatives of the capitalist mode of production, and as such its analysis tends to dissolve into contingent explanations in which almost any outcome becomes possible.

Humanist approaches

'Humanism' is also something of an umbrella term that covers a number of diverse strands of research. Certain elements of the humanist approach can be traced back to Carl Sauer and the Berkeley school of cultural geography, Vidal de la Blache and the French regional school of geography, and the ethnographic surveys of 'natural areas' carried out by Park and the Chicago school of sociology. However, recent developments in humanist geography have mainly resulted from an engagement with the so-called 'philosophies of meaning' – idealism, phenomenology and existentialism (see Johnston, Chapter 1.3).

Humanists have generally been united in their criticisms of positivist approaches to theory construction, including those implicit in the first wave of behavioural studies. Whereas positivists assert the validity of a general scientific method appropriate to the natural as well as the social sciences, humanists insist that the social sciences are qualitatively distinct. The subject matter of the social sciences is endowed with subjective meaning, and the social sciences cannot escape from an attempt to understand those meanings and the way they affect behaviour and action. Thus many humanists have argued that in spite of its achievements behavioural geography was at best a transition to the more satisfactory, more anthropocentric perspectives of humanistic geography. The central focus of the new approach is upon the ways in which humans experience and interpret their surroundings. The objective of research is to uncover the difference layers of meaning in the landscape in order to capture that experience, rather than constructing abstract statistical models of behavioural regularities.

Putting the humanist alternative into practice is fraught with difficulties. Humanist methodologies are 'methodologies of engagement, methodologies that enable the researcher to understand and interpret the subjective meaning contexts of individuals and groups in their own millieu, in as non-obtrusive manner as possible'.[4] Interpretation and understanding depend upon 'verstehen', the ability to empathise with individuals and groups in different social contexts. This often requires extensive participant observation by the researcher, which reinstates the centrality of field work but in a radically different sense: it may even require the development of extended relationships with those under study.[5]

Humanist approaches have been subject to criticisms from a variety of angles. Humanist geographers have been accused of focusing on the unique and the trivial, with methods that are incapable of transcending the subjectivity of the researcher. They have also been accused of focusing almost exclusively on the experience of individuals and small groups, and neglecting broader structural constraints on social behaviour. Humanists, it has been argued, lack any general theory of social life adequate to understand the way in which material forces mould values, intentions and meanings. Humanists have accepted the thrust of some of these criticisms, but have nevertheless insisted that none are essential to humanism which, they claim, *can* encompass social structures and constraints and *can* establish generalisations that transcend the subjectivity of the observer. Matters are made more complicated, however, by continuing disagreements amongst humanists themselves over the fundamentals of their approach. Not only are there tensions between idealism, phenomenology and existentialism: there are also significant disagreements within them.[6]

WHICH WAY FOR URBAN GEOGRAPHY?

Our review of different theoretical approaches has necessarily been something of a breathless gallop through the dense undergrowth of urban research, pointing out only some of the more outstanding trees as we passed. We conclude by standing back from the detail and commenting briefly on a number of more general issues.

Growth and fragmentation

The period since the late 1960s has clearly been one of rapid development, but also one of growing diversity and fragmentation. A variety of different approaches has emerged and vigorous debates have developed between supporters of contending positions. This has been both a source of strength and weakness in urban studies. Diversity and debate can be healthy in exposing deficiencies and challenging orthodoxies. It can also be a source of weakness if research becomes bogged down in broadsides between entrenched positions, with little room for a constructive exchange of ideas. On balance, however, the benefits of diversity and debate have far outweighed the negative effects. Urban geography has become a much more lively and stimulating subject area than it was twenty years ago.

The excavation of philosophical underpinnings

The opening up of debates has forced urban geographers to plunge deeper into basic philosophical and methodological issues to a far greater degree than fifteen years ago. The different approaches we have outlined have complex links to underlying philosophies such as positivism and phenomenology, for example, and debates have often been pitched at this more abstract level. Johnston has tried to relate the diversity of approaches in geography to three underlying philosophical and methodological frameworks, namely positivism, structuralism and humanism.[7] In the present context, our ecological and neo-classical approaches could be largely subsumed under positivism, and much of the neo-Marxist literature could be subsumed under the structuralist heading. There is, however, a danger of over-simplification in pushing this classification too far. Marxist approaches, for example, cannot be exclusively classified as structuralist because positivist, structuralist and humanist strands, as defined by Johnston, *all* find expression in complex ways *within* the Marxist tradition itself. The disentangling of different philosophical roots and the clarification of the fundamental areas of dispute continues to present real challenges to all urban geographers.

Integration into the social science mainstream

The last decade has seen the increasing integration of urban geography into the mainstream of the social sciences. Urban geography was for long dependent on selective borrowings from economics (conventional neo-classical economics) and sociology (the Chicago school), often uncritically retaining theories long after they had been criticised and largely abandoned in their original areas. The adoption of neo-Marxian and neo-Weberian approaches in particular has opened up much broader areas of economics, sociology and politics to urban geographers. There has been more inter-change of ideas between geographers and other social scientists, and key disputes and debates in the social sciences have been more quickly reflected in debates in urban geography. In the process the boundaries of urban geography have been pushed back and have become less clear-cut.

The uncertain status of urban geography

The opening up of the subject to wider debates and the blurring of its boundaries has also raised in a more acute form the whole question of whether 'urban geography' has any separate, distinctive identity. Challenges have come from several directions.

The adoption of Marxist approaches has, on the whole, been subversive of the concept of a separate urban geography. In Marx's original writings the city emerges as a significant locus of economic and social changes in pre-capitalist modes of production, necessitating a specific theory of the urban. Under capitalism, however, the city becomes largely an expression of wider economic and social processes, the place where the broader, contradictory tendencies of capitalist development become most fully developed. The city therefore tends to disappear as a specific object for theoretical analysis. It is true that Castells did attempt to salvage a distinctive field of urban study with a new focus on collective forms of consumption, but this theme became much less prominent in his later work. And, certainly, other Marxists, such as Harvey, have been less concerned with salvage operations, integrating urban change into frameworks that are simultaneously urban, regional, national and even international in their spatial scale.

The adoption of Weberian approaches has had a somewhat similar effect. Weber, like Marx, saw the mediaeval city as a distinct economic, political and ideological configuration, but regarded the capitalist city as an expression of wider social processes not specific to urban areas. This perspective is reflected in Saunders' neo-Weberian critique of urban sociology. Saunders lists four attempts over the past 70 years to identify particular social processes with the distinctive spatial form of the city. These attempts have found expression in the view of the city as an ecological community (the Chicago school), as a cultural unit (Louis Wirth), as a system of resource allocation (Pahl) and as a unit of collective consumption (Castells). All these attempts, Saunders argues, have failed. He concludes by relegating much of the traditional concern with the influence of space on social relations to a minor category of inquiry – 'spatial sociology'. The major themes of social inquiry are reserved either for 'urban political economy' (the significance of urban space for capital accumulation) or for 'non-spatial sociology' (the study of social consumption processes, competitive struggles and local politics).[8]

This view may be contrasted with John Urry's claim that space rather than time is becoming the most important dimension in contemporary capitalism. Although the hypermobility of capital enables production processes to spatially transcend the city, Urry argues, urban areas are becoming increasingly significant sites for the reproduction of labour power. Although urban areas are no longer internally integrated through production linkages, they are integrated through a network of circulation, consumption and household reproduction patterns that Urry terms the sphere of 'civil society'. This shift in the way urban localities are structured has widespread impacts on local class structures and forms of local politics.[9]

This debate clearly poses important questions for urban geographers. It would appear that the future status of urban geography partly depends on clarifying the distinctive role of cities in advanced capitalist economies, and partly on clarifying the role of space in the development of social relations. Does space have an independent effect on social relations, or are spatial relations largely determined by social relations? If, as many assert, there is a reciprocal or even dialectical relation between social and spatial relations, how is this relation manifested in the specific context of contemporary cities?

THE FUTURE: CONVERGENCE OR COMPLEMENTARITY?

Some of the most important areas of debate and development at the moment lie along the boundaries between contending positions (the debates between neo-Weberians and neo-Marxists over theories of class and the state, for example). The focusing on common problems from different directions opens up the possibility of convergence or complementarity between approaches, although there are dangers in the casual yoking together of disparate approaches rooted in different philosophical positions.

Looking to the future it seems more likely that progress will be made through focusing attention on *key problems* that cut across different positions. One that is attracting a great deal of interest at the moment concerns the relationship between 'structure' and 'agency'. More and more authors are calling for an approach that avoids the extremes of structural determinism on the one hand, and a simple voluntarism (in which society is the outcome of the intentional actions of individuals) on the other (see Gregory, Chapter 1.4). The 'structure-agency' problem not only crops up in debates between the behavioural, neo-Marxist and neo-Weberian approaches we have outlined. It also appears in debates *within* these approaches, as for example in the emerging internal critique of structuralist Marxism by 'critical' or humanist Marxists. However, much of the discussion remains at a highly abstract level: we have yet to see how this latest round of theoretical engagement will find expression in a new generation of empirical urban research.

NOTES AND REFERENCES

1. David Ley, *A Social Geography of the City* (New York: Harper and Row, 1983) p.8.
2. M. Castells, *The Urban Question: a Marxist approach* (London: Edward Arnold, 1977) p.126.
3. On urban managerialism and corporatism, see R. E. Pahl, *Whose City?* (Harmondsworth: Penguin, 1975) Part 3, and S. Leonard, 'Urban managerialism: a period of transition', *Progr. Hum. Geogr.*, 6 (1982) pp.190–215.
4. Ley, *op. cit.*, p.217.
5. See Ley, *op. cit.;* Ulf Hannerz, *Exploring the City: inquiries toward an urban anthropology* (New York: Columbia University Press, 1980); Peter Jackson, 'Urban ethnography', *Progr. Hum. Geogr.*, 9 (1985) pp.157–176.
6. See J. Pickles, *Phenomenology, science and geography: spatiality and the human sciences* (Cambridge: Cambridge University Press, 1985)
7. See R. J. Johnston, *Philosophy and human geography: an introduction to contemporary approaches* (London: Edward Arnold, 1983) and his chapter in this volume.
8. Peter Saunders, *Social Theory and the Urban Question* (London: Hutchinson, 1986); Peter Saunders, 'Space, the City and Urban Sociology', in

Derek Gregory and John Urry (eds) *Social Relations and Spatial Structures* (London: Macmillan, 1985) pp.67–89.
9. John Urry, 'Social Relations, Space and Time', in Gregory and Urry, *op. cit.*, pp.20–48.

FURTHER READING

Two accessible texts which offer surveys of modern urban geography are David Ley's *A Social Geography of the City* (New York: Harper & Row, 1983) and John Short's *An Introduction to Urban Geography* (London: Routledge & Kegan Paul, 1984). Peter Saunders's *Social Theory and the Urban Question* (London: Hutchinson, 1986) also offers an interesting reappraisal, though it is more advanced.

The best way to tackle the work of Manuel Castells is by *sampling* his *The City and the Grassroots* (London: Edward Arnold, 1983); for David Harvey, the most accessible texts are two collections of his essays published under the general title *Studies in the History and Theory of Capitalist Urbanization* (Oxford: Basil Blackwell, 1985): the first is *Consciousness and the Urban Experience*, which has a more 'humanistic' flavour, while the second is *The Urbanization of Capital*, which has a more 'structural' character.

3.2
Dismantling the Barriers: Past and Present in Urban Britain

Richard Dennis
University College, London

Richard Dennis is Lecturer in Geography at University College, London. His teaching and research interests are in urban geography and social geography, both past and present, and he is the author of *English Industrial Cities of the Nineteenth Century* and (with Hugh Clout) *A Social Geography of England and Wales.*

INTRODUCTION

Since the 1960s one of the major growth areas in the humanities has been urban history, associated with the trend to write history 'from below', to concentrate on the everyday experience of 'the common people', and reflecting historians' discovery that the recent past, which in Britain is mostly urban, can be just as interesting as the predominantly rural remote past. Moreover, because recent urban history is quite amenable to 'amateur' research, employing the plethora of registration and tax documents – censuses, ratebooks, electoral rolls and pollbooks, trade directories, and birth, marriage and death certificates – compiled by our Victorian ancestors, it has benefited from the enormous surge of popular interest in genealogy and local history.

This interest in the recent past has been shared by human geographers, whose formal historical training has often been as amateurish as that of local and family historians. Traditionally, historical geographers were concerned with the distant past, with rural settlement and agricultural systems. They examined medieval towns as market centres for surrounding rural hinterlands or as foci of long-distance trade; but they rarely considered the internal structures of pre-industrial towns, if only because most British towns were too small to boast an identifiable 'spatial structure'. All this work was firmly empiricist, intent on reconstructing what the past was like, regardless of any conscious theoretical or ideological perspective.

By contrast, and with few exceptions, the new urban historical geography is strongly theoretical, more concerned with generalisation than the uniqueness of particular places, more urban than historical in its inspiration. The exceptions are associated with historical geographers who transferred their allegiance from tenant farmers to tenant builders, from the morphology of field systems to the morphology of urban development, and from enclosure (and the ensuing redistribution of land) to compulsory purchase, slum clearance and the consolidation and subsequent resale of urban land. Whether their orientation is rural or urban, medieval or modern, they employ the same empirical methods to interpret the same sorts of sources: estate records, deeds, government reports.[1]

For the majority, however, their theoretical perspective derived, *firstly*, from the ecological and microeconomic models of 1960s urban geography; *secondly*, from behavioural geography – studies of the decision to migrate in contemporary society prompted parallel studies of past migration and mobility; *thirdly*, from the managerialism popularised by Ray Pahl and particularly employed to examine the activities of 'gatekeepers' who control access to different sectors of the housing market. Thus, studies of the behaviour and ideology of today's planners, developers, builders, estate agents, building societies and local authorities could be matched by studies of landowners, builders and different kinds of private landlord in the eighteenth and nineteenth centuries. *Latterly*, there is a perspective derived from structural Marxism, where the internal structure of cities is interpreted as a reflection of wider social and economic processes, especially the evolution of class structure. In the context of contemporary urban geography, a much fuller discussion of these different approaches is included in the chapter in this volume by Keith Bassett and John Short (Chapter 3.1).

Some structuralists claim that there is nothing specifically urban about urban processes; they are merely processes *in* cities. But in the most recent versions of structuralism the 'urban' has regained some independent significance, as more than just a container of social processes. Urban problems, such as inner-city decay and chronic housing shortages, are regarded as permanent, structural conditions associated with specific characteristics of urban life; as elements in the inevitable contradictions of industrial and post-industrial capitalism. (For elaboration of these ideas, see Roger Lee's discussion of the changing role of cities in contemporary society in Chapter 2.4.)

THE PAST IN THE PRESENT

One important effect of Marxist analysis in geography has been to reinstate the historical dimension as central to our understanding of the present. In the 1960s and early 1970s the functionalist approach of locational analysis tended to disregard the past, or at best treat it as successive cross-sections. Processes of transition from one cross section to the next were either inferred or treated purely mathematically. In contrast, Marxist analysis is about action and reaction, conflict and change. Present conditions reflect the imperfect resolution of past contradictions and the changing balance of power between different factors of production. Hence we cannot understand the present without reference to the past.

Moreover, the division of history according to modes of production, variously labelled 'feudal' or 'pre-capitalist', 'mercantile capitalist', 'industrial capitalist' and 'advanced' or 'monopoly capitalist', points to the unity of the nineteenth and twentieth centuries in British history. Most conventional, classical location theory (for example the ecological models of the Chicago School, Von Thünen's and Alonso's land-use models and Weber's industrial location theory) is most appropriately applied to 'industrial capitalism', which reached its peak in Britain in the late nineteenth century and is certainly in decline today.

Despite superficial differences in technology and living standards, there are close parallels between processes operating in all capitalist societies, in the past as well as the present. Explanations of, and policy responses to, economic problems in the 1840s, the 1880s, the 1930s and the 1980s are not all that different. At a regional scale, as well as in the contrast between East End and West End in major cities, distributions of poverty and unemployment in the 1980s are much like those in late Victorian Britain. In the provision of housing we have returned to nineteenth-century 'solutions', based on the assumption of a responsible private enterprise providing for those who can afford new housing, the hope of 'levelling up' whereby the poor benefit by occupying the dwellings vacated by the better-off and the encouragement of self-help together with some discreet state support for ostensibly philanthropic provision for the deserving poor.

In Victorian London 'five per cent philanthropists' (housing companies restricting their annual dividend to shareholders to no more than 5 per cent) depended on central government to provide long-term, low-interest loans, and on local authorities to supply at cut-price slum clearance sites which they had previously purchased at full market value. Likewise, in the 1980s, housing associations may appear more like private enterprise than council housing, but they are just as dependent on the state for financial support: loans and grants from the Housing Corporation and subsidised land from local authorities. Fundamentally, the illusion has been maintained, in the 1980s as in the 1880s, that 'housing problems' are an isolated component of the economy that can be solved by individual initiative.[2]

Some parallels between the late nineteenth century and the present are almost uncanny. Arguments in favour of the abolition of the Greater London Council in the 1980s replicated those levelled against the establishment of its predecessor, the London County Council, in the 1880s. Debates about rate reform have surfaced regularly since the mid-nineteenth century. In the 1890s, as in the 1980s, there were substantial rate increases, as the growth in local government expenditure, most of it on services prescribed by central government, outstripped the growth of rateable values, and as central government tried to reduce its contribution to local finance.[3] The victims of successive rate squeezes may not be the same – small businesses today, housing landlords then. But the moral is still clear: we *can* learn from the past, at least to the extent of anticipating the problems associated with different courses of action.

Victorian governments gradually recognised the social injustices of rampant *laissez-faire*, legislating in favour of municipal and state interventions that protected the poor and set limits for the promotion of *responsible* capitalism. In the 1980s, the pursuit of a more selective version of 'Victorian values' emphasising only self-help, individual entrepreneurship and the supremacy of the free market, is restoring those injustices that late Victorian state intervention was intended to eradicate: the division of the population into Disraeli's two nations of wealth and poverty, the subordination of welfare issues in the interests of economy and productivity, and the elimination of enterprises that are socially desirable but economically marginal.

UNDERSTANDING THE PAST

Contrary to these recent trends to demonstrate the continuity and congruence of past and present, urban historical geography in the 1970s was more concerned with *contrasting* past and present cities. An evolutionary model of urban structure was favoured, contrasting Sjoberg's pre-industrial city, in which the rich lived centrally and the poor on the periphery, or Vance's mercantile capitalist city, where craft guilds played critical roles in organising the residences and workplaces of different occupational groups in distinctive 'quarters'. These were contrasted with the 'modern' city of Burgess's concentric zones, Hoyt's sectors or, more elaborately, the multi-dimensional cities of factorial ecology, in which economic status, family status and ethnic status assume independent and contrasting spatial patterns. The model was most clearly presented by Duncan Timms in *The Urban Mosaic*, but its historical implications were spelled out in an important article by David Ward, 'Victorian cities: how modern?', which not only reported on the state of the debate but also set the agenda for research that has continued into the 1980s.[4]

To operationalise models of 'modernisation' or of 'cities in transition' necessarily requires small-area data for the past that are as abundant and as susceptible to statistical analysis as modern census data. Hence research has concentrated on the period for which census enumerators' books are available, currently 1841 to 1881. In some respects, these books provide better information than the modern census; because information is available on named individuals, researchers can create their own units of spatial analysis, such as blocks or grid squares, as alternatives to the enumeration districts to which households were originally assigned, and their own cross-tabulations (for example, relating birthplace to household structure, or head's occupation to those, if any, of other household members). But the enumerators' books have also proved to be a straitjacket, their ready availability discouraging researchers from exploring periods or aspects of society ignored by census officials.

In recent years, more imaginative use has been made of the census, linking addresses recorded in census books to those listed in other sources (ratebooks, for example, which indicate the value of a dwelling and whether it was owner-occupied or rented), or linking names from the census with names recorded elsewhere – in pollbooks which recorded who was entitled to vote and, prior to the Secret Ballot Act of 1872, how they voted; in directories which until late in the nineteenth century recorded only the 'principal inhabitants' and provide a useful means of distinguishing employees, who were rarely included in directories, from the self-employed, who used them as a form of advertising; in marriage registers and the membership records of clubs and churches, which allow some estimate of patterns of social interaction. All this is time-consuming and sometimes tedious work, although analysis has been made easier by the use of computerised methods of record linkage, but it will yield far more interesting and locally meaningful results than straight multivariate analysis of census data.[5]

Whatever the limitations of nineteenth-century censuses, they are as gold compared to the mixture of sources available for the reconstruction of pre-industrial city structures, where researchers make what they can of hearth tax returns, rentals and occasional counts of communicants, baptisms, marriages and burials. For years before 1800, therefore, these minimal quantitative sources can yield no more than approximate cross-sectional descriptions. Processes can be established only from individual documentary accounts. But for the nineteenth century processes as well as patterns may be quantified, particularly using techniques of record linkage, to trace individuals or properties through *successive* censuses, ratebooks or directories. Consequently, attention has gradually shifted from estimating the modernity of past patterns to comparing past and present processes.

An example: housing and mobility

Certain characteristics of present-day residential mobility were also typical of the mid-nineteenth century. The elderly moved less frequently than the young; the poor moved over shorter distances than the rich; the last to arrive were often the first to leave. But there were also differences; the overall mobility rate was at least twice today's; the poor moved much more frequently than the rich, albeit over very short distances, whereas council tenants nowadays move rather less often than homeowners.

These contrasts in rates and patterns prompt us to compare the nature of housing markets then and now. In the nineteenth century 90 per cent of households were rented from private landlords; only about 10 per cent were owner-occupiers. Since World War One private renting has steadily declined in importance, owner-occupation has increased to include about 60 per cent of the population, and council housing has grown to accommodate almost a third of households.

Most nineteenth-century private tenants could move at a week's notice, for they had no solicitors' fees or estate agents' commissions to pay, and there were usually plenty of empty houses from which to choose. Moving house was easy and no serious consequences followed from making a bad choice: you could always move again at little expense. Twentieth-century owner-occupiers have to think much more carefully before moving – a wrong choice could prove very costly and a marginal improvement may not justify the expense – and they may be frustrated from moving by being caught in a chain. Council tenants, too, find it difficult to move, particularly between houses owned by different local authorities. Those who remain in privately-rented accommodation have more security of tenure than tenants in the nineteenth century, so are less subject to arbitrary eviction; and rent control offers some incentive for tenants to stay put rather than move and risk having to pay substantially higher rents.

Of course, there are other reasons for declining rates of residential mobility. Instead of moving, owner-occupiers can extend their property as their income or household size increases. Shorter working hours and greater everyday mobility mean that employees no longer need to live close to their workplace, and may not need to move house if they change jobs. In the absence of a welfare state, poor Victorian families were obliged to seek cheaper accommodation in times of crisis; but they were unlikely to move long distances, beyond the limits of localities in which their credit was respected, and where they could expect help from neighbours.

Overall, however, there are close links between housing tenure and mobility, leading us, in our explanation of changes in mobility, to ask *why* the distribution of housing tenure has changed. Why was private renting so much more appropriate in the nineteenth century? Why was council housing only introduced on a major, nationwide scale after 1919? Why was owner-occupation so little regarded in the nineteenth century, even among those who could afford to own their homes, yet is now desired by almost everybody and encouraged by all the major political parties?

In attempting to answer these kinds of questions, British urban geographers have discarded ecological models, which not only over-emphasised consumer choice but also were originally developed to fit North American cities, where the housing market was very different from Britain, especially with respect to the level of public housing provision. Instead, a focus on the political economy of housing has been favoured.

Britain's building industry has always been under-capitalised, most builders needing to sell their most recently completed houses before embarking on further purchases of land and materials. In the absence of a large middle class who either wanted, or could afford to buy their own homes, the private landlord was a vital intermediary between builder and occupier. Short-let renting was admirably suited to a system of industrial production in which workers had little job security and wages fluctuated from one week to the next.

Yet housing landlords never had many political allies. They were a less powerful lobby than landowners, and they commanded fewer votes than tenants. So they gained little sympathy when their profits were squeezed – by rising interest rates (most landlords owned their houses on mortgage), growing rate demands and, after 1915, rent control. After World War One few landlords wanted to acquire more property, yet there was an immediate housing shortage of 600 000 homes, while the return of survivors from the trenches, associated with the lack of jobs in a peacetime economy and increasing demands for female equality, promoted a fear of social unrest. Central government was obliged to subsidise housing for lower-income groups, builders were forced to seek new customers for their houses, and building societies had to find new kinds of borrower to whom they could lend some of the massive influx of funds that were diverted from industrial investment during the depression.[6]

We should also ask what high mobility rates meant to the labouring classes in Victorian and Edwardian cities. Did they regard their dwellings as 'home' as sentimentally as many Victorian ballads or dutifully embroidered samplers of 'Home Sweet Home' imply? Their possessions were so few and their mobility so frequent that we may doubt their attachment to the particular dwellings which they temporarily occupied. Much more important was the sense of belonging to a locality in which they could rely on friends and relatives for help at times of crisis, expect credit at local shops, and make good use of their local knowledge, whether of scandal or of vacancies in job or housing markets. We can use some of the sources already mentioned – marriage and church or club membership records – to reconstruct the bare bones of community structure, but this kind of question is also tailor-made for the attention of humanistic geographers.

EXPERIENCING THE PAST

Other processes, too, such as the *process* of residential segregation of different classes or social strata, also demand a marriage of quantitative analysis and humanistic sensitivity. The growth of humanistic geography has provided another way in which historical research has re-entered the mainstream of human geography. Denis Cosgrove shows earlier in this volume (in Chapter 2.2) how we can interpret the meaning of past landscapes, such as urban plans, that have survived into the present.

Equally important is our reading of how past observers interpreted their surroundings. Much of the art and literature examined by humanistic geographers dates from the eighteenth and nineteenth centuries, when painters and novelists were acutely aware of their physical and social environment. So we can turn to the works of Dickens, Disraeli or Mrs Gaskell to understand the impact of industrialisation on urban society, to George Gissing or Arthur Morrison for a sense of life among the poor in late Victorian London, to Arnold Bennett for an invaluable picture of provincial respectability, to the paintings of Camille Pissarro for an interpretation of London suburbia in the 1870s. Of course, all these sources are dangerously élitist or atypical – the product of unusually gifted, sensitive and generally comfortably-off artists, whose views may not have corresponded with those of the average urbanite. Yet they are no worse distortions of reality than those imposed by census enumerators who pigeonholed the population into 'households' whatever their domestic state, or by ourselves as we group together families according to our definition of their 'class' or their 'ethnicity'. Moreover, it is possible to find personal accounts of urban life penned by less distinguished or unusual authors. Recent years have witnessed the discovery and publication of numerous working-class diaries, describing their writers' 'action space' – where they worked, worshipped, shopped, drank, visited friends. And the current boom in oral history provides valuable information on housing and living conditions in Edwardian England, albeit viewed with hindsight by respondents who were only children at the time.[7]

Figure 3.2.1 derives from *A Hoxton Childhood*, an autobiographical account of growing up in East London before and during World War One.[8] The account has been checked against contemporary street directories (to ascertain the locations of pubs, schools and workplaces mentioned by the author), electoral registers (to check precise addresses) and maps (to locate streets of working-class housing long since replaced by high-rise flats). The confined world of Edwardian working-class families is obvious, as is the frequency of short moves necessitated by changing family circumstances – marriages, bereavements, unemployment or family quarrels. Suburbanisation (moving to Walthamstow) was forced by the lack of suitable accommodation in Hoxton during the post-1918 housing shortage discussed earlier – a graphic demonstration of the interaction of structural change with individual experience.

In various ways, therefore, we can see how historical and contemporary human geography have much in common, and much to contribute to one another. The past is fascinating in its own right and we should devote time to reconstructing it as it was understood by contemporaries. But history is also about re-interpreting the past in the light of the present, identifying structures and processes to which contemporaries were blind. And, as we learn about the past, so we see our own condition through freshly opened eyes.

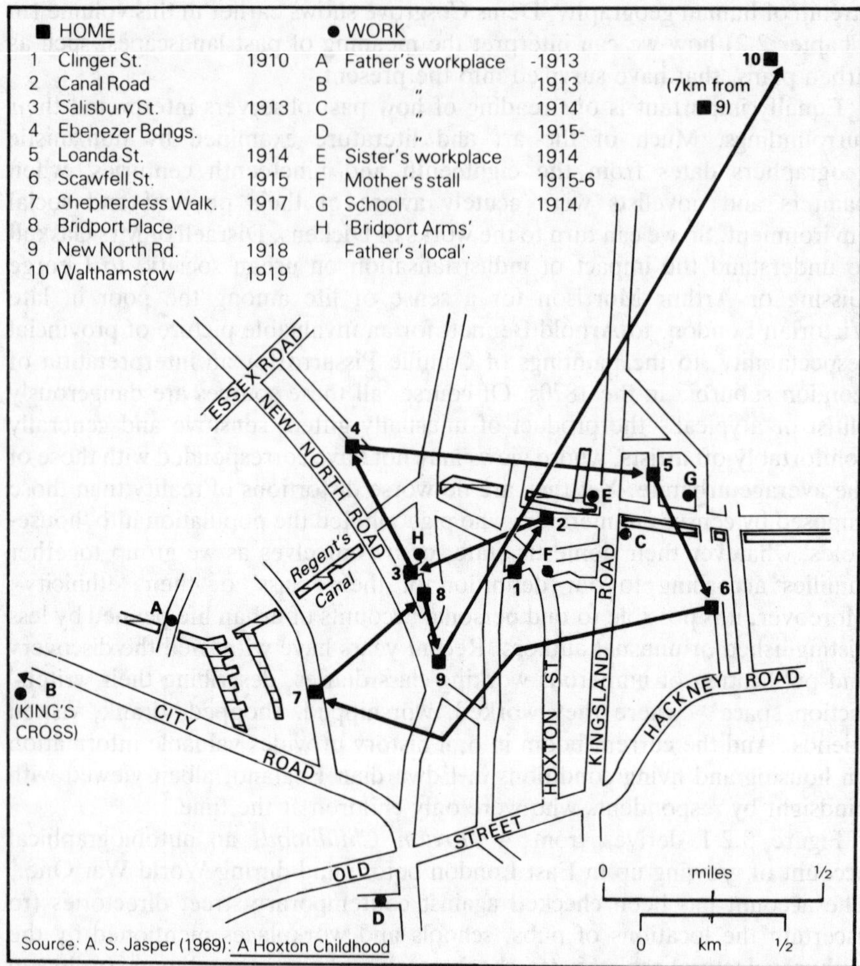

FIGURE 3.2.1 *Home and work for the Jasper family in London's East End, 1910–11*

SOCIAL STRUCTURE AND SPATIAL STRUCTURE

There have been numerous studies of residential segregation in nineteenth-century cities, most of them using a classification of occupations into five socio-economic groups that was derived from the Registrar General's classification for the 1951 census. This may be adequate for identifying the extremes of wealth and status, the growing business and professional classes, initially living centrally in Georgian terraced houses, but later moving to exclusive high-status suburbs such as Edgbaston in Birmingham or Endcliffe in Sheffield, contrasted with the unskilled, casually employed poor, following a transient existence in inner-city slums. But it fails to differentiate among the mass of skilled manual workers, self-employed craftsmen and small shopkeepers in the middle of the social hierarchy.

In theory, the census recorded employers with the numbers of men, women, boys and girls in their employment. In practice, this information was only sporadically included, so that it is often impossible to distinguish between, for example, a 'woollen spinner' who owned or managed a substantial mill with dozens or even hundreds of employees, another who was self-employed or employed a few journeymen in a small workshop, and a third who was a mill operative. As a result, in most studies more than half the employed population is assigned to the same 'middle' class, and the overall structure of society is depicted as barrel-shaped or egg-shaped, or fat in the middle, with few members of each extreme class (see Figure 3.2.2(i)). Moreover, the same classification is applied to 1881 as to 1841, regardless of technological changes that altered the status of occupations in the interim, or of consequent changes in class consciousness.

In contrast to these quantitative studies, social historians have concentrated on the unstable nature of class relations – the making (and subsequent re-making or un-making) of the working class, the emergence of a lower middle class, itself divided into a petty bourgeoisie of self-employed craftsmen, dealers and shopkeepers, a junior non-manual group of teachers, clerks, agents and salesmen, and an aspiring middle class of labour aristocrats, such as the skilled engineers who made and maintained the machines that were responsible for the deskilling of many other industrial workers. The process of deskilling and the demands of the Victorian economy for labourers of various kinds – in building, on the docks, in markets – produced a social structure that was more pyramidal than oval (see Figure 3.2.2(ii)).[9]

While we may be able to rank occupations by income or even status, it is much more difficult to determine where, if at all, to draw the boundaries between distinct 'classes'. Yet this is a necessary foundation if we are measuring the degree of residential segregation. For guidance, we may turn to contemporary observers who variously interpreted society as two-class (the rich and the poor of Disraeli's *Sybil*; the bourgeoisie and proletariat of Marx and Engels' *Communist Manifesto*) or three-class (usually corresponding to the interests of land, capital and labour); to the classifications of early social investigators, such as Booth's and Rowntree's identification of different degrees of poverty; or to the models of social historians.

Among the latter, Neale constructed a five-class model comprising the conventional upper and middle classes but, beneath them, a 'middling' class of upwardly mobile, independently minded, skilled workers and two working classes, one 'deferential', the other 'proletarian'. The former included, according to Neale, most agricultural labourers and female workers, who 'knew their place' and accepted their lowly status and poor conditions. The latter comprised industrial workers conscious of the need to improve their lot through unified, class-based, political action. The fluidity and ambiguity of status was denoted both by the labelling of a 'middling' class and by Neale's recognition of upward and downward social mobility linking the classes in his model (Figure 3.2.2(iii)).[10]

Unfortunately, cross-sectional occupational information on its own is seldom sufficient to warrant the allocation of a household or an individual to a particular class. We require additional information on behaviour – on patterns of intermarriage, on the membership of churches and associations, on political activity and voting habits. We can then group together people with similar behavioural profiles and examine *their* residential distribution.

A few geographers have exploited census information more fully in efforts to define class more sensitively. This is done, for example, by supplementing occupational data with information on the employment of servants, the education of children, the acceptance of lodgers, and the employment of wives and children in paid work outside the home. But we really require more studies linking individuals in a variety of records. Patrick Joyce, a social historian, examined the voting behaviour of various occupational groups living in different neighbourhoods in several Lancashire towns. Linking the pollbook for 1868 (the first after the Second Reform Act had enlarged the electorate, and the last before the passage of the Secret Ballot Act) to the 1871 census, he found that neighbourhood transcended occupation in the determination of political behaviour. In the streets surrounding a cotton mill owned by a Liberal industrialist, there were Liberal majorities among all kinds of worker; in the neighbourhood around a Tory-owned mill, each occupational type returned a Conservative majority. These findings suggest the survival of 'deference' even among the urban proletariat, and question the value of assigning workers with the same occupations but living in different areas to the same 'class'. Indeed, we may even argue that in choosing to live next door to one another, workers with different occupations were identifying themselves as belonging to the same class.[11]

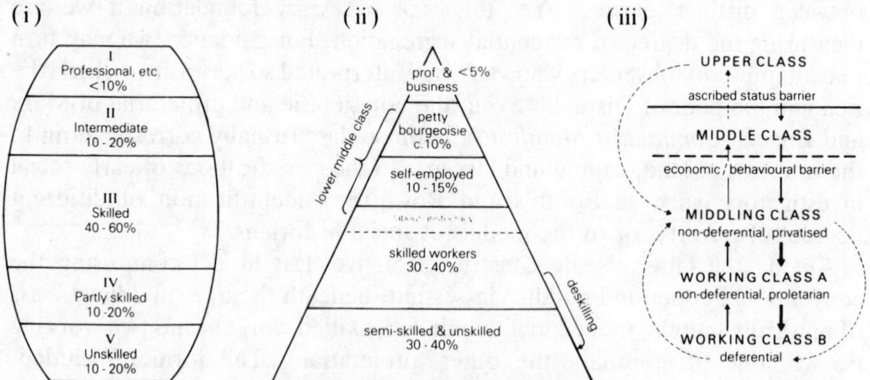

FIGURE 3.2.2. *Alternative models of class in 19th century cities*
(i) based on the Registrar-General's 1951 classification
(ii) a specifically urban alternative
(iii) simplified from Neale's five-class model

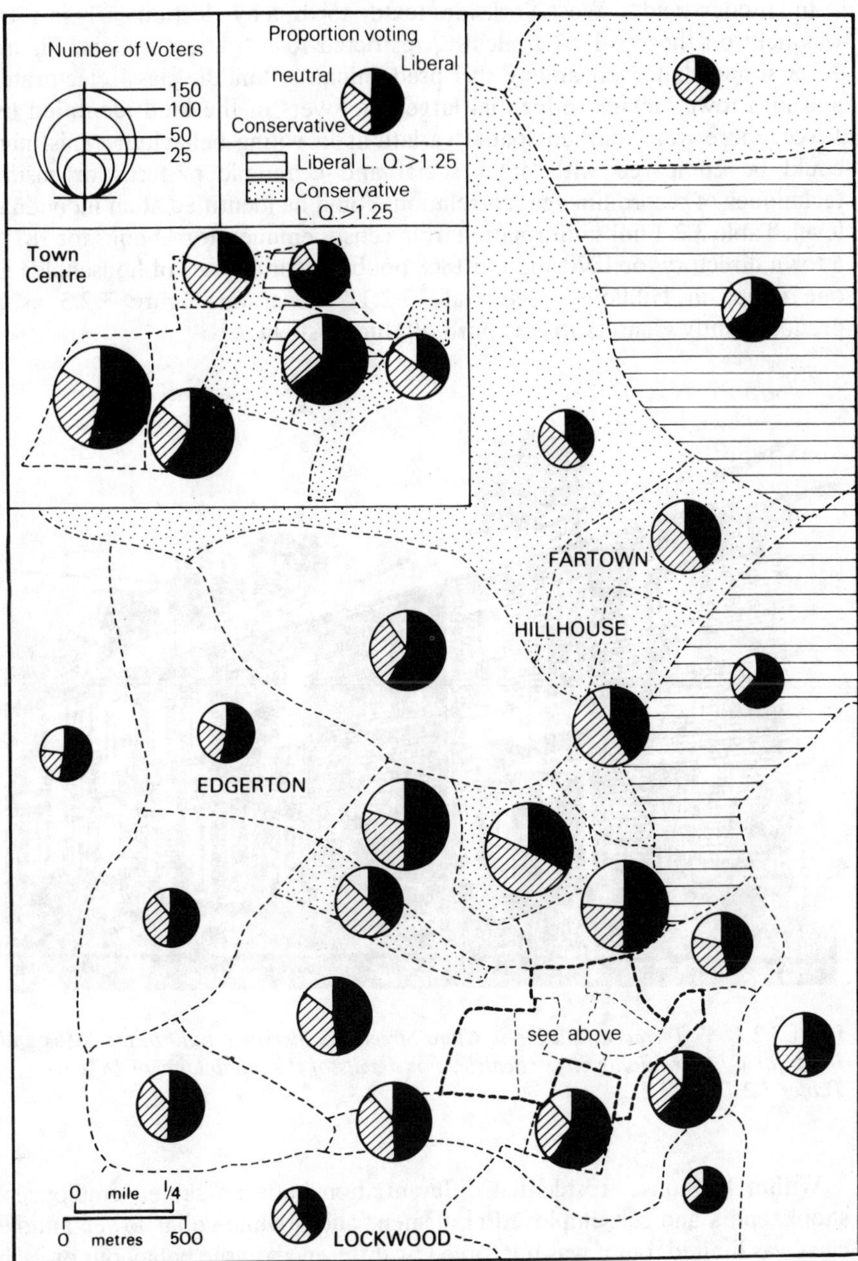

FIGURE 3.2.3 Voting behaviour in Huddersfield in 1868, identifying (i) districts where the proportion voting Liberal or Conservative was more than 25% above the average for the Borough and (ii) the number of electors and the proportion voting for each candidate in each district.

In Huddersfield, a West Yorkshire textile town, a by-election early in 1868 was held on the pre-1867 franchise, restricted to £10 householders. Figure 3.2.3 shows that even among this predominantly 'middle-class' electorate, and in a town lacking influential large employers of the kind identified by Joyce, there were marked spatial variations in voting behaviour. This map could be compared with other social and economic patterns or, using techniques of record linkage, correlations could be identified at an individual level. Table 3.2.1 links information from census enumerators' books for 1871, a town directory for 1870 and the 1868 pollbook for a series of households in one street in Hillhouse (see plate 3.2.1) shown on Figure 3.2.3 as a predominantly Conservative suburb of Huddersfield.

PLATE 3.2.1 *Terraced housing in Clara Street, Huddersfield built in the 1850s and 1860s for a lower middle-class clientele. For details of the inhabitants in 1871 see Tables 3.2.1 and 3.2.2*

Within Hillhouse, residential differentiation between skilled employees, shopkeepers and self-employed craftsmen, and a white-collar lower middle class was limited, but it was reinforced by differences in the behaviour of each group. Tradesmen were more likely to belong to non-conformist churches, clerks and salesmen were more likely to vote Conservative (see Table 3.2.2). The children of neither group were likely to marry into the ranks of labour aristocrats.

TABLE 3.2.1. *A comparison of census, directory and pollbook entries for Clara Street, Hillhouse*

Name	*Census occupation*	*Directory occupation*	*Directory workplace*	*Voting behaviour*
Wm. H. Bedford	engineer employing 14 men and 1 boy	ironfounder and insurance agent	Harrison & Bedford, ironfounders & engineers, Phoenix Iron Works, Leeds Road	Con.
James Hirst	flock mart	flock dealer	Marshalls'Yard, Westgate	Lib.
George Savile	hairdresser employing 3 men and 3 boys	hairdresser	Saville & Barlow, hairdressers & perfumers, Lion Arcade, John William Street	Con.
Charles Smeeton	draper	draper	Cooper & Smeeton, wholesale & retail drapers, 1 Kirkgate	Con.
Henry Marriot	chemist	manufacturing chemist's	—	Lib.
Enoch Heppenstall	dyer	dyer	Heppenstall Bros., cotton & woollen dyers, Turnbridge, Quay Street	
Thos. G. Woodhead	woollen manufacturer	woollen cord manufacturer	Woodhead, J. D. & Bros., woollen & Bedford cord mfrs., 23 King's Head Bdngs., Sheepridge & Turnbridge	Lib.
Samuel K. Hurst	woollen manufacturer	manager	—	Lib.
Joseph Mellor	livery stable keeper	cab proprietor	S. & J. Mellor, cab proprs. and livery stable keepers, Chancery Lane	Con.
Edwd. J. Billing	clerk	cashier	—	
Edward Dawson	draper	—	—	—

SOURCE Census enumerators' books, 1871, RG–10—4370;
William White's Directory, 1870; Huddersfield Poll Book, 1868

TABLE 3.2.2 *Residence and voting behaviour in Hillhouse, Huddersfield circa* 1870

Occupation of household head	% heads in each group	% electors in each group	% in each group voting		
			Lib	Con	Neutral
Professional	2	3	40	60	0
Merchants, manufacturers	6	19	47	38	16
Clerks, agents, etc	14	23	30	58	13
Shopkeepers	11	25	47	45	9
Master craftmen	10	16	48	33	19
Skilled & unskilled	55	15	56	39	6

SOURCE: Census enumerator's books. 1871, RG–10–4370
William White's Directory, 1870
Huddersfield Poll Book, 1868

If we are to understand the *meaning* of residential segregation, we must examine its relationship to other kinds of behavioural segregation, to segregation in time as well as space, and we must be sure that the categories to which we assign people were meaningful to *them*. Nor should we regard segregation as a *symmetrical* construct: the segregation of rich and poor is not experienced in the same way by both groups.

Both modern social planners and Victorian idealists have regarded 'segregation' as the antithesis of 'community'. The latter is always treated positively, equated with harmony, tolerance, balance and friendship; the former is invariably negative, associated with self-interest, intolerance, prejudice and discrimination. But reality is never so black and white. 'Segregation' and 'community' are different sides of the same coin. 'Community' develops among segregated populations, indeed it defines them, and it involves gossip, dissent and conflict. So we should regard residential segregation, on which geographers have concentrated so exclusively, as just one aspect of the social geography of cities, and one which cannot be studied in isolation.

HOUSING CLASSES

Because the census provides so little information on housing, the historical geography of housing has generally been researched independently of the historical geography of social structure. Yet in modern social geography, the organisation of the housing market is assumed to underlie the spatial distribution of different economic and ethnic classes. While studies of 'gatekeepers' in the modern housing market have concentrated on the managers and allocators of already existing housing, such as estate agents, building society managers and local government officers, in nineteenth-century studies the activities of landowners and builders have attracted most attention.

Different landowners pursued varying strategies in releasing their land for development. The tenure under which land was sold (whether freehold or some kind of leasehold), the imposition of restrictive covenants, limiting the kinds of building to be erected or the uses to which they could be put, and the size, shape and location of building plots all affected what was built where and who came to occupy what was built. Some dissenting voices have been raised, arguing that landowners and developers were really prisoners of the free market, that their plans succeeded only when they corresponded with demand, and that builders, rather than landowners, set the social tone of housing estates, sometimes erecting houses substantially better than the minimum standards specified by the landowner, at others finding loopholes in the covenants so that they could jerry-build where there was no middle-class demand.

Nonetheless, development strategies *did* affect the social geography of towns. In Huddersfield the Ramsdens, who owned most of the town centre, granted 'tenancies at will', whereby tenants had no *legal* security of tenure, and refused to allow the building of back-to-back houses, a common feature of other West Riding towns. The builders of high-class villas were deterred from building on Ramsden land until they could obtain more secure terms; and the building of cheap working-class dwellings was displaced on to other estates, on the outskirts of the town, where back-to-backs were permitted.[12]

There has been less research on the activities of Victorian housing managers. In contrast to our tenurially tripartite housing market, the vast majority of dwellings in Victorian cities were privately rented. It might be argued, therefore, that the only criterion governing access to housing was ability to pay. But, just as there are different 'housing classes' within each of the major tenures today so, in the past, there were different kinds of landlord, accommodating different kinds of tenant.

We know most about institutional landlords who kept rent books and tenants' registers, whose minute books record their strategies for selecting tenants, collecting rents and dealing with miscreants. Some gave evidence to inquiries such as the Select Committee on Artizans' and Labourers' Dwellings of 1881–2, and the Royal Commission on Working-Class Housing of 1884–5. So we know who were housed in early local authority housing schemes, in philanthropic tenement blocks and in some other privately financed but easily identifiable developments, such as model colonies built by employers, early building society projects and carefully managed aristocratic estates. Even in these cases, however, our knowledge is often limited to the *outcomes* of management decisions, recorded in the list of residents in a census enumerator's book, or in our calculation from a tenants' register of the turnover rate. We can only infer the decision-making process from the resulting pattern, or take at face value the statements made in annual reports or evidence to government inquiries.

But it is possible to 'read between the lines', applying a geographical imagination to problems and sources which have generally been regarded as the preserve of historians. Institutional landlords are unusual in that they commonly selected and acquired the sites on which they erected buildings which they subsequently continued to own and manage; small, private landlords were more often buying houses that they had not personally commissioned. Nonetheless, all types of landlord displayed their intentions and, indirectly, their ideology, in the sites or buildings they chose and, equally important, those they ignored or rejected.

The Peabody Trust provided housing 'for the poor of London'(see plates 3.2.2 and 3.2.3). In practice this meant the respectable poor living in nuclear families, but initially the Trust expected to find such tenants scattered

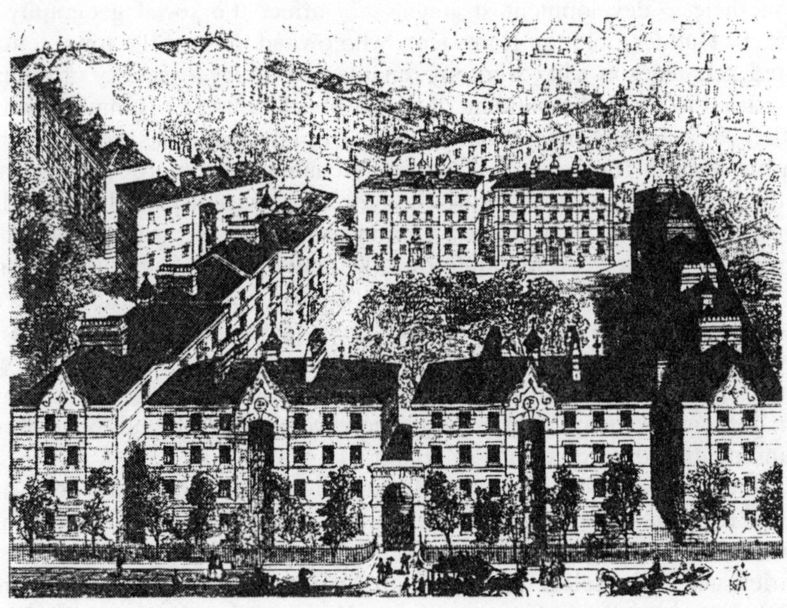

PLATE 3.2.2 *Peabody Square, Blackfriars Road, South London opened in 1871. Note how the estate turned its back on the surrounding slums, providing a safe and supervised environment in its courtyards, which doubled as gardens and playgrounds.*

PLATE 3.2.3 *Peabody Square, Shadwell, East London, opened in 1866. The labourers and their families, depicted in sober recreational activities were, no doubt, as much a figment of the artist's imagination as the figures who adorn artist's impressions of today's modern architecture.* (*Source*: Mansell Collection)

throughout inner London. Their first four estates, constructed in the 1860s, were at Spitalfields, Islington, Shadwell and Westminster (see Figure 3.2.4). In most of these and later estates, demand for rooms substantially exceeded supply, and there were few problems of rent arrears or filling vacancies. An exception was Shadwell, close to the London Docks, where, three years after opening, a quarter of the tenements remained vacant. Rents were reduced to attract tenants, whose earnings averaged 10 to 15 per cent less than those of other Peabody tenants; the estate was struck by a lethal epidemic of scarlet fever and the first superintendent was dismissed for embezzlement and forgery.

Thereafter, the Peabody Trust ignored Dockland in its search for 'poor' tenants, and was only lured back in the late 1870s, when it acquired a site near the Royal Mint, as part of a 'job lot' of six slum clearance sites offered by the Metropolitan Board of Works. The Trust was most interested in purchasing sites in Clerkenwell and the West End, while the Board was eager to offload East End sites as quickly as possible, to demonstrate that its clearance and redevelopment policy really was benefiting poor people living in poor areas of the metropolis. In the ensuing compromise, whereby the ratepayers of London effectively subsidised the Peabody Trust and other housing agencies to the tune of £1.2 million – the difference between the price paid *by* the Board to slum landlords and landowners, and the prices paid *to* the Board by the philanthropic housing trusts and companies which acquired the cleared

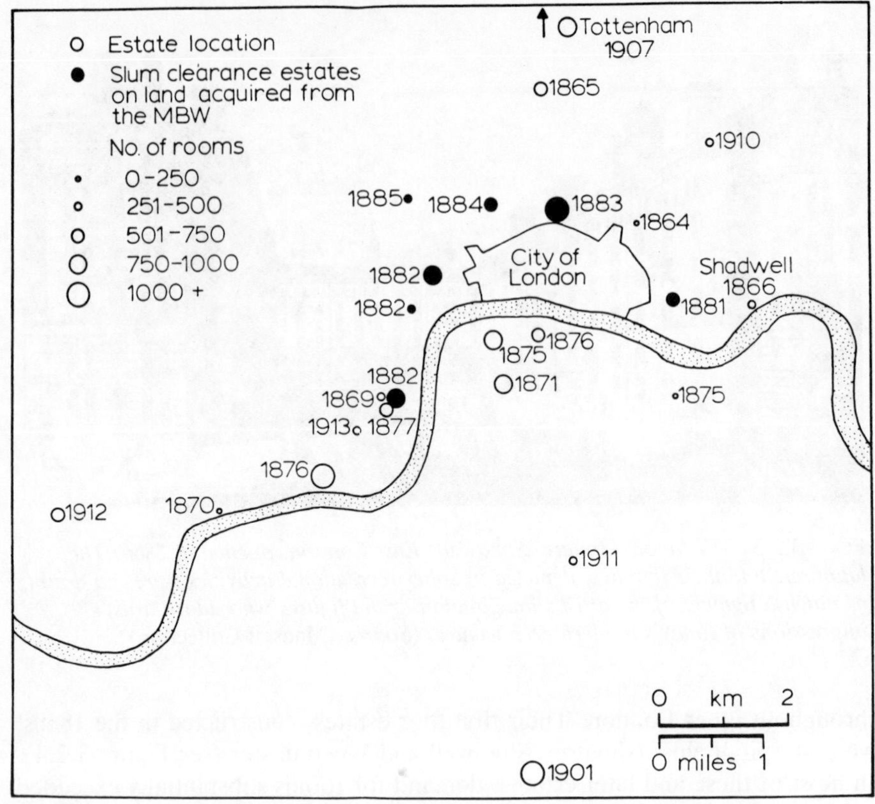

FIGURE 3.2.4 *The distribution of Peabody Trust estates in inner-London, 1864–1914, showing the opening dates of each estate.*

sites – we get a fascinating glimpse of the ideology and strategies of the different parties involved in housing reform.

While institutional landlords were locally quite important – in parts of inner London more than a quarter of dwellings were provided by philanthropic landlords, in some Lancashire towns more than 10 per cent of housing was owned by major employers – they were nationally insignificant, except in the model of management they provided for ordinary landlords. Most private landlords owned only a few properties, restricted their activities to one part of one town, and had other, more lucrative, business activities – as accountants, solicitors, builders, skilled craftsmen and tradesmen.

However, the scale of *management* was probably larger than that of *ownership*. Many owners employed agents, who not only collected rents but also advertised for, selected and evicted tenants, perhaps guaranteeing a fixed level of income to the owner, irrespective of problems over arrears, empties and moonlight flits. Rented houses were frequently bought and sold. Researchers in West Ham noted that 'the numbers of houses belonging to any agent vary very much from year to year. Cottage property is frequently bought and sold. An agent may be managing a hundred houses one month, and perhaps only a dozen the next, and *vice versa*'. In the seventeen years covered by their study (1888–1905), the collective management responsibilities of thirteen agents ranged from 846 dwellings in late 1889 to 5824 in 1904.[13]

Although some historians have begun to research the economics of renting and the class struggle between landlords and tenants,[14] few geographers have been tempted by the possibilities offered by a judicious combination of quantitative and literary evidence. Using ratebooks we can identify the distribution of houses owned by individual landlords, and measure the rate at which property changed owners, and the frequency of residential mobility associated with different kinds of property. Linking ratebooks to censuses, we can establish the characteristics of different landlords' tenants and infer the effects of management policies by examining the rate at which dwellings filtered down to poorer tenants. We could also plot the movement of households between tenancies. Did tenants move between properties owned by the same landlord or managed by the same agent? So, even if the only *direct* information we can obtain on management practices is in the earnest manuals of advice on how property *ought* to be managed, we could infer enough from the outcomes of management to rival our knowledge of the present-day rented housing market.

Contemporary novels offer another perspective on the management of housing. Arnold Bennett, for example, specialised in just that kind of modest respectability in which every other person had a minor stake in the property market. In *Hilda Lessways* Mrs Lessways' resolve to collect the rents of her cottage property herself is dismissed by her daughter with the comment that 'You'll be too hard, and you'll be too easy, too . . . You'll lose the good tenants and you'll keep the bad ones, and the houses will all go to rack and ruin, and then you'll sell all the property at a loss.' Management was a subtle art. But Bennett also showed that even skilled landlords and agents could not defy the demands of the market indefinitely. However carefully the Lessways managed their cottages, the reaility was that 'Calder Street's going down – it's getting more and more of a slum. And there'll always be a lot of bother with tenants of that class.' Even their houses in Lessways Street, substantial dwellings 'rated at from twenty-six to thirty-six pounds a year; beyond the means of artisans and petty insurance agents and rent-collectors', were not immune. The Lessways' agent advised selling while they still had some value: 'Your houses are too good for that part of the town; that's what's the matter with them. People who can afford £25 a year – and over – for rent won't care to live there much longer.'[15]

Bennett wrote from the owner's or manager's perspective. Other novelists offered an interpretation from below.[16] The contrast between them again prompts questions of whether there is any 'objective reality', or whether one perspective is 'more geographical' than another.

AFTERWORD

I have expressed some dissatisfaction with what urban historical geographers have actually achieved. But I have also indicated the scope for an exciting future as the inhibiting barriers around 'urban geography' and 'historical geography' are dismantled. We need to be more adventurous and more critical in our use of sources. We need to be better historians. We cannot explore the past unconscious of our present and we should not interpret the present as if there was no past.

A NOTE ON SOURCES

All the nineteenth and early twentieth-century sources mentioned in this chapter are easily accessible in local libraries and record offices. Most local history libraries have microfilm copies of census enumerators' books for their areas and many councils have deposited ratebooks in local records collections. Although both enumerators' books and ratebooks are in manuscript, their standard layout minimises the problem of interpreting uncertain handwriting. The popularity of local authority and WEA classes in local history, and the increasing use of oral history as a form of psychotherapy, mean that most towns now have accounts of everyday life in the 1920s and before.

NOTES AND REFERENCES

1. On urban morphology, see J. W. R. Whitehand (ed.) *The Urban Landscape* (London: Academic Press, 1981).
2. On housing in Victorian London, see A. S. Wohl, *The Eternal Slum: Housing and Social Policy in Victorian London* (London: Edward Arnold, 1977).
3. K. Young and P. Garside, *Metropolitan London: Politics and Urban Change 1837–1981* (London: Edward Arnold, 1982) discuss the history of London government; M. J. Daunton *House and Home in the Victorian City: Working-class Housing 1850–1914* (London: Edward Arnold, 1983) reviews the problems of landlords faced with rising rates.
4. D. Timms, *The Urban Mosaic: Towards a Theory of Residential Differentiation* (Cambridge: Cambridge University Press, 1971); D. Ward, 'Victorian cities: how modern?', *Jnl. Hist. Geogr.*, 1 (1975) pp.135–151.
5. R. Dennis and S. Daniels, '"Community" and the social geography of

Victorian cities.' *Urban History Yearbook,* 1981, pp.7–23. The *Urban History Yearbook* and the quarterly *Local Historian* provide regular articles on sources and techniques of analysis.

6. Daunton, *op. cit.*; P. Kemp, 'Housing landlordism in late nineteenth-century Britain', *Environ. Plann.* 14 (1982) pp.1437–1447; M. Swenarton, *Homes Fit for Heroes* (London: Heinemann, 1981).
7. J. Burnett, *Useful Toil* (London: Allen Lane, 1974); R. Roberts, *The Classic Slum* (Manchester: Manchester University Press, 1971); T. Thompson, *Edwardian Childhoods* (London: Batsford, 1981).
8. A. S. Jasper, *A Hoxton Childhood* (London: Barrie and Rockcliff, 1969).
9. R. J. Morris, *Class and Class Consciousness in the Industrial Revolution 1780–1850* (London: Macmillan, 1979); R. Gray, *The Aristocracy of Labour in Nineteenth-century Britain* (London: Macmillan, 1981).
10. R. S. Neale (ed.) *History and Class: Essential Readings in Theory and Interpretation* (Oxford: Blackwell, 1983).
11. P. Joyce, *Work, Society and Politics: The Culture of the Factory in Later Victorian England* (Brighton: Harvester, 1980); see also D. Ward, 'Environs and neighbours in the "Two Nations"': residential differentiation in mid-nineteenth century Leeds', *J. Hist. Geogr.*, 6 (1980) pp.133–162.
12. J. Springett, 'Landowners and urban development: the Ramsden estates and nineteenth-century Huddersfield', *J. Hist. Geogr.*, 8 (1982) pp.129–144. Other important studies include M. J. Daunton, *Coal Metropolis: Cardiff 1870–1914* (Leicester: Leicester University Press, 1977) and David Cannadine, *Lords and Landlords: The Aristocracy and the Towns 1774–1967* (Leicester: Leicester University Press, 1980).
13. E. G. Howarth and M. Wilson, *West Ham: A Study in Social and Industrial Problems* (London: J. M. Dent, 1907) pp.61–2, 84.
14. For example, Daunton, *op. cit.*; D. Englander, *Landlord and Tenant in Urban Britain 1838–1918* (Oxford: Oxford University Press, 1983).
15. A. Bennett, *Hilda Lessways* (London: Methuen, 1911) book 1, chapters 1 and 2, book 2, chapter 2.
16. Novels 'from below' include George Gissing, *The Nether World* (London: Smith, Elder, 1889) and A. Morrison, *A Child of the Jago* (London: Methuen, 1896).

FURTHER READING

The progress of urban history can be charted by comparing H. J. Dyos (ed.) *The Study of Urban History* (London: Edward Arnold, 1968) and D. Fraser and A. Sutcliffe (eds) *The Pursuit of Urban History* (London: Edward Arnold, 1983).

Two reviews of urban historical geography are H. Carter, *An Introduction to Urban Historical Geography* (London: Edward Arnold, 1983) and Richard Dennis, *English Industrial Cities of the Nineteenth Century* (Cambridge: Cambridge University Press, 1984).

3.3
The Rain on the Roof: A Geography of the Urban Environment

Ian Douglas
University of Manchester

Ian Douglas is Professor of Physical Geography at the University of Manchester. His teaching and research interests in urban geomorphology and urban environmental problems generally have grown from a concern with the impact of people on geomorphic processes. He has recently published *The Urban Environment* (1983) and is co-editor, with Tom Spencer, of *Environmental Change and Tropical Geomorphology* (1985).

THE FUTURE URBAN GEOGRAPHY

In 1970 the United Nations suggested that by the year 2000 more than 50 per cent of the world's population would be urban and two-thirds of that urban population would be in the developing countries. Huge, complex, diverse cities, bigger than any now known, will become the environment in which most people will live. Mexico City may have over 30 million people by the year 2000, Tokyo 24 million, Sao Paulo 23 million and Shanghai 22 million. The people of these cities will live in an environment created by human endeavour, often made unpleasant by the side effects of human activity, frequently full of risks derived from crowding, inadequate housing and poor sanitation and yet by no means immune from the extremes of natural processes, as the earthquake damage to Mexico City of 19 September 1985 so tragically emphasised.

The future urban geography is thus not that of the declining inner cities of the old industrial conurbations of the western world, but the hectic tumult of growth, overcrowding and environmental deterioration of the cities of low latitudes, of countries like Brazil, China, India and Nigeria. Such cities have to be re-examined, not through the conventional frameworks of social area anlysis, class, ethnicity and industrial location, but as pulsating, vibrant, evolving, changing expressions of people's achievements, ambitions, hopes, fears and failures. The external, material form of those activities and attitudes of mind is the physical and biological city of people, buildings, goods and living organisms making up the urban habitat or living space.

THE URBAN HABITAT

Such a habitat approach has been developed into the study of cities as ecosystems, using the term 'ecosystem' in the general sense of a system of interacting and interdependent parts with inflows and outflows of energy. The general ecosystem approach is valid for analysing flows of energy, water and materials, including nutrients, and for studying the niches and sub-habitats occupied by different groups and types of people and other organisms. But in other respects the ecosystem approach is inadequate, because a city cannot be seen as an evolving, more or less self-sufficient system of biotic and non-biotic components. Cities are far from self-sufficient and could not support their people for more than a day or two without a massive input of renewable and non-renewable natural resources from rural areas. Cities in this sense are *dependent systems*, relying on exchanges with surrounding areas. One analogy that has been over-used is that of the city as a monster organism consuming vast quantities of oxygen, water and organic matter, fossil fuels, wood and foods, and releasing wastes into the atmosphere, hydrosphere, soil and surface layers of the lithosphere.

But the city is directed, governed and managed. And since it is dependent on finance, both public and private, to sustain its life support functions, including care of the sick and removal of noxious wastes, the city can be threatened by financial crises, like those which racked New York in the mid-1970s and Liverpool in 1985. Urban economic dynamism not only sustains urban life but also affects the quality of habitats, of living conditions within the city. From the apartment complexes of Soviet cities to the sprawling suburban bungalows of Los Angeles, living conditions reflect the economic and political systems of city and national governments.

Yet those economic and political systems respond to the problems caused by the environmental conditions they have created. Concern over the environmental consequences of the Industrial Revolution in Britain led to the Public Health Act of 1870 and subsequent by-laws regulating the types of houses which could be built, which transformed the nature of British cities. Evolution of the urban ecosystem is not inevitable, therefore, or unstoppable. To take another example, one of the most important planning goals in Britain since 1945 has been the containment of urban growth through the designation of Green Belts, and yet in many cases these policies have merely resulted in the outward expansion of the journey-to-work zone, facilitated by technical improvements in transport such as railway electrification and motorway construction, and an increasing disparity in living conditions between deprived areas of the inner city and the other suburbs. Such contrasts are nowhere near as great as those between the affluent South Western suburbs of Mexico City and the squatter settlements to the North, but they still show how the physical form and living conditions of the city reflect both political economy and technical change.

URBANISATION AND THE ENVIRONMENT

For all that, cities continue to attract people. In Mexico there is a free public health service, but good health care is only readily available to the poor in the major city. Despite the difficulties in getting work and finding a place to live, many poor people move to the big city to offer their children a better chance for health and future happiness. At the same time, many of those who recognise the opportunities and facilities the city offers are also disturbed by the environmental and social problems which beset it. Paul Bairoch has suggested that the most livable cities with reasonable job prospects are those of less than 600 000 people. More employment opportunities and a wider range of jobs are to be found in cities of between one to two million people, but in such cities there are far greater inconveniences to daily life. Metropolises of over two million face tighter job markets, high pollution levels, high crime rates and burgeoning housing problems. Beyond two million inhabitants, so Bairoch argues, employment conditions start to deteriorate, except for income, and the general conditions of life worsen dramatically.

Despite these pitfalls, half-million cities grow into million cities and urbanisation proceeds apace. The proportion of the people of Asia and the Far East living in cities rose from 20 per cent in 1960 to 29 per cent in 1980. These growing urban populations require more energy, water, food and materials. Industrialisation requires the construction of roads, bridges, dams, power plants, irrigation schemes, airports, harbours, docks and terminals, and all of these need land, power and building materials. Consumption of energy and water grows more rapidly than the human population (see Figure 3.3.1). In developing urban areas, 200–400 litres per capita per day of water are required for domestic purposes, whereas rural people use 40-80 litres per capita per day. The bigger the city, the larger the per capita consumption, as industrial use and public use in fountains, parks, street-cleaning and fire-fighting all expand. If public supplies do not expand quickly enough, unofficial groundwater abstraction may deplete subsurface aquifers and even lead to subsidence, as in Bangkok where parts of the city are subsiding more than 10 cm per year. Where local supplies have become inadequate, massive inter-basin transfers are necessary, as in Kuala Lumpur where a million people now depend on water from four major river systems (see Table 3.3.1). Mexico City, at over 2000 m altitude, relies on water pumped up from both the Atlantic and the Pacific Coast drainage systems of Mexico, consuming large quantities of energy merely to ensure adequate water supplies.

Ideally, the water supply system should expand ahead of urban development, and with it the waste collection system of sewers and drains. In many modern cities, however, this ideal is not achieved. Even in affluent Tokyo, the sewage systems covered only 36 per cent of the urban area in 1968, reaching only 5.5 per cent of the population in some suburbs, and in 1973 only about 12 per cent of the people of Greater Manila in the Philippines were served by sewers.

The material demands of the urban population are the cause of profound changes in the physical character of the city and its surroundings. Modification of the natural flows of energy, water and materials goes hand in hand with the creation and maintenance of artificial flows of the same commodities. The character of the land surface changes, affecting the radiation balance, the rainfall-runoff relationship, sources and supplies of sediments and solutes, infiltration and groundwater levels, soil chemistry and plant and animal habitats. Such changes are both continuous and episodic. The impacts become apparent irregularly, often in extreme or unusual climatic conditions such as floods caused by exceptional rains whose height and duration is affected by the large proportion of impermeable rooved and paved surfaces in the urban catchment area. Similarly, temperature inversions can trap the gaseous pollutants and particulates emitted by urban chimneys and exhausts, causing smogs. Both floods and smog lead to accidents, damage, injury and even loss of life, which in turn place demands on urban services.

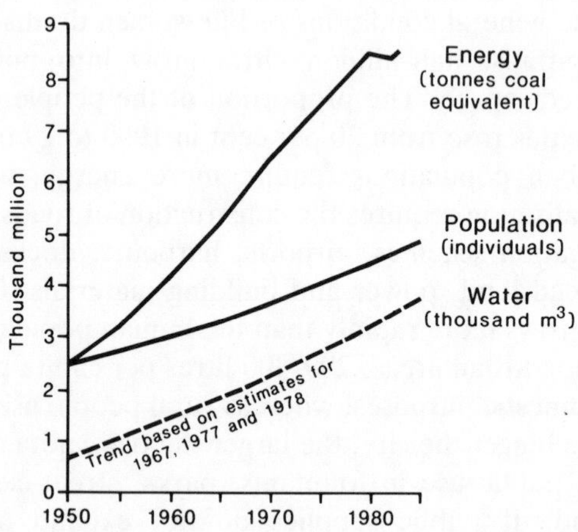

SOURCE: Council for environmental quality and Department of State (1982) *The Global 2000 Reports to the President* (Harmondsworth: Penguin); Foley, G. (1976) *The Energy Crisis* (Harmondsworth: Penguin); United Nations (1985) *Demographic Year Book 1984* (New York: United Nations)

FIGURE 3.3.1 *Global growth of population, energy consumption and water use since 1950*

TABLE 3.3.1. *Growth of Kuala Lumpur and Klang water supply system using storages on the Klang, Langat, Batu and Semenyih Rivers*

Date	*Source*	*Yield* / *Ml day* $^{-1}$*
1977	Available from Genting Kelang Reservoir	136
1977	Available from other sources	83
1979	Completion of Stage III of Langat project	477 (maximum)
1983	Sungai Batu (reservoir mainly for food control)	114
1984	Sungai Semenyith	345

* Ml day $^{-1}$ is a hybrid unit used by British water engineers as a metric equivalent of m.g.d. (million gallons per day). The derived S.I. unit in which these yields should be reported is $m^3 s^{-1}$. To convert Ml day^{-1} to $m^3 s^{-1}$ multiply by yield 1.157×10^{-2}.

SOURCE Douglas, I. (1984) 'Water and sediment issues in the Kuala Lumpur ecosystem', *in* Yip Yat Hoong and Low Kwai Sim (eds) *Urbanization and Ecodevelopment with special reference to Kuala Lumpur* (Kuala Lumpur Institut Pengajian Tinggi, Universiti Malaya) pp. 101–121

CONTROL AND THE URBAN PHYSICAL SYSTEM

The 'urban growth → physical change → people-induced hazard → impact on people and services' chain of actions and responses indicates the value of an environmental systems approach to cities. As the essays in *Horizons in Physical Geography* show, physical geography is concerned with the interplay of energy, water and biogeochemical cycles at or near the earth's surface. The character of the earth's surface at any particular place in time is, in effect, the temporary state of that interplay *and its reaction with the prevailing socio-economic political systems*. One way of beginning to analyse the workings of the city is thus to look at the various people-modified cycles (see Table 3.3.2), taking particular account of the artificial supplies of energy, water and materials. In some parts of high latitude cities with particularly high levels of energy use, especially central business districts and areas around power stations and heavy industrial plants, artificial heat emission exceeds incoming solar radiation in mid-winter (see Table 3.3.3). The significance of artificial water supplies varies, but in many low latitude cities, the bulk of the natural water input by precipitation occurs in a few major storms each year, so that the objective of water management is to evacuate excess water as quickly as possible rather than retain it for use in later dry periods. Waste production varies not only between cities but also from one part of the city to another, so that, for example, one Melbourne suburb produces over 3 times as much as that of another (see Table 3.3.4).

Explanation and understanding of such temporal and spatial variability helps in the design of schemes to alleviate urban environmental problems. But it is just as important to examine the ways in which these problems developed as a result of human activity and hence see how they might be resolved by technological developments and legislation. It is often difficult, however, to decide which of these two is most effective in improving the environment. Air pollution in British cities is a good example, since it had begun to decrease as a result of a change from coal to oil and gas for domestic heating and to oil and electricity for industrial power *before* the Clean Air Act led to the declaration of smokeless zones (see Figure 3.3.2). On the other hand, photochemical smog abatement and a decrease in nitrous oxides in urban air seems to have *followed* legislation on motor vehicle exhaust emissions, although the 1973 world oil crises led to the design of more efficient, less wasteful engines.

Difficulties of this sort in identifying the real controls on the urban physical geographical system have probably done much to hold back the development of a truly comprehensive urban geography. But unless they are tackled, urban physical geography is likely to remain a part of the earth sciences, allied with environmental geology and civil and sanitary engineering, and concerned with describing and explaining natural systems as modified by urbanisation, the limitations to urban expansion posed by natural conditions and the response of natural systems to new urban developments.

An alternative to this approach, I suggest, is to look at the historical evolution of the urban environment in terms of the urban growth-physical change-human impact succession. Let me give a simple example.

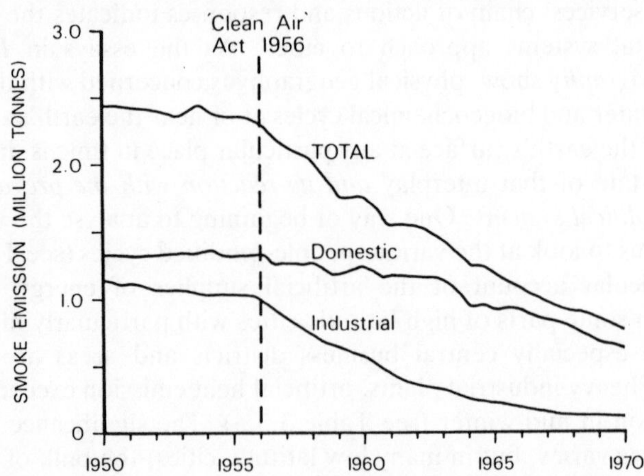

Source: Salmon L. Atkins D. H. F. Fisner E. M. R. Healy C. and Law D. V. (1978) 'Retrospective trend analysis of the content of UK air particulate material 1957–1974', *Science of the Total Environment* 9, 161–99

Figure 3.3.2 *Trends of smoke emissions in UK*

TABLE 3.3.2. *The energy, water and materials cycles of cities*

The surface energy balance of an urban area

$$Q_S + Q_F + Q_I = Q_L + Q_G + Q_E$$

where Q_S = rate of arrival of radiant energy from the sun

Q_F = rate of generation of heat due to combustion, metabolism and dissipation in machinery

Q_I = rate of heat arrival from the earth's interior

Q_L = rate of loss of heat by evaporation, ie, provision of latent heat

Q_G = rate of loss of heat by conduction to soil, buildings, roads, etc

Q_E = rate of loss of heat by radiation

The urban water balance

$$P + D + A + W + E + R_S + S$$

where P = precipitation including rain, snow and hail;

D = dew and hoar frost

A = water released from anthropogenic sources, more particularly combustion

W = piped, surface and subsurface water brought into the city

E = evaporation and transportation

R_S = natural and piped surface and subsurface flow out of the city

S = change in water storage in the fabric of the city

The urban materials budget

$$M_s = M_o + W_f = W_a = M_c + M_r$$

where M_s = materials supplied to the city

M_o = materials exported from the city

W_f = solid and liquid waste materials

W_a = atmospheric pollutants discharged from the use of the materials

M_c = amount of materials converted through heat production or other processes

M_t = net addition of materials to the urban fabric and stock.

SOURCE Author

TABLE 3.3.3. *Total solar radiation, urban consumption and anthropogenic heat release*

Latitude	*Location*	*Total solar radiation*				*Urban energy consumption*	*Anthropogenic heat release*	
		24 – hr mean flux density		*Total daily pulse*		*Daily mean*	*Daily means*	
							Summer	*Winter*
		W m⁻² → $W\ m^{-2}$		$MJ\ m^{-2}$		$MJ\ m^{-2}$	$W\ m^{-2}$	$W\ m^{-2}$
		June	*December*	*June*	*December*			
62°N	Irkutsk	237	7	20	0.5			
54°N	Edmonton	255	30	22	2.6			
52°N	Calgary						2	19
51°N						322		
43°N	Madison	260	56	23	5			
42°N	New York City					1494		
	Manhattan					5029	40	200
34°N	Los Angeles					662		
22°N	Hong Kong City					1035	24	
19°N	Poona	237	190	20	16			
4°N	Kinshasa	160	200	14	17			
34°N	Sydney					61		

SOURCES: Douglas, I. (1983) *The Urban Environment* (London: Edward Arnold)
Miller, D. H. (1981) *Energy at the Surface of the Earth* (New York: Academic Press).

The evolution of the urban environment: the case of Manchester

Manchester's early industrial expansion was accompanied by acute environmental problems. When De Tocqueville visited Manchester in the 1830s he had the following impression: 'A sort of black smoke covers the city. The sun seen through it is a disc without rays . . . The fetid, muddy waters, stained with a thousand colours by the factories they pass . . . wander slowly round this refuge of poverty.' Engels said much the same in 1844, and by the 1860s the bed of the Irwell had been so raised by refuse and cinders dumped in its channel that the main sewers and mill drains became blocked at high discharges and serious flooding occurred after rain. Riverside factories often had chutes down which ashes were ejected directly into the river: 75 000 tonnes of cinders were dumped in the river alone. The gravel bars which formed after every major storm interrupted navigation and further reduced channel capacity, so increasing the flood risk even more.

TABLE 3.3.4. *Mean weights (kg per capita per week) in each waste category in seven districts of Melbourne surveyed in 1974–5(I) and 1977–8(II) and interpolated annual trends over the period*

Waste category	*Kelior*		*Whittlesea*		*Springvale*		*William-stown*		*Croydon*		*Coburg*		*Prahan*	
	I	*II*	*I*	*II*	*I*	*II*	*I*	*II*	*I*	*II*	*I*	*II*	*I*	*II*
Paper products	0.29	0.38	0.44	0.37	0.76	0.67	0.40	0.40	0.53	0.42	0.76	0.80	1.86	1.69
Food wastes	0.92	1.17	0.99	1.13	1.18	1.43	0.81	1.12	1.12	0.78	1.58	1.61	1.84	2.30
Garden wastes	0.03	0.11	0.09	0.08	0.13	0.11	0.10	0.17	0.02	0.02	0.16	0.27	0.44	0.47
Steel	0.12	0.20	0.18	0.21	0.24	0.26	0.17	0.24	0.31	0.25	0.30	0.22	0.30	0.44
Aluminium	0.01	0.01	0.01	0.02	0.02	0.02	0.02	0.02	0.02	0.01	0.02	0.03	0.02	0.03
Other metals	0.00	0.00	0.00	0.00	0.00	0.00	0.00	0.00	0.00	0.00	0.02	0.00	0.02	0.00
Glass	0.19	0.39	0.31	0.29	0.39	0.61	0.21	0.34	0.51	0.33	0.50	0.46	0.94	1.06
Rags	0.02	0.02	0.02	0.04	0.06	0.06	0.04	0.04	0.06	0.02	0.06	0.03	0.08	0.09
Timber	0.00	0.00	0.00	0.00	0.00	0.01	0.00	0.00	0.00	0.00	0.00	0.00	0.02	0.00
Plastics	0.04	0.02	0.08	0.10	0.11	0.21	0.06	0.13	0.09	0.13	0.10	0.14	0.14	0.22
Inert wastes	0.05	0.06	0.04	0.01	0.02	0.07	0.11	0.08	0.10	0.01	0.02	0.06	0.04	0.11
Totals	1.67	2.46	2.17	2.25	2.91	3.45	1.98	2.54	2.74	1.97	3.52	3.62	5.68	6.40
Three-years trend (% per annum compound)	+13.8		+1.2		+5.8		+8.6		−11.6		+0.9		+4.1	

SOURCE: Schaller, C. W. and Wallwork, B. (1979) 'Waste disposal in the Melbourne metropolitan area', *Search*, 128–32

By 1870 a clear association between levels of water pollution and infant mortality appeared to exist in different parts of Manchester and Salford. In response to criticisms of the housing conditions of the poor, attempts were begun to permit municipal action to alleviate the problems (see Table 3.3.5). Changes in transport, especially the construction of suburban railways and tramways, enabled workers to live further from their workplaces and thus eased the pressure on inner city housing. Bye-laws led to improved standards of housing. New technologies and the drive of visionary engineers led to new water supply schemes and new sewage systems.

By the end of the nineteenth century, Manchester had a well-developed infrastructure of railways, canals, sewers and tramways. The city's prosperity provided income through the rates to support a high level of public service provision including parks, hospitals and colleges. The 1920s and 1930s saw the southward expansion of suburban housing, much of it municipally owned and linked to the tramways by motor buses, and ultimately the planning of the satellite city of Wythenshawe. Developments in the catchments of the Irwell, and its tributaries, the Irk and Medlock, involved reservoir construction and flood mitigation works which reduced risks of inundation in Manchester and Salford.

The expansion of Manchester came to an end after 1945. Areas of derelict land, the newly quiet waters of the Salford and Manchester docks, the redundant railway yards converted to car parks – all testify to the deterioration of the urban fabric. That this coincided with a great fervour for environmental improvement is ironic. However, massive programmes of urban rehousing, derelict land reclamation, river valley improvement, canal rejuvenation and conservation of historic buildings have brought large new green areas into the formerly fully built-up inner city zones, and this has changed the albedo, the distribution of pollutant sources and the rainfall-runoff relationship. New manufacturing processes in new locations and consequent changes to traffic flows have altered the spatial distribution and type of heat and pollutant sources, and so transformed the pattern of energy, water and geochemical flows. The search for new land for housing has meant building on hillsides mantled with boulder clay, and this has caused problems of both drainage and mass movement. Upstream urbanisation has produced downstream flooding on urban streams, because eighteenth and nineteenth-century culverts and bridges are too small for late twentieth-century peak flows.

All of these pressures on the nineteenth-century infrastructure have come at a time of financial stringency, and yet problems like sewer collapses, decay of Victorian bridges and roofs demand urgent action. Sustaining the functioning of the people-made flow systems of the city thus competes for resources with the social, housing, education and health needs of the people. The physical system is thus irrevocably interwoven with the socio-economic and political system.

TABLE 3.3.5. *Municipal actions to improve social conditions in Manchester and adjacent areas*

1752	Establishment of Royal Infirmary
1775	Act for widening and improving several Manchester Streets
1792	Board for Commisioners with powers to construct sewers set up in Manchester
1796	House of Recovery established. Voluntary Board of Health established in Manchester by Drs Ferriar and Percival
1828	New act affecting environmental issues gave separate Commissioners to Manchester and Salford
1830	Police Act gave new powers of control to the Commissioners
1833	Manchester Statistical Society founded to assist in social improvement of the manufacturing population
1838	Publication of Dr James Black's survey of Bolton
1844	Borough Police Act requires owners of both new and existing properties to provide sanitary conveniences satisfactory to the Council
1845	Act promoting the health of the inhabitants gave Borough Council powers to control waste disposal and carry out integrated sanitary improvements
1860	Bolton Council acts to clear River of rubbish
1867	Salford Council appointed a river inspector to track down polluters and persuade them to cut their discharge
1868	Medical Officer of Health begins 4-year programme of closure of 2400 cellar dwellings
1870	New City Health Department established in Manchester
1871	Ballard's report on sanitary and social conditions in Bolton
1872	Salford began construction of Sewage works
1885	Salford Corporation took proceedings under 1876 Rivers Pollution Prevention Act against 28 local authorities calling on them to purify their sewage before discharging it into the Irwell
1891	Mersey and Irwell Joint Committee formed to compel local authorities to provide sewage treatment facilities

SOURCES: Bracegirdle, C. (1983) *The Dark River* (Altrincham: Sherratt,); Corbett, J. (1907) *The River Irwell* (Manchester: Heywood); Pooley, M. E. and Pooley, C. G. (1984) 'Health society and environment in Victorian Manchester', in Woods, R. and Woodward, J. (eds) *Urban Disease and Mortality in Nineteenth Century England* (London: Batsford,) pp. 148–175; Redford, A. (1940) *The History of Local Government in Manchester* (London: Longmans Gren,) 3 vols; Saxelby, C. H. (ed) (1971) *Bolton Survey* (East Ardsley, Wakefield: S. R. Publishers,); Thomson, W. H. (1967) *History of Manchester to 1852* (Altrincham: Sherratt,)

Phases of system modification

While Manchester has gone through four phases of physiographic system modification, most third-world cities are only entering phase three, during which old colonial-style city centres are being converted into modern central business districts. However, many cities are forced to adopt massive public works schemes to alleviate such problems like subsidence, traffic congestion and flooding. In Mexico City, deep drains are being constructed 80 m below ground level to remove waste and stormwater and avoid the subsidence in the near surface alluvia which has disrupted the original drains and caused local flooding. The city has also constructed a metro system to alleviate traffic congestion, but still two million cars eject their exhaust gases into the often still montane air of the Mexico basin to produce brown-yellow fogs which persist all day.

In cities like Mexico City, wide variations in air quality, water problems and noxious nuisances occur over the urban area. In most large cities of Asia, Africa and Latin America, at least 30 per cent of the population live in slums and squatter settlements. In Indonesia, an estimated 70 per cent of Jakarta's new growth continues to be absorbed by new unplanned communities on the periphery of the cities. In India the slum population was estimated to be 46.2 million in 1980. Working from the present trend, the United Nation's economic and social commission for Asia and the Pacific estates that by the year 2000, two-thirds of the region's urban population or almost 500 million people will be living in slums and squatter settlements. These are the very communities that often suffer the worst consequences of changes in energy, water and material flows. A sound geography of cities needs a programme to examine these within-city contrasts.

A PROGRAMME FOR URBAN PHYSICAL GEOGRAPHY

Urban physical geography needs a process orientation and an historical dimension. I will consider each of these in turn. The process orientation looks at the detail of the flows of energy, water and materials, while the historical dimension is concerned with the evolution of the present physical form and terrain of the city, both natural and people-made, and with the possible impacts of future changes, again including both natural events like major floods, tidal waves, earthquakes, volcanic eruptions, and people-induced events like subsidence or coastal-erosion after harbour works, land reclamation, excavation, land-fill, drainage pollutant emissions or large heat sources.

The process-oriented urban physical geography would have to examine flows and their relationships to urban physical form at four or more different scales (see Table 3.3.6).

Micro-scale

Appreciation of the impact of urbanisation on environment may well begin at the micro-scale in and around individual buildings. Diversion of winds around buildings takes a characteristic pattern which can readily be detected by a pedestrian passing a side of a building facing an incoming wind. Some of the wind striking the building is diverted upwards and over the building, but much is forced round the side. The windward side of the building may well show a variation in the degree of weathering of stone or concrete, or in the density of lichens on old roof tiles. Drainage may vary from building to building and one side of a building may have wetter adjacent soil than the other. Some buildings face precipitation directly to storm water drains, other roofs lead to stormwater detention tanks within the building designed so as not to increase the peak discharge off-site beyond that which existed before construction, while yet others, especially on houses in the tropics, shed water to an open concrete apron and drain discharging directly into roadside drains and thence into the people-modified natural drainage system. By asking simple questions such as: 'What happens to the rain that falls on the roof?', the whole nature of the hydrological cycle in the urban context may be appreciated.

The heating and cooling of the interiors of buildings provides an excellent opportunity to analyse relative human comfort. Different styles of buildings in Singapore – from traditional kampong (or village) houses on stilts, through to old colonial houses with high pitched roofs and wide verandahs to modern government flats and luxury air conditioned apartments – vary in bioclimatic conditions according to whether or not air flow is impeded; the traditional, more open buildings are in fact more comfortable than the modern structures.

Around and on individual buildings varied habitats for organisms occur, from insects to the plants which colonise crevices in walls or debris in guttering. House plants attract their own communities of insects and micro-organisms. These familiar physical and organic phenomena provide the readily observed components of the flow and storages which operate at other scales.

Meso-scale

Census tracts, social areas, housing estates, industrial zones, small first- and second-order stream catchments provide formal and functional units in which to examine processes such as airborne particulates, dry fall-out, precipitation chemistry, noise levels, rainfall-runoff relationships, sedimentation and water quality, semi-domesticated animals and weed invasions. If health statistics, such as perinatal mortality, are available at enumeration district or some sub-ward level, it is possible to examine their association with environmental, social and lifestyle statistics, although it is often difficult to find suitable

TABLE 3.3.6 *Interaction between urban form and flows and processes at four different scales*

Scale	*Micro-scale*	*Meso-scale*	*Macro-scale*	*Mega-scale*
Approximate areal magnitude	10–1000 m2	0.000–1 km2	1–10 km2	10–1000 + km2
G-scale value	13.7–11.7	11.7–8.7	8.7–7.7	7.7–5.7 +
Type of area	In and around individual buildings and structures	Census tracts Housing estates Industrial zones	Topographic units in urban areas, valleys, ridges, escarpments	Urban stress as a whole Conurbations, Metropolitan regions
Energy flows	Effects of structures on winds, insolation, reflection. Thermal comfort of different house styles	Effects of land use density and ground cover on heat emissions, albedo and radiation balance	Influence of aspect on solar radiation receipt and of water bodies on winds and heat island development	Urban heat islands and wind regimes
Water flows	Runoff from roofs, droveways, yards; individual wells and groundwater pumping	Stormwater drainage including grassed water-ways, separate or combined sewers	Chanelisation and stormwater detention reservoirs, multiple use of river valleys	Urban-induced rainfall Modification of regional groundwater levels; downstream effects of urban runoff and interbasin transfers on major rivers
Materials flows: a) airborn pollutants	Emissions from domestic grates, industrial chimneys, individual vehicles	Concentration of exhaust fumes along major roads, impact of factory emissions on local communities. Dust from construction and demolition sites	Effects of topography on concentration and movement of pollutants and scouring effect of winds	Urban dust domes; emission of oxides of nitrogen and sulphur producing downwind, transfrontier and even intercontinental acid rain
b) water-borne pollutants	Point-source emissions from individual premises	Pollutants from local septic tanks and aeration ponds; sediment in roadside and construction site runoff	Pollution of urban lakes by atmospheric fallout (eg lead) and siltation of lakes and streams	Impact of urban stormwater runoff, including heavy metals, and sewage treatment effluent on major rivers. Oceanic discharge of inadequately treated sewage
c) solid wastes	Rubbish disposal at factories, warehouses and reatail outlets. Illicit dumping of domestic refuse	Community rubbish dumps and garbage depots	Site problems of noxious waste disposal: dangers of groundwater contamination from landfill	Regional waste disposal management such as the use of gravel pits near Didcot for London's rubbish. Ocean dumping of sludge from municipal sewage
Geomorphic effects	Subsidence of individual buildings over old mines, quarries and landfill sites	Foundation problems on glacial deposits and buried karst. Swelling clay problems. Elimination of minor channels	Mass movements on unstable hill slopes. Floodplain delimitation and flood risk estimation	Regional subsidence due to removal of liquids, such as water, brine or petroleum (as at Houston, Texas). Relationship of urban areas to sea level change
Biological effects	Insects and vermin in individual buildings. Bacterial contamination. Character of individual gardens	Effect of housing conditions on health and well being. Influence of working environment on human and other life forms	Plant and animal invasions of derelict urban land. Planned valley reclamation schemes, urban parks	Adaption of birds and animals to urban living. Evolution of strains of disease vectors resistant to pesticides. Urban stress-related diseases

environmental quality indicators: point observations of air pollution levels, linear records of noise levels or stream pollution are difficult to convert to representative areal measures. Even so, studies of urban lead levels have indicated the importance of variations at the meso-scale. Lead concentrations are usually highest along busy streets and much lower away from traffic centres. Smells, on the other hand, can be more pervasive, but their distribution varies with wind directions.

Despite the difficulties of coping with some environmental indicators, areas within cities can be characterised by a range of physiographic variables, such as probability of flooding, mass movement, earthquake damage and swelling clay problems. Geomorphological and soil mapping facilitates assessment of urban land capability. Individual parcels of land can be described in terms of terrain, hazard risks and pollution levels. In this way, physiographic information can be added to a conventional social area analysis in order to explore people-environment relationships in the city.

More excitingly perhaps, neighbourhood awareness can be heightened so that people are made aware of their own community and its environment and are encouraged to improve their areas and to scrutinise any planning proposals which may affect their lives. This may extend to an awareness of the impact of events outside their area on them, and to the effects of their actions on other people. In all environmental questions the question of type of impact is important (see Figure 3.3.3). In urban areas the type 4 impacts (inadvertent, off-site) are all too frequent, usually implying that improvement in one area, for one group, has meant deterioration of conditions for another group off-site, down-wind or downstream. Such linkages indicate the value of examining major segments, river basins or land system within a city as a whole.

Type of Action	Location of Effect: On Site	Location of Effect: Off Site / Downstream
Deliberate	1	2
Inadvertent	3	4

FIGURE 3.3.3 *Types of on-site and off-site environmental impact*

Macro-scale

Some cities are dominated by large physical features, such as the valley of the Yang-tze at Chongqing, China, the Danube at Budapest, or the former Lake Texcoco at Mexico City, but others straddle several smaller features, such as the hills and valleys of Greater Los Angeles or the San Francisco Bay area. Major physical features at this scale influence urban climate, as in Sydney where the configuration of the harbour and Botany Bay affect the diurnal wind and photochemical smog patterns. Yet within such an area the various river basins and plains, plateaux and hills have their own particular problems. One river system, draining a particular set of lithology and land uses, will have a different régime to another. One terrain system may be more prone to instability problems than another. Recognition of the particular processes operating in a given system and the way in which their interaction creates the present conditions and levels of hazards at particular places within the overall system reveals the interdependence of the meso-scale components. Again, let me give a simple example.

The Thames Valley is a dominant feature of the London area, yet the growth of the city has profoundly modified the river and its tributaries. Runoff from the paved and roofed urban area has increased peak river flows, while narrowing of the channel by embankments has raised the height of peak tides. Subsidence, due to a combination of natural tectonic processes, abstraction of groundwater and compaction by the mass of buildings, has slightly lowered the city centre relative to sea levels with the result that many major buildings, such as the Houses of Parliament and Somerset House, were at risk of flooding during exceptional North Sea storm surges.

The Thames tidal barrier is a good illustration of the operation of macro-scale urban physical geographical systems. The barrier at Greenwich, downstream of the City of London, was constructed to protect the city from the flood which might be produced by a North Sea storm surge raising the height of an exceptional Spring Tide, coincident with a discharge down the river. The need for the barrier arises because the city has encroached upon the floodplain, so narrowing the flood channel while at the same time urban drainage has increased peak stormwater discharges. Peak expected flood heights are now above street level along the Embankment. Abstraction of groundwater from the chalk beneath London has lowered the water table by up to 60m in places. Some subsidence caused by this pumping adds to that caused by the weight of structures and the natural geological subsidence of South-East England. The overall subsidence adds to the relative height of the probable maximum flood in relation to city streets. The value of the property and the presence of so many important buildings, including the Houses of Parliament and Somerset House, in the flood hazard zone led to public pressure and political will for an expensive protective structure, not to eradicate the problem, but to prevent it affecting the city centre. The building of the barrier has implications for people living and working along the river downstream of Greenwich, as when the Barrier stops the storm surge in the estuary the height of the water downstream of Greenwich will rise. A protective wall up to the expected storm surge height has had to be built along both banks of the estuary. Many people who had a good view of the river now have a good view of the wall!

Mega-scale

This involves an examination of the overall environmental changes imposed by cities, paying particular attention to such phenomena as the urban heat-island, the pollution-shed (dust or dome) and the influence of urbanisation on precipitation.

Here too an example can illustrate the approach. Los Angeles is often though to be typical of large urban areas with photochemical smog problems, yet the case of Los Angeles is in fact complex in both genesis and distribution. The chemicals emitted to the atmosphere – nitric oxide, carbon monoxide, sulphur dioxide and hydrocarbons – vary in source location and in time of peak emission. Their distribution is affected by the prevailing winds, generally from the coast to inland areas, stronger in summer than in winter and with their trajectories related to topography. More nitric oxide and sulphur dioxide are emitted in winter than in summer. Vehicle emissions are greatest during the morning rush hour, but the secondary contaminants, aldehydes and ozone, which are the result of photochemical reactions which increase with the duration of the sun, reach peak concentrations around midday.

In the Los Angeles areas the stationary sources of pollution, chiefly power stations, oil refineries and heavy industries, situated mainly in the south and southwest coastal area and in the East San Fernando Valley, are the main sources of sulphur dioxide and nitric oxide. Motor vehicle emissions are particularly concentrated around Los Angeles itself, but the highest atmospheric concentrations occur east of that area and over the eastern portion of the San Gabriel Valley. During the day, oxidants drift eastward towards the Riverside and San Bernadino areas. The space-time drift of the zone of highest concentration of oxidants is characteristic of this type of pollution in cities in warm subtropical latitudes. It iilustrates how the mega-scale phenomenon of smog can only be explained using many components of urban geography: physical, economic and social.

Mega-scale physical characteristics have wider effects, such as the urban emission of sulphur and nitrogen to the atmosphere leading to acid rain, and additions of carbon dioxide to the atmosphere caused by the burring of fossil fuels.

THE HISTORICAL DIMENSION

Cities are rapidly evolving phenomena and changes in the built environment may produce responses in natural systems which have such severe repercussions that they create a need for further economic investment in hazard mitigation works. This interaction between human action and natural systems is exemplified by the lower Thames basin as described above, by Venice with the subsidence caused by water abstraction, and by Zeebrugge with coastal erosion as a result of harbour construction. A good, meso-scale example is provided by the changes on the Sungai Anak Ayer Batu in Kuala Lumpur, Malaysia (see Figure 3.3.4).

Under the original rain forest conditions, the Anak Ayer Batu would have been a narrow, meandering stream with a relatively low sediment load. It would have had few tributaries, but would have received much of its annual discharge as base flow and delayed return flow by subsurface water movement. When the land was converted to rubber plantations and weeded between the trees, gully development increased peak flows and led to channel enlargement. Decades later, the plantations were cleared for housing development, with large areas being left bare for long periods of time. Intense tropical rains washed large volumes of sediment into the stream during storms, causing high flood flows with concentrations of suspended sediment exceeding 80 000 mg l^{-1}. This dramatic change transformed the Anak Ayer Batu from a deep, narrow, gently sloping braiding stream to a wide, shallow, relatively straight and steep channel. A small reservoir constructed downstream of the construction area acted as a sediment trap and filled within two years of completion.

New guidelines for urban drainage design introduced by the Federal Territory authorities led to the conversion of some tributaries into concrete-lined storm drains. Paving and planting of the new housing area has reduced peak sediment load, but peak discharges are still higher and cause much bank erosion downstream of the channelised reaches. The roofs of some squatter houses on the floodplain are now below the top of the artificial channel and so reducing channel capacity and hydraulic efficiency and again increasing flood risk.

This sequence of disturbance, channel adjustment, metamorphosis and channelisation shows the temporal and spatial links of physiographic processes and urban growth. The costs of downstream land holders have been high, including both short-term disruption, such as the inability of students and lecturers to move from one part of the University of Malaya campus to another during flash floods, and long-term investment in bridge and bank protection works to prevent the undercutting of major structures. Some people caused the changes, other people suffered from them. Costs had to be met. Developers could pass on their channelisation costs to clients; downstream owners could litigate for compensation for their costs. But whatever happens, the city dweller is intimately involved with the urban ecosystem and the urban water flows.

Most cities have complex environmental relationships of this type. To take another example, in the nineteenth century the towns in Greater Manchester built extensive brick-lined sewer systems to cope with sanitation problems. By the end of the 1970s Greater Manchester had begun to measure the

SUNGAI ANAK AYER BATU, KUALA LUMPUR
sequence of channel change

Before construction :– meandering channel

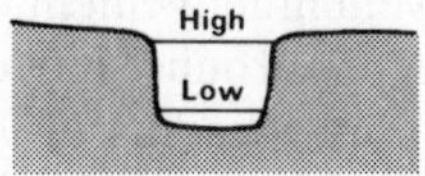

After construction :– braided channel

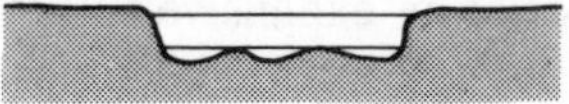

Design channel, stonework encased in concrete

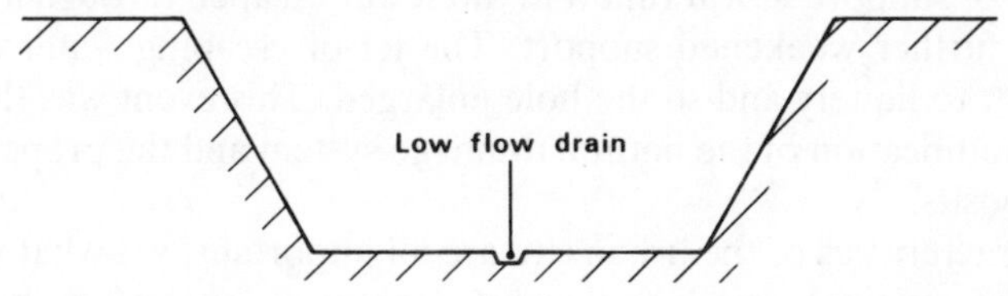

Design channel after two years or more

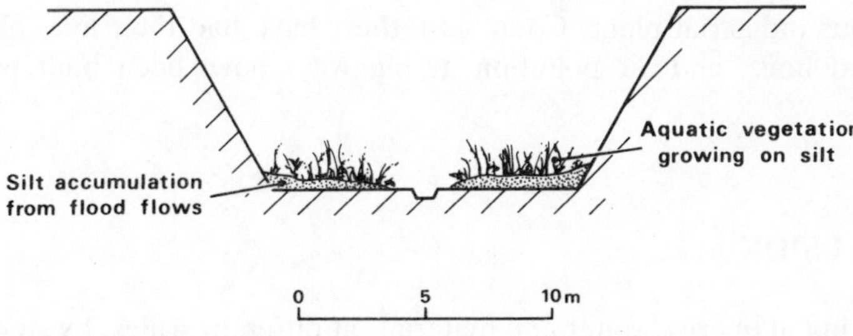

FIGURE 3.3.4 *Sequence of channel changes due to urbanisation of the Sungai Anak Ayer Batu Catchment, Kuala Lumpur*

magnitude of sewer collapses by the number of double-decker buses which would occupy the hole. But some of these collapses were intimately related to geomorphic conditions. A classic example is provided by the subsidence at Fylde Street, Farnworth, on 12 September 1957, where at 0710 hours, after prolonged heavy rain, a small hole appeared in the street. The hole grew in size during the day, and by evening movement ceased, leaving a crater 40 m long, 6 m wide and 4 m deep. Ground movement had occurred over a roughly semi-circular area within a radius of 75 m from the original hole. Seventeen houses were damaged beyond repair and 121 houses had to be evacuated. The hole was created by the collapse of a sewer following the line of the former Farnworth Hall Clough, a small first-order right-bank tributary of the River Croal, which had been filled. The stream was incised into a 3.5m thick bed of glacial silt in the delta deposits of the Croal overflow channel between a layer of sand and gravel above the boulder clay below. The silt has many of the characteristics of an expansive soil. When dry it is stiff and can bear a considerable load, but when wet it becomes plastic and then changes to a silt of individual minute particles colloidally suspended in water.

The sewer runs parallel to the bed of the former Clough, crossing it at three places. The groundwater table was high, and near the surface after rain. Some groundwater moved through the old streambed gravels and washed fine particles through the matrix, thus weakening the support of the sewer. With this failure of support, storm runoff in the sewer escaped through longitudinal joints and further weakened support. The jet of escaping water caused the adjacent silt to liquefy and so the hole enlarged. This event was the result of both the modification of the natural drainage system and the properties of the glacial deposits.

The characteristics of the urban site are all important, yet what was a good site for the original small settlement, centuries ago often becomes an inadequate site for the modern city. Technology is applied to conquer the natural difficulties and legislation is imposed to prevent occupation of unsuitable areas. Yet in so many cities, poor people move illegally into high risk areas such as floodplains, potentially unstable slopes and, as the events of 1984 in Bhopal and Mexico City tragically showed, the surroundings of hazardous industrial plant. Countless others have had their lives altered by increased noise and air pollution as highways have been built past their homes.

CONCLUSION

By looking at energy, water and materials at different scales, by studying the effects on those flows of both topography and the location of human activity, by analysing the consequences of changes in urban activity and adjustment of the biophysical systems over time, a greater understanding of people-environment relationships can be developed (see Table 3.3.7). Geography

TABLE 3.3.7 *Urban environmental changes and their hydrologic consequences during four types of land-use transisiton*

Change in land or water use	*Possible hydrological effect*
Transition from pre-urban stage	
Removal of trees or vegetation Construction of scattered city-type houses Drilling of well Disposal of domestic and sanitary wastes	Decrease in transpiration and increase in peak storm runoff. Increased siltation of streams. Some lowering of water table. Some local additions to soil water and contamination of aquifers
Transition from early urban to middle-urban stage	
Bulldozing of land for mass housing topsoil removal	Accelerated land erosion, stream sedimentation and aggradation. Elimination of smallest streams.
Construction of housing estates, paving of streets and building of stormwater drains Discontinued use and abandonment of shallow wells	Decreased infiltration, increased flood flows, lowered ground water levels, reduced base flows.
Diversion of nearby streams for public water supply	Decrease in runoff between points of diversion and disposal.
Untreated or inadequately treated sewage discharged to streams	Water pollution and death of equatic biota. Water quality deterioration.
Transition from middle-urban to late-urban stage	
Percent of area roofed and paved increased by more intensive urban land use. Increasing waste discharges and import of water from other areas. Channelization. Provision of sewage treatment facilities. Larger, deeper groundwater wells. Increased industrial and commercial water use.	Intensification of high storm runoff peaks. Increased water pollution and consequent biological impacts. Increased flood damage. Changes in channel geometry and sediment load. Reduction of flooding in channelized reaches, more flooding down-stream. Further lowering of groundwater levels. Possible subsidence.
Transition from late-urban to urban renewal stage	
Removal of old mass housing and derelict industrial premises Landfill and reclamation: removal of old waste dumps. Revegetation. River Valley improvements	Increased infiltration and possible recovery of groundwater levels. danger of contamination by leachates from old noxious industrial wastes. Danger of erosion during reclamation. Possible changes in channel stability downstream. Stabilisation of hillslopes.

Note For a fuller version of this table see:
Douglas, I (1983) *The Urban Environment* (London: Edward Arnold) Table 5.2, pp. 60–61

ought to have played a much bigger role in the environmental issues of the 1970s. It must be ready to lead in the coming urban environmental crises. The schools and universities of the future will have to orient their teaching of the biological and earth sciences towards the conditions that the bulk of the world's people experience every day: those of complex urban areas. Physical geography will become that of the city first and that of mountains, forests, coasts, ice-caps and oceans second.

FURTHER READING

Some of the ideas discussed in this chapter are developed in more detail in Ian Douglas, *The Urban Environment* (London: Edward Arnold, 1983). Two other books provide useful general surveys: M. Hough, *Urban Form and Natural Process* (Beckenham: Croom Helm, 1984) and a collection of essays edited by I. C. Laurie, *Nature in Cities* (Chichester: John Wiley, 1979). For a detailed discussion of urban climatology, see H. E. Landsberg, *The Urban Climate* (New York: Academic Press, 1981). An illuminating study of the geomorphology of urban landscapes outside Western Europe is R. U. Cooke, D. Brunsden, J. C. Doornkamp and D. K. C. Jones, *Urban geomorphology in drylands* (Oxford: Oxford University Press, 1982).

PART IV
LANDSCAPES OF PRODUCTION

Introduction

The essays in this section are concerned with the re-making of economic geography. 'Economic geography' first appeared as a distinctive sub-discipline at the end of the nineteenth century, at a time when the so-called marginalist revolution was displacing political economy in favour of simply 'economics'. The suppression of the political had far-reaching consequences, of course, not least because it was combined with a shift away from the sphere of production to an analysis which centred on the system of exchange. Individuals were supposed to enter freely into price-fixing markets, where their transactions were regulated by price-signals to ensure that supply and demand curves would intersect to sustain a general equilibrium. Although these models described an undifferentiated world, a spaceless universe empty of human geography, they were nevertheless translated more or less directly into locational analysis in the middle decades of the twentieth century.

The essays in this section seek to reverse these manoeuvres by reclaiming some of the most vital traditions of political economy. All of them recognise that the economy cannot be studied in isolation; economic processes spiral in and out of cultural, social and political structures. All of them insist on the centrality of production to economic analysis; far from stasis and equilibrium, they chart a world in constant motion, riven by contradiction and struggle. And all of them accentuate the salience of spatial structure to the diversity of ways in which people make their living; the differences that make up human geographies are not so many exceptions to a general model but are instead structurally implicated in the transformation of the global space-economy.

Doreen Massey and **Richard Meegan** begin with a deceptively simple thesis and then seek to show how its focus on the spatial division of labour can illuminate the complex industrial geography of Britain. In their view, an approach of this kind clarifies the ways in which firms both produce and *use* spatial inequalities as part of their search for conditions favourable to profitable production and continued capital accumulation: in other words – and as a matter of fact rather than any special pleading on behalf of the discipline – *geography matters*. Their argument revolves around the identification of successive waves of investment and disinvestment in the economic landscape, which are combined in different ways to produce the contemporary mosaic of 'uneven development'. Seen in this light, as Derek Gregory argued in Chapter 1.4, areal differentiation is firmly back on the agenda of geographical inquiry: but the uniqueness of particular places now has to be explained through the changing systems of interdependence in which they are embedded.

John Harriss and **Barbara Harriss** develop a parallel argument about agricultural change in the Third World. They draw particular attention to the connections between the peasant household and the wider economy, and juxtapose the 'logic' of peasant production to the often contradictory imperatives of those social groups who seek to appropriate the surplus produced by the household. They also emphasise that this is about more than economics: the relations of production which they describe are *social* relations, and the restructuring of peasant agriculture necessarily reaches into the very heart of the local community. But they also track back in time and out across space to emphasise the *diversity* of agrarian economies. It makes little sense, so they suggest, to ship models of agricultural transformation from the First World to the Third World and expect them to survive the journey intact: the classical model of agricultural transition, however well it might work in explaining the rise of capitalism in Western Europe, is likely to break down on the unmade roads of Africa, Asia and South America.

In one sense, **Nigel Thrift** and **Michael Taylor** spin their argument across the other two chapters: they show that in the late twentieth century there can be no simple separation of First and Third Worlds. Their case rests on a spectacular example. They focus on multinational corporations, which function as planned economies in all but name: they have considerable economic and political power, and possess their own internal markets and transfer systems stretching across time and space. The geography of multinational corporations has been a stock-in-trade of economic geography for many years now, of course, but Thrift and Taylor go beyond the usual reconstructions to highlight the extraordinary volatility of these vast spatial systems and to pinpoint their impacts on particular places. In effect, they argue that there is an *historical geography* of multinational corporations.

In the wake of the world recession, when competition became still more cut-throat, most multinational corporations were obliged to rationalise their organisation and to reorganise and diversify their operations. Once they had slimmed down and sub-contracted many of their activities, the successful ones emerged as *global* corporations – 'cruisers' rather than 'battleships' – integrating production, administration and marketing on a global scale and wired in to the new international circuits of financial transfer. This restructuring took place on a large scale, but it was epicentred on the rise of world 'regional cities', control centres within the global information network, and its shock-waves were probably felt most acutely at the local level. 'Cities like Bristol and Kuala Lumpur are quite different in numbers of ways,' Thrift and Taylor observe, and yet 'their economic fortunes are tied together by the levels of activities of multinational corporations'. Here too differentiation and integration are two sides of the same coin.

4.1
Spatial Divisions of Labour in Britain

Doreen Massey and Richard Meegan
Open University and CES Ltd

Doreen Massey is Professor of Geography at the Open University. Her teaching and research interests focus on industrial geography, and her publications include *Spatial Divisions of Labour* and *Geography Matters!* (with John Allen). **Richard Meegan** works for CES Ltd., and his publications include *The Anatomy of Job Loss* (with Doreen Massey).

INTRODUCTION

Both the regional geography of the UK and the way in which we analyse it have been undergoing profound changes over the last two decades. In many ways the two things have been linked. Changes in the geography of employment posed questions which our old theories of industrial location and of regional inequality were quite incapable of answering. In this chapter, therefore, we are going to explore both sets of changes, albeit very briefly, and use an account of changes in Britain's industrial geography to highlight some of the ways in which analysis itself has been transformed. We begin, however, by enumerating some of the most important ways in which the analysis of industrial geography and of regional employment patterns have been developing.

Perhaps the most important change of all has been an increasing consciousness of the need to integrate a geographical analysis with an understanding of the process of *production* (see Lee, Chapter 2.4). This is the very first principle of what, in very general terms, can be called 'a spatial division of labour approach' which seeks to understand the role of space and spatial differentiation in the evolution of the production process and its attendant social relations (of ownership, control, function and status). Starting from the premise that production is distributed and organised systematically over space and that, in a fundamentally capitalist society, the system's rationale is the pursuit of profitable production, this approach attempts to clarify the way in which spatial inequality is both produced and used by firms in their search for conditions favourable for profitable production and continued capital accumulation. Central to the approach is the notion of waves or rounds of investment and disinvestment in the economic landscape. Successive waves of investment are attracted to locations offering adequate opportunities for profitable production, while locations in which these opportunities have been exhausted see a process of disinvestment set in motion. And, at any one point in time, the prevailing balance between these different rounds of investment and disinvestment is reflected in a particular form and pattern of geographical inequality. This geography is itself transformed in turn as new waves of investment respond to the potential it offers for continued capital accumulation (see Gregory 1.4).

SPATIAL DIVISIONS OF LABOUR: SOME UNDERLYING PRINCIPLES

There are a number of important features of the way in which the nature and dynamics of spatial uneven development are conceptualised in this approach. In the following six paragraphs we simply list six further principles which follow from the primary focus on production.

The 'spatial division of labour' approach explicitly links regional and local development to processes operating at broader spatial scales. As we have already argued, the spatially-selective layering of rounds of investment is seen as the outcome of the continual search for profitable production and the approach recognises that this search, and the processes of capital accumulation which drive it, take place in a national and, as Nigel Thrift and Michael Taylor show in their chapter (Chapter 4.3), an international arena. The internal geography of the UK is influenced by, and itself influences, national and international economic development.

There is another point about this wider context, however, which is equally important. This is that it is not just an *economic* context which must be considered, but a whole constellation of technical, social, cultural and political factors. Industrial location and urban and regional industrial change are not just economic questions; industrial geography must not be separated off from wider issues of social processes and social geography. In many ways this means that the study of regional industrial change is now far richer and more integrated into developments in society as a whole.

An implication of all this is that ideas of what is an adequate 'explanation' in industrial geography have also been transformed. No longer is it adequate simply to point to lists of 'location factors' as an explanation of shifting patterns of employment. It also means, in particular, that the understanding of 'labour' as a location factor has been enriched and elaborated. The appreciation of the enormous complexity of 'labour', and of the way it is constructed and operates, as a location factor, is one of the important means by which industrial and employment geography have become far more closely integrated into an understanding of social changes more widely.

It is important, then, that the analysis of regional employment change takes as its starting point an understanding of wider social changes, at international, national and local level, than has perhaps previously been the case. But it is also important that we recognise the *active* role that geography and geographical variation themselves play *within* those wider social and economic changes. Thus at any given time spatial differentiation, itself composed of the varied 'uniqueness' of different localities, may itself encourage further change, discourage some developments and/or actually modify the way in which the effects of a particular process are felt 'on the ground' in different locations. Similarly, firms may actively *use* geographical differentiation in their attempts to maintain viability.

We have mentioned the 'uniqueness' of localities. An important aspect of this approach is the way in which it attempts to hold together both an understanding of general processes of regional change – the broad patterns – with an appreciation that within those broad patterns specific regions and localities retain their individuality, though this itself will be transformed over time. Local uniqueness, it is argued, is constructed within a wider system of interdependencies, within wider spatial divisions of labour. The individuality and uniqueness of different localities is seen as reflecting, on the one hand, the effects of the successive layering of different rounds of investment and as acting, on the other hand, as a potential catalyst for future rounds of investment. Moreover, this individuality is rooted firmly in a wider system of interdependence in which the development of one location is inextricably tied in with that of another. And what that means is that the 'success' of one region may well be dependent on the 'failure' of others. A change in analytical approach, therefore, both by linking regional employment change to wider changes in society and by stressing the interdependence of 'unequal' places also changes our understanding of the policies necessary to attack urban and regional problems. No longer can we rest content with policies which seek merely to shift 'jobs', undifferentiated by type, from one part of the country to another.

Finally, the superimposition of different spatial divisions of labour means that both the *pattern* of regional geography and the *form* of inequality may change over time. As the systems of interdependence change so will the roles that different places play within those wider systems. 'Urban and regional problems' are far more than questions simply of the *levels* of employment.

Seven principles in all, then, which underlie some of the ways in which the analysis of industrial geography has been changing. In the next section these principles are used in a brief exposition of the major shifts in the British 'regional problem' between the mid-nineteenth century and the early 1960s. In the third and final section we examine them in greater detail in the context of the most recent transformations since the mid-1960s.

FROM INDUSTRIALISATION TO DECLINE

It was during the depression of the inter-war years – with its still haunting images of demoralised unemployed workers slouched on the street corners of Northern industrial towns and the Hunger Marchers converging on the relatively prosperous South – that the phrase 'the regional problem' became firmly fixed in the political and social lexicon. The geography of the depression was particularly stark, with glaring disparities in living standards between the 'depressed areas' and the rest of the country. How, then, can the idea of 'spatial divisions of labour' help throw light on this traumatic example of spatial uneven development? For a start, it forces one to look for explanation outside the 'depressed areas' themselves. To understand their depressed state it is necessary to understand Britain's changing position in the international division of labour and the implications of this for the particular geography of production that had been created by the rounds of investment of early industrialisation.

Industrial revolution and sectoral spatial concentration

Britain's leading position in the world's political economy was established by colonial appropriation and reinforced by industrialisation. The country was gradually incorporated into a new international division of labour; a shift which involved the transformation of a largely self-sufficient agricultural-based domestic economy into one dominating, but at the same time increasingly dependent upon, world trade in the new manufactures of the 'Industrial Revolution'. Britain, in the middle of the nineteenth century, was indeed the 'Workshop of the World'. But this workshop was itself based on a particular geographical organisation of production, a particular spatial division of labour. The mechanised factories producing the goods for the world market, being largely steam-powered, developed near to supplies of coal and water. Areas came to specialise in particular industries and the production of particular goods. The mining villages in the coalfields of Durham, Lancashire, the Midlands, South Yorkshire and South Wales provided the basic fuel for the factories. The West Riding of Yorkshire became synonymous with woollen manufacture and Lancashire with cotton. Steel meant Sheffield, while Northumberland and Durham in the North East and the Clyde in Scotland built the ships that dominated the world's merchant and military fleets.

In many traditional accounts of this growth of regional specialisation in particular branches of production great stress is placed on the geography of natural resources. Coal and water in these accounts are often seen as the dominant 'location factors' determining the geography of production. What such explanations miss, however, is the fact that the location factors in question were only important, and can only really be understood, in the context of a broader historical process. Coal and water were being exploited by a factory system at an early stage in its development. The relatively undeveloped state of its production technologies and the correspondingly undeveloped division of labour effectively called for the geographical concentration of the whole process of sectoral production. Thus, the owners, managers and workers in the different sectors were all to be found in the regions in which production was concentrated. Such a spatial division of labour can be called '*sectoral spatial concentration*'. Moreover, this production was geared towards, and integral in the development of, a national and international market economy. It was in precisely this context that coal, for example, was so important; both for direct export and in the manufacture of goods for sale abroad.

Sectoral spatial concentration in these industries was inextricably linked with the broader international division of labour, its further development being reliant upon the country's continuing economic and political domination of world trade. The Great Depression of the 1880s provided a first glimmer of just how tenuous this link was. Increasing restrictions on exports to overseas markets (at a time when the domestic market remained unprotected) and growing competitive pressures from rapidly industrialising countries like Germany and the United States, depressed Britain's basic industries. It was the period between the two World Wars, however, when the country's vulnerability to recession in the world economy became most dramatically apparent.

The Depression and uneven development

The First World War completely disrupted international trade, and after it was over the basic industries were unable to regain their previous shares of the world market as countries previously important for imports switched to domestic production and raised protective barriers. Trade was further depressed as the impact of the financial crash in the now dominant United States reverberated throughout the world economy, revealing at the same time as it shattered the close integration and interdependence of the economies of the industrialised nations. But the story does not end with these international economic developments. Domestic politics also had a decisive role to play.

Thus it was a *political* decision by the government of the day to keep the country on the Gold Standard. The result was an over-valued pound which restricted exports in general and dealt, in particular, a near-fatal blow to the coal-exporting regions. This serves to reinforce our plea for an approach to the geography of industry which integrates economic and wider social processes. The economic plight of the 'depressed areas' of the inter-war years (or for any other period) cannot be understood in isolation from the broader social and political context.

Given the dominant spatial division of labour – sectoral spatial concentration – it was the Northern industrial regions, once the source of the nation's prosperity, which bore the brunt of domestic retrenchment and contraction.

And given the prevailing sexual division of labour in the sectors most seriously affected, and the patriarchal nature of social and political life more generally, the 'regional problem' of the time came to be defined by localised concentration of unemployed male workers. In this way, then, the 'regional problem' is best understood as the social expression of Britain's declining status as a world economic and political power, and the associated decline in the productive base that had helped to bolster its original pre-eminence.

Yet, overall, the economy was still growing, albeit at a much slower rate, and new layers of investment in a wide range of new industries were being put into place. And just as the decline of the old rounds of investment had been spatially specific, so too was the growth of the new. The bulk of the new investment took place in the South East and the Midlands, whose large concentrations of population provided both a potentially major market for the rapidly growing consumer goods industries and a 'new' source of factory labour. The transformation was dramatic: from having the highest rates of unemployment at the outset of World War One, London and the Home Counties had the lowest in the depths of the 1930s slump.

The inter-war period thus marked the beginnings of a major shift in the pattern of regional interdependence within the UK, with the erosion of the previously industrially dominant position of the Northern regions and the rise of new manufacturing centres, particularly in the conurbations of the South East and the West Midlands. A new pattern of sectoral spatial concentration was thus taking shape – led by different sectors in different regions – in which spatial uneven development was reproduced. The domestic political response was a first attempt at regional policy, but in the end international political developments proved to be far more influential. It was rearmament for World War Two which resuscitated the North's basic industries. And, after the war, the political emphasis on engineering for export and reliance on coal for fuel extended this reprieve – but not for long.

Post-war rounds of investment

The recession of the late 1950s saw the resumption of heavy job loss in the industries and regions that dominated the sectoral spatial concentration of early industrialisation. And the politics of the time were again important. Thus cutbacks in the coal-mining industry were intensified by the growing substitution of oil for coal – a shift motivated as much by the political desire to reduce dependence on the latter as by the then relative cheapness of the former. Meanwhile, the waves of investment that the manufacturing conurbations had received in the inter-war period were being 'topped-up' by further rounds, particularly in vehicles and electrical engineering, and by the growth in both State-run service sectors (education and health) and private ones (especially retailing). But the resumption of decline in the old basic industries and the reinforcement of growth in the Southern half of the country did not lead to the opening of a 'North-South' divide anywhere near as wide as it had been in the inter-war years, because of the further evolution of the spatial division of labour in which the Northern regions were integrated in a new way.

The 1950s and early 1960s were a period of unprecedented growth, and geography had an important role to play in this expansive growth. The 'depressed areas' of the 1930s received a large share of manufacturing investment in the immediate post-war years, in many cases in the ordnance factories set up as part of war-time dispersal of production. And the 1950s and early 1960s saw further investment in the branch factories of expanding sectors like engineering and clothing. The question is, of course, 'Why did these investments go to the peripheral areas?' Much of the answer lies in the problems (for industry) which were developing within the existing division of labour. The dominant position of the South East and Midlands in the sectoral spatial concentration of the inter-war years, reinforced by post-war manufacturing expansion, meant employers in these regions were faced with an increasingly 'overheated' labour market. The relative strength of labour in the central regions, together with heightened 'militancy' and wage claims, put increasing pressure on costs. Firms were increasingly adopting multi-plant structures and the siting of branch plants in the peripheral areas, with the latter's abundant and relatively cheap labour, provided them with both a flexible and an economic means of expanding capacity.

Regional policy also had a role to play in this investment – with, for example, the siting of car plants in Scotland and Merseyside and steel works in Scotland and South Wales being perhaps the most notable examples. And it was these new waves of manufacturing investment, in the context of extensive national growth, which did much to lessen the impact of the continuing decline of the old basic industries and which help to explain why the 'North-South' divide was not as pronounced as it had been in the 1930s.

But by these means new regional interdependencies were being formed and a new spatial division of labour was beginning to take shape. Central to this was the increasing 'external control' of production in the peripheral regions. The new investment in the latter was increasingly in the shape of branch plants controlled from Head Offices located predominantly in the central regions. In this aspect of the evolving spatial division of labour, then, there was a major transformation of existing social relations of production within the peripheral regions, with the gradual removal of the functions of ownership and control as part of the new form and pattern of regional inequality. Moreover, the new branch plants in the peripheral areas – in terms of production and labour processes, employment and occupational breakdown and broad function in their companies' overall production set-up – were much the same as their counterparts in the same sector in the central regions. They were 'clones' of each other, each branch in general producing a whole product or group of products and the employment structure of the different branches, in which male employment frequently dominated, was therefore the same.

THE LAST TWENTY YEARS

Since the mid-1960s the urban and regional geography of the UK has been undergoing a further transformation. The structural changes in internal geography, once again, can only be explained in the context of wider changes, both nationally and internationally.

Since the 1960s and the end of the long boom, the weaknesses of Britain's economic structure have become increasingly apparent. The UK's place in the international division of labour – itself changing – has been shifting, and this has had dramatic effects on the country's internal geography. But it has not been a single or simple continuous shift; there have also been major changes within the period, in the relation between the British economy and the world economy, and in political strategies within Britain. And these changes too have had their geographical repercussions within the country. From the start, then, both international context and national politics must be fundamental to our analysis.

The period between 1963 and 1973 was distinctive in many ways. While the British economy was clearly in trouble the world economy was still growing. The Wilson government was committed to a relatively interventionist strategy for economic recovery, with the emphasis on science and technology, on the physical modernisation of capital, and on size (big was beautiful). To complement this strategy of 'modernisation' there was also a policy of social-democratic reform – there was public sector growth, and a relatively active regional policy. All these characteristics of the period had implications for the changing geography of the country.

There were a number of elements to this changing geography, and we can only deal with a few of them here.

Decline and decentralisation

One of the most important changes was a dramatic decline in jobs for men in the old industrial peripheral regions (now designated Development Areas). In particular, there was a major loss of jobs in coal-mining. It is a loss which can only be understood in a political context, for it was intimately related to Wilson's strategy of 'modernisation', one element of which was the 'up-dating' of old, basic sectors of the economy (often nationalised or soon-to-be-nationalised). In some areas, such as Durham, the result of this element of national political economic strategy was a massive loss of what were then relatively well-paid jobs for men, in regions highly dependent on such jobs and sectors.

A second major change in the industrial geography of the country was the, now notorious, relative decentralisation of jobs from the South East and West Midlands towards both the Development Areas in particular and less urbanised areas more generally. As is now well documented, these jobs (in industries such as electrical engineering, electronics, clothing and services, including arms of the Central Government) were largely low-paid, designated as low-skill and low status and for all these reasons largely assigned to women. They were often the 'production-only' branch-plants of wider organisations. The question we must ask is: why did this decentralisation take place? One answer frequently given is 'regional policy and cheap female labour': in other words an answer in terms of location factors. Once again, our approach would be to say that while both of these were important, they were only *factors* in a wider process. And any real *explanation* has to get to grips with understanding that *process*.

One way into this is by asking 'why did the decentralisation take place *then*?'. Already this helps us refine our answer, and enables us to see 'location factors' as both socially-constructed and as part and parcel of wider changes. In a sense, both of these location factors were indeed relatively new in their operation. For political, as well as economic, reasons regional policy had recently been strengthened. Wilson came to power with a solid pro-Labour vote in the coal-mining areas, yet his strategy of modernising the pits was clearly going to throw out of work many members of his social and political base. The evidence is that regional policy was one way of cutting through this contradiction. There would be losses in mining, but regional policy would see to it that new jobs arrived in the regions. For the government this therefore helped push through one arm of national economic strategy, and had the additional potential advantage, by spreading employment more evenly across the country, of undermining the bargaining power of workers, particularly in the West Midlands, where labour markets were 'tight' (that is, where labour was in a relatively strong position). Nonetheless, from their point of view, male unions in the regions saw the increase in regional policy as some kind of victory, or at least compromise. It was therefore ironic when the jobs which arrived were low paid and 'for women'.

It was doubly ironic because in many ways that second location factor, 'cheap female labour', was itself constituted, or certainly increased, precisely by the decline in jobs for men which regional policy was supposedly to help rectify. The story is now well known. These coal-mining regions are typified by particularly patriarchal relations: women had been confined even more than usual to the private sphere, there had been little paid work available for them. In part this in turn resulted from the character of the jobs for men. There was little paid work for women in part because there was so much unpaid domestic labour to be done as wife or mother of miners; shift-work increased the difficulties of both partners in a couple working outside the home; and the very 'masculinity' of the jobs men did (after women had been specifically barred from doing them) contributed to the patriarchal mythology and the confinement of women to the home. All of which meant two things: first, that the decline of jobs for men made it both more possible and more necessary for women to find paid employment (that is, it helped create the reserve of female labour, the much quoted 'location factor') and, second, it created a reserve – very attractive to industry – of green labour, without direct previous experience in capitalist relations of production (see also McDowell, Chapter 2.3).

It may seem that we have come a long way from the decentralisation of jobs from central to peripheral regions. Yet our whole point is that you *have* to go a long way (indeed this is already a simplified account) – for changes in industrial geography can only really be understood, not by citing a handful of location factors, but by analysing them as an integral element in wider changes in society as a whole.

Moreover, there is also a whole other thread in the answer to the question 'why did decentralisation take place at that time?'. For not only were there changes in the geography of location factors, there were also, even more importantly, changes going on in industry itself. And here changes at the international level become integral to the explanation. For large sectors of British industry were at this time facing increasing international competition. The clothing industry in London, for instance, found itself caught between two changes in the international division of labour. On the one hand it was increasingly under threat from cheaper imports, and consequently needed to cut its costs. On the other hand, the young women on whom it was accustomed to rely for its labour force were increasingly being attracted by jobs in London's burgeoning international financial and service industries. The clothing industry could not afford the wages to stop them leaving. Many large firms moved out, seeking cheaper labour elsewhere, either in the peripheral regions of Britain or in the Third World. In other industries, such as electrical engineering/electronics, the decentralisation also involved changes in the technology of production. Changes in location and changes in production were often mutually-reinforcing, the technological change enabling locational change by shifting the nature of labour-demand, and the locational change enabling management to introduce the technological change without the possibility of open confrontation with unions.

What is important to notice here is that in both these sectors, and in many others of the British economy at this time, industry was actively using geography, in this case locational change, as part of its strategy for survival in the face of increasingly hostile international conditions. Geographical change was not simply an effect of the problems of the British economy, it was one element in British industry's attempt to combat those problems.

This single example, of decentralisation of jobs, has therefore demonstrated the first five of the seven principles we mentioned in the opening sections. It is necessary to examine changes in production; it is necessary to examine processes at different spatial scales, including the international; these processes are not only economic; and it is only as part of such processes that we can use 'location factors' as an element of a real explanation; and finally 'geography' was an active element in the changes and not merely their passive outcome.

The net result of all these shifts was, of course, significant social change. In the industrial peripheral regions the old, male, heart of the working class, and of the labour movement, was severely fragmented. The balance between male and female employment changed. And there were signs, possibly reflected in the Womens' Action Groups of the 1984/5 coal strike, of a shift in gender relations and the emergence of women on to the industrial and political scene. Over the course of a century and a half these regions have radically changed their positions in the national and international divisions of labour. No analysis of their changing industrial structure, nor of their evolving social and cultural characteristics, can ignore this changing interrelationship with the wider world. The 'uniqueness' of these regions is precisely bound up with (which is not to say totally explained by) their place in a wider system of interdependencies.

That it is 'uniqueness' can be illustrated by the fact that the same new 'layer of investment', the decentralisation of jobs for women, also affected other regions. The South West is an example. It too was increasingly drawn into the position of being a production-only branch-plant outpost, with growing numbers of jobs similar to those also decentralising to the coalfields. But here the social and economic effects were entirely different. This is an illustration of the sixth principle which we outlined at the beginning. The same *general process* (the decentralisation of jobs for women) was combined with different existing unique characteristics in different places, and different *unique outcomes* resulted.

The decline in well-paid jobs for men in the old coalfields, and the growth of jobs for women both there and in many of the non-conurbation areas of the country, were two elements in the changing spatial division of labour in Britain in the 1960s and early 1970s. There were many other elements, too, none of which there is room to deal with in detail here. But there is one point worth stressing: that this is not a 'deterministic' approach. This has already been hinted at in one way in the discussion of uniqueness – local outcomes are not mechanistic results of processes going on at wider spatial scales. On the contrary, both the outcomes and the general processes themselves are moulded by what is going on at local level. Further, the spatial changes we have documented cannot simply be accounted for by 'the recession' (any more than they can be by 'location factors'). Rather they are explained by industry's and the government's particular responses (in which spatial change was integral) at that time *to* the recession. They are not, in other words, an automatic response to 'wider economic forces', but the result of a response to those forces which has been channelled through political interpretation and, more generally, the state of play of social relations.

Two other major geographical changes in this period can also be seen in this light: the growth of a high-tech 'sunbelt' and the increasingly heightened degree of spatial concentration of upper managerial strata in and around the London area are clear reflections of the understanding at the time, in industry and in government, of the way out of Britain's economic problems – new technology and a more concentrated ownership pattern, a strategy of technocratic modernisation, were to be the saviours of UK industry.

All this together meant that considerable changes took place in the pattern of uneven development within Britain. Regional sectoral specialisation was reduced as were, on some measures, inter-regional unemployment relativities. As the social structure changed so did its geography, in particular with the increasing spatial concentrations of the growing technological-professional and managerial strata. Nor was it just that changes in the social structure produced a new geography. 'Geography' had its own influence on the nature of the social structure itself. While changes in production enabled, for instance, the geographical separation of R and D from the shop-floor, the spatial separation which emerged must surely in its turn have reinforced the social separation.

Changing forms of inequality

Nor was it only the *pattern* of uneven development which was changing; so also was the *form* of its underlying social relations (our seventh principle!). The most obvious aspects of this were perhaps the combination of the increasing degree of external control with the increasing separation between regions of different parts of the production process within the same industry. The electronics industry provided the archetypal industry with its (not totally unrealistic) caricature of a single company with headquarters in London, R and D along the M4 Corridor or around Cambridge, and production in a Development Area. This, then, is a more complicated set of inter-regional interdependencies than the simple branch-plant structure which dominated inter-regional company-forms in the 1950s. In this 'part-process' inter-regional geography the problems of peripheral regions are different. These regions continue to be subject to external control, but now they are not part only of an administrative hierarchy which is controlled elsewhere, they are also tied in to a very definite, company-specific, *production* hierarchy (see Thrift and Taylor, Chapter 4.3).

Intra-national locational change was one element in British industry's, and the British government's, strategy for economic recovery in the 1960s and early 1970s. By the last years of the latter decade it was clear that this technocratic, social democratic route had not worked. While elements of the changes of the earlier period continue to be important, the dominant geographical changes in the 1980s are very different from those of twenty years ago. There are many reasons for this. The international context is very different. Since 1973/4 British economic decline has been set against a world economy which is itself in a fluctuating state of crisis. Moreover, within Britain the dominant political understanding of that decline, and of how to deal with it, has shifted radically. Monetarism and anti-interventionism in the economy have replaced planning, technology and social reform.

One obvious element of this, and one with clear geographical implications, concerns state expenditure. Wilson's strategy of modernisation, for which the short-term price was going to have to be paid by the working class in terms of job-loss and wage-restraint, was coupled with a programme of social-democratic reform. State expenditure in areas such as health and education increased considerably. So did employment. Indeed, these sectors were the only cases in the 1960s where major employment changes did not exacerbate the newly-emerging forms of spatial inequality. In health, social services and education the geography of job quality, as well as numbers, is probably more equal than in any other sector of the economy (which is not to say that there is social equality within these sectors, but simply that the different strata are spread more evenly geographically). The cutbacks in the 1980s are thus reducing the effectiveness of one of the only countervailing tendencies to the newly-increasing forms of spatial inequality. In particular they are reducing the main source of skilled jobs for women in 'the regions'. Nor is there now an active regional policy.

More generally, the combination of the changing international economic situation with the changing internal political situation has meant that many of the processes of change of the 1960s are now very much more muted. Since the late 1970s the dominant change in the geography of the British economy has been brought about by *deindustrialisation*. The loss of manufacturing jobs has spread from the inner cities, to the outer cities, to whole regions – such as the West Midlands and the North West – to include even some of the plants established in the decentralisation of only twenty years before. Although in many ways a clear geographical pattern, the geography of deindustrialisation again cannot be explained by 'location factors'. In this case, on the whole, the pattern of job-loss has been moulded by characteristics of *production* (where the oldest plants are, for instance, and in which the highest levels of trades-union organisation) more than characteristics of *location*. Once again, therefore, the major change in the geography of industry can best be analysed in the context of *international* shifts, a changing *political* climate, and the characteristics of *production* itself.

Once again, too, the changing geography of industry is not just the *result* of these wider processes – it is part and parcel of them. To take an example: it is clear from what has been said already that trades-unionism in the UK has taken a severe battering during the recession. Two of its old geographical heartlands (the heavy-industrial peripheral regions and the major conurbations) have been particularly hard-hit by employment decline. At times, indeed, differential levels of union organisation and/or militancy have been an element in determining the geography of job-loss. Capital has used locational change, whether actual or relative, not only to reduce its costs but also to combat union power. Moreover, the same process is underway even in the areas of growth in the 1980s British economy. The M4 Corridor and the Cambridge area have become notorious for their low levels of unionism. There are many factors contributing to this, including for instance the nature of the new labour processes, but among those factors are undoubtedly the specific history of the areas, and their very separation from the old regions of industrial trades-unionism. Further, even in those areas of industrial trades-unionism, and in particular the old industrial development areas, such is the desperation for jobs that, given that 'regional policy' is based on areas competing against each other, 'sweetheart agreements' between single unions and management are now increasingly common, as a means of workers in one area (and union) winning jobs at the expense of those in another.

Britain's changing place in the international division of labour reinforces this process with, for example, Japanese companies bringing with them their own forms of social relations. The future of industrial relations in Britain is a contested arena in which 'geography' is a central component. In this, and many other ways, spatial reorganisation is not just a reflection of, but an integral element in, wider social change.

FURTHER READING

The approach outlined in this essay is described and developed in much more detail in Doreen Massey and Richard Meegan, *The Anatomy of Job Loss: the how, why and where of employment decline* (London: Methuen, 1982) and Doreen Massey, *Spatial Divisions of Labour: social structures and the geography of production* (London: Macmillan, 1984). For a sympathetic critique and extension, see Alan Warde, 'Spatial change, politics and the division of labour', in Derek Gregory and John Urry (eds) *Social Relations and Spatial Structures* (London: Macmillan, 1985) pp.190–212. A useful collection of essays which charts other aspects of the 'new economic geography' is Allen Scott and Michael Storper (eds) *Production, Work and Territory* (London: Allen and Unwin, 1986).

4.2
Agrarian Transformation in the Third World

John Harriss and Barbara Harriss
University of East Anglia and University of Oxford

John Harriss is Senior Lecturer in Development Studies at the University of East Anglia. He has carried out extensive field research on agrarian problems in India, Sri Lanka and Indonesia. He is the author of *Capitalism and Peasant Farming: agrarian structure and ideology in northern Tamil Nadu*; and editor of *Rural Development: Theories of Peasant Economy and Agrarian Change*.

Barbara Harriss studied geography and agricultural economics at Cambridge, and then taught geography at the Cambridgeshire College of Arts and Technology before starting the practice of field economics, particularly on agricultural marketing, in India, Sri Lanka and Bangladesh. She has taught the social science component of a master's degree in applied nutrition at the London School of Hygiene and Tropical medicine, and is now Lecturer in Agricultural Economics at Oxford University. She is the author of *The Marketing of Foodgrains in the Sudan-Sahelian States of West Africa, Transitional Trade and Rural Development, State and Market* and of *Exchange Relations and Poverty in Dryland Agriculture.*

PEASANT PRODUCTION AND ECONOMIC DEVELOPMENT

The historical geography of the advanced capitalist countries may be understood as the story of the dissolution of peasant production. While there was considerable variety in the organisation of rural production in Europe in the pre-industrial era,[1] and though changes took place in different ways and over different periods, it is possible to interpret them in terms of the model of 'agrarian transformation' which we lay out in this essay. Our interest, however, is in the analysis of economic and social change in the 'Third World', and a major theoretical and empirical question concerns the relevance of this essentially historical model of transformation to the study of contemporary development. The conception of agrarian transformation that we elaborate must not be treated in a deterministic fashion. The future of the Third World cannot be read off from the future of medieval Europe, as we show in the later sections of the essay (see Taylor, Chapter 5.1 for a more general discussion of this question).

Peasant production has two defining characteristics:

a) It is carried on by people who are themselves workers, engaged in cultivating the land but who are also owners of at least some of the resources, the tools and equipment (the 'means of production') which they use.[2] Although they are labourers therefore, the circumstances of their labour are substantially different from those of people who are employed in places of work and who use resources and equipment belonging to somebody else. The main objective of such peasant producers is to satisfy their own livelihood requirements and usually those of their households, for a household is commonly the basic unit of both production and consumption in peasant society.[3] They may meet livelihood requirements either by the direct production of food and raw materials, or by selling what they produce in order to purchase their necessities or, of course, by a combination of both. Further, although labouring with resources which they own is characteristic of peasant producers, it is possible that at some times both adult women and men and sometimes their children also work for other people in return for some kind of remuneration (food, beer, money) and in turn that they engage others to work for them. Producers of this broad type have existed over long historical periods and over large parts of the world.

b) The second important characteristic is that peasants have usually been subordinated politically and economically to other groups within the societies of which the peasants have formed a majority: groups like landlords, merchants or urban based political leaders to whom a part of the peasant produce has had to be handed over in the form of rents, tithes or taxes.

STRUCTURAL TRANSFORMATION AND THE DISSOLUTION OF PEASANT PRODUCTION

This form of production has tended to be dissolved (broken down and replaced) in the course of modern history with the development of capitalist industrialisation (see Lee, Chapter 2.4, for a more general discussion). Historically, economic development has involved increasing specialisation of economic activity, and (often) the formation of increasingly larger units of production, taking advantage of economies of scale. Together with these changes in the scale and specialisation of activity, there has been a major change in its location too, as spatial concentration has occurred and urbanisation has accelerated.[4]

Now it is generally true that the economies of poorer countries are predominantly rural, with a very large share of their labour forces engaged in agriculture (see Table 4.2.1).[5] Economic development may therefore be conceptualised as entailing a transformation of the structure of a society and economy, such that fundamental shifts occur in the type, quantity and location of production and in the way in which the labour force is employed.[6] The continuing predominance of the peasant form of production in a society is evidently antithetical to this transformation.

Historically there has been a major movement of people out of such agricultural production and into other activities. Peasant agriculture has supplied workers, either encouraged to leave the land by the possibility of higher incomes in non-agricultural employment or forced to leave by loss of the ownership of the means with which to work themselves, and by the absence of alternative means of livelihood. This same process has helped to create a market for the products of specialised manufacturing, as increasingly more people have become dependent upon purchased goods instead or upon things produced domestically. A further, vital aspect of the transformation is that some 'surplus' (production above that which is immediately required for the reproduction of the producing unit) is transferred from rural peasant production into non-agricultural activities. Without such a transfer of resources it will generally be impossible for these other, increasingly specialised activities to become established. Agriculture must supply food and raw materials, some of them perhaps for export, and often resources for investment as well. The latter may be mobilised through taxation, from the savings made by rural producers with surpluses or by means of an invisible transfer, such as takes place when the 'terms of trade' – the relative prices of agricultural and non-agricultural goods – move against agricultural commodities.

Economic development in the now advanced economies, and the process of structural transformation which it has entailed has thus been intrinsically bound up with the expansion of the monetised, market economy. And expanded commercialisation has tended, historically, to bring about a dissolution of the peasant form of production. It is this process which is referred to as 'the agrarian transformation', and it may be seen as both a condition for and a consequence of economic development.

COMMERCIALISATION AND PEASANT PRODUCTION

Commercialisation means that people must sell at least some of what they produce and purchase some of their requirements. It depends to some extent

TABLE 4.2.1 *Basic development indicators*

	Population (millions) mid 1981	*GNP per caput* US $ 1981		*Share of GDP originating in agriculture*		*Percentage of labour force in agriculture*	
		US $ 1981	*Av. Annual growth % (1960–81)*	*1969*	*1981*	*1960*	*1981*
Low income countries	2210.5	270	2.9	48	37	77	70
China and India	1681.5	280	3.5	48	33	74	69
Bangladesh	90.7	140	0.3	58	54	87	74
Ethiopia	32.0	140	1.4	65	50	88	80
Tanzania	19.1	280	1.9	57	52	89	83
Middle income countries	1128.4	1500	3.7	24	14	62	45
Zimbabwe	7.2	870	1.0	18	18	69	60
Korea (rep)	38.9	1700	6.9	37	17	66	34
Brazil	120.5	2220	5.1	16	13	52	30
Industrial market economies							
UK	56.0	9110	2.1	2	2	4	2
Japan	117.6	10080	6.3	13	4	33	12
USA	228.8	12820	2.3	4	3	7	2

SOURCE: World Bank (IRD), 1983, (4)

upon the creation of market places in the physical sense and of means of communication between them. Although markets have existed for a long time, even in parts of Africa (for example) which are sometimes thought to have been characterised by a purely 'subsistence' economy until this century,[7] the process of commercialisation has occurred rather rapidly in some parts of the world in the recent past. In Turkey, for example, accounts of rural conditions suggest that as recently as 1950 very many village people sold virtually nothing and purchased only small amounts of a very restricted range of commodities. By the end of the 1950s, however, and partly as a result of the development of infrastructure by the state, many more village shops had sprung up and both the amounts of produce marketed and the range of goods purchased by villagers had great increased.[8] Over the same period the Turkish industrial economy expanded substantially. Part of the reason for state investment in rural marketing infrastructure was in order to ensure that adequate supplies of food and agro-industrial raw materials flowed to the cities and were available for export to earn foreign exchange necessary for the finance of industrialisation.

As the commercialisation of a rural economy takes place, and purchased items enter increasingly into the domestic economy of peasant producers, this economy undergoes *commodification*. The whole circuit of reproduction of the household comes to depend increasingly upon buying and selling things, and ultimately land and labour also become 'commodities'.

The process of differentiation

Commodification is likely to increase the extent of socio-economic differentiation amongst the peasantry. Some societies of rural household producers (as in parts of Africa, for example, in the colonial period) have been relatively egalitarian, with only restricted differences in assets and income between women and men within households and between households. Others (like Indian society, organised around the strong social hierarchy of the caste system) have been markedly inegalitarian. But no matter what the extent or the kind of differentiation that existed historically, it is likely to be increased as commodification proceeds.[9] Some households, as they become more involved in production for the market (perhaps as a result of a need for cash to pay taxes imposed by the state), because of shortages of labour power at critical times, because of limitations in the amount or quality of land that they control, or as a result of sequences of bad years, or because of adverse terms of trade, become progressively less able to meet the costs of their essential requirements. Perhaps as a result of financial debts that they have incurred in trying to make ends meet, they are finally unable to retain control of land and other resources. They are thus *pauperised*. When they no longer own any of their own means of production, they have been *proletarianised*.

At the same time it is possible that some other peasant producers, by virtue of the resources at their disposal (such as the power to command more labour than others) are able to make profits from the sale of produce. They may then be able to purchase more land from others, or to make other kinds of investments so as to enter into a virtuous spiral of expanding income and investment, possibly diversifying and becoming (to give common contemporary examples) traders, bus operators, cinema owners, landlords of urban property, or even industrialists. They become members of the *bourgeoisie*, the class of property owners. Thus it comes about that the society of rural producers, from being one in which all or almost all households produce on their own account, is changed into one in which there are marked differences between those owning sufficient resources to be able to produce a surplus and to employ others, and those who no longer own the means of production and who must work for others. At a certain stage, of course, there may be many who still produce with their own means of production, existing alongside the rural bourgeois class and the rural proletarians.

We have just outlined a process which is generally known as the *differentiation of the peasantry*. It should be noted that while any society may be described as being 'differentiated' – that is as showing socio-economic differences – the term 'differentiation' is used here to refer to a *processual model* of the coming into being of quite distinct classes among rural producers as an outcome of commercialisation and commodification. The process is summarised in Figure 4.2.1.

The categories shown in Figure 4.2.1 refer to distinct classes among the peasantry. '*Rich peasants*' are those who, though they are still engaged in the work of cultivation themselves, employ others and may be able to realise surplus production over and above current consumption requirements. '*Poor peasants*', on the other hand, are those who work for others, certainly to a much greater extent than they employ other people to work for them. They are most unlikely to be able to realise surplus production for themselves, and are probably unable to meet their own livelihood requirements without engaging in wage work. '*Middle peasants*' are those who *both* hire and sell labour, or who may be able to make out with their own resources without having to rely extensively upon working for others, or needing to engage others to work for them. There is mobility between the classes, and the middle peasants in particular may be especially susceptible to movement downwards into the ranks of the poor and landless (tenant) peasants. Over time there may be a tendency towards the crystallisation shown in the diagram as the formation of a rural bourgeoisie in opposition to a proletariat. This represents the final dissolution of peasant production.[10]

The Green Revolution and the differentiation of the peasantry

Thus far we have presented an ideal typical model of agrarian transformation, and there are in fact very few parts of the world – if any at all – where differentiation and transformation have occurred in precisely the way we have described. Rather we have elaborated upon what appears to be entailed in

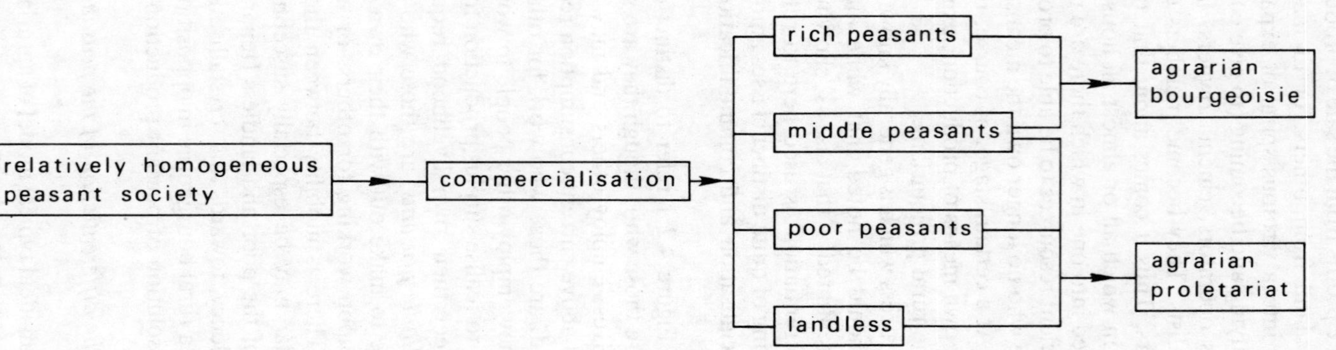

FIGURE 4.2.1 *The differentiation of the peasantry*

economic development involving increasing specialisation and scale of production. The model may be used in the analysis of the agricultural revolution in Britain,[11] or of the 'green revolution' in the Third World now. But the historical and geographical circumstances of these 'revolutions' are very different, and it is extremely important to take account of *context* when making use of models such as the one we have outlined.

The reality of the tendencies of differentiation may be appreciated, however, from analyses of the effects of the so-called 'green revolution' in Asia and Latin America in the 1970s. This term refers to the introduction of new agricultural technology consisting of initially imported higher yielding varieties of major food crops (especially wheat, maize and rice) in association with assured water supplies, with fertilisers and other agrochemicals generally required for their successful cultivation.[12] This new technology has often increased output levels, but the extent to which rural people have benefited from this is disputed. It seems that in many areas the new technology has made agriculture very much more profitable for some (mainly rich peasants, previously well-endowed with resources), but that it has actually contributed to the pauperisation of others. The basic reason for this has been that the use of the new technology has required much more involvement in markets than did the old. Seeds, fertiliser and chemicals, and often irrigation water, have had to be purchased where they were not before. While it is undoubtedly possible for peasants owning or renting only small pieces of land to take advantage of the productive potential of the new technology, it also needs only a little miscalculation or ill-luck with the weather, or with relative prices of inputs or outputs for the out-turn not to be commensurate with the cash input requirements of the new varieties, thus leading to indebtedness and perhaps to pauperisation. It is not of course the fact of producing for the market in itself which has this sort of effect, but involvement in commercial production under circumstances of already unequal access to and ownership of the means of production.[13]

We have shown that agrarian transformation may be understood as a condition and consequence of economic development, and observations of the effects of the 'green revolution' show how the process of differentiation may be encouraged by commercialisation. But the economic history of the advanced economies shows that some peasants survive, while patterns of agrarian transformation in the contemporary Third World appear to be highly diverse.

The introduction of the 'green revolution' technology has in fact etched out differences in the social relations of production in agriculture, and the patterns of change associated with them (on the concept of 'social relations of production' see Lee, Chapter 2.4), and it has intensified inter-regional contrasts. In India, for example, in the period which saw the introduction of the new technology:

> Agricultural growth began to be concentrated in the irrigated areas and assured rainfall regions, increasing rather than reducing in the process the income disparity that had already existed between these and the rest of the countryside . . . Irrigated areas in the major river basins such as those of the Indus and Ganges in the north, of the Godaveri and the Kaveri in the south, and some assured rainfall areas at the foothills of the Himalayas along the northern plains, Assam valley, and western coastal plains, all together covering about 14 per cent of the gross cropped area of the country . . . recorded more than five per cent per annum growth in their agricultural production over the trienniums 1962–63/64–65 to 1970–71/72–73. At the other end there were 25 per cent of districts located mostly in the regions of the central plateau and around its fringes together covering 27 per cent of the country's gross cropped area where agricultural production was in fact declining . . .[14]

Contrasts such as these result from the prioritisation of crops in agricultural research systems. Millets and pulses come low down the list and are allocated relatively fewer research resources, while they pose difficult technical problems for plant breeders and agronomists. These regional contrasts also reflect differences in the extent and rate of adoption of new technology and they are to be understood in terms of the different agro-climatic endowments of different regions, *and* variations in the social relations of production. We describe below circumstances in which the agricultural economy is dominated by mercantile capitalists, and explain how these may hold up the expansion of agricultural production. There are other factors involved too, including the characteristics of the technology itself (for example, higher yielding varieties of rice suitable for either the flood conditions or the seasonally drought-affected regions of Bengal have yet to be developed); and differences in the policies towards agriculture adopted by governments (which mean, for example, that wheat farmers in the Indian Punjab have received relatively more favourable prices for their wheat than the Bengali farmers for their rice).

In many cases it seems that transformation on the lines of our model is not taking place. In the remainder of this chapter we aim to provide a sketch map of the empirical diversity of agrarian economies.[15] We believe both that an adequate geography of agrarian economies must take account of the social relationships of production with which we are concerned here (set within a world-systems historiography something like that referred to in Taylor, Chapter 5.1); and that geographical research informed in this way may contribute to the elucidation of the empirical diversity. A vital geography of *pays* must often be concerned with the extent of, and the reason for, the persistence of peasant production as we have defined it.

THE LOGIC OF PEASANT PRODUCTION AND ITS SURVIVAL IN WESTERN AND EASTERN EUROPE

Peasant production, or rural petty commodity production – production that is carried on by direct producers (workers) who own the means of production – has persisted partly because it is a relatively 'efficient' form of production, especially in agriculture. It has come to be appreciated latterly that peasants may understand their environment much better than outside 'experts',[16] and that *resistance to government sponsored programmes for change may be due not to 'stupidity' or 'ignorance' but to a sound appraisal of technical constraints*.[17] In studies of agrarian change, as in other areas of geographical research, much more weight has come to be placed on understanding the ideas (and the significance) of the people actually involved in the social processes we study.

There is also a range of factors to which attention was drawn by A. V. Chayanov, an important Russian economist of the early part of this century.[18] Chayanov's work was rediscovered in the 1960s and thought to be of special relevance to Third World studies, because of similarities between the circumstances of late nineteenth-century Russia and present day (so-called) 'developing' countries. Chayanov pointed out that in peasant society the household is usually a unit both of production and of consumption. A number of consequences follow from this. Peasant producers' objectives are different from those of capitalists. The difference is simply expressed as follows:[19]

the capitalist firm accounts for itself in these terms:	the peasant household accounts for itself in these terms:
TVP-RM*:-CL = profits	TVP-RM = Total Returns

(where: TVP = total value of the product; RM = costs of raw materials used in production [and RM*: = these costs *plus* depreciation on fixed investment goods]; and CL = costs of labour – the wages or other costs of maintaining and reproducing labour)

The peasant household remains viable so long as total returns are at least equal to the actual subsistence costs of the labour necessarily used in the process of production. Peasant household production will be efficient so long as total returns remain equal to, or are greater than the *opportunity cost* of labour: or in other words greater than the income that the household workers could earn in alternative forms of employment. Rural petty commodity production can remain in existence so long as the total returns to producers are at least sufficient to permit them to reproduce themselves (that is to feed, clothe and shelter themselves well enough to allow them to survive). So long

can make a living which in their perceptions is at least equivalent to the alternatives available to them, they will remain engaged in this form of production. *But note that this means that they do not necessarily have to make 'profits' to remain producing*. They will work using their own means of production for the equivalent of a wage comparable to available alternatives. It may be argued that it is this characteristic of peasant production which makes it, in fact, a very suitable form of agricultural production from the point of view of urban, industrial capitalists because it means that agricultural products may become available at prices which reflect the costs of raw materials and wages and do not include an element of profit.[20]

At the same time there are reasons why capitalists may not find agricultural production an attractive avenue for direct investment, in particular its riskiness, its susceptibility to hazard and the fact that it is still subject to natural biological and climatic cycles, which make it difficult to speed up the rate at which money capital circulates. These reduce the possibilities of profit.[21]

It has also been possible for agricultural capitalists to take indirect advantage of some economies of scale without having to take land away from the direct control of peasant producers. This can be done via systems of *subcontracting*, under which peasant producers supply processing plants owned by a big firm. The Nestlé company offers one example. Already at the beginning of this century,

> It owned in Switzerland two big factories for making condensed milk and a factory for making malted milk. The latter . . . processes 100,000 litres daily, produced by 12,000 cows and coming from 180 villages. These 180 villages have lost their economic autonomy and have become subjected to the house of Nestlé. Their inhabitants still appear to be proprietors but they are not longer free peasants.[22]

Agribusiness corporations organise the production of many commodities in this way, supplying inputs to and exercising technical control over production carried out by apparently autonomous, individual, small farmers.

These are among the factors which account for the persistence of houshold petty commodity production in the advanced economies of Western Europe, in a context in which there has nonetheless been a major shift of the working population out of agriculture. It is noteworthy too that household production remains important even in those Eastern European economies where agriculture has been subject to collectivisation. In Hungary, for example, the private plots of collective farm workers and others are estimated to account for about one third of total agricultural production from only 12 per cent of the total agricultural land.[23] The organisation of the entire agricultural economy is based upon the interrelations of such small-scale production where labour is used intensively, and large scale collectivised units, specialised in the production of cereals and fodder crops, where mechanisation confers advantages to larger units.

PAUPERISATION AND THE PEASANTRY IN THE THIRD WORLD

The circumstances of the persistence of peasant production in Third World countries are varied and mostly rather different. Commercialisation and commodification were encouraged by the interventions of colonial states; in parts of sub-Saharan Africa like Tanzania and Zambia, for example, by road and rail building and by the imposition of hut and poll taxes which were partly intended to stimulate the formation of a wage labour force for work in plantations and in mines; or in the Indian subcontinent by policy on the taxation of land and later by the encouragement of railway construction and, in some areas, of irrigation, which opened the way to more specialised commercial cultivation.

Commercialisation and commodification have fostered the differentiation of peasant producers, but agrarian transformation has rarely proceeded so far as the elimination of petty commodity production. Rather are the agrarian economies of Third World countries characterised by masses of pauperised peasant producers.

Part of the reason for this is the high rate of population growth which restrains the overall rate of transformation of the social and economic structure:

> The Western European countries and Japan reached that 'structural transformation turning point' without any significant increase in the size of the agricultural labour force. The rates of growth of total population and labour force were only about 1-1.5 per cent, so that a moderate rate of growth of non farm employment was sufficient to absorb the annual additions to the labour force . . . Today's developing countries, however, are experiencing substantial growth in the size of their farm labour force because of rapid growth of total population and labour force combined with a high initial share of agriculture in the total labour force.[24]

At the same time the kind of industrial development which has been taking place in most developing countries, even where industrial growth rates have been at historically high levels, has not generated a high and substantial demand for labour. Where the emphasis has been on 'import-substituting industrialisation' (as virtually everywhere in Latin America, Africa and South Asia) capital equipment has had to be imported from the advanced economies. The type of machinery and equipment involved has been capital rather than labour intensive, biased against the employment of labour. Where rural people have been pauperised in ways like those depicted earlier and have left the countryside, it has often been to enter not full-time wage work but various kinds of casual and 'informal' work in big cities. Others have remained in the rural economy as landless wage workers earning minimal incomes.[25] There are then demographic and broader economic conditions which restrain the progress of agrarian transformation, conditions which substantially derive from the location of Third World countries within the world system (again see Taylor, Chapter 5.1).

Merchant capital

There are also conditions within the agricultural economy itself. Where there are large numbers of small producers, owning limited resources of land and equipment and operating in hazardous environments, there is a strong likelihood that they will come to be dependent upon advances of cash or raw materials from landlords, merchants or money lenders, or people who combine these functions. We call them *merchant capitalists* (as distinct from capitalists who directly organise and control production).

In India, for example, study of the economics of production on farms in different size classes shows that it is often *the smallest and the largest farms* which are most extensively commercialised and most dependent upon purchased inputs. But the significance of this market involvement is very different for the two types of farmer. The very small farm holders are primarily dependent on wage work for their livelihoods. They do not own sufficient means of production to be able to produce enough to live on, but they still sell relatively more of what they produce than do those who own somewhat more resources. Their sales do not constitute a marketable surplus because they subsequently have to buy back food, often at higher prices than they were able to obtain for their own sales. They are 'compulsively involved' in the market.[26] Their circumstances are such that they probably have to borrow, in cash or in kind, in order to obtain food during the lean periods of the year before harvests (and these periods may be prolonged where there is a long dry season and/or no irrigation facilities), or in order to meet the costs of production on their own small holdings. They are then compelled to sell their produce immediately after harvest in order to repay at least some part of the debts they have incurred.

Advances in cash or kind may have been obtained from richer landholders, from merchants, or from specialist money lenders. For the poor cultivator a vicious circle of persistent debt is easily entered, while for the landholder/ merchant capitalist supplier of credit it may be possible to get on to an escalator of profit. The landowner/merchant, for example, may obtain bulk supplies of agricultural produce at lowest prices during the post-harvest glut and subsequently may make speculative profits by waiting to sell in the lean season when prices rise. In parts of West Bengal, for example, the inter-seasonal price differences for paddy are 30 to 50 per cent, in parts of sub-Saharan Africa they may sometimes exceed 100 per cent.[27] It is not necessarily advantageous to the monied rural capitalist in such circumstances to foreclose on the debts of impoverished peasants. It is more profitable for them if they are able to appropriate the peasants' crops cheaply, than directly to take over agricultural production themselves. Calculation of the rate of profit in different activities in a region in south India helps to make this point (see Table 4.2.2).

TABLE 4.2.2 *Average rate of profit in sectors of the agrarian economy in North Arcot District, South India*

Sector	*Average annual rate of profit 1972–74 (%)*
Agricultural commerce (weighted av.)	24
Agro-processing (mainly rice milling)	15
Interest rates on money lending	12 – 25 (av. 18 – 20)
Agricultural production	4 – 11

SOURCE: B. Harriss, 1979, p.49

In these circumstances, many poor peasant producers may remain in existence by virtue of their relationships with merchant capitalists, who can profit more from trading than from productive investment in agriculture. And indeed the agrarian class structure of the South Indian region has remained fairly stable for a long time. The incidence of landlessness has increased – in 1891 there were only 2 labourers to 11 cultivators, while in 1971 there were 9 labourers for every 11 cultivators. But there is no evidence for increased concentration amongst the holders of land. A small class of rich peasant/merchant/money lenders nourished by its capacity to procure surplus from the great majority of small landholders (75 to 80 per cent of the total throughout the period) has exercised economic and political control over this rural economy for at least a century. The latters' ownership of resources is hardly sufficient, is frankly insufficient, to meet their livelihood requirements.[28] The dependence of peasant producers on monied capitalists, in circumstances like these, may mean they are not truly independent at all. The circuit of production becomes dependent upon advances. There are many instances of close control over commoditised production of inedible or agro-industrial crops being exercised by merchant capitalists, even though the actual work of cultivation is done by apparently independent petty producers.[29]

Such conditions lead to the reproduction of massive and widespread rural deprivation and poverty to the benefit of a class of landlords or rich peasants or merchant capitalists. Their economic and political power, and the conditions of rural poverty in themselves, probably constitute a major constraint upon the development of the national economy as a whole in some countries. The total supply of agricultural products is almost certainly less than it might be, because impoverished small cultivators are unable to improve the quality of their means of production. And deficiencies and fluctuations in agricultural supply limit the potentialities for development in the remainder of the economy.[30]

The economic growth linkages of agriculture

So long as these conditions remain in force it is difficult to see how the potential for economic growth that economists perceive, in principle, with 'green revolution' technology, can be realised.[31] Liberal economists argue that because the new technology consists essentially of seed and fertiliser, it is almost infinitely divisible and therefore neutral to scale. It should be possible for it to be used with approximately equal relative benefit by large and even very small farmers. The small increments in individual income that will follow will represent a massive increase in aggregate potential demand, thus stimulating the growth of other economic activities and setting the economy off into virtuous circles of highly employment-generative growth. It will thus hasten the structural transformation of the economy.

This is an attractive argument. But it neglects both the fact that it is sometimes difficult for those lacking finance like poor peasants to gain access to the new technology;[32] and the possibility that when they do make use of the new technology, the additional income derived from it flows predominantly to the landlord/rich peasant/merchant class upon which the mass of petty producers remains dependent because of their need for advances with which to pay for the technology. The consumption expenditure of the mercantile class is such as to generate only restricted growth of essentially luxury, not mass consumption goods, manufactured in a few metropolitan cities. Of course our argument is schematic and is not intended to imply that the 'green revolution' must necessarily, and in all places, run out in this particular way. But neither should the effects of the dominance of agrarian societies by small élites be ignored.

Production and reproduction

The continued existence of masses of pauperised peasants may be seen as functionally effective for certain large-scale capitalist enterprises, however, if not for general economic development. In conditions like those of much of Latin America, where there is a very marked contrast between the small number of large agricultural estates (*latifundia*) and the very large number of smallholdings (*minifundia*), it may be possible for the owners of the large estates and other enterprises to obtain supplies of wage labour at a very cheap rate. This is because the wage labourers (male or female) continue to produce a part of their means of subsistence from their own smallholdings. This is how domestic (predominantly female) productive and reproductive labour subsidises capitalist production. It is thus possible for governments to implement and maintain cheap food policies without depressing total output precisely because the availability of cheap or unvalorised (female) peasant labour keeps up the profitability of large-scale capitalist agriculture.[33] Where women are responsible for the production of staples (as in Africa where they are estimated to produce 60 to 70 per cent of all food),[34] their lack of title to land (and thus security for credit for new technology) and their lack of time for training (in a male-dominated system of agricultural extension) may help to explain the widespread stagnation of food production.

Another problem is, of course, that smallholding production is unstable. With population growth in circumstances of limited availability of land, holdings may be subdivided, and also pushed out into environmentally marginal areas for cultivation, such as hill slopes and arid regions, provoking environmental degradation.[35] This affects both productive resources (land) and reproductive resources (fuel and water) and the work burdens associated with them. In this way the ecological basis of smallholding production may be undermined. Part of the reason why governments have begun to intervene with the object of 'developing' smallholder agriculture, by implementing rural development projects which generally offer credit and new inputs, may be to try to ensure the continuation of a form of production which significantly subsidises capitalist development, as well as to satisfy political objectives.

Food crises

The human consequences of retarded agrarian transformation under the impact of commercialisation may be tragic, undermining the capacity of many rural households to provision themselves in such a way as to cope with food crises. In some regions this results from the replacement of patterns of mixed cropping by commercial monocropping. This has happened in Southern Chad, where it played a major part in causing famine in 1984:

> For the first time the south of Chad has not been spared. Certainly, in this region too, the rains were feeble and arrived late, but this is not the basic reason. If a part of the south is suffering from famine it is because, paradoxically, it is too rich. The cotton harvest of 1983-84, which reached 165,000 tonnes, was beyond expectations. The peasants then neglected their traditional crops, like millet, in order to cultivate cotton which was more profitable. In addition, a certain lack of foresight meant the peasants stored less than before (but this was at least in part because of military insecurity in the region) . . . Some Arab merchants have been able to

> speculate: purchased at 4,000 francs from the peasant, the market price of a sack of millet reached 25,000 francs CFA a few weeks later . . .[36]

This particular case illustrates general tendencies which play a part in the explanation of many famines: the breaking down of cropping patterns and cultivation and storage practices which permitted some protection against climatically-induced fluctuations (as happened in the Sahelian countries badly affected by drought and famine in the early 1970s);[37] and the consequences of speculative trading in foodgrains which include putting the price of staples beyond the reach of poorer people (which seems to have been the most important immediate cause of the disastrous Bengal famine of 1943).[38] Failure of rainfall and reduced output may play a part in the causation of famine, but it is the way in which this environmental factor is mediated through the particular social organisation of production and distribution of food (including distribution within the household) which is the catalyst of disaster. (See also Taylor's discussion of Watts's work on Famine in Hausaland, in Chapter 5.1 of this book.) The Chad example also reveals the importance of political and military upheaval. The Bengal famine of 1943 came about as a result of changes which were amongst the effects of World War Two upon the Indian economy; while the significance of civil war in Ethiopia, and of the military expenditure associated with it, in accounting for the existence of famine there has gradually come to be appreciated.[39]

CONCLUSION

We have shown how 'agrarian transformation' on the lines of the model we elaborated to begin with may effectively by blocked in the Third World, and have referred to some of the consequences of this. It cannot be emphasised too much, however, that there is enormous diversity in patterns of transformation. The geographical tradition emphasises the peculiarity of place, and the analysis of specific processes of agrarian change is a fruitful field for geographical research. We have suggested that such analysis must be dynamic and attempt to explain the way in which units of production are reproduced over time; and the relationships between types of activity and between classes of people which are involved.[40]

The main analytical aspects to which we have referred are these. First, the *technical nature of agricultural production* itself, and in particular its susceptibility to environmental hazard and its seasonal character.[41] Second, the predominant form of agricultural production is the *peasant household*, a petty commodity-producing unit in which workers themselves own some means of production. This imparts a specific logic to its activity. Empirical analysis must take into account the composition of households, the ways in which all household labour is used, and the ownership, control and use of other resources to meet livelihood needs. The analysis can then open up to consider the relationships between households. The third element in analysis is therefore that of *market relationships*, in which the way surplus is appropriated from peasant production is of major concern. The structure and behaviour of markets for inputs, peasant produce and consumer goods are relevant here. The analysis thus proceeds from the level of the household to that of the regional and national economy. The final element concerns the *relationship of agriculture with the rest of the national economy within the world economy*, where the terms of trade between agricultural and non-agricultural products will be found to explain many spatial phenomena.[42]

Acknowledgements

We would like to thank Gavin Williams, Derek Gregory and Rex Walford for their helpful comments on a draft of this chapter, although we alone are responsible for its final content.

NOTES AND REFERENCES

1. For a striking essay on the distinctiveness of the English agrarian economy, see A. Macfarlane, *The Origins of English Individualsim* (Oxford: Basil Blackwell, 1979).
2. The best general introduction to the study of peasants remain E. Wolf, *Peasants* (Englewood Cliffs, N.J.: Mc-Graw-Hill, 1966) and T. Shanin (ed.) *Peasants and Peasant Societies* (Harmondsworth: Penguin, 1981). See also the conceptual discussion in J. Harriss (ed.) *Rural development: theories of peasant economy and agrarian change* (London: Hutchinson, 1982).
3. There are valuable discussions of the varying nature of the household in Harriss (ed.) *op. cit.*, and K. Young, C. Wolkowitz and R. McCullagh (eds) *Of Marriage and the Market* (London: Conference of Socialist Economists 1981).
4. For a more general discussion of development, see Lee, Ch.2.4, and G. Kitching *Development and Underdevelopment in Historical Perspective* (London: Methuen, 1982).
5. See also M. Kidron and R. Segal, *The New State of the World Atlas* (London: Pan, 1984) Map 34.
6. See B. F. Johnston and P. Kilby, *Agriculture and Structural Transformation: economic strategies in late developing countries* (New York: Oxford University Press, 1975): B. F. Johnston and W. C. Clark, *Redesigning Rural Development; a strategic development* (Baltimore and London: Johns Hopkins University Press, 1982).
7. An outstanding critique of such stereotyped notions of the African past is A. Hopkins, *An Economic History of West Africa* (London: Longman, 1973).

8. P. Stirling, *Turkish Village* (London: Weidenfeld & Nicolson, 1965).
9. In some cases commodification may be associated initially with reduced inequality, as in parts of Latin America where it has involved the break-up of large estates. But the later history of these cases may well see subsequent differentiation of small producers on the lines described in this section. See C. D. Deere and A. de Janvry, 'A conceptual framework for the empirical analysis of peasants.' *Am. Jnl. Agric. Econ.*, 61 (1979) pp.601–11.
10. See Harriss (ed.) *op. cit.*
11. For a brief review of parts of the literature, see M. Overton, 'Agricultural revolution? Development of the agrarian economy in early modern England.' In A. R. H. Baker and D. Gregory (eds.) *Explorations in Historical Geography: Interpretative essays* (Cambridge: Cambridge University Press, 1984) pp.118–39.
12. On the 'Green Revolution' see B. H. Farmer (ed.) *Green Revolution? Technology and change in rice-growing areas of Tamil Nadu and Sri Lanka* (London: Macmillan, 1977); K. Griffin, *The Political Economy of Agrarian Change* (London: Macmillan, 1979) (2nd edn).
13. Harriss, *Capitalism and Peasant Farming: Agrarian Structure and Ideology in Northern Tamil Nadu* (Bombay and Oxford: Oxford University Press, 1982).
14. Indian Council of Social Science Research (1980) p.11.
15. A useful source for geographers on agrarian change in West Africa is P. Richards, 'Farming systems and agrarian change in West Africa', *Progr. Hum. Geogr.*, 7 (1983) pp.1–39 and P. Richards. *Indigenous Agricultural Revolution* (London: Hutchinson, 1985). On South Asia, see Farmer, *op. cit.* and B. H. Farmer, *South Asia: an outline* (London: Methuen, 1983). Hill's comparison of the patterns of agrarian change in Nigerian Hausaland and in a part of South India also offers valuable source material: P. Hill, *Dry Grain Farming Families* (Cambridge: Cambridge University Press, 1982).
16. R. Chambers (ed.) Rural development: whose knowledge counts? *IDS Bulletin* 10 (1979) No 2; Richards, *op. cit.*
17. See, for example, A. Coulson, 'Agricultural policies in mainland Tanzania.' In J. Heyer, *et. al.* (eds) *Rural development in tropical Africa* (London: Macmillan, 1981) pp.90–120.
18. Chayanov's major work, translated as *The Theory of the Peasant Economy* (Homewood, Ill: Richard M. Irvin, 1966) is discussed in Harriss (ed.) *op. cit.*
19. This formulation follows A. Saith and A. Tainkha, 'Economic decision-making of the poor peasant household.' *Economic and Political Weekly* Annual Number (1972).
20. K. Vergopoulos, 'Capitalism and peasant productivity', *Jnl. Peasant Studs.*, 5 (1978) pp.446–465.
21. S. Mann and J. M. Dickinson, 'Obstacles to the development of a capitalist agriculture', *Jnl. Peasant Studs.*, 5 (1978) pp.466–81.

22. Cited in Harriss (ed.) *op. cit.*
23. These data are from Dr G. Varga, Deputy Director, Research Institute for Agricultural Economics, Budapest.
24. Johnston and Clark, *op. cit.*, p.40.
25. B. Roberts, *Cities of Peasants* (London: Edward Arnold, 1978).
26. This phrase is suggested by J. Bharadwaj, *Production Conditions in Indian Agriculture* (Cambridge: Cambridge University Press, 1974).
27. Harriss (ed.) *op. cit.*
28. B. Harriss, *Transitional Trade and Rural Development* (New Delhi: Vikas, 1981).
29. See, for example, S. Amin, *Sugarcane and Sugar in Gorakhpur; an inquiry into peasant production for capitalist enterprise in colonial India,* (Oxford: Oxford University Press, 1984).
30. See, for example, *Accelerated development in sub-Saharan Africa: an agenda for action* (Washington DC: IBRD, 1981); A. Mitra, *Terms of Trade and Class Relations* (London: Frank Cass, 1977).
31. Johnston and Kilby, *op. cit.* and J. A Mellor, *The New Economics of Growth: a strategy for India and the developing world* (Ithaca and London: Cornell University Press, 1976).
32. T. J. Byres, 'The new technology, class formation and class action in the Indian countryside', *Jnl. Peasant Studs.*, 8 (1981)pp. 405–54.
33. This argument is elaborated by A. de Janvry, *The Agrarian Question and Reformism in Latin America* (Baltimore and London: Johns Hopkins University Press, 1981).
34. E. Trenchard, 'Female work burdens in Africa and their implications for health and nutrition', in J. Momsen and J. Townsend (eds) *Geography and Gender in the Third World* (London: Hutchinson, 1986) pp.153–72
35. On the politico-economic determinants of soil erosion, see P. Blaikie, *The Political Economy of Soil Erosion* (London: Longman, 1985).
36. *Le Monde*, 3 October 1984.
37. See M. H. Glantz (ed.) *The Politics of Natural Disaster: the case of the Sahel drought* (New York: Praeger, 1976).
38. See A. K. Sen. *Poverty and Famines; an essay on entitlement and deprivation* (Oxford: Clarendon Press, 1981).
39. Ibid.; B. Currey and G. Hugo (eds) *Famine as a Geographical Phenomenon* (Dordrecht and London: D. Reidel, 1984).
40. For an elaboration and illustration of the following argument, see Deere and de Janvry, *op. cit.*
41. For an extended treatment of the impact of seasonality see R. Chambers, R. Longhurst and A. Pacey (eds) *Seasonal Dimensions to Rural Poverty* (Frances Pinter: London, 1981).
42. For a model treatment of the way in which the different analytical levels we have distinguished are linked together, see H. Friedmann, 'The political economy of food; the rise and fall of the post-war international food order', *Am. Jnl. Sociol.*, 88 (1982) Supplement.

FURTHER READING

A short paper which elaborates upon the framework outlined here and illustrates it with data from Peru is C. Deere and A. de Janvry, 'A conceptual framework for the empirical analysis of peasants', *Am. Jnl. Agric. Econ.*, 8 (1979) pp.601–11. The only student text in this field is D. Goodman and M. Redclift, *From Peasant to Proletarian* (Oxford: Basil Blackwell, 1981). Some of the most important articles in the field, including both theoretical and empirical work, and with extensive introductions and guides to reading, will be found in J. Harriss (ed.) *Rural Development: theories of peasant economy and agrarian change* (London: Hutchinson, 1982).

4.3

Battleships and Cruisers: The New Geography of Multinational Corporations

Nigel Thrift and Michael Taylor
University of Bristol and Bureau of Transport and Communications Economics, Canberra

Nigel Thrift is Reader in Geography at the University of Bristol. His teaching and research interests are in urban geography, economic geography, time-geography and social theory. His publications include *Timing Space and Spacing Time* (co-edited with D. Parkes and T. Carlstein), *Times, Spaces and Places* (with D. Parkes), and *The Price of War* (with D. Forbes). He is a co-editor of *Environment and Planning* and a member of the editorial board of *Society and Space*.

Michael Taylor works for the Bureau of Transport and Communications Economics, Canberra, Australia. His teaching and research interests are in industrial geography. His publications include *Industrial Organisation and Location* (with P. McDermott); *Fiji: Future Imperfect* and with Nigel Thrift, *Multinationals and the Restructuring of the World Economy.*

INTRODUCTION

It is the beginning of another bleak, winter's day in Bristol. All over the city people are settling down to work. In Severnside, ICI's plant is producing ammonia and fertilisers through snakes of pipes and hissing stacks. You can tell by the yellow green plume of smoke hanging over the works. Down the road in Avonmouth, Commonwealth Smelting is a similar hive of activity churning out zinc and lead. Meanwhile, five miles away, among the terraces and crescents of the salubrious area of Clifton, the partners and employees of the accounting firm of Price Waterhouse sit in their office hard at work preparing audits.[1]

It is eight hours later in Kuala Lumpur, and the day's work is coming to an end. It is winter in Malaysia as well, but the city is hot and humid. The thunder clouds have built all afternoon, but the late afternoon deluge has not eventuated as it had the previous day. In Petaling Jaya, the new town attached to the south-western corner of 'KL', the employees are streaming out to join the bustle and madness of the traffic. International Diecasting's 77 employees are leaving the heat of the electroplating and diecasting works and Kris Metal's 197 employees are leaving the metal products plant and the assembly of louvres, aluminium doors and windows. Not a stone's throw away, more than 300 people are leaving ICI's paints plant to join the throng of cars, taxis, buses and Bas Mini. Meanwhile, on the eleventh floor of their office block in the centre of KL, Price Waterhouse's partners and employees are clearing their desks in air-conditioned comfort before plunging into the heat and fumes of the concrete canyons that are growing by the minute in the city's construction boom.

Cities like Bristol and Kuala Lumpur are quite different in numbers of ways, but their economic fortunes are tied together by the levels of activities of multinational corporations like ICI, Rio Tinto-Zinc (the ultimate cover of Commonwealth Smelting, Kris Metals and International Diecasting) and Price Waterhouse.[2] For example, in Bristol at least 58 per cent of total manufacturing employment is directly controlled by British and foreign-owned multinational corporations.[3] In Kuala Lumpur the comparable figure for Malaysian and foreign-owned multinational corporations is in excess of 75 per cent. And the influence of multinational corporations on these cities' economic fortunes hardly stops here. The indirect effects on employment are just as crucial. In Bristol, for example, ICI's Severnside plant gives £2 million-worth of work a year to local contractors, while CRA's Avonmouth plant provides £1 million-worth of business for the city's docks.

In this chapter we will consider how the geography of multinational corporations has changed over the last fifteen years, with special reference to the three British-owned multinational corporations already mentioned: ICI, Rio Tinto-Zinc and Price Waterhouse.[4] Each of these companies employs substantial numbers of people both in Britain and abroad, so that there can be no dispute as to their importance.

ICI is often seen as one of the flagships of British industry, whose financial fortunes are even now regarded as a barometer to the stock market. It is an institution in its own right – all recent Chairmen have been knighted during their term of office. The corporation is a vast conglomerate that makes almost the complete range of chemicals and chemical-related products, including agricultural products like fertilisers, fibres, general chemicals, explosives, organic chemicals, paints, petrochemicals, pharmaceuticals and various plastics. Its sales and profits depend now on four main markets: in order, the UK, Western Europe, North America and Australia and the Far East.

Rio Tinto-Zinc is similarly something of a British institution. Its board of directors has its quota of knights and lords. The corporation's chief interests are in natural resources, particularly the mining and smelting of metals like aluminium, iron ore, zinc, tin, gold and silver, as well as the extracts of uranium, coal and oil. Its sales and profits depend on the markets (again, in order of importance) in the UK, Japan, North America and Western Europe.

Finally, Price Waterhouse is the largest accountancy firm in the world. It specialises in the auditing of some 220 large corporations (including ICI), but it also has interests in activities like management consultancy, tax consultancy, and services to central and local government. Its main markets are, in order of importance, North America, the UK, Western Europe, Australia and the Far East. Together, the geographies of these three corporations have substantial impacts on the economic and social fortunes of many workers around the world, both directly and indirectly.

WHY ARE MULTINATIONAL CORPORATIONS SO IMPORTANT?

Multinational (or transnational) corporations are not a new development. They have been in existence for a very long time. Fifty years ago they were already an important economic force. In 1926, the year of ICI's formation out of the merger of four companies, ICI was operating in Canada and Australia, Rio Tinto-Zinc was operating in South Africa and Australia and Price Waterhouse was active in the United States, as it had been since the turn of the century. But if such corporations were a potent economic force 50 years ago, their importance is even greater now.

Economic power

At present, multinational corporations wield enormous economic power. That power comes, first of all, from the sheer scale of the economic transactions that multinational corporations make around the world and the consequent influence corporations have on urban, regional and national economies. For example, ICI – the 45th largest multinational corporation[5] – has consolidated sales that are nearly as great as the GNP of East Germany. And ICI is a mere sprat compared with the really large multinational corporations like Exxon, General Motors and Ford (the first, second and fourth largest multinational corporations respectively). Both Exxon and General Motors have consolidated sales nearly as large as the GNP of prosperous Switzerland, while Ford's consolidated sales are almost as great as the GNP of Finland and greater than the GNP of countries like South Korea or Greece.[6]

Such large organisations as these require extensive planning and coordination in order to keep plants supplied with raw materials or component parts, markets supplied with products and offices supplied with information.

Therefore, multinational corporations have become planned economies with vast *internal markets* within which raw materials, component parts, products, money and information are continually circulated. (For example, it is reckoned that Ford, at any one time, has more than 12 000 tonnes of components in transit between its plants in Europe alone).[7] A good part of this circulation of raw materials, component parts, products, money and information crosses national borders and registers as part of a nation's imports or exports. Thus, in 1977, 39 per cent of all the United States' imports and 36 per cent of all its exports could be attributed to transfers within multinational corporations. In 1980, 23 per cent of all the UK's exports could be similarly attributed.

In all, it is reckoned that one third of all world trade is made up of internal transfers of this sort.[8] These transfers provide nation states with resources (in the form of taxes and customs duties). They also provide multinational corporations with ways of avoiding payments to nation states, for example through the mechanism of 'transfer pricing'. When products and services are supplied between separate parts of the same organisation, an internal or 'transfer' price has to be struck. Manipulation of these prices, which are paid not only for goods and components but also for services like accounting and intangibles like royalties and licence fees, can reduce profits in one part of the organisation and increase them in others, causing losses and so helping in the avoidance of taxes and duties.

But multinational corporations' economic power does not come simply from the scale of their economic transactions and the consequent dependency of nation states on these transactions for revenue. It also comes from the actual ownership or control of assets, whether these be plants, warehouses, offices, hotels, mines, forests – the list is almost endless. Multinational corporations' ownership or control of natural resources produces the most striking facts. Take the case of minerals. Multinational corporations own 67 per cent of the world's bauxite resources. Seven large multinational corporations between them account for 23 per cent of the world's copper production.[9] Rio Tinto-Zinc, the 137th largest multinational corporation,[10] owns 40 per cent of the world's known resources of molybdenum (which makes borax) as well as enormous resources of bauxite, iron ore and other minerals. The corporation already has interests in seven North Sea oil fields, and in 1984 it acquired 29 per cent of the shares of Enterprise Oil. If it can arrange the other 71 per cent, then the corporation will be taking a good part of the income from North Sea Oil in the future.[11]

Of course, multinational corporations do not have to own particular assets to control them. In industries like agriculture and hotels multinational corporations are often just as happy to arrange marketing and management deals with the governments of nation states. Thus, in the late 1970s approximately 80 per cent of the exports of agricultural commodities from developing countries remained under the control of multinational corporations, because although the governments of developing countries had acted to acquire the ownership of their own areas of agricultural production they had been unable to break into the marketing of this produce.[12]

Another way in which multinational corporations can exert economic power is through employment. The numbers in the workforces of the multinational corporations are often considerable. For example, in 1984 ICI employed 115 600 people world-wide. Rio Tinto-Zinc employed 74 004 people. Even a smaller multinational corporation like Price Waterhouse employed 26 500 people. It is reckoned that, all told, multinational companies employed about 44 million people in the world in 1980.[13] However, the indirect employment generated by multinational corporations is clearly much greater than this figure. No one has ever been able to calculate how great.

Through the employment strategies they adopt, multinational corporations can clearly have considerable influence on the lives of many people. That the governments of nation states recognise this fact is shown, in the present economic climate, by the enormous range of incentives that urban, regional or state and national arms of government are willing to offer. In Britain, the list of incentives designed to attract foreign multinational corporations is long and includes start-up grants, the attentions of regional development agencies and the like.[14] In Malaysia, the government has set up four 'export processing zones', which are enclaves designed to make life easy for multinational corporations. There are four parts to the incentive package used to attract multinationals to these zones: duty free imports of raw materials and capital equipment; streamlined customs formalities; the provision of infrastructure facilities, especially factories, and land which is often leased at well below market rates.[15]

Political Power

Some commentators have given the impression that the economic power of multinational corporations is almost unlimited, that they possess 'global reach' which transcends the power of nation states. In this vision of the world, the managements of multinational corporations simply snap their fingers and governments stand to attention. Such a vision is a gross exaggeration, with the possible exception of a few of the smallest, poorest developing countries. The relationship is more complex and more subtle.[16]

First of all, governments have many sanctions that they can (and do) apply to multinational corporations. For example, governments provide some of the largest markets for multinational corporations (think only of the world armaments trade). Then again, government can quite often restrict the activities of the multinational corporations by means of import quotas, local content agreements and all sorts of other regulations; it is still extraordinarily difficult, for example, for non-Japanese multinational corporations to operate in Japan. Or, at the limit, governments can close the operations of multinational corporations down.

Second, governments routinely promote the interests of their 'own' multinational corporations over those of others, both at home and abroad. For example, governments may insist that development aid is linked to the services of 'their' multinational corporations. Or if the investments of these corporations are threatened, they may take action to protect them which, at the extreme, can still take the form of armed interventions. The result is that the power of multinational corporations is intimately linked to the power of their nation states in the world at large.

Finally, multinational corporations may want to minimise the attention of governments, including their own. Nowhere is this point made more clearly than by the present international financial system. This whole system, with its many markets for clearing the monetary transactions of multinational corporations from one country to another, with its lending, borrowing and share markets soaking up the $270 billion of available credit that multinational corporations have at their disposal each year, and with its 'futures' markets which allow multinational corporations to minimise the risk to their transactions presented by shifts in commodity and foreign exchange prices, exists *because* of nation states. If nation states had not set up their own national currencies and their own rules and regulations, concerning what and how many economic transactions could cross national borders and would be subject to taxes and customs duties, there would be little need for an international financial system.[17]

So the relationship between multinational corporations and governments is by no means one of narrow dependency. Rather it is one of complex interdependence.[18] In certain situations, the multinational corporation acts as an extension of the interests of the nation state, in others the nation state acts as an extension of the interests of the multinational corporation. In yet other situations, the two have no interests in common.

THE REACTIONS OF MULTINATIONAL CORPORATIONS TO THE WORLD ECONOMIC CRISIS

Much greater attention has been paid by human geographers to the geographies of multinational corporations since the beginning of the 1970s. The reason is obvious enough. There has been a major worldwide recession and a consequent drop in demand for many of the products and services that multinational corporations offer. Their profits have been hit and, for the first time after a long period of growth that began after the Second World War, many corporations have had to think seriously about rationalising their activities.

In the period of growth between the end of the Second World War and the early 1970s, the existing multinational corporations relentlessly expanded their operations overseas. One study found that, out of the 315 largest multinational corporations to be found in 1950, 81 per cent operated in less than six countries. By 1970 the proportion had changed drastically. By then, 88 per cent operated in more than six countries. Indeed, nearly 25 per cent operated in more than 20 countries.[19] So, by the early 1970s, there was a considerable number of large multinational corporations which had sprawled across the world without, on the whole, giving much thought to overall strategy. Rather like Topsy they had simply grown, extending outwards to more and more countries, often with more of an eye to which countries *other* corporations were operating in than to profit. When the economic recession hit, these corporations' responses were hampered by their very size. Size means that it is much more difficult to mount a coordinated turnaround. Size means the corporation has to fight harder each year, as it becomes bigger and bigger, to obtain the same percentage of profit, and size means that the number of countries into which these multinational corporations can expand and expect to get a profit becomes fewer and fewer. In some cases, multinational corporations had actually reduced the number of countries in which it was possible to operate at a profit in the products in which they had specialised.

As if all this were not bad enough, snapping at the heels of these large corporations were a whole series of smaller, more adaptable multinational corporations. Corporations now tend to become multinational at a much earlier stage in their history than previously, so as to get at lucrative overseas markets as soon as possible. (For example, many quite small British electronics firms would find it hard to survive if they could not make inroads into the United States market early on.) As a result of this phenomenon, multinational corporations based in all kinds of nations previously known only as targets for multinational corporation expansion began to appear. *Third World Multinationals* from the newly industrialising countries like Malaysia have become a frequently commented upon phenomenon.[20]

But, worst of all, a whole series of large Japanese corporations, which had previously produced only in Japan and penetrated the overseas markets only via exports, now began to become large multinational corporations. Right through the 1970s and into the 1980s the plants and offices of Japanese multinational corporations began to spring up in most of the larger cities of the world.[21] In Bristol, for example, Hyfil, a subsidiary of Toray Industries, set up operation in 1976 making carbon fibre goods. In Malaysia; Japanese electronics firms including Matsushita, Toshiba and Sanyo have moved into the Free Trade Zones of Penang, Kuala Lumpur and the Kelang Valley. In Kuala Lumpur itself Japanese influence is felt most strongly in construction and traded services. These Japanese corporations were a formidable source of competition, with an enormous hoard of assets and extensive diplomatic and economic back-up from their government.

The experiences of ICI and Rio Tinto-Zinc in the 1970s and early 1980s underline these arguments. Both corporations were hit by a lack of demand for a number of their key products, particularly in the UK market, and increased competition. All through the 1970s ICI was plagued by overcapacity, but its Waterloo came in the period from 1979 to 1983. A number of products suffered market losses, most particularly petrochemicals, plastics, organic chemicals and fibres. In 1982, for example, petrochemicals and plastics lost £139 million. Only agricultural products, pharmaceuticals and oil continued to make substantial profits. Rio Tinto-Zinc had had more generalised problems throughout the 1970s and into the 1980s. Its troubles stemmed almost entirely from lack of demand for nearly all its range of minerals as industry throughout the world ran down.

HOW THE WAR WAS WON

Less demand from the markets of the world, plus more competition from more multinational corporations, equals economic warfare. The cosy cartels and the unwritten agreements between competitors that had made so many countries easy places to make profits in during the 1950s and 1960s were dissolved. Whereas before the 1970s the water had looked warm and inviting, now it was full of sharks.

Strategies

Faced with this situation multinational corporations followed three main inter-related strategies. The first and most pressing thing they had to do was to *rationalise* their activities. They had to decide which products or services to continue with and in which countries they would continue to make or market those products or services. In other words, multinational corporations had to have a coherent *worldwide* strategy.

The second thing they had to do was to consider how to *reorganise* their production, administration and marketing more efficiently so that a worldwide strategy could become possible. There was no room now for 'spare capacity'. Most multinational corporations implemented five programmes, to varying degrees. First of all, they increased the level of automation in their operations, for example through the use of robots. Second, information systems were made more explicit so that, for example, at any time the management could know exactly what a plant's profits and prospects of profit were. Third, the line of command was rejigged. In particular, more responsibility was given to management in a new tier of 'regional headquarters offices', which became responsible for many of the operations of a multinational corporation in a particular 'region' of the world (for example, Europe, Latin America and Asia).[22] Correspondingly less responsibility was given to the management at plant or branch office level; their role was often reduced to the day-to-day running of the plant or a branch office and the preparation of statistics with which to inform upper level management elsewhere. Fourth, multinational corporations began to think more seriously about which functions needed to be kept inside the corporation with the result that there has been an increase in subcontracting, both of production and administration. Finally, and probably of most geographical significance, multinational corporations have, partly as response to the preceding programmes, begun to coordinate these plants and offices more self-consciously. Before the beginning of the 1970s many multinational corporations ran their overseas operations as a series of smaller versions of operations in the home country. But with the stimulus provided by the recession and the means provided by technical innovations in transport (containerisation, aircargo) and telecommunications, they began to systematically integrate their plants and offices to form hierarchies of production and administration functioning on a world-region or even global scale.

Chains of production are arranged so that different parts of products are made at particular plants and then shipped to other plants for intermediate or final assembly. The spatial extension of these chains of production means, in turn, that the parts being made by plants can be more closely tailored to local circumstances. So, for example, products that are made via a series of levels of intensive, repetitive tasks can be assigned to developing, low wage countries, or to low wage regions in developed countries, while products that require more skill to make are assigned to plants in developed countries or to high wage regions in developed countries.[23] This kind of integration of production is particularly advanced in industries like textiles, electronics and automobiles. But integration does not have to stop at production. Recently, marketing has also become integrated on a world-region or even global scale. For example, global advertising campaigns are now becoming more popular on the grounds that international companies need clearly identified international brands.

The third thing multinational companies needed to do to climb out of the recession was to cast around for new ways of making money. One obvious way was to *diversify* into new products and services as they moved out of products and services which no longer made sufficient profit. This is an avenue that a number of multinational corporations have gone down. Another avenue which nearly all multinational corporations have followed in the 1970s and 1980s came from the realisation that it was possible to make money just by having money. Many multinational corporations now make considerable profits from speculation on the international financial markets, for example through currency dealing, share buying and selling and property dealing.

Outcomes

The changing geographies of ICI and Rio Tinto-Zinc over the last fifteen years show these three strategies of *rationalisation, reorganisation* and *diversification* in action. For ICI, the first priority was a substantial rationalisation of the capacity for making unprofitable products like petrochemicals, plastics, organic chemicals and fibres. Plants making these products were closed or production was chopped back. Rio Tinto-Zinc, with its heavy dependence upon natural resources, found it more difficult to rationalise than ICI. However, it could mothball some mines, and close some smelters. This it did.

In addition, both ICI and Rio Tinto-Zinc reoriented their operations (and their employment) towards countries where the opportunities for profit were greater. In both cases this has tended to mean the booming market of the United States. For example in 1984 ICI paid £625 million for Beatrice Chemicals, one of the largest chemical corporations in the United States. Rio Tinto-Zinc has also expanded its capital investment programmes in the United States. Other areas of the world too felt the attention of ICI and Rio Tinto-Zinc in their search for more profitable markets, among them the cities of the Far East, including Malaysia. Through Conzinc Holdings (Malaysia), Rio Tinto-Zinc expanded in Malaysia by buying Kris Metals in 1979, starting diecasting operations and buying interests in two tin dredges in 1980 and by buying into Lysaght Corrugated Pipe in 1982.

Both corporations have also reorganised their operations on a worldwide scale. ICI has been particularly active. Thus many of its more important plants are being extensively automated. Its new plant at Wilhelmshaven in West Germany is a case in point. It is an enormous plant, yet it employs only 40 process workers on any one shift. ICI has also become more willing to subcontract out parts of its production and administration. For example, it has offered selected managers a guaranteed consultancy contract if they leave the company payroll, thereby becoming self-employed. Administration has also been reorganised. ICI is now organised in world region divisions, each with their own regional headquarters office. And, within these divisions, production is being integrated. For example, the new plant at Wilhelmshaven was opened not only to gain access to local markets and cheaper energy supplies, but also to become a focus for West European chemicals production. Similarly, a plant opened at Corpus Christi, Texas in 1980 is intended to become the focus of North American chemicals production.

Finally, both ICI and Rio Tinto-Zinc have diversified into new products. ICI has concentrated much of its effort on speciality chemicals and new pharmaceuticals. Rio Tinto-Zinc has bought into oil and gas production and into consumer products that can be associated with its current metals production (for example, Everest Double Glazing, which calls for aluminium). In addition, both corporations have become heavily involved in speculating on the international money markets. The result of these strategies has been that, by 1984, both corporations were again making healthy profits,[24] although Rio Tinto-Zinc was still cursed by reduced demand for metals.

For Price Waterhouse, in contrast to ICI and Rio Tinto-Zinc, the 1970s and early 1980s have been a halcyon time; the corporation has grown continually, partly because of its aggressive search for custom. But much of the boost in its growth has, in fact, come from the global restructuring of other multinational corporations to meet the stringencies of the recession. Thus Price Waterhouse has benefited from the subcontracting of these corporations' administration. It has been able to expand its tax consulting, management consultancy and other services partly because of this trend. Then again, Price Waterhouse has benefited from the regionalisation of administration. It has piled up extra customers in many cities around the world because its worldwide network of offices mirrors that of many international corporations. And it has gained from the increasing financial sophistication of many multinational corporations, who now require the greater financial expertise which corporations like Price Waterhouse can provide.

FROM BATTLESHIP TO CRUISER: GLOBAL CORPORATIONS

By the time multinational corporations like ICI and Rio Tinto-Zinc had instigated the variety of changes described above, they began to look quite different from the way they had before the 1970s. The difference means that they are now often called by a new name – *Global Corporations*[25] – to distinguish them from their forebears.

There are three main distinguishing marks. First global corporations are slimmed-down beasts. Generally, they have cut their workforces back, through rationalisation of various plants. Those plants and offices that are left tend to employ fewer people doing the same amount of work as before, or more. At the same time, global corporations probably employ more people indirectly, because they subcontract out more of their production and administration. Second, global corporations now operate a worldwide strategy that integrates production, administration and marketing on a global scale. Their executives continually criss-cross the globe, checking and analysing to make sure the profits keep up to the mark and that the corporation's internal market (which, because of the need to integrate products, has probably become more extensive in many corporations) runs smoothly. Third, global corporations have become more and more financially-oriented. Their headquarters resembles nothing so much in function as a bank. The global corporations' methods of appraisal are fiscal.

What have been the main geographical consequences of these changes? There have, of course, been many, including, for example, a worldwide increase in business travel (which has, in turn, given a boost to a number of industries in which multinational corporations are prominent, such as hotels) and the increased importance of the telecommunications and information processing media like telex, satellites and computers, needed to keep tabs on far-flung global operations. But there are three geographical consequences which have been of particular importance, because they affect the workforces of multinational corporations.

The first consequence has been that the workforces of multinational corporations have become more international than ever before. In 1971 the average foreign share of employment amongst the 350 largest multinational corporations in the world was 39 per cent. By 1980 this figure had risen to 46 per cent and, already, a considerable number of the multinational corporations employ well over half their workforce outside their home country.[26] Nowhere is this trend to greater internationalisation of the workforce better illustrated than amongst British multinational corporations, spurred on by the continuing lack of demand in their home market. In 1984 ICI's foreign share of employment was 49 per cent, and this figure continues to increase. Although Rio Tinto-Zinc would be expected to have a high overseas component to its workforce because of its mining operations, still the figure for its foreign share of employment in 1984, at 76 per cent, is exceptionally high and again is increasing. Price Waterhouse has the greatest proportion of its workforce overseas, at some 88 per cent.

The second geographical consequence stems from greater integration of administration within multinational corporations, and with it the locational sifting of management and marketing jobs. For a long time now, the offices of multinational corporations in which most management jobs are to be found have tended to congregate in particular 'world cities'[27] along with the offices of multinational banks, and other 'producer service' corporations. The advantages for the management of multinational corporations of forming 'corporate complexes' within these cities are obvious enough. They include easy access to finance, advice, information, telecommunications, social contacts and the like, all of which increases the management of a multinational corporations's awareness of their environment, likelihood of making correct decisions and ability to influence the decisions of others. But recently the number and scale of these world cities has grown, especially as multinational corporations have instigated a tier of regional headquarters officers in order to be able to scan their global activities properly. This is because the corporations have expanded into new countries and the corporations have shown increasing propensity to subcontract their administration and marketing to producer service firms. Cities like Hong Kong, Singapore, Los Angeles, Honolulu and Miami now all have rapidly growing corporate complexes which were hardly in existence in 1970, based on their function as centres of control of the plants and offices of multinational corporations in particular regions.[28] Thus Hong Kong and Singapore are favourite centres for control of the plants and offices of multinational corporations of all nationalities operating in Asia and the Pacific. For example, ICI has a regional headquarters office in Hong Kong and Rio Tinto-Zinc has a regional headquarters office of one of its subsidiaries in Singapore. Los Angeles and Honolulu are favoured by United States-based multinational corporations as centres of control for the Asia and Pacific region, while Miami is a favoured centre of control for United States-based multinational corporations operating in Latin America. These new world cities have come to share some of the same trends that are also evident in the older world cities like London and New York: a large office property market, a rapidly growing producer service

service sector, a growing young professional middle class that fills the jobs in this sector, and a corresponding appetite for 'gentrified' housing, smart restaurants and cocaine.

The third geographical consequence stems from the greater integration of production and with it the locational sifting of the workforce, especially the workers in manual and routine clerical jobs. There are now clearly fewer of these jobs and they are more likely to be geographically dispersed. Production is being decentralised, both functionally and geographically. In certain industries like textiles, electronics and automobiles, there is a tendency for multinational corporations to decentralise the part of production that requires repetitive tasks to plants in low wage developing countries, and this tendency has been heralded as the beginning of a 'new international division of labour'[29] in which the manufacturing industries of developing countries like Malaysia take on a permanent tributary role. In reality, this tendency is still very tentative and could be wiped out if the cost of automation were to tumble to the point where it matches that of this low wage labour. Already Malaysia is experiencing the closure of electronics firms in its Free Trade Zones, accompanied by the loss of large numbers of jobs.

THE COSTS FOR LOCAL ECONOMIES

The results of the restructuring by multinational corporations over the last fifteen years have obviously been felt most acutely at the level of individual plants and offices. The result of the global reorganisation of multinational corporations has been that these plants or offices are now more likely to be compared one with the other, and more often. Some plants and offices will appear more central to the corporation (and therefore more likely to stay open), whereas others will appear quite peripheral (and are therefore more likely to be closed). Further, because the comparison is more likely to be fiscal in character, a plant or office may well be closed because it is not making sufficient profit, rather than because it is running at a loss.

The net result of these considerations, in the case of British multinational corporations, has been that British plants and offices have been more likely to suffer because of the general increase in the internationalisation of multinational corporations, coupled with the dire state of the domestic market. Certainly, much of the increase in unemployment in the regions of Britain since 1970 has now been traced to the activities of British multinational corporations withdrawing their operations from Britain.[30]

All is not gloom, however, as the different experiences of the Bristol plants and offices of ICI, Rio Tinto-Zinc and Price Waterhouse have shown during the recession. ICI's Severnside plant had two advantages. First, it was quite modern. Most of the plant was built in the 1960s. Second, the greater portion of the plant is now used for making agricultural fertilisers, and this has been a market in which ICI has been able to continue to make profits. Even so, ICI's agricultural division has seen a decline in its employment from 13 009 in 1970 to 6833 in 1984, but the Severnside plant has not shared in this cutback. Its employment has remained steady at about 650 from 1975 to 1985, although the number of contractors on site has declined by about 100. The future of the plant looks reasonably assured, but the pressures on the plant are now increasing for two reasons. First, competition in agricultural products is increasing in the UK market, especially as a result of the entry of a Norwegian multinational corporation, Norsk Hydro, which has taken over the UK fertiliser business of Fisons. Second, there is a possibility that ICI might in the future consider moving some of its operations to the United Arab Emirates, where natural gas is cheaper. At present Severnside would not be affected, but this may not always be the case.

Rio Tinto-Zinc's Avonmouth zinc smelting plant has had a much rougher time. The plant, established during the 1914–18 war but extensively modernised in 1965 in collaboration with ICI and Fisons, has suffered from the general worldwide fall in demand for zinc. By 1982, the plant's poor performance had made it a prime target for rationalisation. The plant lost £10 million in that year, putting its 1000 workers' jobs in jeopardy. The crunch came in July 1983 when the plant was put forward as a candidate to be cut by a newly formed EEC cartel of zinc producers, in order to deal with a Europe-wide overproduction of zinc. Finally, 'only' 300 jobs were cut and the plant's productivity was sufficiently boosted by these redundancies to enable it to carry on. In 1984 it produced 86 000 tonnes of zinc and 36 000 tonnes of lead – about the same amounts as in 1983, but with 30 per cent fewer workers.

In contrast to the gradual decline in jobs at the ICI Severnside plant and the more dramatic cuts at the Rio Tinto-Zinc Avonmouth plant, Price Waterhouse's Clifton office has continued to take on staff through the recession. There are now six partners and 65 staff. The office specialises in audit (including the account of a large Bristol-based multinational corporation, the Dickinson Robinson Group and the Port of Bristol Authority) and management consultancy.

In all, the Bristol experience of British multinational corporations' activities has been a fairly happy one when compared with other harder-hit cities in Britain like Birmingham or Manchester. Meanwhile, in Kuala Lumpur and the Free Trade Zones of Malaysia, the impact of multinational corporations has been equally diverse. There are two important aspects to the economic climate in Malaysia and both involve government. First, the government has sought to encourage foreign investment through an open door policy, in an attempt to emulate the Singapore success story. Central to this policy has been the creation of Free Trade Zones mainly around Penang, in the north of the country, and in the Kuala Lumpur-Klang Valley area. Second, a fundamental tenet of the new policy that has been adopted is to increase the role of ethnic Malays rather than ethnic Chinese within the formal economy. This has had the effect of diluting foreign ownership (but not control) in companies outside the Free Trade Zones, to bring about 'Malayanisation' and increase the involvement of government within the economy through Federal and State-owned corporations.

Price Waterhouse has been able to ride on the economic boom that has occurred in Malaysia in the 1970s, and is only now beginning to falter in the mid-1980s. The boom has involved more than industrialisation. It has also brought massive urban development in Kuala Lumpur in the form of office blocks and vast estates of terraced townhouses. This real estate boom has been paralleled by massive government involvement in the economy. All this has created a climate conducive to the growth of Price Waterhouse. The company now has two offices and 12 partners in Kuala Lumpur, and other offices in Ipoh, Johor Baru, Kota Kinabalu, Malacca and Penang.

Rio Tinto-Zinc's interests in Kuala Lumpur are held indirectly through its Australian subsidiary, CRA, and Conzinc Asia Holdings based in Singapore. However, perhaps the most important aspect of this ownership structure is that it has always been in a state of flux, especially in the past ten years. Rio Tinto-Zinc was first interested in Malaysia for its tin, as it has the best deposits of this mineral in the world. Until the late 1970s investments were mainly in tin dredges, tin leases and subleases, some of which were on the outskirts of Kuala Lumpur. Diversification came in 1978, when the corporation moved into metal fabrication in Kuala Lumpur. Kris Metal, Kris Naco and Kris Aluminium were bought, producing steel louvres, pressed metal products, sliding doors, window frames and other architectural aluminium products. These companies now employ 197 people. Diecasting began in 1980, also in Kuala Lumpur, in a joint venture (employing 77 people) involving another South East Asian firm and other associates of Rio Tinto-Zinc. In 1982 a stake was also bought in Lysaght Corrugate Pipe, a subsidiary of the Australian BHP corporation. In terms of profits, this diversification in Malaysia has been far from successful. Lack of success coupled with Malaysian foreign investment policy brought more restructuring in 1983 and 1984, which took the form of great reductions in equity holdings through the issue of $M22 million worth of shares.

ICI has been more restrained in its investments in Malaysia and has only one large paints plant employing 309 people in Kuala Lumpur. However, the case of Conzinc Asia Holdings' investments in Malaysia shows clearly how multinationals treat their peripheral operations in developing countries as assets to be bought, sold and exchanged often in quick succession.

However, corporations like Rio Tinto-Zinc and ICI first invested in Malaysia when it was a British colony, and these are not the corporations upon which the country has based its recent and rapid industrialisation. This growth has been based on electronics and textiles firms that moved into the Free Trade Zones that have been established. They have created thousands of jobs, mainly assembly-line jobs for young, unmarried women. This has brought large numbers of women from rural communities to work in the new factory environment. The price of this success is now being realised as the companies are beginning to pull out of the zones, leaving behind more redundant workers than incoming firms can absorb.

CONCLUSION: EXPORT AND SURVIVE?

This chapter has, of necessity, taken a quite narrow, 'economic' view of the geographies of multinational corporations. Many of the topics deserve a more detailed treatment too. Even so, it should be clear that multinational corporations are a worthy object of study, with discernable impacts on almost every city and region in the world. Cities like Bristol and Kuala Lumpur are examples picked almost at random. There are many other cities to choose from.

But stop: multinational corporations are more than a 'worthy object of study'! In Britain the subject of multinational corporations is now absolutely vital to national economic survival. As British multinational corporations continue their push abroad, and as they become more and more likely to be owned and even run by foreign interests – 20 per cent of ICI's shares are now in American hands and one of the corporation's directors is the President of the Toshiba Corporation – so it becomes more and more legitimate to ask: which of their plants and offices are likely to be left in Britain in ten or twenty years' time? As John Harvey-Jones, the £287 000 per year plus share options Chairperson of ICI puts it: 'When the UK industrial base largely collapsed what could we do? We had either to shut the whole bloody company down or export to survive.'[31] The problem now is whether the geography of multinational corporation survival and the survival of Britain can ever be made to intermesh again.[32] What can we do?

Acknowledgements

Keith Bassett provided us with considerable information on various aspects of the running of the Bristol ICI and Rio Tinto-Zinc plants.

NOTES AND REFERENCES

1. Information on the Bristol plants of ICI and Rio Tinto-Zinc comes from the following sources: Annual Reports of ICI; Annual Reports of Rio Tinto-Zinc and CRA (Rio Tinto-Zinc's Australian subsidiary which is responsible for the running, through its subsidiary AM+S, of the Commonwealth smelting plant); local newspaper cuttings; plant guidebooks; interviews. Information on Price Waterhouse's Bristol office comes from its Annual Review; The Company Office Directory; Crawford's *Directory of City Connections* and interviews.

2. Information on the Kuala Lumpur plants of ICI and Rio Tinto-Zinc comes from a variety of sources including: Annual Reports of ICI; Annual Reports of CRA (Rio Tinto-Zinc's Australian subsidiary that controls Kris Metals, International Diecasting and other interests in Malaysia through Conzinc Holdings (Malaysia) Sdn Bhd); plant directories; the Federation of Malaysian Manufacturers' 1984 *Directory*. Information on Price Waterhouse in Malaysia comes from the International Directory of Offices, Information Guides and Staff Handbooks.
3. K. Bassett, 'Corporate structure and corporate change in a local economy: the case of Bristol', *Environ. Plann. A,* 16 (1984) pp.879–90; K. Bassett, 'Economic crisis and corporate restructuring: multinational corporations and the paper, printing and packaging sector in Bristol', in M. J. Taylor and N. J Thrift (eds) *Multinationals and the Restructuring of the World Economy* (Beckenham: Croom Helm, 1985) pp.311–343; J. Hillier, 'Multinational control in the Bristol economy', *Area* 17 (1985) pp.123–7.
4. Information on the world-wide operations of ICI, Rio Tinto-Zinc and Price Waterhouse comes from the following sources, unless otherwise stated. For ICI: Annual Reports; newspaper reports; A. M. Pettigrew, *The Awakening Giant: continuity and change in ICI.* (Oxford: Blackwell, 1985); I. M. Clarke, *The Spatial Organisation of Multinational Corporations* (Beckenham: Croom Helm, 1985). For Rio Tinto-Zinc: Annual Reports, newspaper reports; F. Walker, *The Bristol Region* (London: Nelson, 1972); M. J. Taylor, N. J. Thrift, 'British capital overseas, direct investment and firm development in Australia', *Reg. Studs.,* 15 (1981) pp.183–212. For Price Waterhouse: Annual Reviews; M. Stevens, *The Big Eight* (New York: Macmillan, 1981); T. Tinker, *Paper Prophets* (Eastbourne: Holt Rinehart and Winston, 1985).
5. J. H. Dunning, R. D. Pearce *The World's Largest Industrial Enterprises* (Farnborough: Gower, 1985).
6. United Nations Centre on Transnational Corporations, *Transnational Corporations in World Development: Third Study* (New York: United Nations, 1983).
7. Robin Murray, pers. comm.
8. United Nations Centre on Transnational Corporations, op. cit.
9. Ibid.
10. Dunning and Pearce, *op. cit.*
11. ICI is similarly active in the North Sea oilfields.
12. United Nations Centre on Transnational Corporations, op. cit.
13. International Labour Organisation, *Employment Effects of Multinational Enterprises* (Geneva: ILO, 1981).
14. For a review, see N. Hood, S. Young, *Multinational Investment Strategies in the British Isles* (London: HMSO, 1983).
15. For more detail, see P. G. Warr, 'Malaysia's industrial enclaves: Free Trade Zones and licensed manufacturing warehouses', in T. G. McGee (ed.) *Industrialisation and the Growth of the Labour Force in Malaysia*

(Canberra: Australian National University, 1986).

16. For more detail, see N. Thrift, 'All change: the geography of international economic disorder', in P. J. Taylor, R. J. Johnston (eds) *A World in Crisis? Geographical perspectives* (Oxford: Basil Blackwell, 1985) pp.12–67.
17. A perfect recent example of this point is the rise of the Eurodollar market in the 1970s: see M. S. Mendelsohn, *Money on the Move* (New York: Blackwell, 1981) and J. Coakley, L. Harris, *The City of Capital* (London: Blackwell, 1983).
18. For a summary of the various competing theories of economic imperialism implied by this discussion, see D. K. Forbes, *The Geography of Underdevelopment* (Beckenham: Croom Helm, 1984).
19. R. Vernon, 'The product cycle hypothesis in a new international economic environment', *Oxford Bulletin of Economics and Statistics* 41 (1979) pp.255–68.
20. S. Lall, *The New Multinationals: the spread of Third World enterprises* (Chichester: Wiley, 1984); L. T. Wells Jr., *Third World Multinationals*(Cambridge, Mass.: MIT Press, 1983).
21. L. G. Franko, *The Japanese Multinations* (Chichester: Wiley, 1983); P. G. Dicken, 'Japanese manufacturing investment in the United Kingdom: a flood or a mere trickle', *Area* 15 (1983) pp.273–84.
22. D. Heenan, 'Global cities of tomorrow', *Harvard Business Review* 55 (1977) pp.79–92; J. H. Dunning, G. Norman, 'The theory of the multinational enterprise: an application to multinational office location', *Environ. Plann. A* 15 (1983) pp.675–692.
23. Thrift, *op. cit.* (note 16).
24. Net profits in 1984 for ICI were £585 million; for Rio Tinto-Zinc £210 million; for Price Waterhouse (est.) £115 million.
25. M. J. Taylor, N. J. Thrift, 'Models of corporate development and the multinational corporation', in M. J. Taylor, N. J. Thrift (eds) *The Geography of Multinationals* (Beckenham: Croom Helm, 1982); Clarke, *op. cit.* (note 4).
26. United Nations Centre on Transnational Corporations, op. cit. (note 6).
27. R. B. Cohen, 'The new international division of labour, multinational corporations and urban hierarchy', in M. J. Dear, A. J. Scott (eds) *Urbanisation and Urban Planning in Capitalist Society* (London: Allen and Unwin, 1981) pp.287–315; J. Friedmann, G. Wolff, 'World City formation: an agenda for research and activity', *Int. Jnl. Urb. Reg. Res.*, 6 (1982) pp.309–344; N. J. Thrift, 'The internationalisation of producer services and the integration of the Pacific Basin property market', in M. J. Taylor, N. J. Thrift (eds) *Multinationals and the Restructuring of the World Economy* (Beckenham: Croom Helm, 1985).
28. H. C. Reed, 'Appraising corporate investment policy: a financial centre theory of foreign direct investment,' in C. P. Kindleberger, D. B. Audretsch (eds) *The Multinational Corporation in the 1980s* (Cambridge,

Mass: MIT Press, 1983) pp.219–244.
29. F. Frobel, J. Heinrichs, O. Kreye, *The New International Division of Labour* (Cambridge: Cambridge University Press, 1980); Thrift, *op. cit.* (note 27).
30. F. Gaffikin, A. Nickson, *Jobs, Crisis and the Multinationals: the case of the West Midlands* (Nottingham: Russell Press, 1984); P. E. Lloyd, J. Shutt, 'Recession and restructuring in the North-West Region 1975-1982', in D. Massey, R. A. Meegan (eds) *Politics and Method: contrasting studies in industrial geography* (London: Methuen, 1985) pp.16–60.
31. Cited in J. Erlichman, 'The Imperial imperative', *The Guardian*, 19 February 1985, p.24.
32. N. J. Thrift, 'Taking the rest of the world seriously' The state of British urban and regional research in a time of economic crisis', *Environ. Plann. A,* 17 (1985) pp.7–24; N. J. Thrift, 'Out of bounds . . . ', *Times Higher Education Supplement*, 12 July 1985, p.15; L. Harris, 'British capital manufacturing, finance and multinational corporations', in D. Coates, G. Johnston, R. Bush (eds) *A Socialist Anatomy of Britain* (Cambridge: Polity, 1985) pp.7–28.

FURTHER READING

We have edited two collections of essays which bear directly on the themes discussed in this chapter: *The Geography of Multinationals* (Beckenham: Croom Helm, 1982) and *Multinationals and the Restructuring of the World Economy* (Beckenham: Croom Helm, 1985).

Nigel Thrift provides a summary account in 'All change: the geography of international economic disorder', in another useful collection of essays, edited by P. J. Taylor and R. J. Johnston, *A World in Crisis? Geographical Perspectives* (Oxford: Basil Blackwell, 1985) pp.12–67.

Finally, there are two special issues of journals which are worth obtaining: D. Evans and R. Kaplinsky (eds) 'Slowdown or Crisis? Restructuring in the 1980s', *IDS Bulletin* 16 (1984) No. 1; A. Simpson (ed.) 'The global economy, trade, aid and multinationals. *Contemporary Issues in Geography and Education* 1 (1984) No. 3.

PART V
REGIONAL GEOGRAPHIES AND GLOBAL PERSPECTIVES

Introduction

The essays in this section take their cue from **Peter Taylor**'s opening declaration that geography is in *crisis*. 'We live in a world in which global issues are paramount,' Taylor announces, 'but where geography has little or nothing to say about them.' In the optimistic years following World War Two, Taylor suggests that the social sciences became committed to the ideology of 'developmentalism'. By this he means a view of social change in which societies are seen as more or less separate entities, with clearly defined boundaries setting one off from the other, and in which each society 'develops' through its own, internal logic – rather like a mainspring uncoiling to set each society off on a set of parallel paths leading away from the 'traditional' and towards the 'modern' world. These models can, of course, be traced back before the global conflicts of the twentieth century, and their marks are all over the pages of the 'New Geography' of the 1960s, but Taylor suggests that the spectacular and, significantly, *worldwide* recession of the late twentieth century has forced a dramatic reappraisal of these orthodoxies.

The result has been a series of new, so-called *dependency theories*, which have substituted various 'exogenous' models for the old 'endogenous' models of social change. The most sophisticated of these, so Taylor contends, is the *world systems approach* proposed by Immanuel Wallerstein. 'If we wish to study social change,' Taylor argues, then, following Wallerstein, 'the entity we must deal with is the world economy.' Individual countries are not 'societies': and this means that it makes little sense to study individual countries or even relations between individual countries. There is instead an overall 'global logic' determined (today) by the operations of an essentially *capitalist* world economy. But this logic is not a supra-historical constant; it has varied through time as 'world-empires' have given way to 'world-economies', and it has sustained a series of shifting core-periphery structures in space. This must mean, Taylor concludes, that the only way in which we can analyse the modern world system is through a reconstruction of its *historical geography*.

Wallerstein's writings have not been without their critics, and the two chapters which follow seek to qualify what they see as an insistent 'economic reductionism' in Wallerstein's account. **Graham Smith** accepts, with Taylor, the need to grasp 'the simultaneity of global and regional processes operating within an historically unfolding framework'; but he also insists that this framework is not fashioned out of an exclusively economic logic. This, he says, 'is to fall back into the trap of the generalising impulse of spatial science'. (And a number of commentators have indeed drawn parallels between Wallerstein's thesis and a generalised systems theory). In Smith's view, therefore, it is important to retain the sensitivity to difference and differentiation which was the hallmark of classical regional geography. In particular, those who emphasise the capitalist world economy all too often minimise *fundamental* differences between the socialist and capitalist worlds, not least in *cultural* and *political* terms. State socialist societies like the Soviet Union 'have followed their own cultural logic of development,' Smith says, 'and have their own [political] ways of organising their peoples and places'. Like Taylor, therefore, Smith seeks to show that an understanding of social life demands an understanding of its geography: the two cannot be separated and assigned to different disciplines. But his is a much more nuanced account, which shows how the administrative stratification of places within the Soviet Union affects the lives of its peoples in strikingly direct ways.

Stuart Corbridge considers the other superpower actor on the global stage, the United States of America. He too has some considerable sympathy with Taylor's argument, but in his view 'the very changes in the capitalist world economy which have eroded national sovereignty in one direction have also encouraged and made possible national economic planning and national economic and political offensives in other arenas'. What is needed in his view is a 'geopolitical economy', an approach which can 'deconstruct' the received categories of 'North' and 'South', 'core' and 'periphery', and so demonstrate the continued salience of national rivalries and national policies within a shifting global framework. He illustrates his thesis through a detailed examination of the operation of the world economy – the very heart of Wallerstein's corpus – and shows the strategic importance of the United States and its 'semi-autonomous powers' to affect the dynamics of the global economy. To be sure, those powers are military as well as economic, but Corbridge's illustration is still sufficient to demonstrate the depth of these new perspectives.

If we duck the challenges posed by these three chapters – if we are unwilling to probe deeply into the multi-level dynamics of global geography – then we will not only never emerge from the crisis which Taylor identifies: we will not deserve to.

5.1 The Error of Developmentalism in Human Geography

Peter J. Taylor
University of Newcastle-Upon-Tyne

Peter J. Taylor is Senior Lecturer in Geography at the University of Newcastle-upon-Tyne. He is the Editor of *Political Geography Quarterly*, co-editor (with R. J. Johnston) of *A World in Crisis: geographical perspectives* and author of *Political Geography: world-economy, nation-state and locality*.

GEOGRAPHY AND THE GLOBAL PERSPECTIVE

Geography is about the world. Well . . . yes, sure, but let's get on with the newest geography and forget the world. If this reaction is only true of a minority of the last generation of geographers – and I believe it to be much more prevalent than that – then it is a massive betrayal of lost opportunities. Let us re-state, therefore, the basic assertion – geography *is* about the world. This should be repeated, *ad nauseam*, every time a new geography emerges out of the intellectual sanctuary of the universities. This antidote may then prevent the current crisis of geography from ever happening again. What is the current crisis? Well, if you haven't noticed it you have been more hypnotised by new geographies than you dare admit. The crisis of geography is that we live in a world in which global issues are paramount, but where geography has little or nothing to say about them. At the very least it is a crisis of self-respect. We need to put the 'geo' back into geography. But before we can do that we need to understand how we came to lose our geo in the first place.

Most of the children who become (and became!) attracted to geography do so because of a fascination with peoples and places beyond their own experiences. This fascination – modern geography's final link with its exploration heritage – can be kindled by imaginative teaching showing how different people in different places live out their lives. This should be a truly educational experience, as alternative modes of life are introduced to broaden the inevitably narrow perspectives of most children. Of course it has never worked just like that. Unfortunately, at the present time, the huge cloud of material inequalities hangs over comparative geography. Our children do experience these faraway places, sometimes before their geography lessons, on their television screens. And the image they pick up is not a happy one.

The mass poverty of the Third World enters their homes every week. They know all too well that the world is divided between people living lives like them and others attempting desperately to survive. Our world is polarised; places are not just different, some are rich and some are so very, very poor. In these circumstances geographical fascination can develop into anything from a smug sense of superiority to a genuine, humane desire to help alleviate the poverty. It is the thesis of this chapter that geography's neglect of a global perspective has meant that, inadvertently, our teaching has contributed more to notions of superiority than to feelings of compassion. This is a very serious indictment. The mitigating circumstances are that human geography stands charged with all the other social sciences. We will present the case against human geography, but this will inevitably mean treading on toes outside our discipline. No matter, geographers should never respect disciplinary boundaries anyway since, if we take them too seriously, we are likely to disappear. So we will set our sights in a broad holistic manner, no doubt mildly reminiscent of the grand geography of the past.

THE WORLD IS NOT A LADDER

One effect of the quantitative revolution was that human geography moved away from its traditional affiliation with the humanities and joined the social sciences. Human geography was reconstructed as spatial science. The irony of this situation was that, just as we enrolled in the social science club, some of the more discerning of the social scientists were beginning to have grave doubts about their membership.

Optimism and the social sciences

What was this social science that geographers were so keen to join in the 1960s? Brookfield has described it as a 'sort of euphoria' exhibiting a 'sublime confidence'.[1] Certainly the geographers of the period caught this mood, but how did the euphoria come about in the first place?

Quite simply, it was a product of the particular context of economic expansion in the 'west' after 1945. Social knowledge was already neatly packaged into three bundles of largely separate ideas termed economics, political science and sociology, and post-war prosperity provided a fillip to all three of these 'social sciences'. This was a period when ordinary citizens of the richer countries were being raised above the poverty line for the first time in history. A new message was becoming generally accepted: things could be done to improve the lot of the ordinary man and woman. In this atmosphere social scientists were in demand as experts on what should be done. And the social sciences responded with their models and theories reflecting the optimism of the times. Yes, they could do what was necessary even if it meant *reversing* the theories of their eighteenth and nineteenth-century heritages. So economics was transformed from the dismal science which justified poverty to a new science of managing economic growth and prosperity. The 'leap into darkness' that political writers in the mid-nineteenth century had feared became celebrated as the popular participatory system of democracy which political scientists now offered as the ideal for all ex-colonies. And, perhaps most intriguingly of all, sociologists reversed their theory through a simple change of signs.[2]

Sociology had been born as a reaction to the social disorder of nineteenth-century European urbanisation. The community of traditional society was set against the problem of the anonymity of modern society. In the twentieth century, especially after 1945, modern society came to be celebrated as the ideal social system with traditional society as the problem. Clearly the optimism of the post-war era permeated the social sciences to such a degree that they were able to turn their theories upside down. These were the sister disciplines human geography was mortgaging its future to. And one of the chief – and essentially optimistic – ideas they took on board was developmentalism.

Developmentalism and modernisation

Developmentalism consists of two primary assumptions. The first asserts that the modern world consists of a large number of relatively autonomous societies. They are viewed as autonomous to the extent that social change within these societies can be adequately understood as processes operating *within* each society. In practice each country or 'nation-state' constitutes such a 'society'. The second assumption is that social change operates as a series of parallel paths for all societies. Hence each society or nation-state can be viewed as occupying a position along this common path. This implies three research tasks: a theoretical project to define the path, an empirical project to allocate countries to the path, and a practical duty to advise governments on how to speed their journey along the path. Each of the social sciences produced developmentalist models which emphasised their own particular contribution to 'development', but all of these models shared the same basic character. At one end of the path was a traditional society which was irrational and non-progressive, whereas at the other end was a modern society that was rational and progressive. The general process of reaching this modern ideal was, not surprisingly, often termed *modernisation*.

Let us briefly illustrate the idea of developmentalism by describing two of its most well-known expressions, Rostow's stages of economic growth[3] and the demographic transition model.[4] Rostow begins with a traditional society and its pre-Newtonian science and hence rudimentary technology. In the demographic transition model we start with 'the high fluctuating stage' where both birth rates and death rates are high, a sort of 'natural' demographic situation. Although seeming to describe quite distinct processes, these two first stages actually have much in common. They invoke characteristics of societies which were once universal, but which are now only to be found in poorer countries. This is the crucial step in equating current societies in the 'Third World' with the situation which obtained in the past in the 'First World'. Once this leap of imagination is achieved the history of the First World can be used as a guide for Third World countries navigating the same path. Hence the subsequent stages of both Rostow's model and the demographic transition model can be developed as highly abstracted histories of First World experience, or to be precise in these cases, particularly stylised histories of England. This means that England and other First World societies who have reached the final stage of 'the age of high mass consumption' and low fluctuating birth and death rates are defined as the policy goals for the less fortunate. This reduces to saying 'if only you were like us, your problems would be solved'. Clearly the optimism of the social sciences of this period were also tinged with an arrogance which is only just beginning to be fully appreciated.

Critique and crisis in the social sciences

So far we have described these models as defining paths to a modern, and most importantly, an affluent society. 'Path' is a rather benign and neutral term. It is adequate for describing the theory, but misses much of the arrogance of the resulting prescription. Let me therefore change metaphors at this point. I want to replace the smooth path by the notion of a societal ladder. All societies can be allocated to the appropriate rung of this ladder. On the bottom rung are found traditional societies, on the top rung are the thoroughly modern societies. I have, of course, added a hierarchy to these models. This has in fact been implicit in the preceding discussion, but I now need to make it explicit for my critique of developmentalism. Put simply, when England was 'traditional' and occupying the bottom rung of the ladder there was no 'high mass consumption' going on above it. Countries that are on the bottom rung today, however, find themselves in a polarised world because the top rungs are occupied. This is where the assumption of autonomous societies is crucial to developmentalism. If social change is indeed pre-eminently a matter of the internal dynamics of each society or country, then clearly the position of other countries on the ladder is irrelevant. But if this assumption is unsound and social processes beyond individual states are important to social change, then 'traditional' societies today are not equivalent to England's situation a few centuries ago. This is the nub of the critique of developmentalism in social science.

This critique was voiced but generally not heard in the post-1945 era of social optimism. All this changed with the end of the post-war economic boom and the onset of a world depression. The social sciences began to lose their optimism. Economics became dismal again as Keynesian ideas fell prey to old orthodoxies with a new name: monetarism. Political scientists gave up promoting liberal democracy in the Third World and settled for 'social order' as an attainable ideal. And sociology suffered a famous crisis. Quite simply, the accepted theories and models of the social sciences could not handle the increasing polarisation of the world. Developmentalism had heralded a new dawn for poor countries, it showed them how to catch up. When it became clear that they were not catching up, developmentalist models became a sick joke. Gundar Frank led the attack in a seminal critique entitled *Sociology of Development and the Underdevelopment of Sociology*. He began by simply asserting:

> This new sociology of development is found to be empirically invalid when confronted with reality, theoretically inadequate in terms of its own classical social scientific standards, and policy-wise ineffective for pursuing its supposed intentions of promoting the development of the under-developed countries.[5]

The remainder of the study justified this position by exposing the inadequacies of the modernisation concept in general and Rostow's model in particular. But Frank had constructive arguments to make too, which amounted to an alternative theory of world polarisation. Instead of all countries following the same path to development, Frank identified two complementary but opposite paths. Whereas the rich countries had indeed shown impressive economic growth, this development was countered by an equally impressive process of under-development in poorer countries. They were experiencing the 'development of under-development'. Peru, for instance, had been a victim of this process for several centuries; it was not catching up and it was being continually under-developed. The bottom rung of the ladder was so crowded because of this process of keeping countries under-developed. And this was not a result of the nature of these particular societies: they were kept on the bottom by those at the top. Development and under-development were twin processes, both necessary for each other's operation in the modern world. Those at the top of the ladder maintained their position through exploiting those at the bottom. The benign path to development was in reality an international dogfight which reflected a history of winners and losers. England was a winner, Peru was a loser.

The crux of Frank's criticism is that the orthodox models 'resolutely avoid the study of the international structure of development and underdevelopment of which the domestic structure is only a part'.[6] This argument has been developed by many writers since 1967, of which the most sophisticated is Immanuel Wallerstein's *world-systems approach*.[7] He is attempting to re-unite social science and history by eradicating the error of developmentalism in a new 'historical social science'. For Wallerstein, the world does not consist of a collection of societies all marching towards modernity. Rather, he identifies just one society in today's world, which he terms the *capitalist world-economy*. This consists of a world-wide division of labour and a world market for commodities plus an interstate system. (Note that the so-called 'Second World' is part of this single world-economy: ask the Polish workers who are paying off their government's debts to 'First World' banks.) The essence of the system is *one economy but multiple polities*. The lesson of this approach is that if we wish to study social change – development or underdevelopment – the entity we must deal with is the world-economy. Individual countries do not constitute 'societies' and therefore are inappropriate as the basis of studying social change.

A simple example will clarify this position. The most important social change being experienced today is the current period of relative economic stagnation. The point is that this is not a British problem, an American problem, a Polish problem or a Peruvian problem: it is something that is pervasive throughout the world. For Wallerstein it is the latest in a series of phases of stagnation in the evolution of the world-economy. He provides us with a holistic global picture of our world set out on a social trajectory in which social, economic and political processes are part of a single overall logic. It is a logic that produces a polarisation spatially represented by core and periphery in the world-economy. In this model, to use more traditional geographical terminology, modern history is interpreted not as a ladder but as a process whereby the world has come to be organised into a single large functional region, initially with a single major node in North-West Europe and latterly becoming multi-nodal with first North America and then Japan becoming important members of the core. Clearly, Wallerstein's scheme is not only bringing history back into consideration: it locates geography at centre-stage instead of being a spatial appendix to conventional social science. In the world-systems approach geography can rediscover its lost geo.

LADDERS IN HUMAN GEOGRAPHY

Models in Geography was published in the same year as Frank's critique of modernisation. Hence Keeble[8] was introducing Rostow's model to a geography audience just as Frank was demolishing it for a social science audience. At about the same time modernisation itself was being added to our geographical concepts by way of a series of 'geographies of modernisation' for different African countries.[9] In line with human geography's new role as spatial science, modernisation was modelled as a 'spatial process' diffusing out from centres to produce 'surfaces' of relative modernisation. And of course the demographic transition became popular among population geographers. Chung[10] provided 'a space-time diffusion' of the demographic transition explicitly showing how different countries were passing through different stages of the model not unlike those Rostow had incorporated within his model.

But geographers did not just apply the developmentalist models of other social scientists, they invented some of their own. I will consider just three of them.

Transport networks

By far the most popular, at least in terms of its reproduction in textbooks, was the Taaffe, Morrill and Gould model of transport expansion in undevelopment countries.[11] They defined 'an ideal-typical sequence of transport development' based on case studies of Ghana and Nigeria. Their diagram of six stages from 'scattered ports' to 'emergence of high-priority "main streets"' is one of the most familiar of 1960s geography. It is of interest to note here that they explicitly point out 'analogies' with Rostow's stages: for instance, 'the development of a penetration line might be viewed as a sort of spatial "take-off"'. Hence although primarily concerned with 'under-developed countries', a final stage reminiscent of 'main street USA' (New York–Chicago) is what they had in mind in their ultimate 'high priority linkages' phase.

In short, this is a beautifully clear geographical developmentalist model and it suffers from all the problems of such models. Transport expansion is treated on a country-by-country basis. All the processes discussed take place within the individual country. The idea that Ghana and Nigeria are part of a much larger global process, and that their transport expansions are merely two small parts of the wider process of creating the modern world 'functional region', is not addressed. In both of these cases their transport was designed as part of a system that terminated in London. But Taaffe, Morrill and Gould were able to override this feature of the process to conclude optimistically with a vision of an integrated and independent transport network, asserting: 'In under-developed countries high priority linkages would seem less likely to develop along an export trunk line than along a route connecting two centres concerned in internal linkage.'[12] Of course in the two decades since these words were written New York – Chicago style 'main streets' have not materialised in the countries of the Third World. Instead, they remain locked into a global transport network where their local transport lines are merely feeders into the larger whole.

Primate cities

A similar developmentalist argument has been suggested for the size distribution of settlements within countries, in order to bring together the seemingly contradictory 'law of the primate city' and 'rank size rule'. Berry provided a neat argument which suggested the primate city distribution was merely a first stage in the development of an integrated city system represented by the rank size rule.[13] The model is superficially attractive since the majority of primate cities are indeed to be found in the Third World. But once again it can easily be shown that by treating city-size distributions on a country-by-country basis the overall processes producing city growth are omitted. Primate cities tend to occur at both ends of imperial linkages, that is Paris and London as well as Dakar and Accra. Basically the world 'functional region' can be thought of as a series of functional sub-regions nesting within the global whole. The creation of colonies, covering nearly all the non-European world, was a political act which brought in its train the construction of these functional sub-regions. The scale of most colonies was such that they could be controlled from and economically linked through one colonial capital city.

It is these capital cities that constitute the primate cities in today's third world. Where the size of the colony was larger than the control span of the times, then several economic centres emerged so that the colony consisted of a cluster of functional sub-regions as in the case of India. The lesson of this short discussion is that the city size distribution of single countries does not evolve towards a rank size equilibrium, but rather represents particular histories of fragments of the world-economy and reflects specific relations operating at the global scale. There can be no simple model because there is no autonomous process operating within countries.

The mobility transition

Developmentalist thinking in geography reached its apogee in Zelinsky's thesis about the 'mobility transition'. In Zelinsky's view: 'There are definite, patterned regularities in the growth of personal mobility through space-time during recent history, and these regularities comprise an essential component of the modernisation process.'[14] The conventional demographic transition was renamed the 'vital transition' (dealing with just births and deaths) and this 'mobility transition' is added as the 'other demographic transition'. Zelinsky provides the most explicit description of developmentalism in geography: in effect, a geography of ladders. The world is viewed as a series of hearth areas out of which modernisation diffuses, so that the Third World's future can be explicitly read from the First World's past and present in idealised maps and graphs of developmental social change. The mobility transition itself consists of five phases from the now familiar 'pre-modern traditional society' through to 'a future superadvanced society'.

By now my critique will have been anticipated. The mobility history of particular countries does not just reflect processes within those countries. Different forms of mobility are the result of processes and opportunities which unfold at the global scale. This is equally true of the other 'transitions' Zelinsky identified – the occupation transition, the educational transition and the residential transition. To interpret these as occurring country-by-country is a gross example of the error of developmentalism. Social changes involving occupations, education and residence are part of the overall process in the unfolding dynamic of our world-economy. Different sectors of that world-economy, core and periphery, experience different types of change as the whole system is continually restructured. This is the essence of Wallerstein's world-systems logic.

NEITHER SNAKES NOR LADDERS BUT TADPOLES

Although we can interpret Zelinsky's identification of multiple 'transitions' as the culmination of developmentalist research in geography, this type of thinking still has a strong hold on human geography. Its demise does not, however, mean we should replace our ladders by snakes.

The most celebrated phrase in the whole debate is Frank's 'development of under-development'. According to Frank, as I have indicated, while development was proceeding in the core the development of under-development was occurring in the periphery. It is easy to see how this can be viewed as snakes and ladders. And much detailed research of processes operating in the periphery has documented the regressive effects of the restructuring of local economies in the wake of European imperialism. In some ways this work is the opposite of the geography of modernisation. Watts, for instance, has studied the famine of the Sahel in Northern Nigeria and finds that contact with the European colonisers, far from heralding a new affluent modern life, is actually directly culpable for the disaster which has befallen these unfortunate people.[15] Although this 'natural disaster' has generally been blamed on drought conditions, Watts points out that these climatic circumstances are a periodic feature of the Sahel. The question therefore arises as to why there is such a disastrous famine this time compared to previous drought periods. Watts finds the answer in the re-organisation of the Hausa society by the colonial power which destroyed the carefully constituted economic and social processes adapted to periodic drought. Traditional methods of risk aversion and margins of security were sacrificed for inflexible state taxes and markets for export. What was created was the new vulnerable people whose members suffered starvation on our television screens through the 1970s.

Surely here we have discovered a 'snake' in the sense that Hausa society has spiralled downwards instead of modernising upwards? This is not Watts' interpretation, and I agree with him. Once taken over by the British colonial power, Hausa society ceased to be an autonomous entity. This pre-capitalist social formation was incorporated into the capitalist world-economy. From that point onwards social change in Hausaland became part of the changes operating in the world-economy as a whole. Hence there *is* no Hausa society moving in a particular direction, either up or down, because that 'society' has ceased to exist. In general, then, a revised geography must not treat the world as a game of snakes and ladders. Frank's development of under-development does not describe an alternative path. Such interpretations perpetuate developmentalist thinking: countries remain the basic unit of change as they slide up and down the games board. The whole essence of the world-systems approach is to break with this tradition.

Nor is it sufficient to postulate inter-dependence as the prime concept around which to organise our ideas. This is emphasised by Brookfield[16] and more recently Reitsma[17] has suggested we go beyond the simple core-periphery linkage implied above and concentrate instead on the wide range of linkages between different types of countries in our modern world. We don't seem to be able to get away from countries, do we? The world-systems approach is not about classifying countries and then investigating the linkages between these different classes. If social change ultimately occurs at the level of the world-economy, that means there is an overall logic *operating at that geographical scale*. It is a logic that is not expressed as inter-dependence between countries; we need to consider the operation of the world-system as a whole.

Wallerstein describes the operation of the world-economy with a beautiful analogy borrowed from R. H. Tawney. This is the 'tadpole philosophy'. Consider a pond which spawns a population of frogs. Every year large numbers of eggs are deposited into the pond to produce masses of tadpoles. From these many tadpoles, though, only a limited number of frogs emerge. The tadpole philosophy is then proclaimed by the successful frogs sitting on their lily pads. Each frog asserts to the spirits of its departed brothers and sisters (who never reached froghood) that if only they had emulated its behaviour they too could have become frogs. Of course, the more arrogant frogs go on to assert that they had special abilities as tadpoles, which marked them out as especially suited to froghood. No matter, the point is that if all tadpoles had been genetically equal, the ecology of the pond is such that only a given number of frogs could develop. It is nothing to do with behaviour or abilities, the key criterion is the quantity of resources available to sustain the population (see also Rees, Chapter 6.1).

Translated into world-systems terms, the tadpole philosophy is our developmentalism. The world-economy has a given quantity of resources at any point in time distributed among all the core and periphery countries. If at this time *every* country adopted perfectly rational policies reflecting their particular self-interest, there will continue to be successes and failures. The world-economy cannot sustain all countries rising simultaneously. In fact, Wallerstein argues that the very success of any one country lessens the opportunities for its rivals. Polarisation between rich and poor is an integral part of the system. He goes on to suggest that the ratio between core and periphery populations has remained approximately constant throughout the history of the world-economy. Hence the expansion of the core in the last century has only been possible with the incorporation of further areas into the periphery. Now that this geographical expansion is complete, movement into the core will be that much more difficult being dependent on other countries vacating their eminent position. Most countries in the world are tadpoles and are destined to remain so as long as the capitalist world-economy exists.

WOT, NO LADDERS!

Human geography has changed a great deal since the 1960s. The questioning of what came to be known as 'positivism' in geography took many forms. The hallmark of current human geography is therefore a variety of perspectives and a distrust of any new conformity. This is no doubt a healthy development for geographical research, but it can be quite confusing for geographical teaching. This is particularly the case where new ideas have not been fully worked out geographically, as is true for the world-systems approach. We stand accused of knocking down models without having anything equivalent to put immediately in their place. Quite simply no fully worked out 'geography of the world-economy' currently exists. We can imagine what such a new geography should look like but it has not, as yet, been produced. This does not lessen the need to eradicate the error of developmentalism in geography, but it does leave us with an incomplete argument. I have chosen to make this point honestly rather than plead shortage of space as an excuse for the limited nature of what follows. Whatever expectations I have built up in previous sections should by now be deflated, so I can safely proceed.

The ideas of Frank and Wallerstein have entered geography largely through debates carried on in the 'geography of development'.[18] This has centred on the relevance of their ideas for researchers specialising in Third World countries and continents. But it should be clear from the above discussions that the world-systems approach is about *one world*, not two or three. Its lessons and prescriptions for research and teaching are just as relevant to those geographers specialising in, say, Britain and USA as in Africa and Latin America. It is just that the failure of the optimistic social science models of a past age are particularly acute in Third World countries, hence the particular concern of 'geographers of development'.

A sub-discipline much more directly in the world-systems firing line is, perhaps surprisingly, traditional historical geography. As Wallerstein has made clear, he is constructing a new historiography to replace the one that has dominated western history since the mid-nineteenth century.[19] A liberal theory of inevitable progress is the one underlying the stylised histories that pass for developmentalist models. Wallerstein's history is very different. Most of recorded history consists of the waxing and waning of 'world-empires' as distinct entities successively incorporating and releasing local mini-systems of hunters, gatherers and rudimentary agriculturalists. These larger world-empires have a structural dynamic which eventually produces their demise. The demise of one of these world-empires, feudal Europe, was instrumental in generating after 1450 a new type of 'world-system', the European capitalist world-economy. This has its own cyclical dynamic, but within that pattern it had geographically expanded to cover the whole globe by about 1900. It is for this reason that we can currently talk about there being only one entity of social change, and to think otherwise is to commit the error of developmentalism.

Inevitably, the world-systems approach must involve a new historical geography. But what sort of geography will be so treated? I believe, with many other recent critics of positivism, that the time is ripe for a revitalisation of regional geography. The regional geography I am thinking of would be set within the world-systems historiography which has just been outlined. Regional geographies of the world-economy would involve description of the society and its geography before incorporation, the nature of the incorporation of the region into the world-economy, the subsequent re-organisation of the old society and its geography as it became part of the larger whole and, finally, the social and geographical changes in the region as it responds to, and contributes to, the cyclical dynamic of the modern world-system. There is much material available in the literature in a wide variety of sources, both geographical and non-geographical, on all of these aspects of most regions in the world, but they have not yet been put together for any one major region. The nearest thing we have to such regional geographies are the particular case studies which are consistent with my previous discussion, such as Watts' treatment of famine in Hausaland. But all the indications are that such new regional geographies are not too far away.

An example: urbanisation and world systems

I think it is important to give one example of an alternative interpretation of some relative familiar geography to illustrate world-systems thinking in geography. In the standard historiography, urban history is largely concerned with a sequence of 'urbanisations' working through time from the early middle-east and classical Mediterranean to medieval Europe and finally modern industrial Europe and America. This is largely adherred to in Harold Carter's recent *Introduction to Urban Historical Geography*.[20] In this study China warrants just three mentions compared with eight for Merthyr Tydfil. Of course no book can be expected to fully cover all historical examples of urbanisation, but any selection does reflect the historiography underlying the study.

The world-systems alternative historiography is represented by the four diagrams in Figures 5.1.1 to 5.1.4. In Figure 5.1.1 circles represent separate world-systems – either world-empires or the incipient European world-economy – as autonomous entities, existing in 1500. Within each world system the dots represent towns of over 30 000 population, and open circles represent cities of over 100 000.[21] In 1500 twelve entitles could be identified, each with their own 'urban system'. Europe has by no means the largest urban system at this time. The other three diagrams show changes in these urban systems for subsequent centuries. In 1600 (Figure 5.1.2) expansion of both the European world-economy and the Islam world-empire are recorded and little change is shown by 1700 (Figure 5.1.3). In 1800 (Figure 5.1.4) on the eve of the great urbanisation subsequent on industrialisation in Europe, the European urban system remains only about the same size as that of the other large world-systems. In fact in 1800 there was only one millionaire city in the world and that was outside the capitalist world-economy – Peking, China.

This sequence of diagrams should help reveal the Eurocentric thinking which dominates much of our current historical geography. Urban population sizes can be interpreted in many ways. They reflect the economic efficiency of the rural populations and their ability to support large urban populations, as well as the ability of the administrative organisation to store and distribute large quantities of food for the town dwellers. On both of these grounds the European world-system of agricultural capitalism was certainly not superior to the other major world-systems as late as 1800. But the important point of this exercise is to first find your 'society' before defining your 'urban system'.

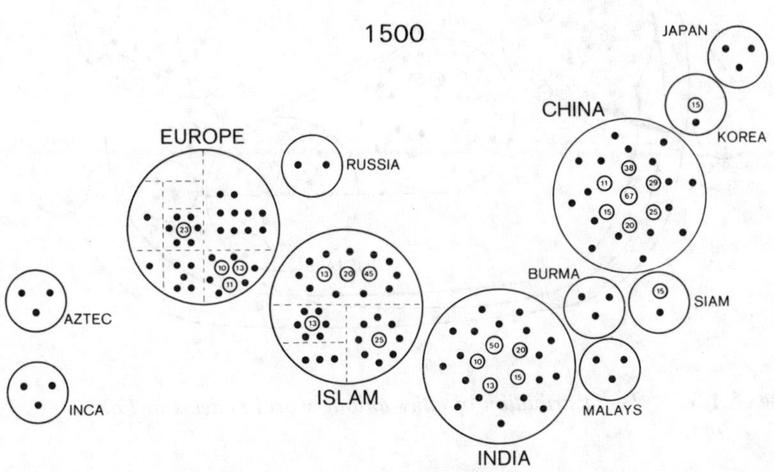

FIGURE 5.1.1 *The distribution of cities among world-systems in 1500.* Each dot represents a city of over 30 000 people. Open ones represent cities of over 100 000. Broken lines show the main political divisions within a world-system. All population estimates are from Chandler and Fox (1974)

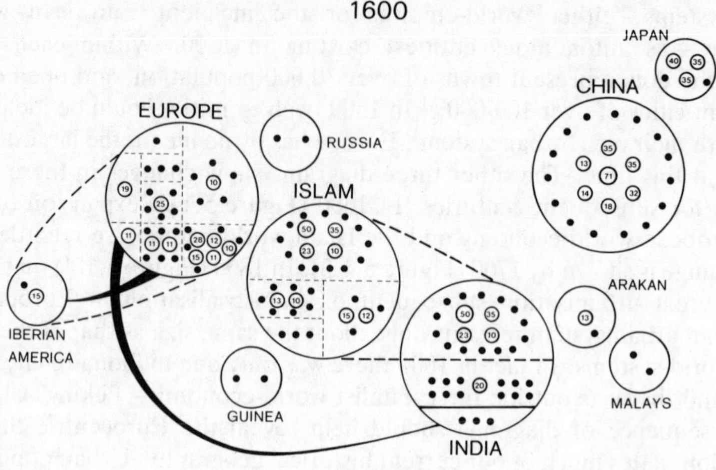

FIGURE 5.1.2 *The distribution of cities among world-systems in 1600*

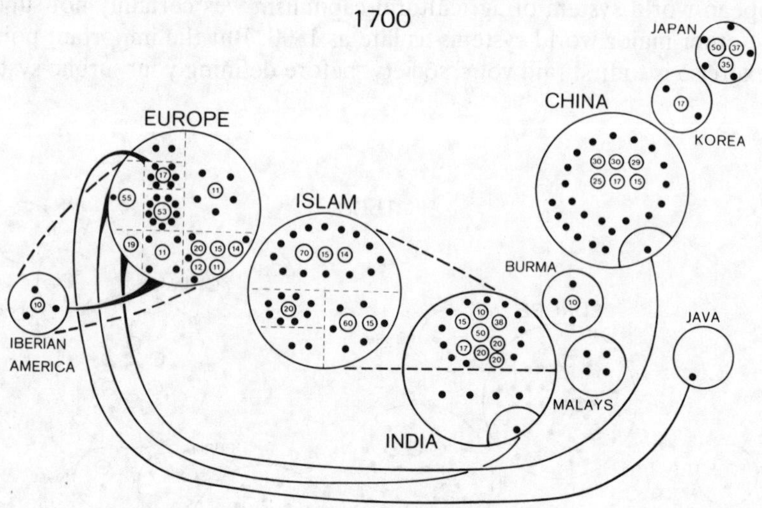

FIGURE 5.1.3 *The distribution of cities among world-systems in 1700*

The European world-economy co-existed with several rival world-systems before they succumbed to its military and economic might by 1900. There are no new facts here, merely a new historiography. Even this one small aspect of historical geography illustrates the revolution in thinking that is the challenge of the world-systems approach.

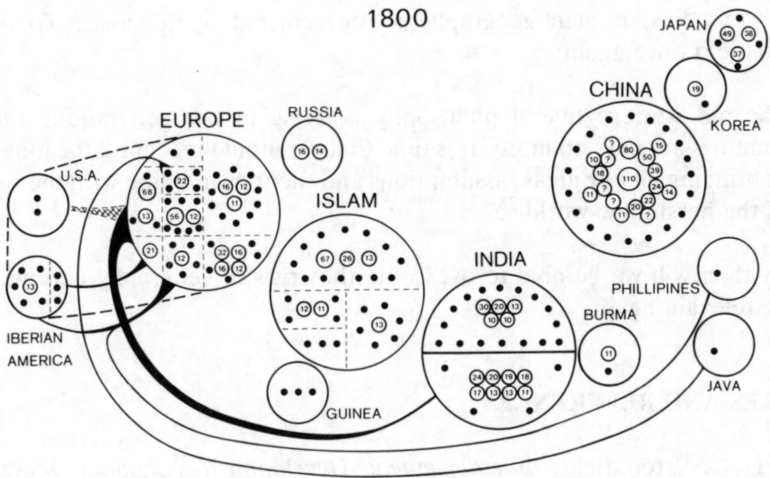

FIGURE 5.1.4 *The distribution of cities in world-systems in 1800*

CONCLUSION

In hindsight it seems incredible just how seductive those old social science ladders really were. I suppose the medium-level abstraction made developmental models ideal pedagogic classroom tools. We all know how easy it was to teach Rostow, the demographic transitions and their geographical variants. Simple and clear visual presentation was obviously another key advantage. But if we are really honest with ourselves, we know that what these models were saying is what we wanted to hear. That is to say, they were sensitively tuned to our underlying philosophy in the 1960s. In those optimistic times we wanted to believe in stairways to heaven. Finally, however, the bubble burst – in Brookfield's words: 'Confidence in the inevitability of progress rose steadily from 1945 to peak around 1960 and collapsed in the late 1960s.'[22] Now we must surely treat those models as interesting intellectual artifacts of a past age of innocence.

To appreciate the changes in geography that have taken place we need only look at the contrasting treatments of Nigeria by Taaffe *et. al* and Watts. We seem to have moved to another world; and in a sense we have – from a world of multiple parallel paths to the modern world-system. The eradication of the error of developmentalism is only one small step, albeit an important first step, to adjust human geography to our current world crisis. To quote Brookfield once again:

> The old western liberal philosophy is dying in our generation, and its comforts are ours no more. It is time that we should recognise the long task of bringing all our ideas, assumptions and theories into line with the reality of the harsh new world.[23]

Only then will we be able to overcome the crisis of geography and make it truly relevant again.

NOTES AND REFERENCES

1. H. C. Brookfield, *Interdependent Development* (London: Methuen, 1975).
2. E. Wolf, *Europe and the People without History* (Berkeley: University of California Press, 1982).
3. W. Rostow, *The Stages of Economic Growth: a non-communist manifesto* (Cambridge: Cambridge University Press, 1960).
4. K. Davis, 'The world demographic transition', *Ann. Amer. Acad. Pol. Sci.* 24 (1945) pp.1–15.
5. A. G. Frank, 'Sociology of Development and the Underdevelopment of Sociology' *Catalyst*, Summer 1967, pp.20–73.
6. Ibid., pp.26–7.
7. I. Wallerstein, *The Capitalist World-Economy* (Cambridge: Cambridge University Press, 1979); idem, *Historical Capitalism* (London: Verso, 1983); P. J. Taylor, 'The world-systems project', in R. J. Johnston and P. J. Taylor (eds) *A World in Crisis: geographical perspectives* (Oxford: Basil Blackwell, 1985) pp.269–288.
8. D. Keeble, 'Models of economic development', in R. J. Chorley and P. Haggett (eds) *Models in Geography* (London: Methuen, 1967) pp.243–302.
9. For example, J. B. Riddell, *The Spatial Dynamics of Modernisation in Sierra Leone* (Evanston, Ill.: North Western University Press,. 1970); but cf. J. B. Riddell, 'The geography of modernisation in Africa: a re-examination', *Canadian Geographer* 25 (1981) pp.290–99.
10. R. Chung, 'Space-time diffusion of the transition model: the twentieth-century patterns', in G. Demko, H. Rose and G. Schnell (eds) *Population Geography: a reader* (New York: McGraw-Hill, 1970) pp.220–39.
11. E. J. Taafe, R. L. Morrill and P. R. Gould, 'Transport expansion in underdeveloped countries: a comparative analysis', *Geogr. Rev.*, 53 (1963) pp.503–29.
12. Ibid., p.514.

13. B. J. L. Berry, 'City-size distribution and economic development.' *Econ. Dev. Cult. Change* 9 (1961) pp.573–88.
14. W. Zelinsky, 'The hypothesis of the mobility transition', *Geogr. Rev.*, 61 (1971) pp.219–49.
15. M. Watts, 'Hazards and crises: a political economy of drought and famine in Northern Nigeria', *Antipode* 15(1) (1983) pp.24–34.
16. Brookfield, *op. cit.*
17. H. Reitsma, 'Development geography, dependency relations and the capitalist scapegoat', *Professional Geographer* 34 (1982) pp.125–30.
18. For example, D. Forbes, *The Geography of Underdevelopment* (Beckenham: Croom Helm, 1984).
19. I. Wallerstein, 'Maps, maps, maps', *Radical History Review* 24 (1980) pp.155–9.
20. H. Carter, *An Introduction to Urban Historical Geography* (London: Edward Arnold, 1983).
21. Urban populations are those estimated by G. Chandler and T. Fox, *3000 Years of Urban Growth* (New York: Academic Press, 1974).
22. Brookfield, *op. cit.*, pp.76–7.
23. H. C. Brookfield, 'On one geography and a third world', *Trans. Inst. Br. Geogr.*, 58 (1973) pp.1–20.

FURTHER READING

A textbook which summarises many of the debates in development geography (and beyond) is Dean Forbes, *The Geography of Underdevelopment* (Beckenham: Croom Helm, 1984), while I have used the world-systems approach in my reconstruction of political geography, *Political Geography: world-economy, nation-state and locality* (Harlow: Longman, 1985).

An indispensable collection of Immanuel Wallerstein's essays is his *The Capitalist World-Economy* (Cambridge: Cambridge University Press, 1979). His *Historical Capitalism* (London: Verso, 1983) is also essential reading: it is a brief essay which outlines the world-systems interpretation of capitalism as an economic, political and intellectual product.

5.2
Privilege and Place in Soviet Society

Graham E. Smith
University of Cambridge

Graham Smith is Lecturer in Geography at the University of Cambridge and a Fellow of Sidney Sussex College. His teaching and research interests are in political geography and the Soviet Union. He has published widely on ethnic nationalism in advanced societies, the Soviet Baltic republics, and on economic and social aspects of the Soviet labour force.

REGIONAL GEOGRAPHIES AND WORLD SYSTEMS

Although regional geography has always held an affectionate place within our discipline, it has become tangential to the great majority of geographic research. There are of course good reasons for its low profile in both the schools and the universities. In the wave of the so-called 'new geography' of the 1950s and 1960s, with its emphasis on generalisations based on geometry and neo-classical location models, there was little room for the study of places and of the peoples who made them. As a profession we are now no longer trained in the broader perspectives of our forebears; our linguistic capabilities rarely extend beyond the arena of the English-speaking world, while sharp systematic divisions of labour within geography have resulted in the analytical fragmentation of societies. Rather than enhancing our comprehension of those complex and inter-related social, cultural, economic and political processes which mould the very fabric of the regions we claim to be studying, such academic specialisation has instead obscured a fuller regional understanding, at whatever scale.

In arguing for a renewed commitment to regional geography, however, I am not suggesting that we come full circle; to do so is to advocate a return to the exceptionalist and encyclopedic regional geography of the past. Rather, as Johnston rightly notes: 'Regional geography must focus on the unique characteristics of the places being studied, but must not express them as if they were singular. This means that regions must not be studied solely as separate entities. They are part of a much larger whole.'[1] Instead of considering a region as somehow irreducibly unique, therefore, because no general statements can be made in reference to it, we should be moving towards developing a regional geography which can be accounted for by a particular combination of general and place-specific processes. So if I understand Johnston's argument correctly, and at the risk of oversimplifying his proposed methodology, what is being proposed is a dialectical approach along the following lines:

1. *Thesis*: We live in *one* world in which no part of the earth's surface escapes from general processes that are operating at the global scale. Economic processes in particular have mapped out an unevenly developed world in which all regions are linked and are part of a cumulatively causal and historically determined process of differential development.
2. *Antithesis*: Yet regions are also distinct and definable, complete with their own particular social, political and cultural forms of organisation and ways of doing things. Institutions, groups and individuals mould the geographies of their own regions.
3. *Synthesis*: Regions are both determined and determining; there is a subtle interplay between those processes operating at the global scale and those which are regionally-specific to particular societies.

Although such an approach offers the possibility of grasping the simultaneity of global and regional processes operating within an historically unfolding framework, however, it also suggests that global scale *economic* processes – based on a capitalist mode of production – is of primary importance. There is no doubt that unequal exchange between societies leads to geographies of differential development, and that this reflects the structuring of social relationships between societies as well as the vested interests of particular political institutions – such as states – which mould the world of inequality. We also know that global capital in the form of, for example, multinational firms, follows a spatial logic with all the different consequences this has for different societies (see Thrift and Taylor, Chapter 4.3). Only the myopic would deny the importance of such economic processes as they cascade through all geographic scales, leaving their uneven and diffuse imprint on the city, the neighbourhood and the workplace. What is at issue, however, is whether regional geographies can *only* be understood by locating each society within a global framework determined by its *economic* position within the world system. Let us then consider this 'world-systems' perspective in a little more detail.

World-systems analysis emerged from dependency theory and, as Taylor shows in his chapter (Chapter 5.1), starts from the assumption that the world is the only meaningful entity within which the history of any particular region can be understood. Rather than viewing the world as composed of a multitude of 'societies' or states, it is instead argued that 'societies' are merely 'parts of a whole reflecting the whole' and that it is this *totality* – one, essentially capitalist economic system with its origins in the seventeenth century – that must be taken as the basic framework within which 'society' can be located. The doyen of world-systems analysis, Immanuel Wallerstein, argues that a society 'no more has a mode of production than does a firm. The concept "mode of production" describes an economy, the boundaries of which are . . . an empirical question.'[2] In the case of the capitalist mode of production, Wallerstein argues, its boundaries are global. From such a perspective it follows that in order to understand the geography of any country – Japan or Jamaica – we must first locate it within the world economy, for it is the interstate system which fundamentally determines what resources are available to any country and how they are distributed internally.

In a world of finite resources, so it is claimed, the logic of capitalism dictates the balance of domination between countries and thereby provides the motivation for military competition between states and the basis for foreign policy. According to this argument, socialist countries – like so-called 'Third World' and advanced capitalist countries – fall into one of three categories along a dominance-dependency continuum which runs from core countries through to semi-peripheral countries to peripheral countries. Socialist countries, Wallerstein claims, are simply 'collective capitalist firm(s),[3] whose positions in the world economy also depend on how effective each has been in competing for power and economic advantage. On this basis, as a core-located country, the Soviet Union is supposed to have more in common with the United States and West Germany than it has with peripherally-positioned Cuba and Mozambique.

Although possessing a seductively holistic framework, such an approach to regional geography reduces differences between countries in both time and space to those economic processes operating at the global scale. This is to misconceive differing local forms of political, legal and social organisation, various cultures, values and beliefs, as little more than regimented appendages to a macroscale hierarchy of world order, and means that in the last resort explanation revolves around the dominance-dependency dynamics of *one* world system. In approaching regional geography in this way, and *contra* Taylor (Chapter 5.1) we fall back into the trap of the generalising impulse of spatial science, and fail to take into account the distinctive histories, cultures and politics of the regions that we study. To squeeze societies into three neat boxes on the basis of a dominance-dependency continuum is to ignore the *fundamental* differences between the socialist world and the capitalist world.

To ignore the differences between these two 'systems' is to erase the distinctive ways in which socialist countries organise their economies, and to suppress the distinctive features of their entire political and cultural life. I am, of course, not arguing that the geographies of the socialist world are somehow unaffected by what goes on in the capitalist world. Societies like the Soviet Union, China and even Albania function as part of one world, economically as well as politically. It is right to be reminded by world-systems theorists that economic conditions within the socialist world are affected by what goes on in the capitalist world, which does indeed dominate world trade and which therefore determines the price of the imports and the exports of the socialist bloc and the volume of their foreign earnings. Such processes do circumvent the activities of state planners in such economies and thus affect the lives of consumers and producers in Kiev and Kraków as well as in Bristol and Kuala Lumpur (cf. Thrift and Taylor, Chapter 4.3).

Food queues in Polish cities are the consequence not only of a countryside starved of effective state investment, but of the need to export food in order to pay that country's gigantic bill for goods imported from the West. What I am suggesting, however, is that, to quote Worsley: 'The world is neither capitalist nor communist, but a system of oppositions based on two major polarities: developed versus underdeveloped, and capitalist versus communist.'[4] On this basis it could well be argued that there is 'an alternative world system' based on the Council for Mutual Economic Assistance (CMEA or COMECON), whose member countries are more dependent on each other than they are on the capitalist world. Certainly this 'system' has its own distinctive hierarchy of states, with the Soviet Union at the core. The latter dominates militarily, economically and politically, with capital and labour flows being of far more significance within this socialist bloc than between it and the capitalist world. And indeed, the intense nationalism displayed by the socialist bloc towards the West, while also helping to map out trading patterns, cannot be simply explained in terms of inter-state competition for scarce resources. To understand how such countries operate within the world economy – let alone what processes structure them – we need to acknowledge *from the outset* that state socialist societies have followed their own cultural logic of development and have their own ways of organising their peoples and places.

TERRITORIAL POWER AND THE SOVIET STATE

In this chapter I want to focus on the Soviet Union, historically the most important of the countries in the socialist world and arguably nearest to the archetypal case. One of the most striking features of the Soviet Union is the economic, social and political power that the state has at its disposal to shape the spatial structure of society and to determine who gets what and where. Through its territorial near-monopoly over the ownership, control and management of resources (including land, technology, wages, education, status and position), the leadership has the ability to manipulate resource allocation and distribution within society in accordance with its own political preferences.

Both the character and the concentration of such territorial power distinguishes the USSR from capitalist democracies where, to paraphrase Goldthorpe: 'economic, and specifically market forces act as the crucial agency within society . . . (and) consequently, the class situation of individuals and groups, understood in terms of their economic power and resources, tends to be the most single determinant of their life chances.'[5] The Soviet state's claim to such a monopoly of highly centralised and coordinated territorial power rests on its commitment to eradicating town-country and region-region differences and removing the inequalities in life chances which these spatial divisions represent. It is, of course, this egalitarian goal of creating a classless society (and full communism), drawing upon the ideas and ideals of its Marxist founding fathers, which also sets such a régime apart from the West.

In the present self-designated period of 'developed socialism', a slogan coined in the mid-1960s, the Soviet political leadership argues that Soviet society has progressed towards the creation of socially equal opportunities between places, and is hence well on the way to removing town-country and region-region differences. While few western commentators would deny the speed at which the USSR has improved the material and social well-being of the average citizen in the post-Stalin period, however, many would dispute that 'developed socialism' is a synonym for social equality. In one of the most exhaustive examinations of official Soviet statistics on urban-rural, inter-urban and regional differences in the USSR, Fuchs and Demko demonstrate that marked socio-spatial inequalities continue to persist. This they attribute to four socio-economic processes:

(1) economic development through location policy prioritised uneven development for both strategic and spatial efficiency reasons at the expense of regional equity through geographic dispersion;
(2) investment in productive sectors has taken priority over infrastructural investment (eg. housing) and this has led to 'underurbanisation' and the consequent emergence of a disadvantaged group of commuters;
(3) the centralisation of social services through economies of scale has resulted in differential access to them;
(4) occupational groups are differentially rewarded through income, and since they are spatially clustered, regional differences in income result.[6]

Although he accepts these statistical findings, Peet is nonetheless highly critical of the way in which Fuchs and Demko explain social inequality. He considers that their 'explanation' is little more than a randomly assembled group of 'factors' with little relation between them, and suggests that we need to move on 'to try and understand what the *structure* of a more *complete* explanation might be'.[7] He is, I think, right to contend that this necessarily involves considering how the state relates to society, who makes what kinds of decisions, on what grounds and in whose interests. Yet at the same time he argues that Soviet society is not a socialist society but rather a 'state capitalist' society. He does not acknowledge the possibility that *new* and *different* social processes to those found under capitalism may be at work and that these might be attributed to the way in which the Soviet state administers its society. What I want to argue, in contrast, is that the processes which have given rise to socio-spatial inequalities in the Soviet Union – and indeed the nature of these inequalities – are qualitatively different to those found outside the socialist bloc. It is only by working towards a theory of the spatial structure of society under existing state socialism (however imperfect that *type* of socialism may be) that we will be able to begin to grasp the nature of Soviet society.

I begin by arguing that the particular developmental strategy adopted by the architects of the modern Soviet state, together with the use of administrative restrictions on the population's geographic mobility, have resulted in the creation of a territorial hierarchy of places which corresponds to social patterns of differentiation between basic groups. While creating unintended problems for the effective utilisation of the labour force to meet the needs of a centrally planned economy, such administrative restrictions play an important part in providing a territorial basis for social stability amongst the privileged and most politically sensitive urban groupings, namely the middle classes and white collar workers.

THE TRANSITION TO SOCIALISM

It has often been argued that, historically, two alternative routes were open to the USSR's urban-centred power élite in deciding how and when to proceed with transforming the backward economy of the mid 1920s – when over four-fifths of the population lived in the private, primarily rural sector – into a fully industrialised and state-owned economy. Advocates of whatever strategy never doubted that the building of socialism was dependent on the expansion of the urban-industrial base, but on what become known as the 'Right opposition', Nikolai Bukharin and his followers advocated industrialisation 'at a snail's pace'. It was only through increasing the production of consumer goods in exchange for lowered prices, so they argued, that the peasantry would be induced to raise and sell more agricultural produce and so contribute to the financing of industrial growth. Such a strategy therefore entailed slow urban growth, required only moderate population migration to the cities envisaged the weakening of the division of labour between agriculture and industry, and thereby held out the prospect of a more equitable balance in living standards. So urban-industrial development was seen as inconceivable without rural development; it was marketable surpluses plus (urban-inspired) rural innovation which was to encourage the co-operation of the peasantry in the process of industrialisation.

On the other hand, adopting policies originally advocated by the defeated 'Left Opposition', Stalin gradually groped his way towards Evgeny Preobrazhensky's theory of primitive socialist accumulation and extensive industrialisation. Ultimately this would entail huge, sustained investments in heavy industry, coupled with the imposition of agricultural collectivisation (1929–32) in order to force the peasantry into both providing the necessary finance for industrialisation and to releasing labour for the sudden industrial expansion. Such a strategy not only led to the long-term down-grading of rural investment, but also to the neglect of small towns and the growth of large cities. Moreover, as this strategy of unbalanced sectoral and spatial growth was preoccupied with developing the economic base of both industrialisation and military power at any cost, it also necessitated savings through the complete neglect of urban infrastructural facilities like housing and of consumer-related industries, and the sacrifice of high urban wages. In short, the particular strategy which led to socialist state ownership of both urban and rural production meant planning for *differential development*.

It is possible to question whether the Bukharinist strategy represented a real alternative for the Bolshevik leadership in the late 1920s, or indeed whether a substantial resource and capital outflow from the countryside to the city took place during the initial phase of industrialisation (1929–1937).[8] It is sufficient for my present purposes, however, to say that it was very difficult for the political leadership to envisage any alternative. Firstly, there was the economic and military vulnerability of the beleaguered Soviet state, the sense of isolation and danger in a world hostile to socialism and the consequent perception of a need to secure a strong military-industrial base with all speed. Secondly, there was the mistrust – based on experience – of a peasantry considered by urban decision-makers to be largely unsympathetic to socialism. Thirdly, there were the ambiguous views of Marx himself on how to build socialism, and an increasingly powerful strain of post-revolutionary thought which considered the coercive apparatus of the state as the only vehicle capable of transforming society. Finally, there was a commitment to an ideal and that meant securing industrialisation sooner or later.

What is central to my argument, however, is that the nature and speed of industrialisation resulted in the release of millions of people from the countryside and their incorporation into labour intensive industry in the large cities. An extremely rapid growth occurred in urban-industrial employment. In 1928, manual and non-manual workers (including members of families but excluding peasants) comprised 17.6 per cent of the total population. By 1939, only two years after the completion of the first two five year plans, this group had risen to 50.2 per cent. The urban population also rapidly doubled: from 27.6 million in 1926 to 61.1 million by 1940 (and increasing the urban share of the total population from 17 to 33 per cent).[9] This rural to urban migration also resulted in unprecedented upward social mobility, for it turned peasants into industrial workers and specialists more or less overnight. Extensive industrialisation therefore necessitated a fluidity of social structure in order to meet the insatiable demands of a modernising urban economy, and a rapidly growing state bureaucracy to administer it. Not surprisingly, Stalin's massive purges also created considerable scope for promotion. Yet despite the state's omnipotent control over the workforce and its indiscriminate use of violence and coercion in order to fulfill its ambitious economic objectives, the importance of expanding opportunities through large-scale investment in education, through shifts from rural to urban occupations, and from semi-skilled to skilled employment, must also have provided an important ingredient for stability, and indeed of support for the régime itself.

As Fitzpatrick notes, for those moving up the social ladder, 'industrialisation was an heroic achievement . . . their own, Stalin's and that of Soviet power – and their promotion, linked to the industrialisation drive, was a fulfillment of the promises of the revolution'.[10] So in addition to a society in which everything was sacrificed in the name of rapid industrial growth – most notably the inability of labour to influence production decisions either at the top or in the workplace – what was also being created was a social structure in which reward, honour and status were tied increasingly to the individual's functional contribution to industrialisation. This not only reinforced the division of labour between town and country, but also generally favoured highly skilled and specialist urban workers over the relatively unskilled who by and large were newly-arrived village immigrants.

Today's fully industrialised society – with two-thirds of its citizenry urbanised – is the direct descendent of the priorities laid down by Stalin. It is a state which, having given power to the very institutions which spearheaded industrialisation, most notably the industrial ministries and the military, continues to ensure that the maximisation of industrial production and the meeting of military interests receive priority. This is to the detriment of those institutions representing non-production needs who, even in a more pluralist but still highly centralised power structure, are unable to provide a counterweight to the pressures for industrial production. Thus sectoral emphasis on heavy industry and on those industries connected with defence continues to keep more balanced sectoral and regional development much further down the political agenda. Such allocative inertia can be legitimised by the political leadership through an emotional appeal to the populace on the past and present vulnerability of the state to foreign invasion.

Yet at the same time we should not lose sight of the substantive political and social changes which are directly connected to the replacement of 'terroristic totalitarianism' as the central basis and driving force for maintaining stability by a less coercive and more paternalistically-minded state. Firstly, under 'developed socialism', the state has linked improvements in standards of living with stability. There has been an impressive increase in personal consumption, whether measured in terms of housing, consumer durables, health services, education or diet. Secondly, although the countryside still remains the Achilles' Heel of the economy, there has been a far greater emphasis on redistributing both economic and infrastructural investments to rural areas. Today agriculture, not least because of its inefficiency, constitutes one of the largest single items in state budgetary expenditure. Moreover, since the mid 1960s, the right to a minimum industrial wage and to an old age pension has been extended to the peasantry.

Yet while all basic social groups have benefited from such policy changes, they have not offset processes which increasingly generate privilege and *de facto* inequality. This, in particular, is related to the fact that with the ending of the USSR's extensive industrialisation, the number of more specialist, primarily middle-class positions in the urban economy and in the bureaucracy, are no longer expanding on the scale that they were during industrialisation. Indeed, as I shall show, one of the consequences of this for 'developed socialism' is that social strata tend to become more hereditary in composition. As I now want to illustrate, this is linked to the occupancy of place in the regional settlement structure and to the way in which the state has attempted to cope with the extraordinary demands by the labourforce for access to the privileges of place. In particular it involves examining the state's use of the internal passport system in administering the inequalities which the Stalinist period created.

THE TERRITORIAL ADMINISTRATION OF PRIVILEGE

During the phase of intensive industrial development, one way in which the state attempted to adjust to a situation in which large cities could no longer cope with the excessive demands on their skeletal social infrastructure, and particularly overcrowding of their housing stock, was to reintroduce the internal passport. Although reinstated in 1932 ostensibly 'to improve the enumeration of the population of towns, workers' settlements and building sites, and free them from persons not engaged in productive labour . . . - kulaks, criminals and other anti-social elements', it became a means not only of weeding out unwanted city residents but also, by excluding the rural population from the right to a passport, of regulating the flood of migration into particular cities.

In the same year the passport régime was extended by the reinstatement of residence permits or *propiska*. In order to obtain a *propiska*, of which a passport is a necessary condition, a migrant wishing to reside in a city has to apply to the local militia. In the event of a refusal, a person must leave within a stipulated time period (at present seven days). In order to qualify for city residence, a passport bearer must be able to obtain housing, which long waiting lists make difficult. Non-issuance has therefore become an important sanction which planners can use in large cities in conjunction with a (largely unsuccessful) scheme of industrial deconcentration. Initially, only Moscow and Leningrad were singled out for the cessation of industrial or demographic expansion, but in 1939 a further five major cities were included. In the post-Stalin years, the number of these so called closed (*zakrytye*) cities subject to either prohibited or restricted industrial and demographic growth has increased dramatically, and, as Figure 5.2.1 shows, now includes more or less all settlements with populations of over 500 000 together with many smaller towns.

Most Western and Soviet studies of large cities conclude that policies designed to restrict demographic growth have not been particularly successful. That practically all the growth of the urban population continues to occur in large cities can be attributed to the way in which powerful industrial enterprises try to maximise production, which in turn enhances their bargaining power and so increases their resource budgets, so that they openly flaunt industrial development restrictions and increase labour demand. Moreover, less powerful local authorities, with few resources at *their* disposal, are only too well aware of the benefits which industrial development brings to their cities (revenue, housing and other services), so that they tend to court industry even more assiduously than their equivalents in market economies.

And so, for the 47 cities designated for no new industrial construction in 1956, population grew in the 1959–79 intercensal period by 2.2 per cent, compared with a 2.5 per cent city-wide average, even though they had far lower levels of natural population increase.[11] It would therefore seem that, given the demand for labour in these cities, migration restrictions are either exceptionally lax or that ways around the *propiska* system can be found, like marrying a resident, moving in with relatives or by finding an employer prepared to turn a blind eye. Yet hidden beneath these glacier-like statistical averages is a passport-*propiska* system which is considered by the ordinary Soviet citizen as an important indicator of status and position in society, and as a determinant of life chances and social well-being. The following extract from Hedrick Smith's book, *The Russians*, gives some indication of its value:

> Klara's family lived in a dingy little provincial town. She was desperate to avoid being sent there or to Siberia on government assignment as a teacher after graduation. She found it impossible to get a job in Moscow because she could not get registered for Moscow housing. But Klara hit upon the scheme of marrying a Moscow lad to qualify for city housing as a wife. One of her close friends told me that Klara paid 1,500 rubles for a bogus marriage to the brother of another friend, never planning to spend a single night with him. In fact, the groom ducked out quickly after the wedding ceremony. All Klara wanted was to use the marriage certification in her passport and six months of 'married life' to obtain her Moscow *propiska*, her residence permit.[12]

We can understand how the passport-*propiska* system regulates life chances and prospects for upward mobility by considering recent passport legislation. Many western commentators (the existence and importance of the passport is rarely acknowledged in Soviet scholarly circles) have identified the September 1974 decree as one which extended the passport to the previously

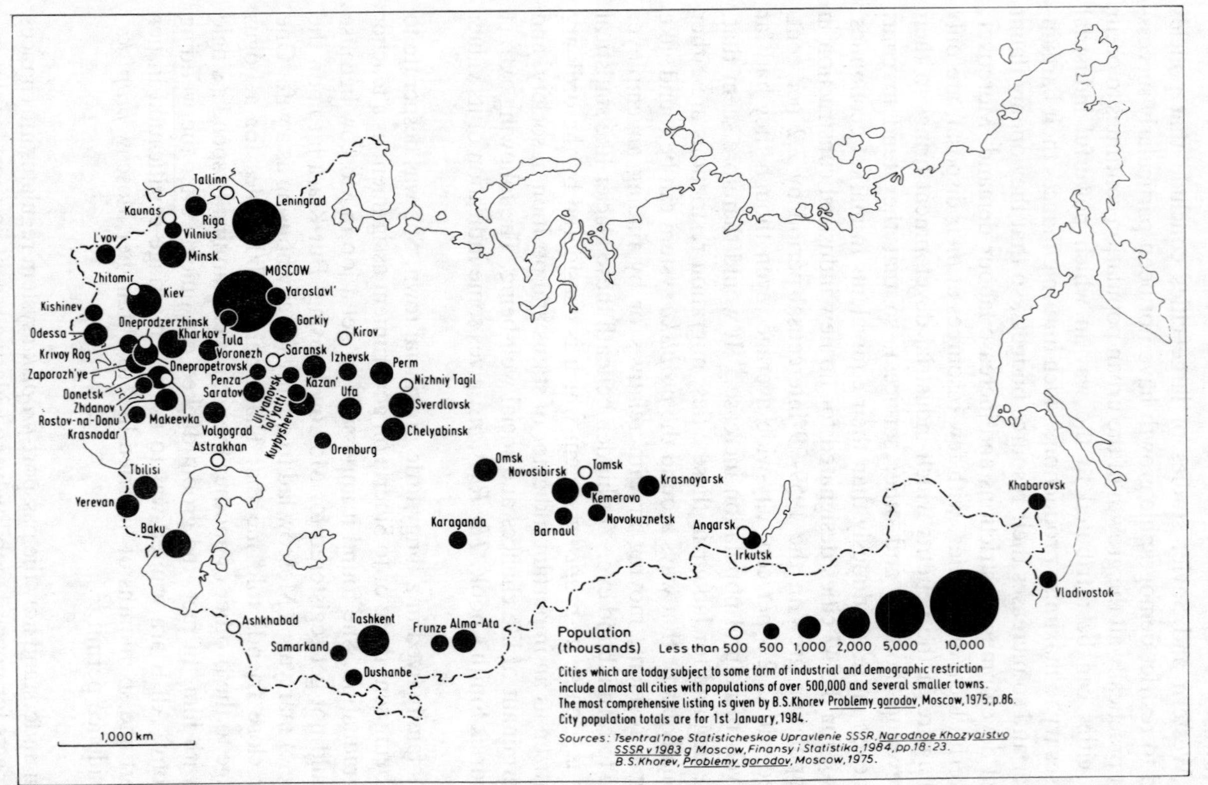

SOURCE: Tsentral'noe Statisticheskoe Upravlenie SSSR, *Narodnoe Khozyaistvo SSSR v 1983* g Moscow, Finansy i Statistika, 1984, pp. 18–23.B. S. Khorev, *Problemy gorodov*, Moscow, 1975

FIGURE 5.2.1 *Soviet cities subject to some form of industrial-demographic restriction*

disenfranchised peasantry. Yet more careful scrutiny of what is proposed in the reform reveals some concessions, but on the whole there is a continuity with previous policy:

> Citizens residing in rural localities to whom passports had previously not been issued shall be issued passports when they depart for other places for long terms; while for departures for terms of up to a month and a half . . . they shall be issued papers of identification (*spravki*) certifying who they are and the purpose of the departure, by the executive committee of the village and settlement Soviets of working people's deputies.[13]

So in spite of the 1974 reforms, the peasantry do not have an *automatic* right to a passport because its issue still remains at the discretion of the local party organisation, the administrative arm of the central state in the countryside. The peasantry therefore remains the only major social group excluded from economic and cultural citizenship: they are deprived of any natural right to geographic mobility and much sought-after residency, and to a free choice of occupation. Their material and social prospects therefore remain bleak in a county whose economic credentials have always been measured in terms of urban-industrial performance.

Among passport-bearing urban residents, the *propiska* has also helped to distinguish between two groups of citizens. In the small and medium-sized towns, citizens are substantially better off than the peasantry in terms of life chances and opportunities for upward mobility, but without a *propiska* they cannot move into the more privileged closed cities. Inhabitants of the latter constitute a privileged stratum for they acquire the right to city residency by birth. Here the standard of living is far higher (particularly in Moscow and Leningrad), the provision of public goods and services greater, and opportunities for upward mobility concentrated. It is therefore not surprising that it is in these cities that one finds an over-concentration of skilled and professional labour. Their continuing industrial development is at the expense of the so-called 'open towns' which, in failing to attract large-scale industrial investment, face poorer employment prospects and receive fewer industry-provided services amongst their disproportionately larger semi-skilled and unskilled populations. Inequalities deriving from social stratification are therefore inextricably inter-related with a tripartite hierarchical stratification of places (see Figure 5.2.2).

The sociologist Victor Zaslavsky is one of the few western commentators to draw attention to the importance of the passport-*propiska* system in regulating upward social mobility, and the consequences this has for territorial stratification between places.[14] He notes in particular that the nature and character of migration is now completely different from the Stalinist years. Then migration was characterised by rapid and mass rural to urban movement, primarily into the major cities and developing industrial centres, whereas since the early 1960s it has become increasingly more complex.

There has been a decline in rural to urban migration and a phenomenal increase in intra-city movement. Stepwise migration, from countryside to small towns and from small towns to closed cities, has also become a feature of the migration process. In Novosibirsk, for instance, it was found that in some years around two-thirds of all rural persons arriving in the city were denied permission to register and settle; many instead settled in the surrounding region's smaller towns.[15] Furthermore, in the Stalinist years the migrants tended to be less educated than the population as a whole, whereas since the early 1960s the typical migrant is generally better educated than the state-wide average. As education is one important route to upward mobility, governmental manipulation of migration, Zaslavsky concludes, has far-reaching consequences for preserving inequalities between places. So I now want to consider how educational opportunities are influenced by the passport system.

Educational opportunities

Education is of far greater importance to upward mobility in the Soviet Union than in most Western countries: formal qualifications determine advancement through the occupational pyramid; higher education in particular opens the door to middle-class employment. Yet although the USSR could be labelled 'a diplomocracy', social and prestige positions are no longer expanding on the scale that they were during extensive industrialisation. Consequently, access to higher education is becoming increasingly competitive. In this scramble for diplomas, social origin plays a decisive part in education prospects. In one major study of thirteen of the largest cities in European Russia, it was found that of students who had completed one year of higher education, 9 per cent came from a peasant-collective farm background, 35 per

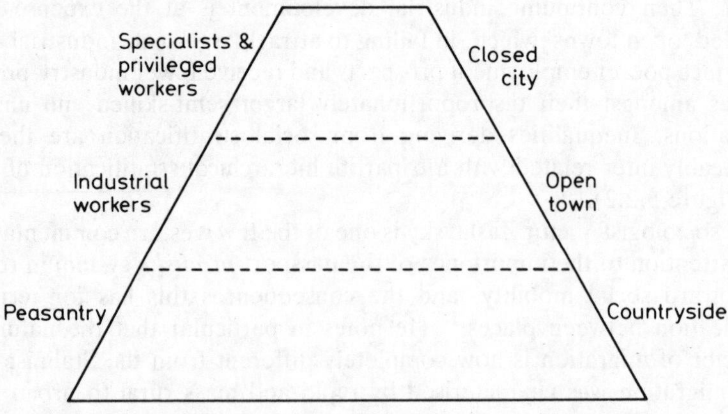

FIGURE 5.2.2 *The territorial stratification of places in the USSR*

cent from an industrial and state farm worker family, while 41 per cent were drawn from the specialist class.[16]

That offspring from the collective farms in particular and the countryside in general are socially disadvantaged is attributable to a number of reasons. In contrast to the big cities, rural schools are poorly staffed and have few resources to realise scholastic potential. Second, cultural values of the family environment tend to be place-specific: less book-orientated homes are less conducive to encouraging a university education, although it is quite evident that despite this, a higher education is seen as desirable and as a necessary condition for 'escaping' from the drudgeries of rural life. Finally, a poor standard of living in the countryside and provincial towns means that there is not the inclination to prepare offspring for the increasingly competitive university entrance examinations which have become a hallmark of the educational system (specialist families lavish up to 1.5 billion rubles per year on private tutoring, a sum equal to one fifth of the total annual budget for general secondary schools).[17]

According to Zaslavsky, such social inequalities between places are becoming fossilised, in part through the passport system. First, he notes that specialists are structurally connected to the system of higher education by virtue of the major universities being located in closed cities. The opportunities for access to all the resources which facilitate university entrance, in combination with the informal urban network which exists for obtaining specialist employment afterwards, ensures the social reproduction of inequality. Secondly, as persons accepted into university automatically receive passports and temporary residence permits, higher education has emerged as one of the few channels to upward mobility open to rural and small town migrants. Clearly, this route to upward mobility is highly selective and is biased towards the young, talented male. By means of the passport-*propiska,* then, the state is selecting and determining the *nature* of migration flow into the closed cities as well as its magnitude, with all the consequences this carries for rural and small town economies and social life.[18]

To this can be added a third important role performed by the passport. The authorities also have the power to determine whether after graduation 'outsiders' remain in the closed city or whether through the graduate placement scheme – in which all those who have completed higher education have to spend three years in a place chosen by the state – they are denied permanent residency. Yet even with this scheme, the state has become increasingly lenient in accommodating the residential wishes of many graduates.[19]

Occupational opportunities

The university-educated urban specialist class, as well as those graduating from eight year 'secondary' schools, therefore have a vested interest in the administered stratification of places, for the abandonment of the passport-

propiska would lead to the loss of many privileges which accrue from closed city residency. It is therefore not surprising to find their over-concentration in such cities and their reluctance to move down the settlement hierarchy. As a result, the occupational structure of closed cities is becoming increasingly imbalanced. *Pravda* recently drew attention to the alarming increase in the number of specialists in Leningrad, the USSR's second largest city, including the over-production of engineers. Moreover, 'the overwhelming majority of Leningraders (graduating from eight year schools) become specialists, while more than half of the city workers are filled by those from outside'.[20] While managing to avoid direct mention of the passport-*propiska* system the Soviet geographer, Khorev, sees the major solution to this unsatisfactory utilisation of specialists not in the abolition of administrative restrictions to mobility but rather, given the fear by many specialists of losing their right to residency if temporarily absent, in 'a guarantee of return' to those leaving cities like Moscow for the purposes of performing specialist work in areas of shortage.[21] So the state continues to administer the basis upon which graduates can remain in closed cities, and indeed guarantees them employment afterwards despite the tremendous economic cost. In preserving this administrative system, it is also providing for the reproduction and over-concentration of the specialist class by means of an expanding educational system and by facilitating differential opportunities according to place. This leads to considerable support from the specialist classes for maintaining the social and political *status quo*.

It is not only those in the professions and in white collar employment who have benefited from the existence of the passport, however, but rather all those industrial workers who have qualified for permanent residency in the closed city. So the place in which one lives can itself make more difference than the job one performs. As income is relatively uniform within each occupational grouping, and as the differentials between strata are not that great anyway, then whether one is a blue collar worker in Moscow or in a provincial town makes a substantial difference. Why is this the case?

In regulating in-migration into closed cities, the demand for industrial labour becomes greater, creating all sorts of informal economies in which the administered price of wage-labour set by the state becomes a fiction. Under such conditions, closed city industrial enterprises which are in constant competition for additional labour in order to meet state-set production targets, find ways of providing other incentives by making available good quality enterprise housing, for example, or by using piecework rates to boost earnings by setting workers 'easy' targets which they can meet comfortably. It is not just simply labour shortages *per se* which give closed city manual workers more power, however, for the economic hold which enterprise managers have over manual workers is seriously reduced as a result of the state's commitment to full employment and the enterprise managers' need to hoard labour in order to ensure completion of plan targets. In the closed cities this not only enforces a 'paternalistic' atmosphere within the workplace (that is, personal considerations and favours asked by the workers) but also militates against a strict enforcement of labour discipline, so that the worker tends to retain some limited and purely negative control over his or her work. This results in an overall reduction in the intensity of labour.[22]

In the open towns, in contrast, labour is in no position to bargain with its feet either with the state or the local enterprise. These 'labour surplus' small towns are also often owned outright by one industrial employer/enterprise; and since small towns have less centrally-allocated resources at their disposal than the big cities, it is the industrial enterprise which provides the necessary housing and other services. Within a 'buyers market' of this kind, the workforce becomes impersonally dependent on and subjugated by the managers of their workplace. The only alternative is to move hundreds of miles away from their permanent home or family, often to live in grossly sub-standard accommodations. Certainly, unemployment is rarely considered as an 'alternative' in a society which has institutionalised the 'right to work' as a social duty – although unemployment benefit is so low anyway that the individual is dissuaded from such a course of action. Yet in towns which fail to attract industry, there is much 'hidden unemployment'; this is especially the case amongst unskilled and semi-skilled women who stay at home due to the absence of local job opportunities.

THE CREATION OF NEW SOCIO-TERRITORIAL GROUPINGS

Not only has the passport-*propiska* system helped to administer the territorial stratification of places but in the process of the state adjusting to the frictions created by its own policies (particularly the chronic shortage of unskilled and semi-skilled labour in the closed cities) it has also helped to structure the rise of additional socially disadvantaged groupings. Murray and Szelenyi have noted that in socialist states adopting a strategy of extensive industrialisation the growth of the urban population can be quite significant, but the expansion of urban-industrial employment is usually much faster.

Studies of Hungary's major cities have shown that, as a result of increasing demographic pressures on a limited housing stock, more and more individuals are forced to commute from neglected rural villages and suburbs with poor infrastructures to their industrial workplaces.[23] So those who cannot gain access to the privileges of largely state-owned and state-administered housing become commuters. The creation of these peasants, who are restratified as workers for eight hours a day is, in effect, a way of alleviating some of the needs of big city industry for semi-skilled and unskilled labour, and is also a response to the supply of housing falling well below demand. In the Soviet Union this process of 'under-urbanisation' is managed by large cities through the *propiska* system, for the pattern of urbanisation in the USSR has also given rise to a distinctive socio-economic commuting class who by and large constitute the more recent exodus from the countryside and the small towns, and whose primarily young population is employed in jobs which demand lower qualifications. In Moscow, this class constitutes about one tenth of the city's labour force.

The demand for unskilled and semi-skilled labour, however, is only partially met by the commuting class. In addition, the *propiska* has also been crucial in administering the creation of another distinct social group who, although resident in the closed city, have only been issued with a temporary *propiska*, and whose sole function is to perform what Khorev calls 'especially unappealing types of work' connected particularly with industry, construction and transport.[24] These 'limit workers', so called due to a system whereby city-based industrial enterprises can file requests for additional personnel (100 000 were requested for Moscow in 1979)[25] are recruited more or less exclusively from the collective farms. This system is seen by its largely young, single and male recruits as an easy way of obtaining access to the privileges of the closed city. Yet due to the power that an enterprise has over their residency, 'limit workers' are at the complete disposal of their industrial manager. Not surprisingly, they are assiduous workers, surpassing set quotas and production plans. In addition, because of their temporary residence status, they cannot seek alternative employment. As if quarantined, they remain in special enterprise-provided housing, because they are debarred from satisfying the necessary residency requirement for a city apartment. Yet their turnover is low. In Moscow approximately one third of the number arriving leave the city,[26] so it would seem that temporary *propiska* are renewed. Given the disdain felt by most Muscovites towards such workers and the conditions under which they live and work, obtaining permanent residency through marriage is rare.

These new under-privileged territorial groupings are a product of the way in which the Soviet Union (and other socialist countries following a similar strategy of early extensive industrialisation) have attempted to readjust to their own system of priorities established in the initial phases of development. It is not just the *scale* of such a massive concentration of economic resources upon industrial productive investments which singles out such socialist régimes, but also their ability, through highly centralised state control and monopoly over territorial resources, to be committed to the clearcut goal of accelerated and sustained industrial development. Moreover, as I have demonstrated, the socio-economic processes which have created these new groupings are entirely different from those which have given birth either to a commuting class in the West or to Southern European *Gästarbeiter*, as indeed are their socio-economic characteristics. One has to refrain, therefore, from using either western models of urbanisation or industrialisation to explain the socialist case, and from drawing too close a comparison between what are entirely different experiences.

IMPLICATIONS FOR TERRITORIAL STABILITY

Clearly there are strong moral and demographic reasons for the abolition of the passport-*propiska* system. In the countryside, it is distorting the age structure of the population and selectively diminishing the number of people of working age. Yet by regulating already high rates of peasant out-migration, some of the short-term needs of the ailing rural sector are met by muddling through on a policy which relies heavily on labour intensification, rather than on having to devote even larger amounts of limited investment capital into increasing labour productivity by means of massive technological and material inputs. Giving the peasanty the unlimited power to vote with their feet, as the state well knows, would lead to far more pressure for greater rural investments and for improvements in rural life-styles, as well as unrestricted mobility adding to even greater strain on urban housing and services. Yet few if any Soviet scholars advocate increasing administrative restrictions on peasant mobility. Rather, most see the solution to the already high labour shortages in the countryside, particularly in parts of European USSR, as a policy of material and social improvement. To this the Soviet geographer, Perevedentsev, adds the introduction of material and psychological incentives to encourage the return of recent urban migrants to the countryside.[27]

However, for the peasantry, rural life continues to be measured with an urban ruler with all the material benefits and social status that big city life entails. Indeed, as Khorev adds, the mass media continue to extol such virtues: 'One example of the insufficiently sober approach to this problem (of large-city in-migration and rural labour shortages) is the delight with which each birth of a new "millionaire" city is announced.'[28] By means of social sifting, then, access to city life can become a reality for those prepared to give up their rural life-styles and roots in the countryside for the more seductive benefits of the city. By holding out the prospect of such a path to social betterment (through, for example, education), but by retaining the passport-*propiska* system, the state has at its disposal an important safety-valve for removing at least one basis of possible rural instability while still being able to commend the virtues of life under a meritocracy.

The sharply increased closed city demand from the mid-1970s onwards for supplemental labour also questions the demographic merits of retaining the *propiska*. Many large cities are coming perilously close to being unable to reproduce through natural demographic means. (In Moscow, the rate of natural increase per thousand population is now 2.5, whereas the countrywide average stands at 8.8, which is also low.)[29] Being unable to replenish this rapidly ageing labour force without removing migration retrictions could undermine economic growth, although at present the filling of this vaccum by a docile class of 'limit workers' has short-term advantages from the point of view of the state. Nonetheless, preserving the *status quo* is one of the few ways in which the state can continue to regulate and control the labour force;

if labour were completely free to determine where it wished to live and work, central planning would become even less effective. Yet the cost of preserving the social conditions in which the specialist classes remain cocooned in the advantages of closed city residency may become too great. Their over-production and over-concentration may no longer be affordable through the state either guaranteeing the cost of education expansion or matching educational qualifications with commensurate closed city employment.

Increased intra-group competition for status positions could therefore undermine social stability as expectations no longer translate into economic reality. But just as we cannot necessarily assume that the removal of the passport-*propiska* system would automatically lead to widespread and organised action from industrial workers presently fragmented and divided by their occupancy of open towns and closed cities, so we must also be careful with Zaslavsky's inference that abolition would lead to a politically restless and mobilised middle class.[30] We should neither over-estimate the power of solidarity within the Soviet social structure, which somehow can be easily detached from the experiences of being part of a state 70 years old, nor underestimate the territorial power at the state's disposal to convince the populace of the necessity of personal sacrifice, however formulated, for the benefit of socialism. There is no doubt, however, that the 'dangers of egalitarianism' that Stalin discerned as fatal hazards to the régime are still acknowledged. In this regard, regulated access to place-specific resource inducements as preferred by the state, and however constituted, provide an important motor for social stability.

CONCLUSION

In this chapter I have argued that we need to refocus our regional lens when considering the study of the socialist world. Rather than viewing its societies through the prism of either a world-systems perspective or western-based models, we must acknowledge from the outset the distinctiveness of socialist régimes. This means beginning at the *societal* scale, reintroducing the significance of *history* into our regional studies, and paying due attention to those *socio-economic and political processes* which make places different. I have also argued that when considering inequalities in Soviet society, *place* should not be viewed in a narrowly spatial sense, but in a social sense too – *for one cannot be separated from the other*. The inequalities which give rise to differences between places can only be understood if we take note of the political strategies adopted by the early Soviet state, and the ways in which subsequent régimes continue to administer them through such means as the passport system. By reflecting on why this is the case and determining whose interests are involved, we are able to explain why place is important to the constitution of Soviet society.

NOTES AND REFERENCES

1. R. J. Johnston, 'The world is our oyster', *Trans. Inst. Br. Geogr.*, 9 (1984) pp.443–59.
2. I. Wallerstein, *The Capitalist World Economy* (Cambridge: Cambridge University Press, 1979) p.220.
3. Ibid., p.68.
4. P. Worsley, 'One world or three? A critique of the world system theory of Immanuel Wallerstein', in D. Held (ed.) *States and Societies* (Oxford: Martin Robertson, 1983) pp.504–25.
5. J. Goldthorpe, 'Social stratification in industrial society', in R. Bendix and S. Lipset (eds) *Class, status and power* (New York: Free Press, 1966) pp.648–59.
6. R. Fuchs and G. Demko, 'Geographic inequality under socialism', *Ann. Ass. Am. Geogr.,* 69 (1979) pp.304–18.
7. R. Peet, 'On "geographic inequality under socialism"', *Ann. Ass. Am. Geogr.,* 70 (1980) pp.280–86.
8. See, for example, R. Bideleux, *Communism and Development* (London: Methuen, 1985).
9. D. Lane and F. O'Dell, *The Soviet Industrial Worker* (Oxford: Martin Robertson, 1978) pp.7–8.
10. S. Fitzpatrick, *Education and Social Mobility in the Soviet Union 1921–34* (Cambridge: Cambridge University Press, 1979) p.254.
11. R. Rowland, 'The growth of large cities in the USSR: policies and trends 1959–79', *Urban Geography,* 4 (1983) pp.258–79.
12. H. Smith, *The Russians* (Aylesbury: Sphere, 1976) p.23.
13. 'On the adoption of the statute on the passport system in the USSR', *Soviet Law and Government,* 14 (1975–76) pp.67–80.
14. V. Zaslavsky, *The Neo-Stalinist State* (New York: Harvester Press, 1982) chapter 6.
15. T. Zaslavskaya, *Migratsiya sel'skogo naseleniia* (Moscow: Mysl', 1970) p.266.
16. Akademiya Nauk SSSR, Institut Sotsiologicheskikh Issledovanii, *Formirovaniye sotsial'noi odnorodonosti sotsialisticheskogo obshchestva* (Moscow: Nauka, 1981) p.102.
17. A. Pravda, 'Is there a Soviet working class?' *Problems of Communism,* 31 (1982) pp.1–24.
18. Zaslavsky, op. cit., pp.141–3.
19. A. Kotliar, 'Sistema trudoustroistva v SSSR', *Ekonomicheskie Nauki* 3 (1984) pp.50–60.
20. *Pravda*, 21 January 1985, p.7.
21. B. S. Khorev, 'Aktual'nye nauchnoprikladnye problemy organicheniya rosta krupnykh gorodov v SSSR', *Ekonomicheskie Nauki* 3 (1984) pp.60–68.

22. F. Feher, A. Heller, G. Markus, *Dictatorship over Needs: an analysis of Soviet societies* (Oxford: Basil Blackwell, 1983) p.75.
23. P. Murray and I. Szelenyi, 'The city in the transition to socialism', *Int. Jnl. Urban Reg. Res.*, 8 (1984) pp.90–108.
24. Khorev, *op. cit.*, p.62.
25. V. V. Grishin, *Izbrannye rechi i stat'i* (Moscow: not given, 1979) p.625.
26. Khorev, *op. cit.*, p.62.
27. V. Perevedentsev, 'Migratsiya naseleniya i razvitie sel'skokhozaistvennogo issledovaniya', *Sotsiologicheskie issledovaniya* 1983 pp.54–61.
28. Khorev, *op. cit.*, p.68.
29. *Vestnik Statistiki* 11 (1984) pp.64–73.
30. Zaslavsky, op. cit., chapter 6.

FURTHER READING

The most comprehensive guide to geographical literature on the Soviet Union is J. Pallot, 'Recent approaches in the geography of the Soviet Union', *Progr. Hum. Geogr.*, 7 (1983) pp.519–42. A novel regional approach to geographical studies of the Soviet Union will be found in D. Shaw, J. Pallot, A. Helgeson, G. Smith and R. North, *The Soviet Union: geography of an administered society* (Harlow: Longman, 1988).

5.3
Debt, the Nation-State and Theories of the World Economy

Stuart Corbridge
University of Cambridge

Stuart Corbridge is Lecturer in Geography at the University of Cambridge and a Fellow of Sidney Sussex College. His teaching and research interests focus on development geography and regional geography, with special reference to South Asia. He is the author of *Capitalist World Development*.

PERSPECTIVES ON GLOBAL DEVELOPMENT

Recent debates on global development have revealed the existence of three clear and competing perspectives. On the political Left there is the radical school, associated in geography with Harvey, Peet and Blaut (among many others).[1] The main tenet of this school is that capitalism (variously defined) is *incapable* of promoting the development of the Third World (however defined). Indeed, most radicals believe that a capitalism centred in certain core countries has actively under-developed the periphery by pillage, by colonialism, and by the sort of neo-colonialism now being directed by the transnational corporations, the World Bank and the International Monetary Fund. In their judgement the capitalist world economy (see Lee, Chapter 2.4 and Taylor, Chapter 5.1) is structured by a host of unequal and asymmetrical power relations which work to the disadvantage of the South in terms of trade, aid, finance, industry, agriculture and just about everything else.[2]

On the political Right, meanwhile, there is the emerging 'new classical' school associated with scholars such as Lal and Beenstock (though with few geographers as yet).[3] In the more optimistic analysis of this group, capitalism is made the *pre-condition* for development in the South. In line with the equilibriating assumptions of neo-classical economics, it is argued that industry and jobs are now flowing to the cheap labour areas of the South, and that trade union action in the North is making the core countries relatively uncompetitive. So long as trading systems remain open and free, this argument continues, and so long as Third World economies respond to open market prices, the future must indeed be a happy one. Talking of this 'world economy in transition', Michael Beenstock maintains that: 'The greatest challenge to the world economic order is coming to terms with the inexorable spread of economic development over the next hundred years.'[4]

Finally, standing between these two perspectives, is the well established liberal/Keynesian-interventionist paradigm, typified in geography by Brookfield's theses on *Interdependent Development*, and more generally by the two reports of the Brandt Commission.[5] The appeal of this paradigm lies in its contention that we are living in an interdependent world, in which North and South have a mutual interest in (managed) inter-hemispheral flows of aid and trade. The Brandt Commission argues that it is in the interest of the North to pump-prime the economies of the South (with aid), so that a developing South might in turn buy goods from the North, keeping the latter out of recession and depression.

For all the deep schisms that divide these development perspectives, however, it is apparent that there is agreement on one basic assumption: *that the modern world system is best theorised in terms of core and periphery, or North and South, or developed and developing*. All three perspectives assume that purely national differences and *geographies*, and national capacities for economic and political planning, are no longer important: the geopolitics of the modern world system is about North and South, or North versus South.

Now there are clearly some good reasons for endorsing this suggestion. The Left, in particular, has shown how industrial, and more especially financial capital, has become 'transnational' in recent years (see Thrift and Taylor, Chapter 4.3), leaving even Northern governments at the mercy of global trends in industrial restructuring, and of capital flight through the Eurocurrency markets. (In effect the Eurocurrency markets consist of deposits of a given currency – and especially the dollar – in countries not subject to the banking regulations that obtain in that currency's 'host' country.) By the same token the Keynesians and the new classical (monetarist) economists have demonstrated both a massive expansion in North/South trade and a synchronisation in global interest rates. In the age of the multinational corporation, the computer and satellite telecommunications, we truly do live in an interdependent world. Decisions taken in Citicorp's New York headquarters affect the lives of slum dwellers in Latin America, and anti-union policies in South Korea affect the employment prospects of shipworkers in Britain.

Having said that, however, I want in this chapter to offer one or two qualifications to this emerging consensus. Without at any time challenging its central truth, I will argue that *the very changes in the capitalist world economy which have eroded national sovereignty in one direction have also encouraged and made possible national economic planning, and national economic and political offensives, in other arenas*. More particularly, I will argue that we must continue to find a place in our accounts for the semi-autonomous powers of the USA. The USA is an enormous and still relatively closed economy which retains vast discretionary powers, both as a result of its size and as a result of the dominant position of the dollar in the world economy. It is also an economy which has been under threat from the relatively more competitive enconomies of the EEC and Japan. It follows that the USA might have good reasons for making use of such powers, as it has to ward off a possible long-term decline in its fortunes. To this extent the USA remains a dominant and dominating geographical actor within the capitalist world system.[6]

Because this argument is rather contentious, and in places rather opaque, it makes sense to present it slowly and in the context of a concrete empirical issue: the global debt crisis. This crisis has an obvious geographical significance – its differential impact has slowed down the development process in Latin America in particular – but I want to use it here illustratively, to examine the strengths and weaknesses of a resolutely 'internationalist' approach to development geography.

To this end the chapter unfurls in three main sections. In the first section the main contours of the debt crisis are outlined, and I consider how these facts might be dealt with by (or how they might compromise) the free market theories of the economic Right. The second section takes this nascent critique a stage further, contrasting the views of Lal and Beenstock with the Brandt Commissioners' strictures on debt and what is to be done about it. Readers will gather that I have some sympathy for the Commissioners' remarks, and for their suggestion that the debt crisis must be solved by a mixture of global economic management and by reflation in the core capitalist countries. Nevertheless, the final section presents a challenge to the political wisdom of the interventionist line. Turning here to the role of the USA, I follow an Italian socialist, Riccardo Parboni, in arguing that the USA has good reasons for resisting the main recommendations of the Brandt reports. (So too does West Germany and the UK but for slightly different reasons.) More generally, I follow Parboni in arguing that the roots of the current global recession, and the most proximate causes of the debt crisis, can be traced back in part to the geopolitical and economic strategies of the United States. It is at least plausible that inter-Northern bloc rivalries are actually deepening today – a conclusion which runs counter to most development thinking.

THE ECONOMIC RIGHT AND THE DEBT CRISIS

The debt crisis became front page news in 1983, when headlines proclaimed that the Third World owed something in the region of 590 billion dollars to the North's governments and banks. The financial papers further recorded that the International Monetary Fund (IMF) was active in the economic management of at least fifteen Southern countries. In the last two years the crisis has slipped from the front pages,[7] but by the end of the decade it is expected to be on the agenda again, and some commentators predict that the scale of the Third World's debt, and the scale of its debt/export ratios, will then be dwarfing present figures. Such commentators talk graphically about a 'debt-bomb' upon which we are all supposed to be sitting, and which threatens both North and South with further underdevelopment and a collapse of the banking system.

Not everyone accepts this thesis, however, or even its less apocalyptic versions. It is thus useful to open our account with the views of the monetarist economic Right: a school of thought which acuses the debt pessimists of adopting a curiously conservative (mis)reading of the role of credit and debt. For theorists like Beenstock or Lal the debt-bomb thesis is suspect in three respects:

1. It ignores the fact that an absolute tenfold increase in Third World debt over the past decade is a nominal figure only. In real terms the South's debt has probably only doubled over this period.
2. This apparently low debt-exposure is not contradicted by the high, and supposedly more threatening, debt/export ratios which alarmists are wont to quote. Lal argues that most of these ratios are meaningless. For as long as a borrower can utilise a foreign loan productively, he says, – that is, to yield a rate of return at least equal to the real interest costs of borrowing – the foreign borrowing can pose no problem. In other words, debt in itself is not a bad thing. Very often, indeed, it is a precondition for development, and the New Right reminds us that it is no coincidence that those countries most often seen as the fuses of the debt-bomb are the very countries which enjoyed the world's highest rates of export growth in the 1970s, as is shown in Table 5.3.1. (It is also worth noting that current Third World debt/export ratios are not so high by historical standards. In the 1910s Canada and South Africa coped with debt/export ratios of over 200 per cent – well above the ratio prevailing in Brazil in 1985.)
3. It is not the case that a return to private commercial lending as the main form of North/South capital flow is 'bound' to precipitate a banking crisis. Monetarists argue that this is to draw a false parallel between the 1980s and the 1930s. In fact things have changed a good deal in fifty years and there are now central banks and inter-bank lines in place to ward off the sort of collapse in domestic money supplies that dogged the 1930s.

These three rejoinders offer a much-needed rebuke to the cruder perspectives on the debt crisis, and we might expect most geographers to take them on board. The discipline might even endorse Lal's conclusion that: 'Much of the talk of a Third World debt crisis threatening the Western banking system is exaggerated. It stems from a misunderstanding in both North and South of the consequences of a return to private commercial lending as the main form of capital flow from rich to poor countries.'[8]

But does it following from this that there is no secular, long-run malaise in the international monetary system? This is a more controversial claim, though it is worth stating that monetarists believe as much. For Beenstock:

> What is going on at present is a liquidity crisis rather than a solvency crisis which is therefore likely to be a *temporary* problem. As global inflation is squeezed out of the system real interest rates will tend to abate and financial distress in the Third World will ease. At the same time global policies of *sound money* . . . will trigger a *spontaneous* global economic recovery as real wages, real interest rates, and real stocks of wealth and money balances revert to *normal* levels.[9]

From this it follows that it is quite wrong to combat a temporary crisis by a new round of institution building – nurturing a world central bank conceived in the spirit of unsound money, says Beenstock – or by strengthening IMF quotas, increasing Special Drawing Rights to the tune of $10 to 12 billion per year, or increasing IMF resources by $10-11 billion under the General

TABLE 5.3.1 *Third world debt and development, 1970–80*

	Average annual growth rates, per cent		*Debt service* as a percentage of:*			
			GNP		*Exports of goods and services*	
Country	*Output 1970/80*	*Exports 1970/80*	*1970*	*1980*	*1970*	*1980*
Mexico	5.2	13.4	2.1	4.9	24.1	31.9
Brazil	8.4	7.5	0.9	3.4	18.9	22.9
Argentina	2.2	9.3	1.9	1.4	21.5	16.6
Venezuela	5.0	−6.7	0.7	4.9	2.9	13.2
South Korea	9.5	23.0	3.1	4.9	19.4	12.2
Chad	−0.2	−4.0	1.0	3.1	3.9	n.a.
Niger	2.7	12.8	0.6	2.2	3.8	2.3
El Salvador	4.1	1.5	0.9	1.2	3.6	3.5
Ghana	−0.1	−8.4	1.1	0.6	5.2	6.0
Ethiopia	2.0	−1.7	1.2	1.1	11.4	7.6

* Debt service is the sum of interest payments and repayments of principal on external public and publicly guaranteed medium and long-term debt.

SOURCE: World Bank – World Development Report (1982), Tables 2, 8 & 13

Agreement to Borrow. That would simply fuel global inflation and signal the fact that certain Northern governments are prepared to be 'monetarist at home but Keynesian abroad [where they] actually accept the central thesis of Brandt'.[10]

BRANDT II: COMMON CRISIS

In fact there is scant evidence of such behaviour. The Brandt Commission's analysis opposes the monetarist interpretation at two points. First of all it joins with the debt-bomb proponents in denouncing the imperfections of the international private capital market that is the altar of the New Right. Secondly, it points up the necessarily contradictory and depressive effects of pursuing monetarist policies of competitive deflation at an international level.

Private capital markets

At first glance the Brandt Commission's strictures on the role of private capital flows are straightforward enough. It is in favour of them so long as they have the support of the international institutions and the central banks. Probe a little deeper, though, and it is clear that there is more to it than this. Because the Commissioners' view of bank lending to sovereign countries has grown out of its reading of the past ten or so years of world economic history, it emphasises three points.

Volatility: It is not the Commissioner's belief that private capital flows can or should be relied upon to provide the lion's share of development finance; still less that it should be made the *raison d'être* of a diminished role for the Bretton Woods institutions.[11] This would quite overlook the fact that present trends towards private finance are less a result of some pilgrimage back to the 'norms' of market economics, than the product of the peculiar, and probably unrepeatable, circumstances that followed the distortion of international economic and financial markets occasioned by the Organisation of Petroleum Exporting Countries [OPEC] in 1973/4. Then, for the first time since the 1930s, the private markets were liberated to play a role in the Third World not just because certain legal restrictions were lifted (which is Lal's point), but because vast numbers of petrodollars were flowing on to the Euromarkets from OPEC members with a limited import capacity. Similarly, it would quite overlook the fact that the World Bank and the International Development Association are meant to serve a rather different set of clients than the private banks. Their customers are not so much the 'credit-worthy' Newly Industrialising Countries, as the Low Income Countries at the bottom of the international league table.

Geographical coverage: or what the Commissioners refer to as the 'herd behaviour' of those banks who followed the lead of their big brothers in lending to just a few countries: notably Brazil, Mexico, Argentina and South Korea. This might well make sense in terms of a simple demand and supply calculus (Mexico demanded $X billion so it got $X billion), but the Commissioners doubt whether the principles of sound finance have been best served by a system which allocated cash as if there was no tomorrow, and which has been divorced from any manner of external control. Yet this is arguably what has happened. Major banks such as Citicorp and Chase Manhattan maintained a strict security on their credit portfolios and now find themselves bereft of the Triple-A credit ratings they once took for granted. More worryingly, many of the countries these and other banks dealt with are now considered major credit insurance risks (see Figure 5.3.1).

Short-term versus long-term debts: Here the Commissioners would point out that whilst it may be true, *pace* Lal, that the ratio of long-term debts to exports in selected Latin American countries is not high by historical standards, this is hardly the point. What matters is that the trend away from multilateral official capital flows has been paralleled by an inevitable contraction in the amortization periods of the loans offered to the Third World. Private banks are not in the business of lending long. (Five to seven years is typical – hence the post OPEC crisis of 1981/3.) The implications of this are two-fold. First, it suggests that a serious mismatch might arise between the long-run needs of developing countries for infrastructural finance, and the recycling timetables of the private markets which prefer an investment profile better suited to short-run debt serving capacities. (One thinks of the apparently wasteful gigantism that lies behind so much of Latin America's public debt: nuclear power plants, hotels, luxury apartment blocks and the like.) Second, it suggests that the dependence of South upon North may be forged anew by tying the development chronologies of the former to the monetary (that is, interest rate) rhythms of the latter.

International monetarism

This brings us to the second, and perhaps more important, debate between Brandt and Beenstock: on the impact of international monetarism. For it is the Brandt Commission's bold charge that the counter-inflationary policies now being pursued by Northern governments, far from providing the conditions of existence of world recovery and Southern development, are actively pulling the rug from under it. This is so for two main reasons.

First, there is the question of recession. To a non-monetarist economist it seems self-evident that high interest rate policies to restrictively control the money supply in any one country – and especially the USA – must induce a copy-cat policy in the policies of its competitors, if only to safeguard their currencies against exchange rate fluctuations set in motion by capital flows to

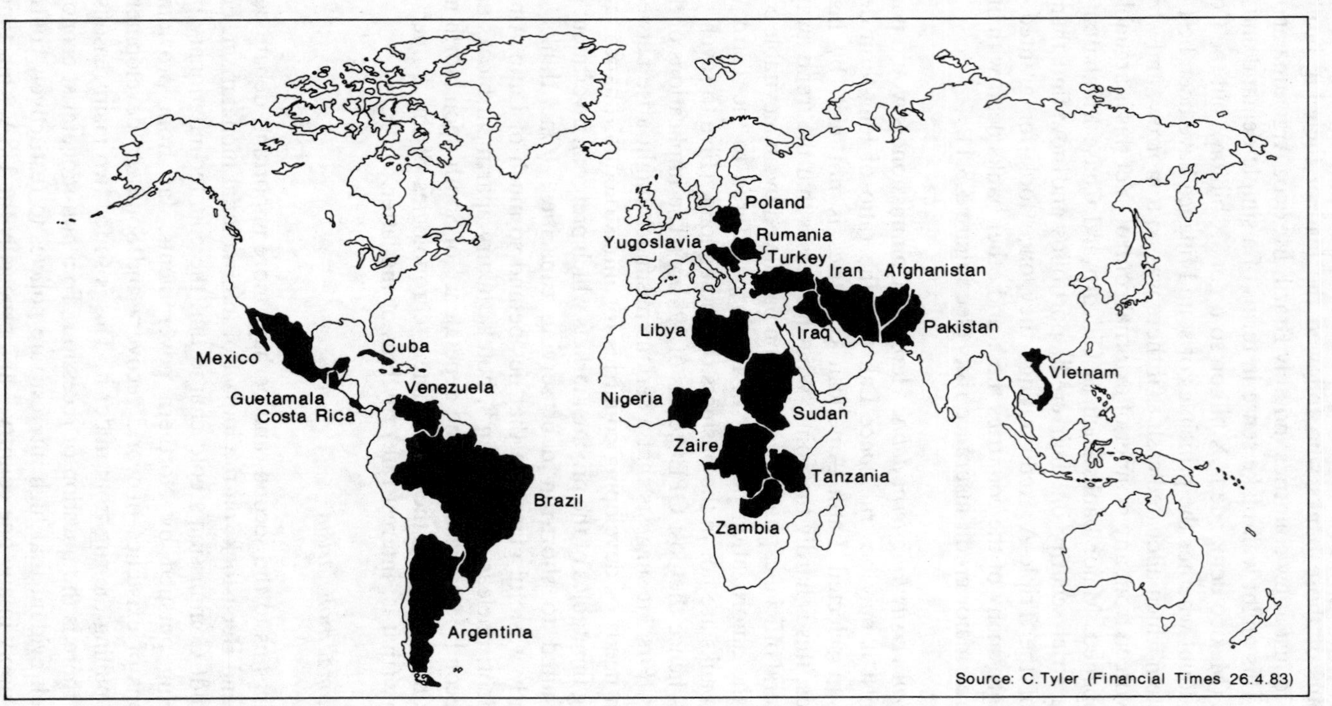

SOURCE: C. Tyler, Financial Times, 26 April 1983

FIGURE 5.3.1 *Countries where exporters have found or may find credit insurance restrictions*

the high interest rate areas. Yet this must in turn set in train the sort of world slump in which we now find ourselves; with the imports of the industrial nations stagnant, with the exports of the developing countries rising at a mere 1 per cent per year (as against 8 or 9 per cent growth rates in the later 1970s), and with real commodity prices at their lowest levels for 30 years. Secondly, there is the question of the direct effect that high interest rates have on the repayment of Third World debt. Here the Commissioners are convinced that the present crisis has emerged because the Third World countries have been made the unwitting victims of a peculiar Catch-22: the sort of scissors crisis shown in Figure 5.3.2.

On the one hand Third World countries have seen their export markets fall away in the wake of the OECD recession. On the other hand, and at the same time, they have been forced to pay off a greatly increased debt burden just as

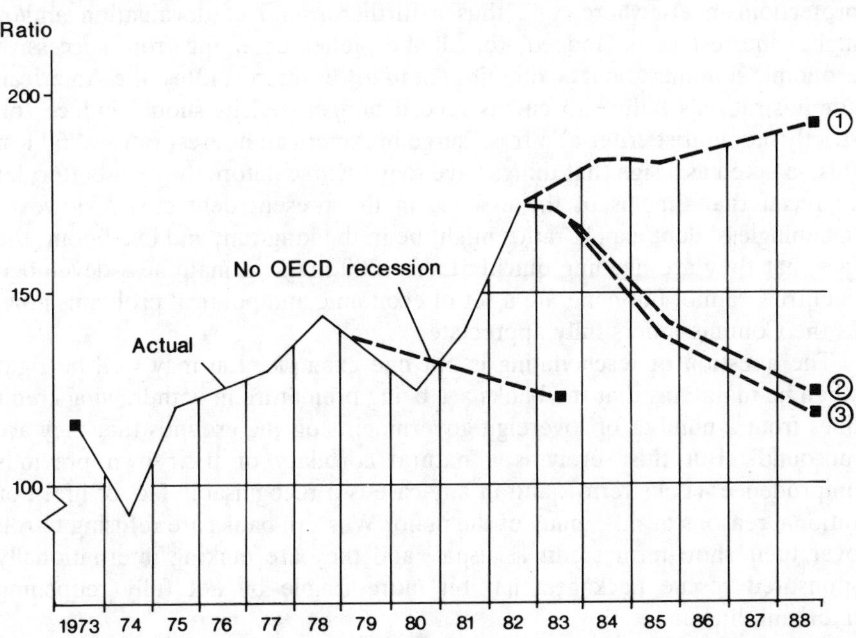

SOURCE: Morgan Guaranty (after Frances Williams)

FIGURE 5.3.2 *The debt/export ratios of 21 major developing country borrowers (average of beginning and end-year total debt as a per cent of exports of goods and services)*

real interest rates rose from 6 per cent in 1976 to 15 per cent in early 1982, and just as the dollar (in which most of the loans are to be repaid) strengthened in the teeth of these same interest rate policies. It has been calculated that for each 1 per cent rise in these interest rates an estimated two billion dollars was added to the developing countries' annual debt bill.

The debt crisis

This is a lot of money in anyone's language and it is the scale of this problem, plus the Commissioners' critique of international monetarism, which has led Brandt to a rather different outlook on the present crisis to that of many Northern governments (Beenstock notwithstanding). In my judgement this strikes a reasonable balance between millenarianism and complacency.

On the one hand it points out the valuable role played by the major banks in recycling the OPEC surpluses to selected (perhaps too selected) countries. But at the same time it stresses the essentially unplanned, and thus volatile, nature of this lending, and the dangers of relying on what both Beenstock and Lal take to be axiomatic: a spontaneous fall in real interest rates leading to a spontaneous world recovery. This simply is not on, say the Commissioners. Any spontaneity in the system is surely of a disequilibriating nature, with counter-inflationary policies in one part of the globe encouraging slump and protectionism elsewhere, and thus a further round of devaluation and/or higher interest rates. Indeed, for all the pieties emerging from successive economic summits about a commitment to lower interest rates, the American administration's failure to cut its record budget deficits should induce (on strictly monetarist criteria) a fresh surge in American interest rates. And lest this be taken as a sign that things have to get worse before they get better, let us recall that time is of the essence in the present debt crisis. However 'meaningless' debt/export ratios might be in the long run, and in a boom, the fact that they are heading quickly to the 200 mark in many less developed countries cannot but generate a set of economic and political problems now, as the Commissioners fully appreciate.

The question of rescheduling is but one example. Lal may well be right when he maintains that the banks are being premature in withdrawing credit lines from a number of sovereign governments on the grounds that they are 'unsound'. But this surely is a natural corollary of their own previous 'imprudence' (Lal's term), and in any case is a recognisable fact of life. For rational reasons or not, many of the major Western banks are refusing to roll over their short-term credit as usual, and they are making internationally sponsored rescue packages that bit more fragile by not fully reopening interbank lines.

Similarly with the IMF. It may indeed be regrettable that the Fund is having to pick up the pieces of just those rescheduled deals, but this is of little consequence when set against the possible political repercussions of such action. For as the Commissioners recognise full well, the IMF intercedes almost invariably to reinforce 'sound money' policies of devaluation and public expenditure cuts; policies which might not only deepen the sinking sands of recession, but which might also provoke just that measure of political resistance which monetarists rightly perceive as a threat to international recovery.

And, finally, what if the worst does come to the worst? Suppose some bank from, say, the American Midwest threatens to pull down the whole interbank house of cards to teach the Communists or the bad-debtors a lesson. (According to one Frankfurt banker, that nearly happened in 1981 when the German banks lived in fear that 'some small US bank was going to play patriot and show those Communists a thing or two by calling in their debt'.)[12] Or suppose that the Latin American countries collectively demand lower interest rates and/or a moratorium. What then? Very likely, the system would survive. As Figure 5.3.3 makes clear, it is stronger than some seem to think. But its stability could only be guaranteed at a price, for the pre-conditions of saving the system in such circumstances would be nothing less than a 'tax' on Northern citizens. Again, this is hardly the ideal way to kick-start the magic circle of spontaneous growth which is so vital to the monetarist case.

Proposals

For all of these reasons, the Brandt Commissioners have come to reject the fatalistic charms of monetarism, and to put forward a set of proposals which go far beyond the anaemic re-equipping of the IMF which took place in 1983.[13] The most important of these proposals are as follows:

1. To at least double the IMF quotas.

2. To secure a major new allocation of Special Drawing Rights (SDRs).

3. To set up an emergency borrowing authority to support developing countries through enlargement and reform of the General Agreement to Borrow.

4. To allow the IMF to borrow increasingly from central banks and from capital markets, whilst encouraging central banks to provide additional short-term deposits to the Bank for International Settlements (BIS), so that its bridge-financing operations might be expanded.

5. To relax the conditionality of the IMF by lessening the exclusive concentration on demand constraints, devaluation and credit ceilings as the main instruments of balance of payments adjustment.

6. To step up the programme lending arm of the World Bank from 10 to 30 per cent of total lending.

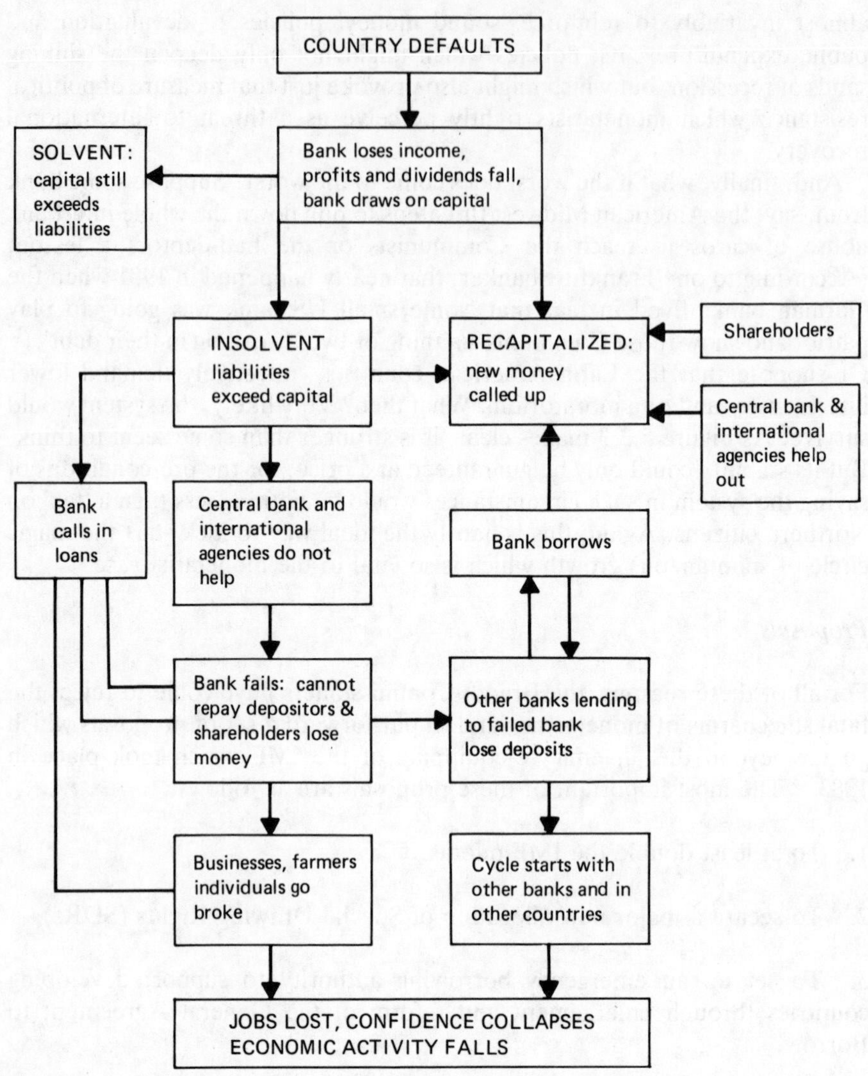

SOURCE: Michael Prest, *The Times*, 3 February 1983

FIGURE 5.3.3 *What happens after a default*

PARBONI AND INTER-IMPERIALISM

Together, these proposals add up to a stinging attack on the institutional structures now governing international finance, while at the same time advancing a Keynesian prospectus for reflating a world economy in slump.

And it is in this spirit that we might commend them. If nothing else, the Commissioners are to be congratulated for demanding a package of direct action for recovery, and for attacking the impotence of the free-market Friedmanites (Beenstock's cries of 'gloomy economics' and 'global dirigisme' notwithstanding).

But global dirigisme depends on global goodwill, and it is on this more practical issue that the Commissioners' programme may fall down. For what their prospectus amounts to is (another) call for the governments of the North to see sense to join together in collective action against the 'common crisis'. At no point do they suspend their belief that the real role of governments, codified in the Keynesian stereotypes, is to tirelessly defend the mechanisms that safeguard the harmony of international relations. Far less do they consider that: 'The crisis [may] not be the result of so-called objective factors [at all] but is fundamentally the fruit of a grand inter-imperialist conflict the stakes of which are the global redivision of economic and political power between the United States on the one hand and the major powers of the second world – Germany and Japan – on the other.'[14]

Perhaps this is to be expected. But it is in marked contrast to the more challenging thesis advanced in Parboni's recent book on *The Dollar and Its Rivals*. Here is a text which not only faces up to current realities (the Cancun failure,[15] the rise of protectionism, US/European conflicts on East-West trade, US opposition to any decline in the dollar standard, and so on), but does so in a way that eschews both the charges of irrationality that course through the Brandt reports, and the stereotypes of American malevolence so often found on the Left. Instead it makes use of a carefully crafted argument to ground a polemic on inter-imperialism in the changing contours of one key geopolitical fact: the unrivalled ability of post-war US governments to ward off the long-run decline of their economy by resort to devaluation and the extraction of financial seignorage.

American financial strategy

Let me elaborate on this, because it is not a common claim in geography. For Parboni it is a truism that the United States has long opposed the philosophy of 'concerted action' which Presidential adviser Feldstein declared to be at the core of international Keynesianism. Throughout the 1950s and 1960s the United States opposed the introduction of the Special Drawing Right (SDR) and even today, when a miserly allocation of SDRs points fleetingly to the future, the USA clings to the hope that its protégé might remain in the mould of its now defunct antecedents: the British Exchange Equalisation Fund and the American Stabilization Fund.

But why should the United States take what Brandt has called 'this negative stance'? This is a question which is less often asked and it is here that Parboni's geopolitics come into their own. In essence his argument runs like this. Consider the position of the US economy at the end of the Second World

War. Undoubtedly it was then at its peak, with a 62 per cent share of world manufacturing output presaging nothing so much as a period of relative decline. The question which then arises is 'What could the United States do to stave off this decline?'. One option open to it would be to ensure that investment and accumulation rates within the USA stayed ahead of its emergent competitors, but given the post-war propensity of US capital to flow out of the country this presupposed an unlikely degree of economic planning. Then again it could act to make domestic investment more profitable by attacking the power of organised labour, but this too raised the prospect of unwelcome political opposition.

However, there was a third option: an international option. By making use of the relatively closed nature of the US economy (its import/GNP ratio of 0.15 is less than half that of its European rivals), the USA could hope to undercut its competitors by a policy of persistent dollar devaluation. This would induce only a limited degree of inflation at home and could be secured by running up huge balance of payments deficits worldwide, and simply printing more dollars to cover them. The only conditions for such action were as follows. First, it presupposed that the USA would act to defend the dominant position of the dollar as the world's generally accepted reserve currency; which it did. (The reason for this is that countries would only allow the USA to build up balance of payments deficits against them so long as the dollar 'alone' could be used by central banks to settle accounts and intervene in foreign exchange markets, and by private firms to conduct international trade.) Second, it presupposed that the USA would if necessary break its Bretton Woods commitments to maintain the value of the dollar at a fixed nominal exchange rate, and to maintain its convertability into gold. This latter agreement was critical because the threat of a rush into gold cautioned US governments against excessive dollar devaluations.

Of course what I have outlined here are only the parameters of US financial action, and I am not claiming that, in practice, the USA has maintained a bullish monetary policy since 1945. Nor should we be blind to the internal quibbles and politicking that shaped US external policies. The fact is that throughout the 1950s US economic supremacy was so assured that its government was content to present itself as a benevolent despot, providing the world with the collective blessing of economic stability while extracting no direct advantages for its own economy. But the 1960s are another matter, for then the United States' economy began to come under pressure from its erstwhile satellites, Germany and Japan. With these two countries biting into its export markets and surpassing its rate of fixed capital formation and productivity growth (see Table 5.3.2), the United States was forced to run up balance of payments deficits just to pay its way (and to sustain the Vietnam offensive). But this induced precisely those pressures that it wished to avoid: a movement into gold, and demands for new international forms of credit.

Clearly something had to give, and give it did on 15 August 1971. President Nixon unilaterally withdrew the USA from its Bretton Woods commitment to

TABLE 5.3.2 *The relative decline of the United States economy, 1950–1977*

a. Annual Growth Rates of Industrial Productivity, 1950–76 (in%)

USA	2.8
JAPAN	8.3
FRANCE	5.0
GERMANY	5.4
ITALY	4.3
BRITAIN	2.6

b. Annual Growth Rates of Total Fixed Stock Excluding Housing, 1950–77 (average of stocks, net and gross, in %)

	1950–70	*1971–77*
USA	3.8	3.0
JAPAN	8.8	7.9
FRANCE	5.4	6.3
GERMANY	6.2	4.8
ITALY	5.1*	5.0*
BRITAIN	3.9	3.7

* net stock only

c. Evolution of Shares of World Exports in Manufacturers (in %)

	1956	*1970*	*1976*
USA	25.5	18.5	17.3
JAPAN	5.7	11.7	14.6
FRANCE	7.9	8.7	9.8
GERMANY	16.5	19.8	20.6
ITALY	3.6	7.2	7.1
BRITAIN	18.7	10.8	8.7

SOURCE: R. Parboni (1981) *The Dollar and Its Rivals* (London: New Left Books) p. 93

maintain the convertability of the dollar into gold. According to Parboni, the significance of this one event cannot be overstated, for what it did was to signal the end of an era. Henceforth, the United States would not use its reserve currency position for the general good, but would instead 'unhesitatingly pursue its own national interest and so become the principal source of perturbation of the international economy'.[16] This worked in two ways. First, by escaping the trap of gold convertability, the United States was free to finance its own deficits with payments in its own currency, without having to resort to financial assets abroad previously accumulated through foreign surpluses. This it did. Between 1970 and 1978 the United States ran up a current account deficit of more than $30 billion, an act no other country could even dream of and one bound to accelerate the international transmission of inflation already under way when OPEC put up its prices in 1973/74 (see Table 5.3.3). Indeed it is Parboni's belief that the mid-1970s rise in raw material prices was largely made possible by the United States' ability to import oil and other commodities at will, by printing more dollars.

At the same time this resort to international deficit financing allowed the Americans to push through a persistent devaluation of the dollar. The main purpose of this was to restore US competitiveness, but its unintended (?) effect was to induce the European economic stagnation of the late 1970s (and

TABLE 5.3.3 *Evolution of some items of the United States balance of payments (in thousands of millions of dollars)*

	(1)	*(2)*	*(3)*	*(4)*
1960/69	+23.3	+41.2	−23.7	+15.5
1970	+0.4	+2.2	−4.2	−7.4
1971	−2.8	−2.7	−4.9	−9.0
1972	−7.9	−6.8	−3.1	+2.2
1973	+0.4	+0.5	−2.3	−0.7
1974	−3.3	−5.3	−5.3	−1.9
1975	+11.9	+9.0	−4.8	−8.4
1976	−1.4	−9.3	−2.4	−6.9
1977	−15.2*	−31.2	−3.5	−4.2
1978	−15.9*	−34.1	−4.0	−16.6
Total	−33.8	−70.2	−34.5	−52.9

(1) Current Account Balance
(2) Balance of Trade (f.o.b.)
(3) Balance of direct investment, of the United States abroad and of foreign investment in the United States, net of dis-investment and re-investment of earnings
(4) Variation of the net position abroad of credit agencies

* As of 1977 the current account includes earnings on direct foreign investment that are re-invested; the unfavourable current account balance is correspondingly diminished

SOURCE: R. Parboni (1981) *The Dollar and Its Rivals*, (London: New Left Books) Table 2

indirectly the world economic slump and international debt crisis of the 1980s). For Germany's response to the increased US competition that ensued was to step up its export drive by extending cheap credits to potential customers and by improving the technological quality of German manufactured goods. Both prongs of Germany's export strategy – cheap credits and industrial restructuring – required domestic (and ultimately European) deflation.

In one way or another, then, the recent financial stategy of the United States has not been a happy one. Outside its shores it has created frightening bouts of inflation and recession, and when set alongside German dominance of the European Monetary System, it has allowed just two major powers to dictate economic circumstances to the rest of the world, often against their best interests. As before, Parboni sums this up best.

> Here again [he says] the preponderance of imperialist interests at the expense of the weak countries is evident. The United States and Germany agree in rejecting any enlargement of official financial mechanisms, which would enable the weak countries to deal more effectively with potential problems related to their concession of credit to newly industrialising countries in order to sell their complex products, or would enable the new countries to go into debt more independently and to select their own suppliers of financing. The various plans to increase official international liquidity have been systematically sabotaged – or in the best of cases sharply reduced in scope – by joint action by the United States and Germany . . . The United States and Germany, in conflict over the maintenance of industrial and technological leadership, join together in the commercial exploitation of the rest of the world.[17]

TOWARDS A GEOPOLITICAL ECONOMY

Of course it may be objected that this is past history, and that since President Reagan came to power there has been such a sea-change in US financial affairs that Parboni's thesis is now out of touch. After all, the *direct* roots of the present debt crisis are to be found in the strong dollar policies of the current US administration, not in the weak dollar era that preceeded them.

In a sense, though, this misses the point – or so I would urge in conclusion. For one thing, it is not apparent that recent events *are* inconsistent with the Parboni thesis. On the contrary, Parboni himself would maintain that the 'monetarist' about-turn of the later Carter/early Reagan Presidencies (it is not a matter of personalities) is very much a product of the long-term contradictions of the weak dollar decade of the 1970s. In effect, it was forced upon the Americans by a new crisis of confidence which shook the dollar in 1978. By this time quite reasonable fears were springing up in the financial community that the strategy of dollar devaluation was promoting a degree of international inflation that made another wave of raw materials price rises inevitable, and it was this that demanded a movement into the mark, yen, Swiss franc or pound simply to preserve the value of long-term assets.

Just as crucially, though, this objection fails to understand the true purpose of *The Dollar and Its Rivals*. The object of this book is not to provide predictions on this or that short-run scenario; though Parboni is clearly not averse to the odd moment of speculation. Rather it is Parboni's intention to provide us with an empirically consistent interpretation of the present crisis which has as its core what I would call a 'geopolitical-economy'. This consists of a number of interlocking prepositions, as we have seen, but the demands it makes of future geographies fall under three main headings.

- It asks us to begin our accounts of development or of crisis by *deconstructing* the received categories of North and South or core and periphery. By all means let us acknowledge that national economic actions are constrained - especially in the South, and especially in the United Kingdom, the centre of transnational finance capital – but let us recognise also that there are still inter-national rivalries shaping the world economy and conditioning the responses of many developed countries to the North/South issue. What we need is a geography which is sensitive to the complex and highly differentiated web of interactions which bind together the capitalist world system and its 'component' nation states.
- It asks us to put particular emphasis upon the geopolitical strategy of the *United States* as a long-run determinant of global development and perturbation. If we do this, and if we guard against Parboni's rather too unitary theory of US policy formation, we may yet avoid the pitfalls of both monetarism and international Keynesianism: on the one hand fatalism, on the other hand disenchantment.
- It asks us to take political economy seriously. This has obviously been a central theme of this chapter, for as geography comes face to face with issues of real political importance – the debt crisis, famine in Africa, devolution, the inner city problem and so on – so it must come to terms with an economic literature which obeys no one God. Increasingly, the geographer will need to understand and to move between competing economic traditions, in the process recognising that the factors which shape space, and the relationships between people and place, are described by literatures which depart markedly in their methodologies and conclusions. As ever this puts an extra burden on the geographer, but this is as it must be. In the 1960s geographers took on board the lessons of the quantitative revolution; today we have begun a critical engagement with the literatures of political economy.

NOTES AND REFERENCES

1. All three authors are represented in R. Peet (ed.) *Radical Geography* (London: Methuen, 1978).
2. The 'South' and the 'Third World' are used interchangeably in this account. They both describe the less developed countries of Central and Latin America, Africa (except South Africa), Asia (except the Soviet Union) and Australasia (except Australia and New Zealand). The position of the developed socialist economies within the 'Northern' bloc is problematic. In this chapter the 'North' is generally taken to mean the major 'Western' capitalist powers of Europe, North America, Japan, South Africa, Australia and New Zealand.
3. An important exception is M. Chisholm, *Modern World Development: a geographical perspective* (London: Hutchinson, 1982).
4. M. Beenstock, *The World Economy in Transition* (London: Allen and Unwin, 1983) p.226.
5. H. Brookfield, *Interdependent Development* (London: Methuen, 1975); W. Brandt, *North/South: a programme for survival* (London: Pan, 1980); W. Brandt, *Common Crisis North/South: co-operation for world recovery* (London: Pan, 1983).
6. To speak of the USA as a 'geographical actor' is to risk an unnecessary anthropomorphism. I use it here partly as a convenient shorthand and partly to emphasise that nation-states can be (and often are) important economic agents.
7. In part because of the success of the so-called 'case approach' (that is, country by country) to the rescheduling of Latin America's debt.
8. D. Lal, 'Time to put the Third World Debt Threat into perspective', *Financial Times*, 6 May 1983, p.18.
9. M. Beenstock, 'The Gloomy Economics of Willy Brandt', *Financial Times*, 2 March 1983, p.23 (emphases added).
10. Ibid.
11. The 1944 conference which founded the International Monetary Fund (IMF) and the World Bank was held at Bretton Woods in New Hampshire, USA.
12. J. Palmer, 'The Debt-Bomb Threat', *Time Magazine,* 19 January 1983, pp.4–11.
13. In May 1983 the IMF's quotas were increased by 50 per cent.
14. R. Parboni, *The Dollar and Its Rivals: recession, inflation and international finance* (London: New Left Books, 1981) p.50.
15. The most important economic summit devoted exclusively to North/South issues was held at Cancun (Mexico) in the autumn of 1981. The Brandt Commission records that this summit 'fell far short of our expectations. It did not even come close to launching the idea of a world economic

recovery programme': Brandt, 1983 *op. cit.*, p.2.
16. Parboni, *op. cit.*, p.50.
17. Ibid., p.138.

FURTHER READING

I have provided a fuller discussion of these questions in my *Capitalist World Development* (London: Macmillan, 1986). Parboni's thesis is described in detail in his *The Dollar and Its Rivals: recession, inflation and international finance* (London: New Left Books, 1981), but see also his 'Capital and the Nation State', *New Left Review* 137 (1983) pp.87–96.

PART VI
POLITICISING THE ENVIRONMENT

Introduction

If, as Taylor suggests, spatial science was indeed committed to 'developmentalism', it certainly had little room for 'environmentalism'. **Judith Rees** seeks to tie these two strands together. The reawakening of concern over environmental resources in the 1960s and early 1970s largely by-passed geography, she says, because most of its formal spatial models assumed that the location and nature of the resource base was fixed and given. And yet, of course, resources are dynamic cultural creations, varying dramatically through time and over space. In order to grasp the significance of this, Rees draws attention to the geopolitical economy of resource exploitation at a global scale. Resource scarcity, she suggests, is much less of a problem for the 'North' than it is for the 'South'. The 'Northern' countries have acted to reduce their dependence on the 'Southern' countries and the dependencies which remain are 'non-symmetrical [and] work against Third World producers'. This is no simple reflection of a brute physical geography: it has, rather, been 'created by a complex of economic, social, demographic, institutional and political conditions'. In a challenging essay, therefore, which draws together themes from virtually every part of the book, Rees shows how resource use is an arena for strategic human action with its own vital political geography.

In a parallel essay, **Timothy O'Riordan** provides four case-studies of environmental action in both 'North' and 'South'. One of his sharpest points is that decisions which affect the environment – even seemingly the most local and commonplace – have wider repercussions and are structured (or, as O'Riordan says, 'framed') differently for different groups of actors *in ways which they may not realise and with consequences which they rarely foresee.* This is precisely why the deep examinations of human geography are so essential and why they are, of necessity, profoundly political. Indeed, O'Riordan goes still further. In his view, environmentalism offers a profound critique of contemporary society. It refuses to fence off 'the environment' as some separate arena for specific interest groups; it draws attention, rather, to the whole complex of society-nature relations which must provide an essential foundation for the construction of a genuinely human geography.

6.1
Natural Resources, Economy and Society

Judith Rees
London School of Economics

Judith Rees took her undergraduate and post-graduate degrees at the London School of Economics, to which she returned as a lecturer in 1969 after a spell teaching in the Agricultural Economics Department at Wye College, London. Most of her research has focussed on the economic aspects of natural resources management, with an initial emphasis on water resources. She has published widely on water economics and management, including a book on *Industrial Demands for Water*, and has acted as a consultant in these areas to a number of government bodies, including the UK Department of the Environment, the Australian Department of Urban and Regional Development, the Egyptian Government and the UNDP. More recently her research has concentrated on environmental planning and on the political economy of mineral exploitation and trade. These research themes are reflected in her teaching at LSE, where she takes courses on resource management and environmental planning at both the undergraduate and post-graduate levels. In her recent book, *Natural Resources: allocation, economics and policy*, she explores the extent to which current resource management systems produce an efficient, equitable and environmentally sensitive allocation of global resources.

During the 1960s there was a renaissance of public and academic interest in a plethora of natural resource problems. These included the physical scarcity of vital energy and metallic minerals; geopolitical threats to mineral supplies; unequal trading relations between the resource exporters of the South and the importing countries of the North; the deteriorating quality of the environment; the depletion of renewable resources, such as soils, fish and forests; and the potentially disastrous effects of changes in global biogeochemical cycles. Despite the fact that geographers once defined their subject as the study of the relationship between human society and the physical environment, this reawakening of concern over natural resources largely by-passed human geography. The subject was at that time preoccupied to the point of obsession with the quantitative revolution, with the search for spatial order and the development of theoretical models of industrial location, land use patterns, urban hierarchies and transport networks. It was commonly assumed that the location and nature of the resource base were fixed and given; the way in which human societies define resources and give meaning to natural systems was largely ignored and the physical environment vanished behind neat optimising rules for the spacing of economic activities and settlements. In addition, and perhaps most importantly, there was almost total neglect of the critical question of how natural resources, and the wealth or welfare derived from them, are allocated between socio-economic, political and cultural groups over space and time. This neglect was evident at all spatial scales – global, national and local.

Although geographical interest in resource management and allocation issues has undoubtedly increased steadily since the mid-1970s, it is still true to say that the contribution of human geographers to the analysis of resource problems has been relatively slight and that there is a comparative dearth of material treating the issues from a distinctive geographical perspective. For this reason alone it is necessary to go beyond the boundaries of geography and to consider work in economics, ecology, political science, international relations and many other academic disciplines. But this wider perspective is also made essential by the nature of the key resource questions. It is clear that an understanding of the problems involved in resource exploitation and the development of management policies cannot be obtained from any one discipline or ideological viewpoint; it must involve inquiry into physical systems, economic processes, social organisations, legal and administrative structures and political institutions.

THE NATURE OF RESOURCES

Although resources are products of the physical system they are defined by human ability and need, not by nature. Human beings evaluate the natural environment and classify as resources those substances, organisms or physical properties which they are technically capable of utilising and which provide desired goods and services. Resources are, therefore, dynamic cultural conceptions. Perceived resources have changed, and will continue to change, dramatically over time, not only in response to increased knowledge and technological innovation but also in line with economic, social and political developments which alter the demand for resource products and services. Historically, the process of cultural change has acted to widen the resource base by giving resource value to previously unusable substances. Bauxite, for instance, only acquired resource status in 1886 when the commercial extraction of aluminium became feasible, while uranium had negligible value until the military and economic importance of nuclear power became evident in the 1940s. However, it is important to realise that the mechanisms which create resource value can also destroy it. Clearly, if changes occur in consumer tastes, lifestyles and needs, or if more effective or lower cost substitutes are developed, then currently important resources, such as copper or coal, could revert to valueless physical substances.

Since resources are culturally defined, there need be no consensus as to what they are at any particular period of time. As socio-economic, political and technical conditions vary over space, and between cultural groups, so too does the set of perceived resources. During the twentieth century the spatial diversity of assessments has undoubtedly declined for the internationally traded metals and energy minerals. As Peter Taylor and Stuart Corbridge have shown (in their Chapters 5.1 and 5.3), the global economy has become increasingly interdependent, and this has meant that most societies accept the resource value of these minerals as defined by the technology and demands of the advanced countries. Such convergence of valuations is one end product of the processes of capital transformation discussed by Roger Lee (Chapter 4.3). Some variations do, however, remain. In the Soviet Union, for instance, which has pursued a minerals self-sufficiency policy for the last 60 years, non-bauxite sources of aluminium, such as nepheline and alunite, are important resources, but these have negligible value elsewhere in the world economy where bauxite is in plentiful supply. Similarly, peat and lignite can be crucial energy resources in some countries (or regions) lacking indigenous supplies of coal, oil or gas and unable to afford to import their fuel requirements.

Internationally agreed assessments of resource value occur less frequently in the environmental resource sector. The cultural significance of landscapes, plant and animal species, or natural ecosystems varies markedly between socities. They are all, to use Denis Cosgrove's words, multi-layered texts 'offering the possibility of simultaneous different readings'. Cross-cultural differences in the 'meaning' attributed to different environments are by no means easy to explain. There is, however, a tendency for the value, or priority, given to resources which satisfy aesthetic rather than immediate material needs to increase with economic wealth. People living at high levels of material prosperity can afford to be concerned with environmental quality and the potential needs of future generations. But such concerns may have little relevance to those living on the margins of subsistence, striving to satisfy their basic requirements for food, shelter and fuel. Having said this, there are societies – like that of the Australian Aborigines for instance – where 'nature' has such a religious significance that its integrity is valued much more highly than the products of resource exploitation. The discongruity between the environmental evaluations of white and black Australians is central to the continuing controversy over the mining of uranium, bauxite and iron ore on Aboriginal lands.

Moreover, for environmental resources there may be no consensus even within one society. An area of badland topography could be regarded by some as a crucial scientific and recreational resource, but to others it could be a valueless eyesore or an erosion hazard threatening agricultural productivity, buildings and local infrastructure (Plate 6.1.1.). Similarly, what is a vital wetland resource to those with interests in nature conservation, could be a costly nuisance to farmers and a complete irrelevance to the vast majority of people. Such differences in valuation lie at the heart of many of the current conflicts over the use and allocation of environmental resources, which are discussed by Tim O'Riordan in Chapter 6.2.

RESOURCE TYPES

It has been common to divide natural resources into two broad and distinct groups: stock and renewable (see Figure 6.1.1). *Stock resources* (all minerals and land) are substances which have taken millions of years to form and, therefore, from a human perspective are now fixed in supply. On the other hand, *renewable resources* naturally regenerate rapidly enough to provide new units of supply within a time-span relevant to human beings. In practice, however, the dividing line between these groups is blurred and it is more useful to think of a *use-renewability continuum* (Figure 6.1.2).

At one extreme, there is a group of resources whose potential supplies are naturally determined, infinitely renewable and unrelated to current levels of use. This most obviously applies to solar, tidal and wind energies and to the global water cycle,[4] although it should be stressed that considerable invest-

SOURCE: By courtesy of the Municipality of Aliano

FIGURE 6.1.1 *Landslide threat: Aliano, Regione Basilicato, Italy*

ment is required to convert potential supplies into useful resource products. To some extent the capacity of air and water to absorb waste materials, and render them harmless, also comes into this use-independent category. In general the environment acts quickly to disperse or degrade pollutants, so restoring these resources to their natural condition. However, there are three important caveats. First, when waste loads exceed the assimilative capacity of individual streams, lakes or air sheds, short-run deterioration of quality does occur. Second, such quality changes can destroy, often for long periods, whole populations of plant and animal species. And third, for the so-called stock pollutants (some forms of radio-active waste, mercury and cadmium, for instance) natural breakdown and cleansing processes may be too slow to be relevant to human beings. The environment, therefore, has a limited capacity to absorb such wastes safely.

At the other end of the use-renewability continuum are the fossil fuels. These are being utilised at rates which massively exceed their natural regeneration and, importantly, they are transformed by use into forms of matter which cannot yield usable energy. For this 'consumed by use' resource set, present levels of consumption must affect the quantity available for future generations.

Between the two extremes on the continuum are a wide range of resources where renewability is no longer naturally assured but is dependent on human management practices. Future availabilities will critically depend on whether

STOCK			FLOW	
Consumed by use	Theoretically recoverable	Recyclable	Critical zone	Non-critical zone
OIL GAS COAL	ALL ELEMENTAL MINERALS	METALLIC MINERALS	FISH FORESTS ANIMALS SOIL WATER IN AQUIFERS	SOLAR ENERGY TIDES WIND WAVES WATER AIR

Flow resources used to extinction

Critical zone resources become stock once regenerative capacity is exceeded

SOURCE: Judith Rees, *Natural Resources: Allocation, Economics and Policy*, (London: Methuen, 1986) p. 13

FIGURE 6.1.1 *Classification of resources*

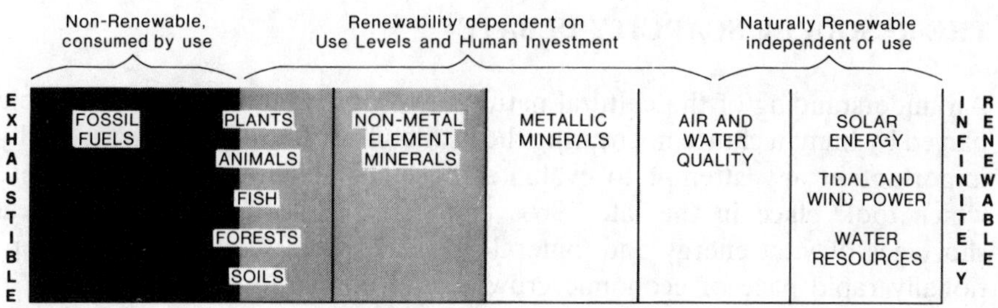

FIGURE 6.1.2 *The natural resources continuum*

utilisation is managed according to the sustainable yield principle (see O'Riordan, Chapter 6.2).

All resources which reproduce biologically are only renewable if the rate of use is at or below the rate of natural replenishment. At higher usage levels, the resource is being 'mined' to exhaustion as surely as any coal or oil stock. If plant, animal or fish populations become very small and dispersed they can reach a *critical zone*, where the depletion process has become too far advanced to be reversed even when all exploitation ceases. It is well known that many species have already been pushed to extinction by over-hunting, pollution and habitat destruction, and many others are endangered. Likewise, although the fertility of soil resources is naturally renewable when land is not used intensively, under all forms of modern agriculture it has to be managed and artificially restored. Moreover, once land has been degraded by soil erosion, salinization and desertification, it is by no means certain that it can be restored to productivity within a humanly relevant time scale, either naturally or through planned remedial programmes. In other words, although all these resources are conventionally classified as naturally renewable, in reality future supplies depend on human choice and can only be assured if usage is controlled or investment occurs in artificial regeneration programmes.

When looked at in this way, these resources broadly belong to the same resource category as the element minerals. In principle, none of the elements are consumed by use: the total amounts available in the global system are roughly constant, taking account of the quantities remaining in the earth's crust, temporally stored in products and discarded in waste dumps. Therefore, theoretically at least, future units of supply can continually be made available, not by natural renewal but by investment in recycling. The technology already exists to allow most metals to be used many times over with little loss of quality;[2] future supplies of metals should not be subject to physical availability barriers, but will depend on the costs of recycling, the level of investment in re-use technologies and on the continued supplies of low-cost energies.

THE RESOURCE SCARCITY DEBATE

An understanding of the cultural nature of resources and of the crucial role played by human choice in ensuring the availability of future supplies is vitally important in any attempt to evaluate the highly polarised scarcity debate which took place in the late 1960s and early 1970s. Fears over physical shortages of vital energy and mineral resources were fuelled by the exceptionally rapid pace of economic growth, and the associated rising trend in mineral consumption which had occurred over the previous two decades. It had been common for mineral use growth rates to exceed 5 per cent per annum, and in some cases rates greatly in excess of this were experienced. Iron ore consumption, for instance, increased by 7 per cent while platinum demand grew at 9 per cent and aluminium use escalated by 9.8 per cent. Many commentators argued that these growth rates were not sustainable, that at best shortages would be a barrier to continued economic development and at worst they would result in the total collapse of society during the early part of the 21st century.[3] These fears over the future state of the world economy were reinforced by a growing concern over the depletion and degradation of supposedly renewable resources, including environmental quality, and over the potentially disastrous effects of anthropogenic (that is, human-induced) changes in global biogeochemical cycles.

This latter set of concerns was also related to the post-1945 surge in the pace of economic activity and resource consumption. In the first place, it was increasingly recognised that the elementary laws of physics on the conservation of matter dictated that resource materials did not conveniently vanish after processing and use. Rather, a mass, broadly equal to that initially extracted, must be eventually discharged, albeit in a transformed state, to accumulate somewhere in the global ecosystem (see Figure 6.1.3). Therefore, as mineral use escalated so too did waste discharge levels, and fears grew particularly over the effects on the atmosphere of the by-products of fossil-fuel combustion (see Figure 6.1.4), and over the accumulation of metal residuals in drinking water and food.

Secondly, as the demand for minerals grew, lower grade deposits were worked, exploitation was pushed into increasingly remote and environmentally sensitive areas, and the scale of operations escalated as modern mass-mining technologies were employed. All these changes increased the potential damage caused by mineral extraction, not only to the physical environment but also to the integrity of distinct cultural groups (controversy arose, for example, over the impact of Alaskan oil developments on Eskimo communities, the disruptive effects of mining on Aboriginal lifestyles, and the cultural changes caused in Papua New Guinea by large scale copper extraction).

Finally, the pace of post-war economic growth and technological change also affected the way human beings evaluated their physical environment; many people became concerned with the quality of their lives and were able

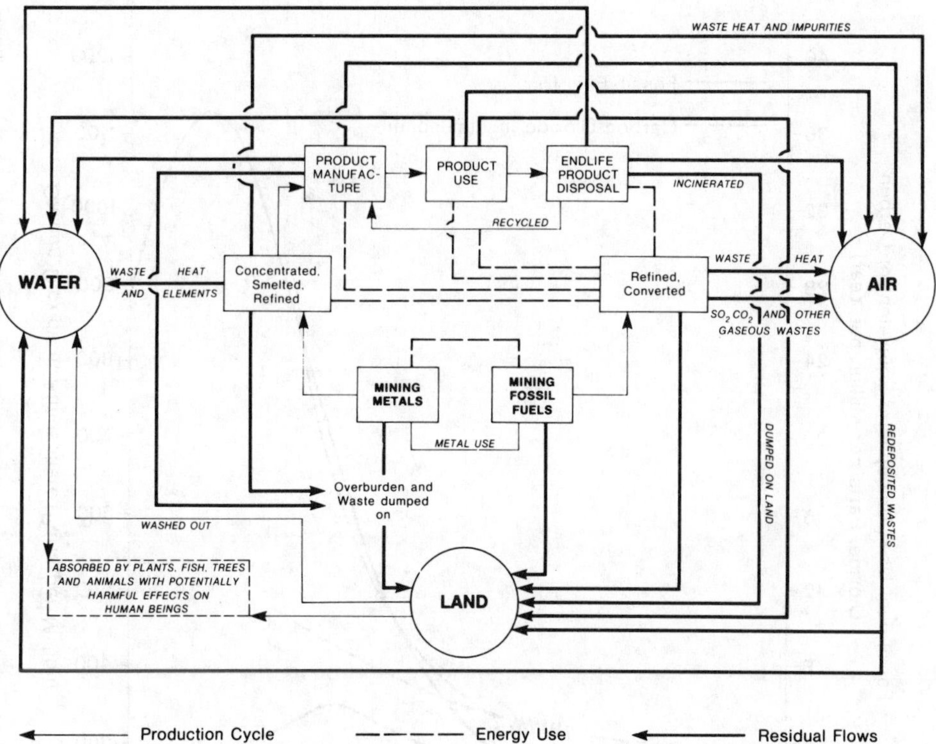

FIGURE 6.1.3 *The closed production and waste disposal cycle*

to afford to turn their attention from the acquisition of material goods towards resources which had aesthetic or recreational value. Therefore, in the advanced nations of the world, industrial, urban and agricultural pressures were reducing the supply of 'natural' environmental quality resources, at the very time when the demand for them was increasingly markedly. Conflicts over their use and allocation between social groups were the inevitable result.

PHYSICAL SCARCITIES

In this chapter I want to focus on the likely adequacy of resources which are incorporated within the economic system of exchange, and which serve to provide material goods and services. Judgements about the continued global availability of minerals and energy supplies differ enormously, and are crucially dependent upon two factors:-

a) the *assumed* total quantity of particular substances within the physical system;

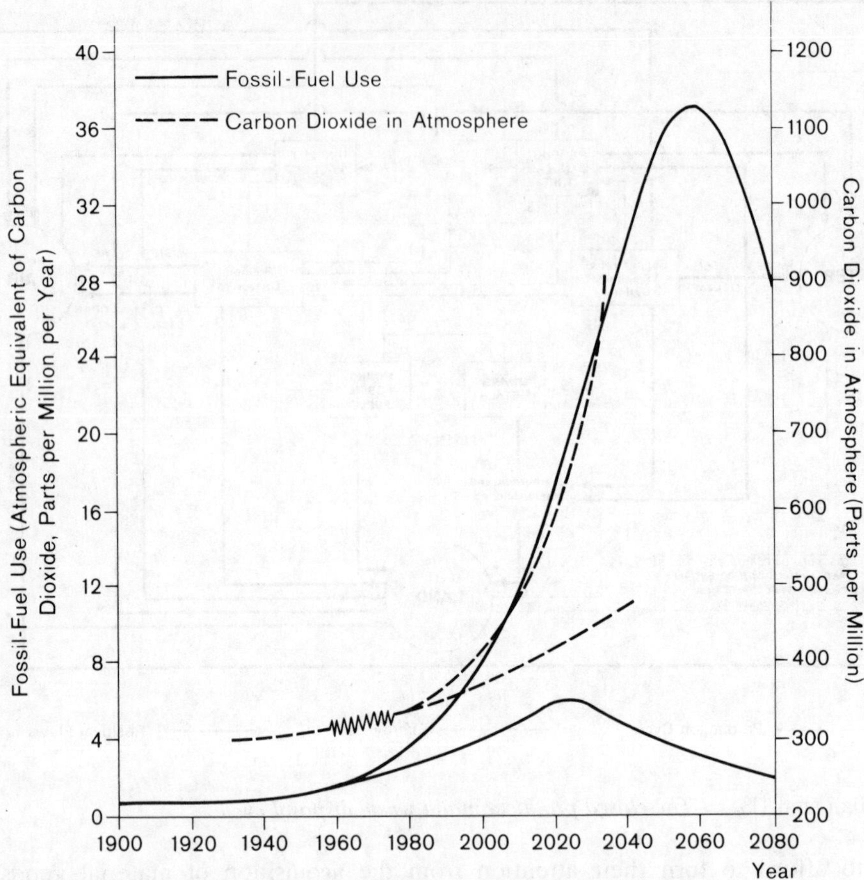

SOURCE: George M. Woodwell, 'The Carbon Dioxide Question', *Scientific American*, 238(1), January 1978, p. 40 (Copyright © 1978 by Scientific American Inc., all rights reserved).

FIGURE 6.1.4 *Projections of fossil fuel consumption and carbon dioxide content of the atmosphere: minimum and maximum plausible rates of increase*

b) the *assumed* role of economic and technological change in altering patterns of consumption and the definition of resources.

By far the most pessimistic prognostications are made when current *proven reserves* are taken to be the total potential supply. These are defined as deposits already discovered and economically extractable under *present* demand, price, political, legal and technological conditions.[4] They are obviously the product of past efforts to locate and appraise deposits (see Table 6.1.1), and are only 'proven' after considerable capital expenditure. Few mining companies are likely to invest in exploration when they have secure title to enough reserves to meet projected demands for the next 20 or so years. Thus, for most minerals, proven reserves simply reflect current consumption levels and the reserve inventory policies of mining companies; they say little about the potential size of the ultimate resource stock. Their use to forecast the life of a mineral clearly involves the highly unrealistic assumption that no successful exploration activity will take place in the future. Moreover, it has to be further assumed that no changes will occur which shift already known but uneconomic deposits (*conditional reserves*) into the proven category. There will, in other words, be no improvements made to extraction, transportation, refining or processing technologies; no changes in the cost and availability of investment capital, labour, machinery, power or other infrastructure services; no variations in the demand for mineral products; no real price increases; and no alterations to the political, legal or economic conditions which affect development costs and risks. Proven reserves are a dynamic concept and any calculations which make them static, at current levels, produce meaningless results.

Having said this, it was by no means uncommon in the early 1970s for analysts to estimate future resource availabilities by crudely dividing proven reserves by the then current annual consumption to obtain a *static life index* (the number of years supply left at present levels of use). Alternatively, an *exponential life index* was constructed by assuming that past compound rates of consumption growth would continue in the future. As Figure 6.1.5 shows, this latter type of calculation normally produced much more alarming results; while bauxite reserves would last approximately 100 years at static levels of use, they would run out within 25 years if demand continued to rise at 9.8 per cent per annum compound, as it had done from 1947 to 1974. Whenever these type of indices were employed, it was inevitably concluded that most of the economically important minerals would be exhausted sometime in the early 21st century and that this would cause the collapse of industrial society.[5] It is easy to show how misguided earlier, but similarly based, projections have been. In 1939, for instance, the US Department of the Interior predicted that the country's oil stocks would be exhausted by 1952; today some 10 million barrels a day (including natural gas liquids) are still being produced and sufficient reserves have already been established to last at least 12 to 15 years. Similar, in 1950 it was estimated that world iron ore reserves would run out in 1970, but by that time there were enough reserves to last another 240 years at the then current levels of use.

Some forecasters have attempted to cover the fact that new reserves will continue to be developed by assuming that ultimately available supplies will be some arbitrary factor of either current reserves (5 times being a popular figure) or current consumption (250 times the 1970 consumption level is used in the well-known World III model of *The Limits to Growth*).[6] It is usually claimed that such allowances for new finds are generous, but on past evidence this is not the case. For instance, in just 20 years, 1950 to 1970, fivefold increases were experienced in the cumulative reserves of most of our widely used minerals, including iron, bauxite, oil and phosphates. In reality, the rate at which new discoveries, technological innovation and market changes have

TABLE 6.1.1 *Stages in the search for and assessment of mineral deposits*

	Stages	*Techniques*
a) Exploration	1) Preliminary topographic and geological investigations of broad regions.	Maps, historic record, air photography, satellite imagery
	2) Identification of target zones	Mapping, field survey, testing superficial materials for trace elements, seismic investigations.
	3) Investigation of small-scale structures and geology of target zones	
	4) Identification of potential prospects	Test-drilling, geo-chemical, geo-physical analysis.
	5) Identification of deposits	
b) Evaluation	6) Assessment of physical characteristics of deposits:– structure, extent, quality.	
c) Commercial Appraisal	7) Analysis of leasing conditions, government regulations, infrastructure costs of factors of production.	
	8) Appraisal of market conditions, interest rates, risk and uncertainty, alternative supply sources, price of substitutes.	
d) Reassessment	New physical data Technological innovation Changing market conditions Changing political climate Changing legal or planning requirements.	

acted to prove new reserves has exceeded, or at least kept pace with, increases in consumption. While it is axiomatic that individual fossil fuel stocks and sources of *new* element minerals must have some physical limit, we do not have the information to determine what this is, nor is there any certainty that the substances will still be regarded as resources when their physical limits are neared. Any model, however sophisticated, which gives a

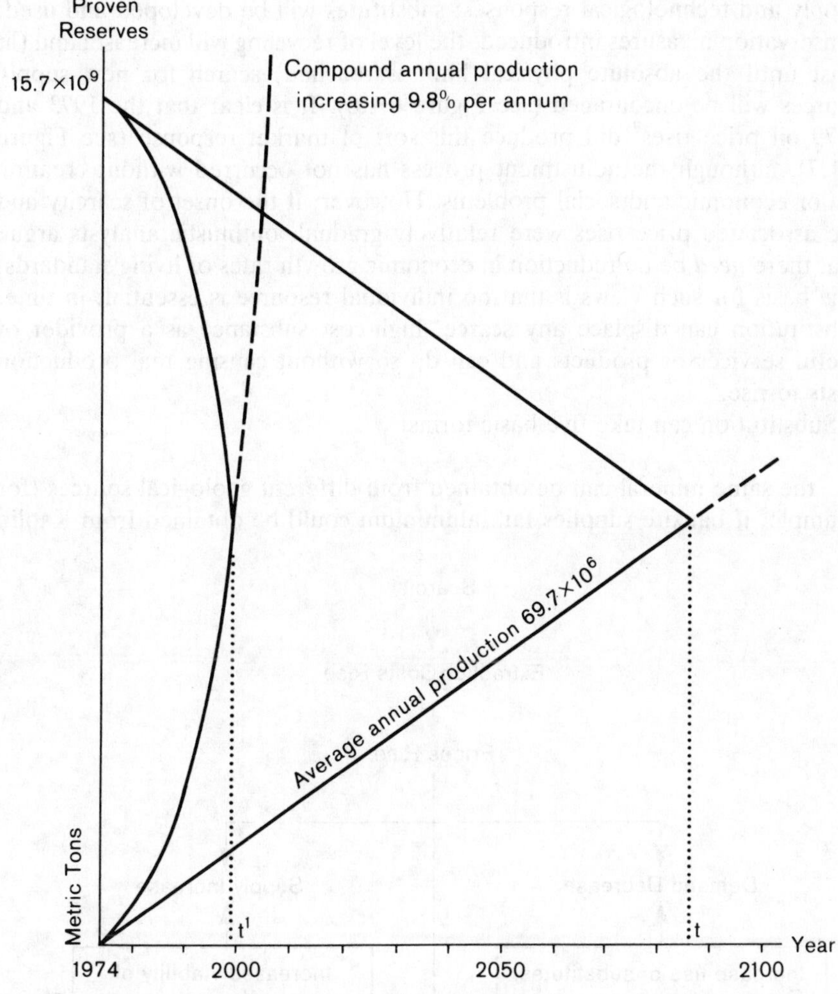

SOURCE: Judith Rees, *Natural Resources: Allocation, Economics and Policy* (London: Methuen, 1985) p. 32

FIGURE 6.1.5 *The life of bauxite reserves using static and exponential life indices*

static physical dimension to the dynamic resource concept is programmed to predict a scarcity catastrophe.

Much more optimistic judgements about future resource availabilities arise from the analysis of the mechanisms which exist within the market system to prevent mineral shortages, and to reduce the economic significance of the exhaustion of particular resource stocks. As any mineral becomes scarce its price inevitably rises, and this will then set in train a whole series of demand, supply and technological responses: substitutes will be developed and used; conservation measures introduced; the level of recycling will increase; and (at least until the absolute physical limit is reached) search for new supply sources will be encouraged (see Figure 6.1.6). It is clear that the 1973 and 1979 oil price rises[7] did produce this sort of market response (see Figure 6.1.7), although the adjustment process has not occurred without creating major economic and social problems. However, if the onset of scarcity and the associated price rises were relatively gradual, optimistic analysts argue that there *need* be no reduction in economic growth rates or living standards. The basis for such views is that no individual resource is essential; in time, substitution can displace any scarce, high-cost substance as a provider of useful services or products and can do so without causing real production costs to rise.

Substitution can take five basic forms:

1. the same mineral can be obtained from different geological sources (for example, if bauxite supplies fail, aluminium could be obtained from Kaolin

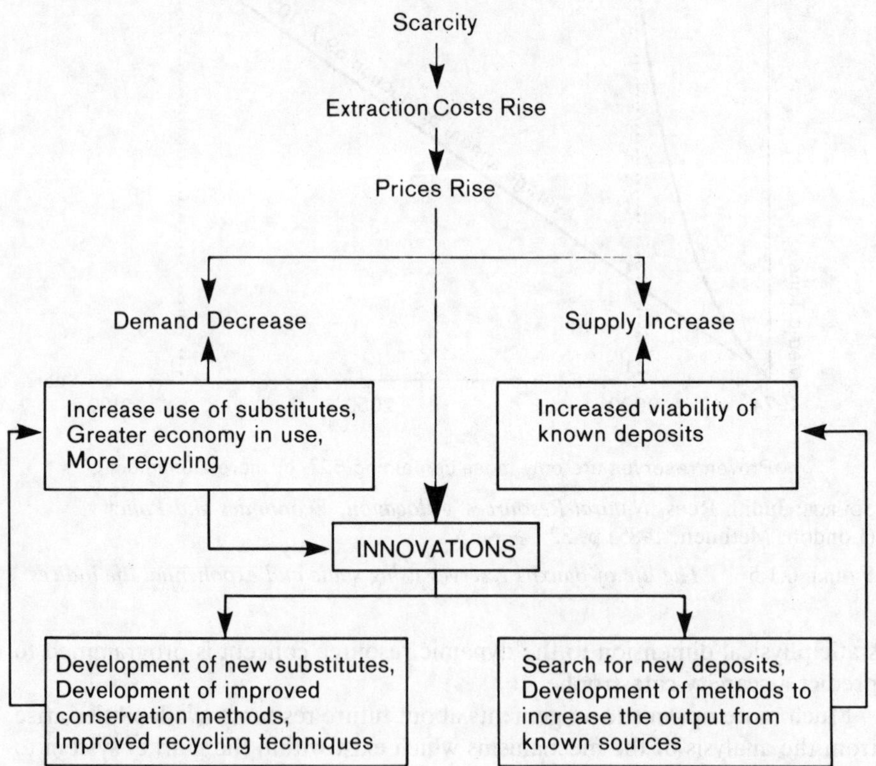

SOURCE: Judith Rees, *Natural Resources: Allocation, Economics and Policy*, (London: Methuen, 1985)

FIGURE 6.1.6 *The idealised market response to resource scarcity*

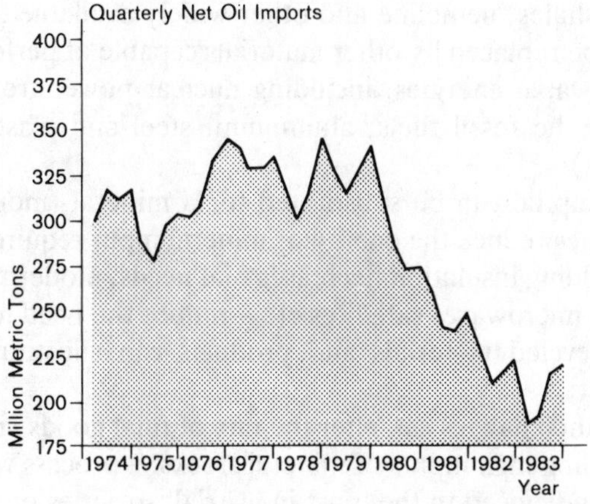

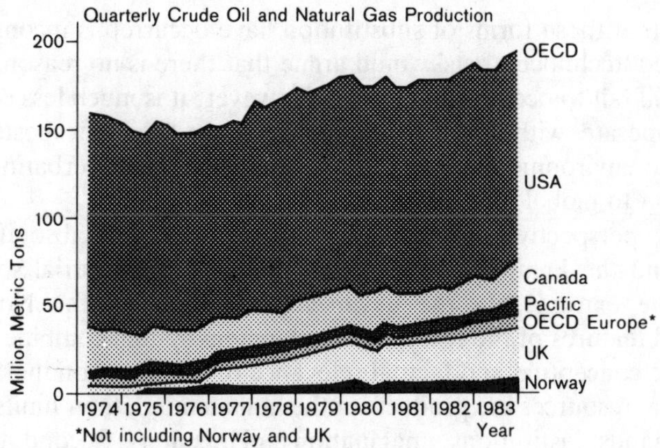

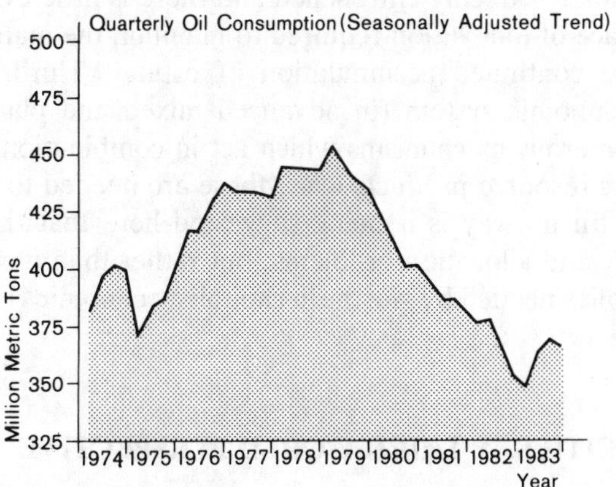

SOURCE: As Figure 6.1.6, p. 89

FIGURE 6.1.7 *OECD: The changing trends of oil and gas imports, production and consumption,* 1974–83.

clays, carboniferous shales, nemeline and other widely available materials);
2. one mineral can be replaced by other materials capable of performing the same end uses (renewable energies, including nuclear power from breeder reactors, can replace the fossil fuels; aluminium, steel and plastics are all substitutes for copper);
3. technology and capital can be substituted for a mineral (more efficient production technologies reduce the energy or mineral input required per unit output, improved building insulation decreases fuel needs, modern communication technologies – microwave, satellites etc – reduce the need for metals);
4. 'second-hand' recycled materials and products can substitute for the freshly mined product;
5. Lifestyle or demand changes can alter the mix of final goods and services away from those needing high inputs of mineral stocks; a process which some argue is already well advanced in the 'post industrial' societies of the North.

The fact that these forms of substitution have occurred is incontrovertible and so-called 'technocentrists' would argue that there is no reason to believe that they will fail to occur in the future. However, it is much less certain that they can operate without imposing major socio-economic costs, without considerable environmental degradation, and without exacerbating the risks of disruption to global biogeochemical cycles.

From the perspective of today, the models predicting absolute physical scarcities and the imminent catastrophic collapse of industrial society look naive in the extreme. In the advanced economies of the North, three interrelated features of the resource development system combine to destroy much of the conceptual and factual relevance of the idea of mineral scarcity. First, natural resources are products of the human mind, their limits are set by human demands, institutions, imagination and ingenuity. Second, the process of technological change is deeply entrenched and there is little evidence of a slackening of the pace of innovation required to maintain the material inputs needed to fuel the continued accumulation of capital. Third, and most importantly, the economic system (in advanced mixed and planned economies) contains numerous mechanisms which act in combination to combat shortages of specific resource products *when* these are needed to sustain the process of growth. In no way is it being suggested here that there are no resource availability and allocation problems, but rather than physical limits on the mineral supplies needed by Northern capitalist economies is not one of these.

PHYSICAL SCARCITIES: A THIRD WORLD PERSPECTIVE

It is not possible to be so sanguine about the physical availability of the resources needed to create economic development in many Third World nations, or indeed to sustain present levels of material wealth. No one can fail to be aware that severe resource shortages are already affecting the basic existence of millions of people. For instance, it is well known that the 90 or so LDCs which do not have indigenous oil or gas production are desperately short of the energy needed to maintain transport and other infrastructure services, and to process agricultural raw materials. Since 1973, the increased price of imported oil has greatly exacerbated their supply and external debt problems (cf. Corbridge, Chapter 5.3). It is crucial to realise that the price they pay for imported energy is determined by the income and demand levels of the North, and this inevitably means that the supplies available to LDCs are severely limited by their ability to pay. As we have seen, the market optimists assume that resource scarcities will be prevented by rising prices which will stimulate investment in new supplies. However, such notions are quite untenable if the price people *can* pay is insufficient to provide the necessary supply incentives; price rises will merely increase the shortage since people will only be able to afford to buy fewer units of supply.

Such supply problems have led to the common suggestion that energy deficient LDCs should locate and develop their own potential oil, gas, coal or hydro-electric power resources thereby attaining some measure of self-sufficiency and freedom from international markets. However, this seemingly simple suggestion is fraught with difficulties. Undoubtedly some LDCs have potentially large hydro-carbon deposits; Botswana, for example, is known to have extensive deposits of coal. But reserves are only 'proved' by investment and remain valueless until effective demands are great enough to warrant the major investments needed to develop production, processing and transport facilities. There lies the nub of the LDC scarcity problem. Many countries lack indigenous capital and have limited ability to raise, and pay for, further foreign loans. Moreover, the private multinational mineral companies, with the necessary capital and technical expertise, will rarely undertake investment solely to meet the relatively low internal demands of an LDC. Their concern is with obtaining economies of scale in production and serving a large international market (see Thrift and Taylor, Chapter 4.3). In such circumstances the potential physical presence of energy or mineral deposits is irrelevant; shortages remain, created by limited effective demand and lack of investment capital.

Clearly, scarcity of minerals and energy is not the only natural resource problem faced by many LDCs. Scarcities of renewable resources can also be critical. Soil erosion and desertification are now widespread phenomena, resulting in marked reductions in agricultural productivity particularly, but not exclusively, in semi-arid areas. Endemic water shortages affect roughly 50 per cent of the world's population and deforestation has already created severe local scarcities of firewood, still the most important fuel source in many LDCs. These are all resources where scarcity is created by management practice and the lack of investment in artificial regeneration programmes. In the water case, for instance, there could be a physically unlimited recyclable supply, as the sophisticated reprocessing technologies employed on space craft demonstrate. Storage and transport can adjust spatial and temporal imbalances between primary water supply and use; the natural cleansing cycle can be accelerated by waste water renovation and the option technically exists to tap the massive stores held in the oceans. Thus scarcity is not a physical problem *per se*, but is created by a complex of economic, social, demographic, institutional and political conditions.

Food, water and timber have clear use value and have long been potentially marketable products, with a recognized price even in the poorest areas of the world. But the mere existence of a use value or price cannot ensure their adequate supply. In part their scarcity is a function of the international distribution of wealth. Just as many LDC consumers lack the effective demand to justify investment in minerals to serve domestic markets, so too they are unable to articulate, within the existing economic, political and financial systems, their needs for the augmentation of renewable resource flows. It would, however, be simplistic to suggest that problems, such as deforestation or the desertification of the Sahel, can be solved merely by throwing massive technological and financial aid packages at them. As the history of the 'green revolution' has shown, investment in increased soil productivity (or the augmentation of other renewable resource flows) has to be accompanied by socio-economic, political and institutional change. Without this the resultant benefits tend to be concentrated in the hands of a relatively small, wealthy élite, and the poorest social groups are 'marginalised' still further, both in economic and spatial terms (see Harriss and Harriss, Chapter 4.2). The marginalisation process frequently forces the poor into the least climatically or geomorphologically favourable areas, such as desert margins or mountain foothills, and this merely serves to exacerbate renewable resource scarcity problems. Vulnerable ecosystems are overused, thus reducing their productivity and so the scarcity cycle goes on.

GEOPOLITICALLY INDUCED SCARCITIES

During the mid-1970s greater salience was attached to the notion that the global distribution of low cost mineral sources was becoming increasingly unfavourable for the advanced capitalist economies. Their long histories of indigenous resource expoitation made it seem likely that in the future a much greater proportion of reserves would be found in the relatively under-explored Soviet Bloc and in the Third World. This would shift 'resource power', exacerbate problems of import dependence and increase the probability that artificial, politically motivated, scarcities could be created to threaten the economic prosperity and military security of the advanced Western nations.

Such ideas appeared vindicated by events in the early 1970s. In 1971, the United States moved into oil deficit and imports rose sharply: Libya, followed by the other OPEC states, achieved a 50 per cent increase in world oil prices between 1970 and 1972. From 1972 to 1974, agricultural and mineral prices rose rapidly, in many cases increasing over 200 per cent in two years.

Morocco used its dominance over phosphate exports to push up prices by 400 per cent in just 9 months (January-June 1974); Jamaica increased bauxite taxes five-fold and, of greatest importance, in retaliation for the re-supply of Israel with arms during the October 1973 war, the Arab oil producers cut output by 25 per cent and placed an embargo on sales to the United States and other 'unfriendly nations', including Japan, Britain and France. Panic buying allowed Iran, followed by the rest of OPEC, to double the crude oil price and double it again just three months later. It became a widely held belief that a major shift in the balance of power had occurred between the industrialised nations and the mineral exporters of the Third World. Even radical commentators saw the possibility of breaking the polarised pattern of global development and celebrated the 'turning point in the history of international relations'.[8] For right wing analysts there was no cause for celebration, however, and they argued that the 'dynamic nature of capitalism' would be impaired as other producer cartels followed OPEC's lead in 'holding the consumer nations to ransom'.[9] Some hardliners even went as far as advocating military invasion of the oil fields and the imposition of embargoes on all exports of food, manufactured goods and investment capital to 'wayward' Third World countries.

With the advantage of hindsight, it seems clear that the resource power debate was misguided, based on a false perception of the fragility of the established economic order and of the real dangers posed by LDC ownership of actual or potential mineral supplies. First, it is necessary to explode a common piece of mythology that, 'it is now the Third World that supplies most of the capitalist world's raw materials'.[10] The facts do not support this view. The advanced western nations are themselves the chief mineral producers and the chief sourcee of their own consumption. Even in the energy sector, the developed capitalist economies produced 69 per cent of their own requirements in 1979, and this figure has increased steadily in the 1980s as the move away from imported oil continues (as in Figure 6.1.7). For most of the metallic minerals, LDCs produce well under a third of world supplies. Figure 6.1.8, which shows the dominance of developed countries in the production and consumption of iron ore, is by no means untypical of the distributions for other metals, although there are exceptions. The major ones are tin, where 68 per cent of world production comes from LDCs, copper (46 per cent) and bauxite (42 per cent), although the LDC contribution in the latter two cases is declining. As far as the non-metallic element minerals are concerned, the LDC's production role is minor, except for phosphates where they contribute about 33 per cent of world supplies. In total the OECD countries rely on LDC exports of non-fuel minerals for less than 15 per cent of their total consumption.

It has to be remembered that a considerable proportion of mineral production never enters world trade, but is produced and consumed in the same country. Even for a major traded mineral such as iron ore only approximately 32 per cent is put on the international market. Furthermore, the major exporters are advanced and not Third World countries. At no time in the last decade did the developed countries take less than 60 per cent of their non-fuel mineral imports from other advanced nations (Australia, Canada, South Africa and the United States being the most important), and by the early 1980s this proportion had risen to 68 per cent. On present trends it is also highly unlikely that LDC contributions to advanced nation consumption and imports will increase significantly in the foreseeable future. The major reason for this is the pattern of investment in the search for new mineral supply sources.

Investment in proving mineral reserves has never, and still does not, take place uniformly over all the potentially mineraliferous areas of the world (see Figure 6.1.9 for the highly skewed pattern of search for oil). Although published data on the level and location of this investment are sketchy and global figures are non-existent, it is evident that historically expenditure has been concentrated in the already developed countries. For a brief period in the late 1940s and 1950s, expenditure did escalate in the Third World, reaching an estimated 57 per cent of the exploration budget of the European group of mining companies and accounting for 53 per cent of US direct investment in mining and smelting.[11] But these proportions have tumbled in the last 25 years. By 1980 LDCs attracted only 20 per cent of European company exploration investment and only 30 per cent of US foreign investment in the minerals sector. Overall throughout the 1970s it appears that some 80 per cent of the capitalist world's expenditure on mineral search went to advanced nations, with the bulk being channelled to four 'safe countries' – U.S., Canada, South Africa and Australia. Since mineral reserves are only proved by investment, this skewed distribution of expenditure must be reflected in the supply and trade patterns of the future.

The production, trade and investment facts in themselves deprive the notion of general LDC resource power of much practical meaning. It is, however, possible to find specific mineral products in which Western capitalist economies are import dependent to a substantial degree (see Table 6.1.2). But does this pose a significant supply security threat? In reality, the ability of LDC exporters to achieve, maintain and use market power to create supply shortages and impose major price rises in limited by four important factors.

The diversification strategies of the major mineral multinationals and consumer governments

The risk of supply disruptions can be significantly reduced by spreading production sites over as many different countries as possible, producing a wide range of substitutable mineral products, and spatially separating investments in mining and downstream processing (see also Thrift and Taylor, Chapter 4.3). (This last also has balance-of-payments advantages for the consumer nations, since crude minerals are less costly than refined products.) Such risk-reducing strategies have always been employed, but their use expanded markedly after 1951, following the costly lesson of the nationalisa-

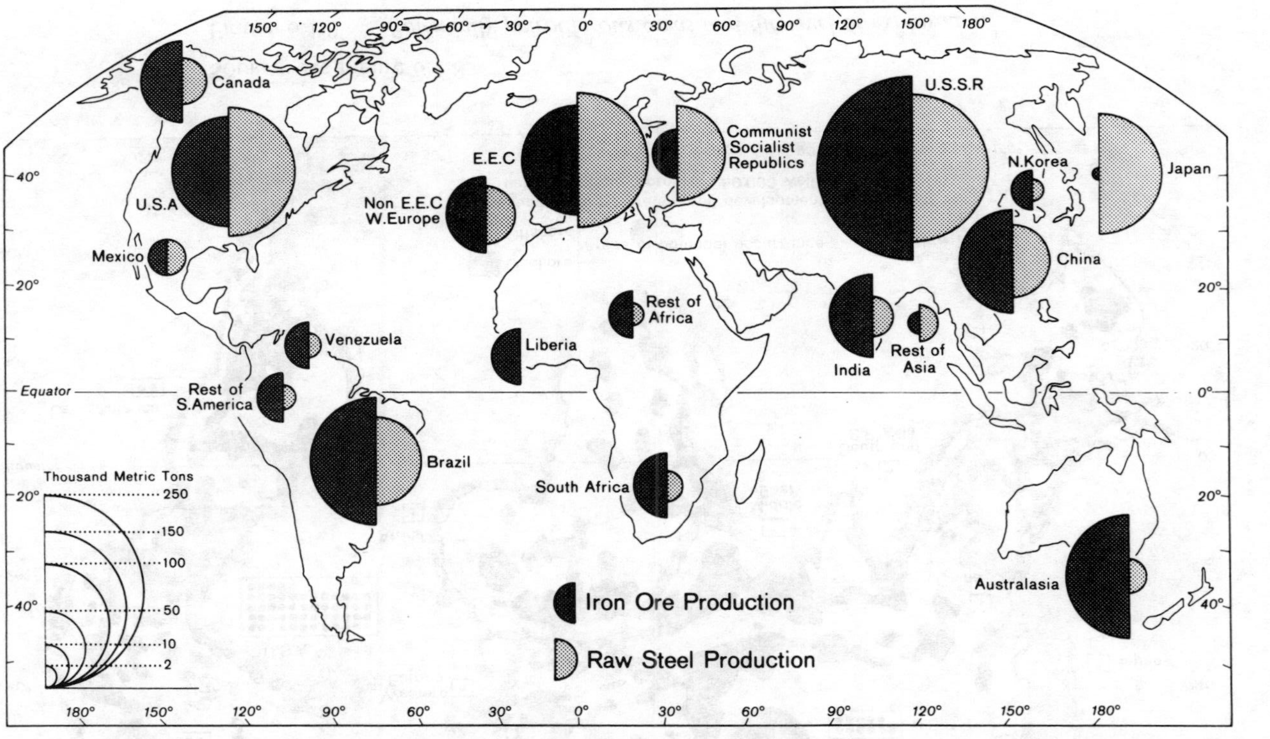

SOURCE: As Figure 6.1.6, p. 23, adapted from P. Odell and K. Rosing, *The Future of Oil* 2nd rev. edn (London? Kogan Page, 1983) pp. 27, 33

FIGURE 6.1.8 *Spatial patterns of iron ore production and steel consumption, 1980–1*

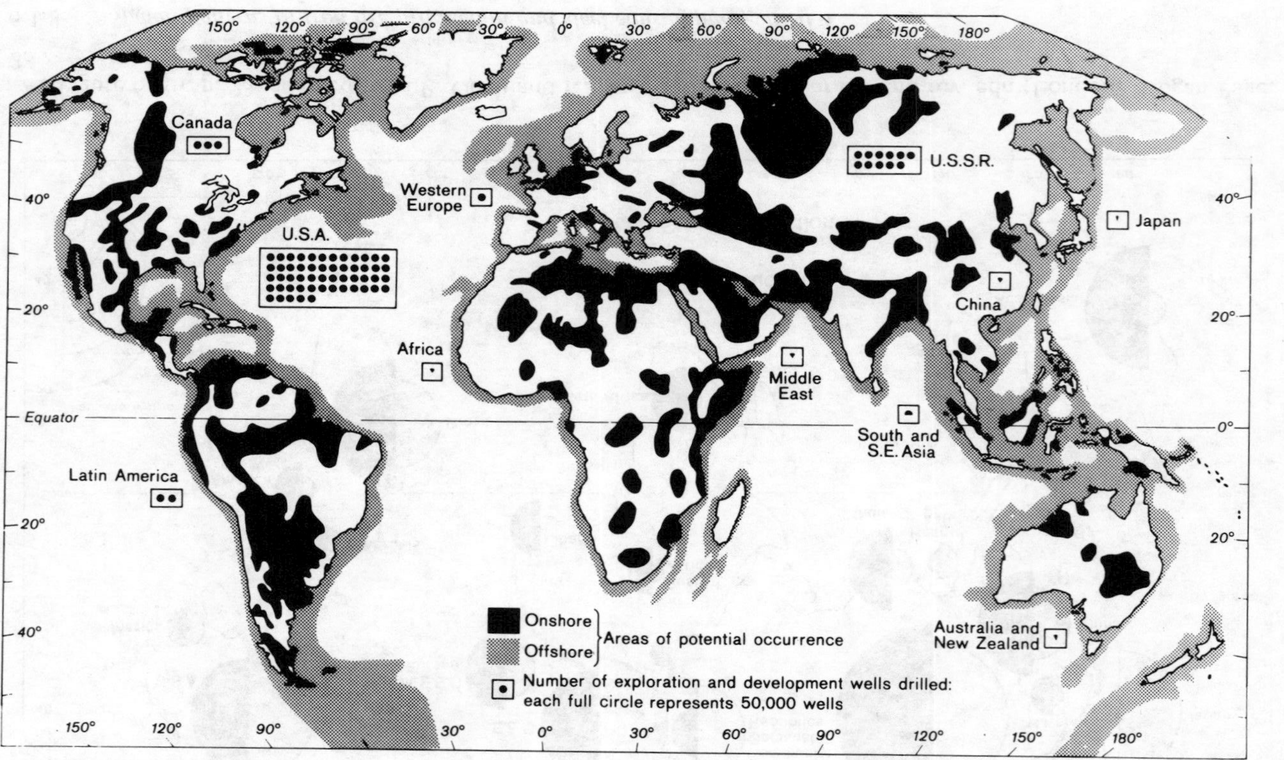

SOURCE: As Figure 6.1.8

FIGURE 6.1.9 *Potentially petroliferous areas and the level of exploration*

tion of the Anglo-Iranian oil company (later BP). The closure of Abadan oil refinery cut the UK's refined oil supplies by 75 per cent and these could only be replaced by adding £300 million to the import bill. Until 1973, diversification successfully coped with the rising economic and political nationalism of the LDCs, the spate of asset expropriations which peaked in the late 1960s, and the greater political instability of many parts of the Third World. Import patterns could be rearranged with comparative ease, causing only temporary price increases, and any supply shortfalls during the adjustment period could be covered by stock piles.[12] While the producer countries remained isolated from one another and were willing, indeed eager, to fill the gap created by the loss of one supply source, then import dependence posed no significant security threats.

The OPEC experience showed that security risks still remained *if* effective producer cartels could be formed. However, source diversification reduces the likelihood that agreements between exporters on prices and market shares will be concluded and, even more crucially, maintained overtime. This is particularly so when very large numbers of producers, with heterogenous political and economic interests, have to be included in the cartel. For instance, the Iron Ore Exporters Association, formed in 1975, was not joined by such major producers as Canada, US, Brazil and Liberia. It had, therefore, minimal ability to push up, or even stabilise prices, as it could not control the quantities exported by such 'outsider' countries.

TABLE 6.1.2 *Metals for which US, Western Europe or Japan were substantially dependent 1981/2*

		Major exporting countries
	Bauxite	Australia, New Guinea, Jamaica, Brazil
	Chromium	USSR, South Africa, Zimbabwe, Turkey
	Cobalt	Zaire, Zambia
*	Copper	Chile, Zambia, Canada, Peru
*	Iron Ore	Brazil, Australia, Liberia, Canada
*	Lead	Australia, Canada, Peru (plus many small producers)
	Manganese	South Africa, Brazil
	Nickel	Australia, Canada, New Caledonia
	Platinum	USSR, South Africa, Canada
	Tin	Malaysia, Indonesia, Thailand, Bolivia
	Tungsten	USSR, Canada, Australia (plus many small producers)
*	Uranium	Canada, South Africa, Australia
*	Zinc	Canada, Australia, Peru

* Minerals for which Western Europe and Japan are import dependent but US is not.
SOURCE: Author

Mining is today a highly capital intensive activity; this means that output cuts produce few cost savings and at times of surplus capacity there is always an incentive to maintain production levels. In such circumstances producer cartels have considerable difficulties in controlling the sales even of their own members, and have no hope of stopping established or new non-cartel members from entering export markets. It is significant, for instance, that Brazil, a small producer of bauxite in 1974, remained outside the International Bauxite Cartel and has subsequently become by far the fastest growing centre of production. In just five years, 1976 to 1981, its output rose from 83 to 560 thousand metric tons per month, making it the fourth largest producer in the Western world. Over the same period IBA members, such as Guyana and Surinam, saw their output and export sales fall absolutely. Further, for many of the major traded minerals, an effective cartel would have to include at least one of the advanced capitalist exporting nations. While Australia, South Africa and Canada have all joined various producer associations, their economies are too deeply enmeshed with the rest of the North to make aggressive supply cuts or price fixing measures a realistic proposition.

The stock-piling policies of consumer governments and companies

Governments in the major industrial nations have for long held emergency reserves of strategic minerals; even in the 1950s it was normal for stockpiles to be sufficient to cover between 6 to 12 months' consumption. In addition, as part of normal business practice, private and public sector industries will hold inventories of the minerals essential to their own production processes, while the multinationals normally carry considerable stocks of the minerals in which they trade. Since 1973, these stockpiles have increased markedly. The US government alone aims to hold stocks of 93 strategic materials against a 3 year military emergency, and most Western nations have adopted similar policies. This means, firstly, any attempts by producers to deliberately withhold supplies have to be extremely long-lasting before the effects begin to bite; secondly, there is time to develop alternative supply sources; and thirdly, consumers can use their stocks to manipulate the market price for minerals. In 1974, for instance, CIPEC (the copper producers' cartel) announced a 10 per cent supply cut, but releases from stocks were used to prevent a rise in market prices. In the same year an attempt by the Soviet Union to double the selling price of palladium merely resulted in large inventory sales which depressed prices. Clearly the existence of these stock piles further limits the effective market power of the exporting nations.

The dependence of the producer countries

Readers of this book will not need reminding that we live in an interdependent world, and it is often contended that the dependency links are symmetrical, with the North being as dependent on the South as the South is on the North. In a resource context, however, it can be argued that whereas the North has acted to reduce its supply dependence, no such reductions have occurred in LDC dependence. In other words, the dependency ties are not symmetrical but work against Third World producers.

The dependence of the LDC exporters takes two forms. First, for many, mineral exports are the prime (and sometimes the only significant) source of investment capital and foreign exchange (see Table 6.1.3). This crucially constrains their ability to sustain sales cuts for significant periods of time, and also makes it less likely that a producer cartel will succeed in maintaining the export limits needed to force up mineral prices; the short-term economic advantages of cheating the cartel are often irresistable. For instance, the International Tin Council has had continual problems with members openly ignoring their export quotas or covertly smuggling their production into neighbouring non-ITC countries. Smuggling from Thailand explains why Burma has frequently had annual export sales five times greater than its total production! Similarly, OPEC is currently having difficulties in maintaining its official prices, with both Iran and Nigeria selling at 'discounts' to sustain sales.

In recent years, as Stuart Corbridge shows in Chapter 5.3, the problems posed by export dependence have been exacerbated by the need to service massive overseas debts. The healthy trade balances experienced by most OPEC states during the 1970s have now evaporated, and OPEC as a whole moved into a balance of payments deficit in 1984. Nigeria, for example, switched from being a net lender to the international banks of $2200 million in 1981, to a net borrower of $2300 million just one year later; servicing this debt now consumes about 40 per cent of oil export earnings. Many of the metal exporters are in an even worse position, requiring over 50 per cent of their total export earnings to repay outstanding loans and the interest on their debt. This situation has been made still more difficult by reduced export volumes and by the falling real market price of minerals. Since 1980 the dollar market price for non-fuel minerals has fallen by 12 per cent per annum, while the oil price has fallen an average of about 15 per cent during the last three years.[13]

The exporting states are also substantially dependent on the western advanced nations for technology, aid, investment capital and manufactured goods. This places further constraints on their ability to sustain aggressive price or supply control measures, since they are exceptionally vulnerable to any retaliatory actions. Moreover, in some LDCs the ruling political élites rely on their economic and military support of the West to maintain their internal power base. Many would argue that régimes such as the Pinochet Junta in Chile simply could not afford to go against the interests of international capital. However, while there may be some validity in such arguments, the point cannot be pushed too far; after all, the first government to raise oil prices in 1973 was the Shah's Iran.

TABLE 6.1.3 *The value of mineral exports as a percentage of all exports from selected Third World countries*

	Country	*Year*	*Fuels* %	*Ores/Metals* %	
*	Algeria	1979	97.7		
*	Bahrain	1979	85.6		
	Bolivia	1977		66.5	(tin and other non-ferrous ores)
	Brunei	1979	99.9		
	Chile	1978		62.7	(mainly copper ores and concentrates)
	Gabon	1977	81.07		
	Indonesia	1980	71.9		
	Kiribati	1979		84.65	(crude fertilisers)
*	Kuwait	1978	88.5		
	Liberia	1978		62.7	(iron ore and related materials)
*	Libya	1979	99.57		
	Mauritania	1975		90.1	(iron ore 70% plus non-ferrous metals)
	New Caledonia	1980		94.8	(pig iron, nickel and other non-ferrous ores)
	Niger	1978		78.3	(uranium and thorium ores)
*	Nigeria	1978	90.27		
	Papua New Guinea	1976		59.9	(mainly copper ores and concentrates)
	Peru	1977		53.3	(mainly copper ore and concenrates)
	Togo	1977		49.4	(crude fertilisers)
	Zaire	1979		73.1	(mainly copper ores and concentrates)
	Zambia	1978		95.8	(mainly copper ores and concentrates)

* These high proportions are typical of those recorded in other O.P.E.C. states.
SOURCE: UNCTAD (1982) *Handbook of International Trade and Development Statistics*, pp. 106–129

The nature of mineral markets

For individual exports or producer cartels to attain and maintain market power, and through this to threaten the security of the consumer states, the following conditions would need to apply:-

a) there are no reasonable cost substitute materials;
b) few opportunities exist for increasing the efficiency of mineral use or for conservation;
c) the mineral must be essential to the industrial base of the importing nation; and
d) the producers must control the output of all potentially important export centres.

If these conditions do not hold, then it is quite possible for producers attempting to control the market, to actually loose financially as a result.

In Figure 6.1.10, a hypothetically elastic[14] demand curve has been drawn for a mineral. Producers faced by such a curve would need to reduce exports markedly to force prices up by a small amount. In the process their total revenue would fall significantly. For most non-fuel minerals, demands are known to be elastic in the medium term, and it has become clear that the demand for oil is also responsive to price, albeit with a time lag while adjustments are made. This responsiveness has resulted in a dramatic fall in the contribution of OPEC oil to the energy needs of the Western world. In 1973, before the price rise, it accounted for some 37 per cent of total energy consumption; today it provides only 18 per cent. The economic mechanisms which operate to mitigate the effects of physical scarcity therefore also work to minimise the risks and longer-term economic effects of geopolitically induced shortages. To borrow the 'tadpole' analogy employed earlier by Peter Taylor in Chapter 5.1, although all the world tadpoles may have been born genetically equal, this equality has long since gone. Once some have become fitter and fatter they acquire the power to remain that way.

THE QUESTION OF INTERNATIONAL DISTRIBUTIVE EQUITY

The debate over the role of the mineral export trade in generating economic growth and reducing spatial inequalities in the distribution of income is a classic case of the blind talking to the deaf. This debate is merely one facet of the larger clash of opinion over the role of capitalism in the development of the Third World.

On the one side, free trade economists argue that the market contains equilibriating mechanisms which work to reduce spatial inequality. Left to themselves, economic forces would ensure that capital was attracted away from the advanced nations, with their high cost labour, and into the LDCs, so generating growth, employment and higher income levels. Trade is regarded as an 'engine of growth and a support for political stability' which 'has advanced the countries that have engaged in it to ever increasing income levels'.[15] Taking this perspective, governments should confine their role to establishing a favourable trading climate and should avoid intervening in the market. Attempts by national governments, or intergovernmental agencies, to promote a 'New International Economic Order' are regarded as counter-productive, fostering inefficient production arrangements and reducing global economic growth rates.[16]

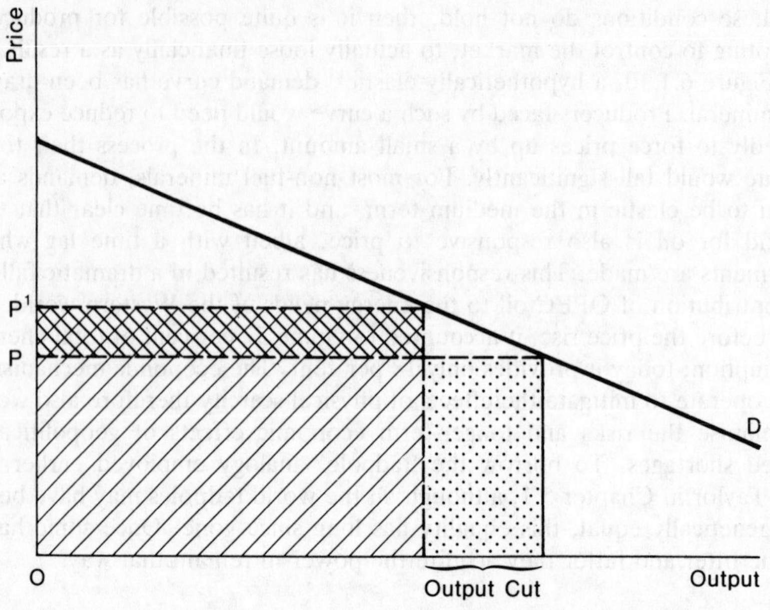
Price
P1
P
D
O
Output Cut
Output
D – Hypothetical Demand Curve faced by a metal producers cartel
With an elastic demand curve, the revenue loss would
exceed the revenue gained due to the price rise from P-P1

FIGURE 6.1.10 *Demand elasticity and the producers' revenue problem*

This is not the view of the international trade system held by most governments in the Third World, nor of the 'dependency' and 'uneven development' schools of theorists. They regard the system of international exchange to be inequitable in two senses: first, it has conspicuously failed to narrow the income gap between rich and poor nations and second, it consigns the LDCs to a position of economic dependence. The whole debate over unequal trade relations involves much wider issues than the way the minerals sector operates. Nevertheless, the value of crude mineral exports *vis-à-vis* manufactured goods and the stability of prices were a crucially important element in the so-called North-South dialogue.

In the 1950s and 1960s it was common to ascribe all the ills of the mineral exporting LDCs to the way the multinational companies, which dominated international trade, operated. First, it was argued that they repatriated a disproportionately high amount of their profits, rather than reinvesting them in the exporting country. A much quoted figure is that before the formation of OPEC in 1960, some 45 per cent of the gross receipts from Middle Eastern oil operations were remitted abroad, chiefly to the US and the UK, and even higher profit 'export' figures have been reported in studies of the copper industry in Chile, Peru and Zambia. To the countries concerned this amounted to 'inequitable exploitation', which deprived them of capital much needed for growth-generating investment. To the companies, it was just payment for their risk capital, technological know-how, equipment and marketing networks, without which the resource had no value. Moreover, high returns on working mines were needed to cover the losses made on exploration and development efforts which did not yield workable finds.

Second, the vertically integrated multinations were accused of manipulating the *transfer price* (paid between affiliates in the same company) of the crude materials to minimise their tax and royalty liabilities; this not only deprived host governments of income but also reduced foreign exchange earnings. Third, the companies were blamed for using inappropriate capital intensive technologies. These not only restricted indigenous employment opportunities, but also required the import of plant, construction materials, equipment, energy and skilled labour. And finally, much of the spin-off developments associated with mining (refining, the growth of equipment manufacturers and service industries) were being 'exported' from the producer country to the developed nations of the North.

For all these reasons, together with their ideological opposition to foreign ownership, LDC governments rejected the notion that free trade in minerals could fulfill their economic growth and national income objectives. A plethora of interventionist measures were, therefore, introduced. These included imposition of much increased export taxes on unprocessed minerals to encourage the indigenous development of smelting and refining; physical export controls (quotas) designed to force price increases; restrictions on imports to promote local construction, servicing and manufacturing industry; major increases in profit taxes (including the removal of tax holidays and similar concessions, plus the imposition of extra taxes on windfall profits); price fixing by producer cartels and asset nationalisation or equity sharing schemes.[17] While such moves have undoubtedly increased the proportion of mining profits accruing to producer governments, they clearly have not brought the hoped-for development in many LDCs, nor have they reduced global income disparities. An exporter government's ability to gain effective control of its mineral production is critically determined by the need to market the products. These markets are still predominantly in the North and, as we have seen, this places severe constraints on the ability of most producers to increase real mineral prices and raise the level of processing which occurs in the mining areas. The adjustment mechanisms which protect the mineral corporations and consumers from physical and geopolitical shortages also serve to place a limit on the aspirations of exporting states.

While Third World states have the role of crude mineral exporters, the system of international trade will tend to exacerbate, not reduce, spatial inequalities. The whole trend in the economic development process is towards the production of increasingly complex processed goods. This means that the prices of basic primary commodities must fall in relative terms as a proportion of the price of final goods; thus reducing the relative incomes of primary producers. However, with some notable exceptions, the success of LDCs in breaking into refining and metal processing has been limited, in part due to internal economic mismanagement but also due to the constraints placed by consumer governments on the import of processed goods. There seems little possibility, therefore, that the resource trade can act to redress global inequalities, unless, that is, strong and effective international institutions are created. This seems unlikely and certainly in the present economic climate there is little evidence to support Tinbergen's optimistic thesis that a global welfare state will develop with the evolution of international institutions to plan and co-ordinate economic development and to pursue social welfare objectives.[18]

NOTES AND REFERENCES

1. There is, however, considerable controversy over whether incoming and outgoing radiation flows could be affected inadvertently by the use of the atmosphere for the disposal of waste products. Pollutants, such as nitrogen oxides and chlorofluorocarbons, could act to increase the inflow of radiation, while increasing concentrations of carbon dioxide (from burning fossil fuels) could prevent the escape of radiation, so producing the 'greenhouse' warming effect. If these changes do occur, planetary temperatures and precipitation patterns will alter and then no renewable resource flows will be natural and unrelated to human activity.
2. It has been argued that infinite recycling is impossible due to the thermodynamic *law of entropy*, which indicates that unavailability (chaos) is an ultimate tendency of the utilisation of specific materials. In other words, minerals may eventually become too dispersed and mixed with impurities during use to be recoverable. However, evidence from the United States suggests that as little as 1 per cent of some metals is dissipated beyond recovery, and some commentators have suggested that the use of solid waste land dumps acts to concentrate rather than disperse the metal: the waste tips of today may become the mines of the future!
3. J. W. Forrester, *World Dynamics* (Cambridge, Mass.: Wright-Allen Press, 1970); D. H. Meadows, *et al.*, *The Limits to Growth* (New York: Universe Books, 1972); E. Goldsmith, *et al.*, 'Blueprint for survival', *Ecologist* 2 (1972).

4. There is in fact no single objectively derived proven reserve figure; what is economically extractable depends upon the commercial judgements of producers. These will vary with the desired rate of return on capital investment, assessments of possible risks to the investment, product pricing policies and production objectives. A state-owned industry may accept a lower level of profit than a private company in order to maintain employment levels or to reduce imports, and this will act to increase perceived proven resources. Moreover, what is a proven reserve in, say, the United States, could be only a conditional deposit if located in a politically risky area – say, Botswana.
5. Goldsmith, *op. cit.*
6. Meadows, *op. cit.*
7. S. Amin, 'NIEO; how to put Third World surpluses to effective use', *Third World Quarterly* 1 (1979) pp.65–72.
8. These were not produced by physical scarcity, but occurred because of the supply cuts and pricing decisions of OPEC, and because of panic buying and stockpiling by the major consumer nations.
9. C. F. Bergsten, 'The threat is real', *Foreign Policy* 14 (1974) pp.84–90.
10. M. Meacher, 'Global resources, growth and political agency', in M. Barrett-Brown, T. Emerson and C. Stoneman (eds) *Resources and the Environment: a socialist perspective* (Nottingham: Spokesman Books, 1976) pp.42–47.
11. This last figure does not allow for the considerable (but unpublished) expenditure made by mining companies within the USA itself.
12. In June 1967, for instance, the Nigerian Civil War and the Six Day Arab-Israeli War shut off areas providing Britain with 80 per cent of her imports; just two months later these had been replaced entirely, chiefly from Iran and the USA.
13. The falling dollar oil price has done little to help the oil importing LDCs, since the rising value of the dollar has wiped out any gains.
14. In economics the concept of demand elasticity is used to describe the way in which the demand for a product responds to changing prices. It is defined as % change in quantity/% change in price. An elastic demand curve is simply one where a price change produces a more than proportionate change in the quantity demanded.
15. S. Burenstam-Linder, 'How to avoid a New International Economic Disorder', *World Economy* 5 (1982) pp.275–84.
16. H. J. Barnett, *et al.*, 'Global trends in non-fuel minerals.' In J. L. Simon and H. Kahn (eds) *The Resourceful Earth* (Oxford: Basil Blackwell, 1984) pp.155–63.
17. The government takes shares in new national production companies and works in partnership with the mining multinationals.
18. J. Tinbergen, *Reshaping the International Order: a report to the Club of Rome* (New York: E. P. Dutton, 1976).

FURTHER READING

A useful source book of information and resources is the *Atlas of Earth Resources* (London: Mitchell Beazley, 1979), and a good general survey of the politics involved is R. J. Barnet, *The Lean Years: Politics in an Age of Scarcity* (New York: Simon and Schuster, 1980). For a more monographic treatment of a particular issue, see R. Bosson and B. Varron, *The Mining Industry in the Developing Countries* (New York: Oxford University Press, 1977).

6.2 Contemporary Environmentalism

Timothy O'Riordan
University of East Anglia

Timothy O'Riordan is Professor of Environmental Sciences at the University of East Anglia. His publications include *Environmentalism* and he had edited editions of *Progress in Resource Management and Environmental Planning*. He is actively involved in the politics of countryside change and has recently conducted a research project investigating the efficiency and effectiveness of the Sizewell B Public Enquiry. This was published under the title *Sizewell B: an anatomy of the inquiry*.

INTRODUCTION

An analysis of the purpose and achievements of contemporary environmental politics is a vast and overwhelming task. Even though there are several good books on the topic,[1] it is still difficult to summarise contemporary environmentalism in any clear and concise way. I have decided, therefore, to use a number of case studies to illustrate environmental issues in both 'North' and 'South', though only passing reference will be made to environmental politics in centrally planned economies.[2] Part of my purpose is to show how geographical approaches to ideology, and to the social meanings that underly human action, can assist in understanding what modern environmentalism is trying to do, why it is so important, and what kind of influence it is having. Stripped of all the rhetoric, I suggest that environmentalism offers a profound critique of contemporary society and that its message is too important to be ignored.

A TALE OF TWO FARMERS

One day in 1984 a Norfolk farmer began to convert 35 ha of poorly drained and unproductive grazing marsh into an arable field producing winter wheat.

From his point of view, the choice was a matter of simple economics. Net returns from beef production were about £56 per ha, but the costs of buying stock cattle were rising and the rates he had to pay for drainage were also likely to rise from around £20 to £36 per ha. In all, then, he could only expect a net profit of some £40 per ha. Wheat production, on the other hand, offered a far more profitable prospect. Even taking out the costs of conversion, he stood to make at least £400 per ha in profit, and possibly £500 per ha if yields exceeded 7.5 tonnes. His bank manager was willing to lend the capital to undertake the conversion: even at 14 per cent interest he could repay his debt within two years. Furthermore, his income was secure because wheat prices are presently protected by the European Community through the intervention price scheme of the Common Agricultural Policy.[3]

The farmer sprayed an all-purpose herbicide on his land to clear it for levelling and ploughing, and hired a contractor to dig out his dykes so that the watertable could be dropped from 75 cms to 2 metres. He had voluntarily notified the local Broads Authority of his actions. The Authority has struggled long and hard to save some 3000 ha of similar marsh in the area, known as Halvergate Marshes, because together they formed one of the great regional landscapes of England – the last major area of traditional grazing marsh.[4] Much of the area had been grazed for over 200 years, and the marshes thus had historical, aesthetic, symbolic and psychological significance. They were very much one of the landscapes of meaning that Dennis Cosgrove mentions in his essay (Chapter 2.2) with national as well as local value. In this particular case, however, the Broads Authority did not object because it was not prepared to pay the price the farmer was demanding in compensation for not ploughing (£555 per ha). Even though the Authority would have paid only 25 per cent of this (the Countryside Commission would have financed the rest), the local authorities which together made up the Broads Authority were unwilling to meet such a cost, because they had been forced to cut back their services by central government restrictions on public expenditure.

Within hours of the land being sprayed, protesters from Broadland Friends of the Earth illegally occupied the property. They sat in front of the excavating machine and hired a landrover so that journalists, photographers and television camera crews could get to the site. Questions were asked in the House of Commons, but Ministers refused to intervene on the grounds that the matter was a local one and that the Broads Authority had made a democratic decision. The farmer duly ploughed and is currently enjoyed his increased profits, 40 per cent of which are provided by the British taxpayer and the European Community. The wheat will probably never be consumed: Europe already has a 10 per cent surplus and is currently storing over 6000 000 tonnes of wheat.

Only five kilometres away another landowner also hired a contractor to deepen his dykes for the same purpose. He was a publican rather than a farmer, who owned 40 ha of marsh and simply wanted to make money quickly and easily. He was not prepared to be bought off, even though the Broads Authority were willing to pay in this case because the dykes contained a variety of ecologically important water plants and insects. Moreover the area was part of a linear strip of grazing marsh, part of which was already protected as a nature reserve. The landowner was in fact eventually forbidden to convert his land. An environmental group, the Council for the Protection of Rural England, obtained legal advice and discovered that engineering operations designed to alter materially the character of the land required planning permission from the Broads Authority. The landowner then settled for an *ex gratia* payment to reflect the loss of potential income, pocketed the money and did nothing to his land.

The first farmer, in contrast, became a political scapegoat, a symbol of the environmental insensitivity of modern agriculture buttressed by the Common Agricultural Policy, and a victim of a *national* policy towards agriculture and conservation that placed the burden for the protection of *national* environmental assets on individuals trapped in a web of economics, not of their making, and on local authorities whose judgement were conditioned by cash limits, rate ceilings and parochial perspectives.

Commentary

These two examples are representative of many that have occurred in the United Kingdom since the passage of the Wildlife and Countryside Act alerted political and public opinion to the forces that enabled farmers to improve their income by, in part, destroying the nation's environmental issues.

First, let us consider three viewpoints – those of the farmer, the environmental activist and the politician. The farmers were taking what John Eyles (in Chapter 2.1) terms everyday decisions. In their world, the decision to convert unprofitable land was entirely reasonable and almost humdrum. But, as Ron Johnston points out (in Chapter 1.3), their decisions were not purely personal: they were, rather, structured or 'framed'. What we learn from this, therefore, is how issues become 'framed' for each group of actors. How someone judges a problem and a solution is conditioned by influences that may hardly be discernible or distinguishable. These forces can be simplified, however, as shown in Figures 6.2.1 to 6.2.3.

As Figure 6.2.1 shows, the decisions which the farmers took were both constrained and enabled. They were *constrained* by the remorseless economics of the Common Agricultural Policy and by the protective barriers of advice and expectation that their own society signalled to them. The advice they got was to increase production, to leave the land materially and economically better off for their successors, and to be progressive. They were *enabled* by the law, substantially a creature of powerful vested interests (in this case MAFF and the agricultural lobby), which guaranteed them against any loss of income whichever course of action they took. They were also

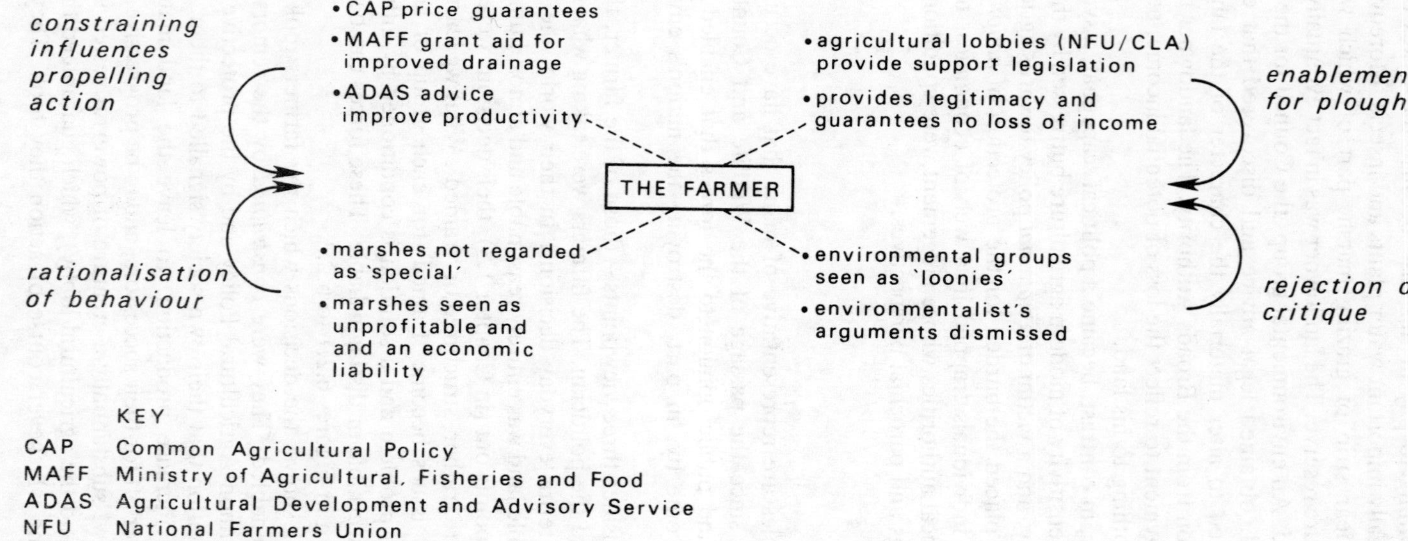

KEY

CAP Common Agricultural Policy
MAFF Ministry of Agricultural, Fisheries and Food
ADAS Agricultural Development and Advisory Service
NFU National Farmers Union
CLA Country Landowners Association

FIGURE 6.2.1 *Issue framing for the two Broadland farmers*

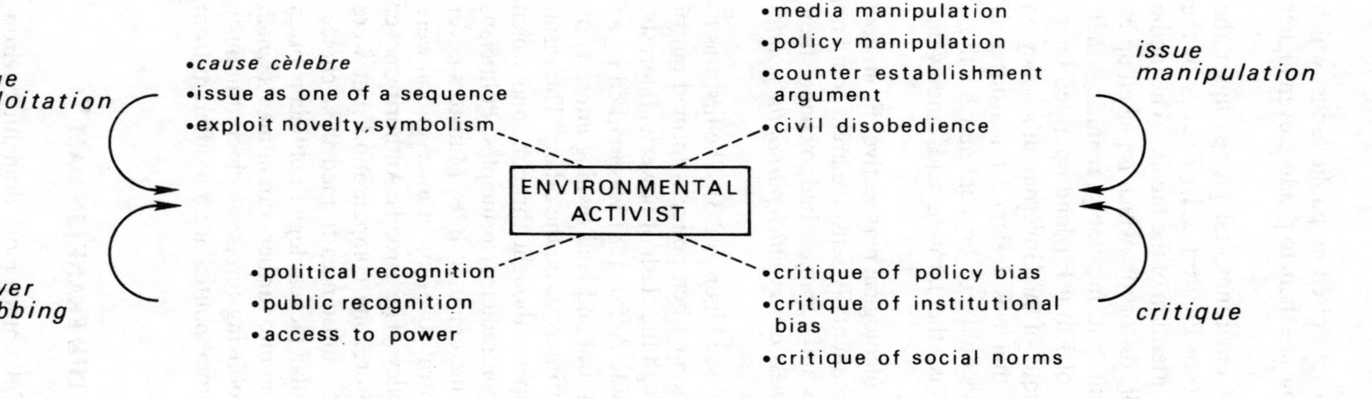

FIGURE 6.2.2 *Issue framing for the environmental activist*

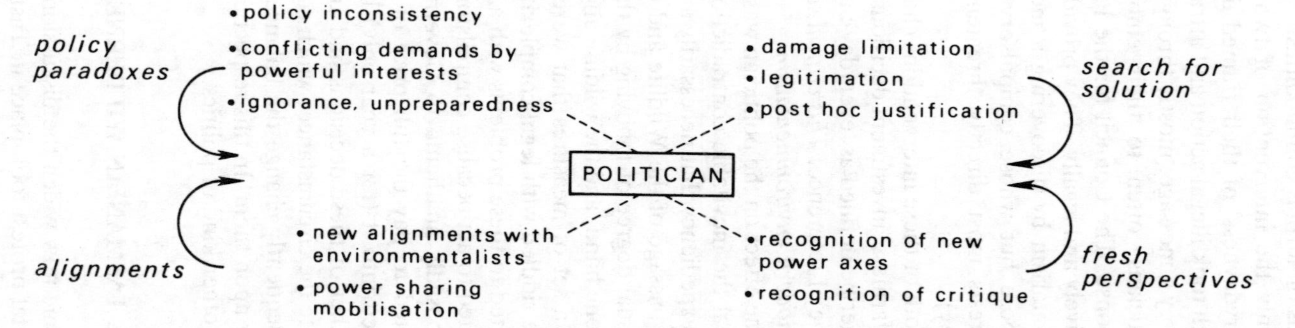

FIGURE 6.2.3 *Issue framing for the politician*

enabled by technological innovation, also subsidised by public funds, which provided the information and skills to encourage them to produce even higher yields of surplus commodities.

Only the intervention of two kinds of environmental groups upset the 'everydayness' of their framed decisions (see Figure 6.2.2). Friends of the Earth took illegal action and attracted the attention of the media.[5] The media convey a message, mostly through symbolic distortion, which is picked up by politicians, often to their embarrassment but inevitably requiring their response. The Council for the Protection of Rural England operated imaginatively and legally. They provided a critique of the Government's policy on voluntarism by discovering a mechanism that was designed for a different purpose but whose compulsory function could not be confined by those interests most directly threatened (that is, the farming and landowning lobby).

Both of these interventions changed the ideological perspective. From now on, farmers' investment decisions in environmentally-sensitive areas could no longer be defined as 'everyday': all owners and occupiers had to change their frame of reference. *This critical self-awareness is very much part of the politics of modern environmentalism.*

The effect on the politician was two-fold (see Figure 6.2.3). The first was to reveal the inevitable contradictions that occur when policy is formed out of the expediency that necessarily arises through the clash of powerful interests. The passage of the Wildlife and Countryside Act of 1981 was marked by an unusual degree of lobbying by the agricultural and land owning interests on the one hand, and the wildlife and amenity interests on the other.[6] The result was a set of measures that were not properly thought through, and which were riddled with legal complexities and contradictory principles. Politicians reacted to these problems with a series of incremental shifts. Ministers never wanted to act because compulsion and central government intervention were supposedly anathema to Government policy. The Broads Authority never wanted to pay the full price of a profit-foregone compensation, but were forced into it (for a year only) because circumstances framed their choice. Neither of these decisions had any particular tactical logic: politicians often create the circumstances which compel them into further commitments which subsequently change the balance of the lobbying forces which continuously bear upon them. In this respect environmental politics are not different from any other kind of politics.

THE TASMANIAN WILDERNESS AND THE FRANKLIN DAM

Let me now widen the discussion. In 1982/3 a much more dramatic environmental protest took place in Tasmania. The stakes were much higher. Some 10 000 square kilometres of temperate forest wilderness, identified by the International Union for the Conservation of Nature as a World Heritage Site, were threatened with inundation as a result of a hydro-electric power scheme.[7] The scheme was backed by the Tasmanian State Government, which had successfully won an election on the issue. In democratic terms, again, Tasmania was acting legally and properly.

The scheme was fiercely opposed by the Tasmanian Wilderness Society (TWS) and by influential international voices of conservation, notably Prince Charles and David Bellamy. Between December 1982 and February 1983 the TWS successfully blockaded the construction equipment while the Commonwealth (federal) Government of Australia attempted to barter with the state. The federal government proposed to grant Tasmania A$550 million, so that the same amount of electrical power could be developed from local coal reserves at no extra cost. The federal idea was to provide equivalent compensation: Tasmania would be no worse off in net energy terms, while Australia and the world would be better off as a result of safeguarding the wilderness. The Tasmanian government rejected this suggestion: it wanted to take an 'everyday decision' within its own frame of reference. Like the Norfolk landowners, the issue was in part about the right to take autonomous decisions.

The interesting feature of this case was the issue of legality. In an historic judgement, the Australian High Court ruled that the federal government had superior jurisdiction over a state government when matters of national or international importance were concerned, and that because Australia was party to the Global Heritage Concept by virtue of passing the Australian Heritage Commission Act in 1975, the federal government was statutorily obliged to protect and defend designated heritage sites from unalterable damage. And in another ruling, the Court also accepted that the Tasmanian Wilderness Society had legal standing to object to the proposed construction because of its economic interest in the Wilderness area. That interest arose because the Society earned income from the sale of postcards and illustrated books of the magnificent forest ecology of the area. This has important implications for future environmental politics in Australia (and possibly elsewhere) because legal recognition should give environmental groups greater political leverage.

Commentary

The Tasmanian case highlights several additional aspects of contemporary environmental politics. The first is the relation between *political autonomy* and *international obligation*. Once again much depends on how a problem is interpreted or framed. There are many similarities with the situation shown in Figures 6.2.1 to 6.2.3, though in this case the actor was the Tasmanian Government. It was propelled into a decision by its determination to champion its legal autonomy. The Tasmanian Government and a majority of the Tasmanian population did not regard the wilderness area as inviolate. They were prepared to safeguard part of the ecosystem as a protected site, but believed that they could implement their electricity scheme and still enjoy a (diminished) wilderness.

This line of thinking is akin to Ron Johnston's analysis of manipulative empirical science, which results in anthropocentric mastery (see Chapter 1.3). What wilderness is left is that which society by 'fair' democratic means determines it to be. Environmental scientists and landscape architects were expected to design the scheme so that it minimised environmental damage, yet guaranteed the low cost electricity necessary to attract industry and create a small number of relatively ephermeral jobs.

The TWS and the federal government, however, were worried about Australia's international standing and its influence in other resource management matters. They both believed that Australia as a nation-state had a moral obligation to safeguard the area – an obligation that was supposed to transcend politics. But lurking behind these high-minded ideals were more down-to-earth political motives. The federal government was also in the middle of an election, and the Labour leader Bob Hawke came to power partly on his 'no-nonsense' platform towards Tasmania. Australian mainlanders had little to lose and a lot to gain by seeing the Tasmanian Wilderness saved. The TWS, on the other hand, sought two objectives. One was a stake in all matters relating to Tasmanian resource exploitation. They wanted to climb up the lobbying ladder and become a much more effective political voice. This is the understandable aim of any interest group, but the TWS, along with other environmental groups, also wanted to change the direction of political thinking. They argued that the dam was simply not required, that electricity could be produced from other sources, that much more investment should be put into electricity conservation and a radical shift in economic activity that would produce wealth through more efficient use of electricity.

We begin now to see the other part of the environmentalist critique – the critical, emancipating perspective also described by Johnston (in Chapter 1.3). The Tasmanian Wilderness was regarded as a symbol of society's unjustified ability to destroy an irreplaceable ecosystem. The Wilderness also became a metaphor for a political shift towards a so-called 'conserver society' – a society freed from the shackles of mindless materialism and consumerism, capable of taking perceptive decisions, and able to adopt forms of economic and social activity frugal in their use of resources and caring for environmental as well as communal well-being.

But there was a second aspect to all this. Explicit in the TWS argument, and also familiar to students of contemporary environmentalism, was the fact that the true 'cost' of the Franklin electricity was not merely the amortised capital involved in the dam, the turbines and the associated roads and housing. The true cost included the loss of the wilderness and the loss of innocence about human superiority and free will. Difficulties arise in trying to establish a value for these costs, which can be compared with the more tangible (and readily quantifiable) benefits of increased availability of electricity.

Again we come back to ideology. The empiricist and positivist look for measures of value that are both observable and quantifiable – for example the additional cost of the next least expensive electricity generating alternative which would provide the same package of benefits. Another possibility, also attractive to positivist economists, is to calculate how much society seems willing to pay to protect such a wilderness or to bequeath it to future generations to decide what to do with it. Recent studies have shown a higher propensity to pay for environmental benefits of this kind – much higher than the valuation of the material benefits associated with the development alternative.[8] A third possibility, also positivist, is to meddle with the discount rates (which determine the value and time stream of benefits and costs). A very low discount rate would ensure that gains or losses that might be more valued in the future than at present are weighted more into the future. A high discount rate demands much more immediate rates of return on interest.

Behind the environmentalists' critique, however, was something closer to what John Eyles and Denis Cosgrove (in Chapters 2.1 and 2.2) are driving at. This is the objective of altering the individual's relationship to the natural world, to the future of the globe, and to a previously unacknowledged acceptance of the forces that shape the everyday world and the surrounding landscape. Part of the environmentalist's motive is to provide a more holistic perspective; environmental conflicts are used as a means for introducing a higher level of critical understanding. The aim is to illuminate how individuals or organisations can act to change the forces that create environmentally or communally destructive behaviour, and to create a more self-aware 'lived world'. In essence, the purpose is to emancipate both the individual, the interest and the interest groups to which he or she belongs from the fetters of what might loosely be termed the 'false environmental consciousness' that trapped the Norfolk landowners and the Tasmanian electorate. Part of contemporary environmental politics therefore is about sharpening critical faculties and changing the basis of hermeneutic understanding. Let us take two further case studies to illustrate this point.

NUCLEAR WASTE AND THE POLITICS OF ENVIRONMENTAL RISK

On the 16 November 1983 the Sellafield nuclear waste reprocessing facility in Cumbria accidentally discharged the residue from tanks which had received the filtrate of radioactive effluent into another set of tanks. These receiving tanks were not designed to take this effluent: the exit pipes became clogged with radioactive crude which the operators flushed out, on at least two separate occasions, into the sea. This discharge contained illegally high amounts of transuranics – toxic radioactive substances – which floated to the surface and contaminated the beaches in the vicinity of the plant. The sludge was also picked up on the clothing of members of the Greenpeace organisation, who were illegally attempting to block the very pipes through which the illegal discharge was taking place. Part of the problem was simply a matter of negligence. Workers on each shift record on a log book what they have been up to and leave instructions for their colleagues on a later shift. These instructions often appear on different pages so are not always read. Workers flushed out tanks containing contaminated sludge because they had not made themselves aware of what the tanks contained.

There is, however, a more insidious aspect to this story. The operators of the Sellafield complex, British Nuclear Fuels plc (BNFL), have been discharging radioactive wastes, including plutonium, for almost thirty years. During that period standards of effluent treatment have been tightened as knowledge about pollutant pathways and thresholds of exposure have altered. Consequently BNFL have been investing in better sludge retaining equipment. The retained sludge is now much more toxic because it concentrates substances that were once dispersed throughout the Irish Sea and shoreline sediment. This means that BNFL are dealing with potentially more dangerous materials, which are more troublesome to store and eventually to bury.

BNFL are caught in an environmental and technological conundrum. The more efficiently they treat their effluent, the more technically difficult it will be for them to dispose of the residuals. This also has important political and economic implications. It will cost BNFL a total of £250 million to improve its processes to meet the requirements now imposed by the Government's two regulatory agencies, the Radiochemical Inspectorate of the Department of the Environment, and the Nuclear Installations Inspectorate of the Health and Safety Executive. About £100 million of this investment can be justified by the necessary upgrading of effluent quality to meet tightened national standards. But the additional £150 million or so was due partly to the problem of increased sludge toxicity already referred to, as well as a result of the public alarm following the much publicised scare over a possible association between the existence of the Sellafield complex and child leukemia in West Cumbria.

The nuclear facility – leukemia connection invokes both political and geographical considerations in its analysis. The geographical element lies in the statistical manipulation of medical evidence across spaces occupied by nuclear activity. The problem is that the relationship simply cannot be proven either way: neither the statistical techniques nor the data base are sufficiently robust and comprehensive to allow for unambiguous interpretation.[9]

Commentary

Doubt and scientific uncertainty form another important element of contemporary environmental politics. Opponents of environmentally risky activities – sulphur and nitrogen oxide emitting processes, asbestos manufacture and removal, lead in petrol or radioactive waste disposal – do not have to prove very much. They need only cast the mantle of suspicion over a risk creator who subsequently has to prove innocence. The great tenet of British jurisprudence is turned upside down: risk creators are guilty until proven innocent. So BNFL can only invest in the most advanced technology in order to confer political legitimacy on an activity that must command public acceptance if the future of the whole nuclear power industry is to remain viable. The benefit of this £150 million is not really in lives saved, but in protecting industrial and political capital. That investment is made by the state, not the consumer, in funding for back-up research and development, in direct grant aid, and in support for a continuation and extension of a fission power programme.

It is therefore no wonder that the marginal cost of saving a statistical life for nuclear power-produced radioactivity is extraordinarily high. It is impossible to place a precise figure on this, but it could be as high as £40 million per computed life. Environmental groups would like to drive this figure up to even more astronomical levels – to make radioactive waste reprocessing so expensive that it cannot be continued, and to make radioactive waste disposal so politically contentious that no satisfactory (and least-cost) site can be found. The way to deal with the nuclear industry, they say, is to make it sit on its own waste products.[10]

As the radioactive waste disposal issue is likely to be one of the two major environmental talking points of the latter half of the 1980s, let me examine a little more carefully why this issue is so contentious. I have discussed one aspect, namely the need of the state to protect a particular form of advanced technology, in this case radioactive waste disposal, which is made necessary by a prior political commitment to civil nuclear power. At the margin of safety determination that technology is not cost effective: safety standards are set by political rather than technical considerations. Empiricism and predictability no longer rule. To scientists trained in analytical, replicable and verifiable judgement this shifting of the conceptual ground is a matter of great worry. No longer can they operate in a climate of assurance and predictability. They bemoan the fickleness of politicians and the uncertainties that confront long-term investments in technologies whose safety standards are expected to be predetermined.

It is this presumption of scientific determinism that most aggravates the opponents of 'big' and risky technology. But we must not forget another important feature of the critique, namely the injustice of placing a greater risk burden on neighbours of the located technology for the benefit of society at large. People who are likely to be faced with a risky or nuisance-creating technology can mobilise opposition across party lines remarkably effectively. This is particularly the case for radioactive waste, but it is becoming increasingly so for all hazardous residues and for major chemical works.

There are four main reasons for this dislike of radioactive waste.

1. It confers no tangible benefit to the local community – no jobs, no rates relief, no kudos, no enticement to entrepreneurs.

2. The technology and the substances are feared because they are unknown and non-sensible – they are foreign intruders in the everyday lived worlds of the local people – and because if anything goes wrong innocent people may get injured or possibly killed. Innocence is a powerful symbol here: people feel they are recipients of decisions which they cannot control or from which they cannot readily escape. Many also believe that their own elected representatives are powerless to put a stop to these developments: politicians are pushed on by the technology itself, by the big egos and organisations that create it, and by the experts who say everything will be all right.
3. But these experts are being proved fallible. Dangers do exist, accidents do occur and attempts to cover up mistakes are often exposed. Fallibility, mischief, deceipt and appalling public relations are proving to be a curse for many risk creators.
4. The last is the obverse of the first, namely there are not only no community benefits, there are significant community costs in the form of depressed house prices, loss of interest amongst potential immigrating employers, and a feeling of intense anger as to why they should be singled out.

The reaction of the waste disposal industry is twofold: one, that the fears are 'irrational' and two, that a better argued case will calm the people down. The industry is wrong on both counts, as anyone who has read the Eyles and Cosgrove chapters will readily appreciate. There is almost a religious rationality to these views – hence the strength and persistence of the opposition to more public relations which serves only to arouse greater suspicion. The whole siting process becomes stalled. This creates an interesting dilemma for a democracy. Does a majority government use its parliamentary superiority to thrust an unpopular decision on a fiercely opposed local electorate? A decision has to be taken because the industry must dispose of its waste if it is to survive. The Government tactic is to legitimate a constrained choice framed by circumstances not entirely of its making, but which it cannot avoid.

The way out is to by-pass the statutory mechanism designed to assist governments to make awkward decisions, namely the public inquiry. In January 1985 the government resorted to special parliamentary procedures to avoid the holding of any planning inquiry for the preliminary test-drilling explorations, necessary to discover the physical suitability of proposed sites. The trouble will come when the inevitable public inquiry is eventually convened for the site or sites eventually selected as environmentally suitable.

How that inquiry is handled should reveal a lot about the political geography of site justification for risky technology. If that inquiry is to be legitimate, it will have to address the two rationalities that at present are unbridgeable. These are the empiricist rationalities of the industry scientists and the critical (and no less scientific) rationalities of environmental groups and local residents. This will require a new approach to community consultation and to community compensation for accepting an element of residual risk. That residual risk is the disturbance to the everyday environment that is not accounted for by protestations that the technology is safe, adequately managed and properly regulated. That inquiry is going to be an exceptionally difficult one to organise and command public confidence.

THE LOSS OF TROPICAL FOREST

Every minute of every day about 18 ha of tropical forest are either cut down for timber or fuelwood and burnt, so that the land can be cleared for local agriculture or for cash cropping by large multinational corporations. Most of the last is for beef cattle production to feed the well-padded bellies of the western hamburger consumer.[11] This destruction carries with it considerable dangers both for local and global economies. Tropical forests provide a number of critical environmental functions that go well beyond harbouring one half of the world's remaining wildlife species. They regulate rainfall, darken the reflectivity of the tropical areas, generate a regular amount of water vapour and control both surface and underground runoff and sediment flows. At the current rate of loss, about half the remaining forest could disappear by the year 2000 and three quarters by 2010. Only remnants would be left in south and northeast Asia and Central America, though parts of the upper Amazonian basin and Central Africa would remain well covered.

The consequences of this loss are alarming. In all probability there would be significant variations in the global water vapour cycle, leading to perturbations in weather patterns and an even greater tendency to unpredictable drought and flood. The implications for both temperate and tropical food production are worrying, mostly because they are unknowable with any certainty. Flash flooding and soil erosion are likely to increase at an alarming rate. Already about one seventh of the world's cultivatable land suffers from severe soil erosion; by 2025 this problem could take about one quarter of this precious resource out of production. The consequences for the rice growing cultures in south and south east Asia are potentially very serious indeed, as alluvial paddies become vulnerable to flooding and silting. Equally serious is the likely loss of up to 1 million plant, insect and animal species. Some of these are known to have enormous value for the food, biogenetics and pharmaceutical industries, while others have considerable economic potential for tourism. There are real economic as well as environmental costs if this devastation of the tropical forest habitat is allowed to proceed.

Commentary

Yet that loss will surely continue: what is uncertain is how the rate of loss will change. What are the forces which encourage a non-sustainable exploitation of a globally critical resource? Two related explanations can be advanced, and I can now widen the discussion to all features of environmental damage in the Third World – soil erosion, desertification and over-grazing.[12] Various propositions have been advanced.

Entitlement and marginalisation In the past local people have always been entitled to a certain amount of tropical forest services – fuelwood, food genes, animal and insect products and land for agriculture and settlement. That entitlement was never legalised, but it had an important cultural dimension. Access to the resource carried with it a covenant for its continued availability. Entitlement and sustainable utilisation went hand in hand. Limiting factors were the level of technology and population size, but there was an important element of collective self-restraint *vis-à-vis* over-exploitation.

The introduction of more environmentally demanding technologies, the loss of land to cash crops, national and multinational ownership, the growth of population and, most recently, the conditions and attitudes connected with aid and economic development have all contributed to a process of marginalisation of indigenous populations. By marginalisation I mean the loss of entitlement to land and to resources through enormous difficulties of access to basic requirements (food, drinking water and fuelwood), and through a position of economic dependency on a landlord, or a money lender or other form of creditor (see John and Barbara Harriss, Chapter 4.2). Poverty, debt and disenfranchisement to local resources all contribute to environmental destruction.[13]

Figure 6.2.4 outlines the forces at work. This is a highly generalised diagram, but it serves to show how various agents involved in the process of trpical forest loss frame the problem in very different ways. The peasant is both constrained into debt and destruction, and enabled to do so by the adoption of some technology (for example pesticides or high yielding varieties). The multinational agency, including bilateral and multilateral lending institutions,[14] often supported by the nation state, sees the forest, or the soil, *not the denuded land,* as an investment to make profit for shareholders. These agencies may be aware of the built-in environmental destruction, but their future profitability need not be affected. They believe that there are other resources to be exploited elsewhere. The national governments are also blinded by circumstances – debt, the need for foreign currency, the prestige of mega-projects, the false faith in environmental rehabilitation out of the profits gained, commitment to arms trading and aid-granting conditions.

One must be careful not to paint too black and white a picture of all this. The temptation is to visualise a pre-imperialist peasant culture sensitive to the value of its environmental resources and capable of building in various

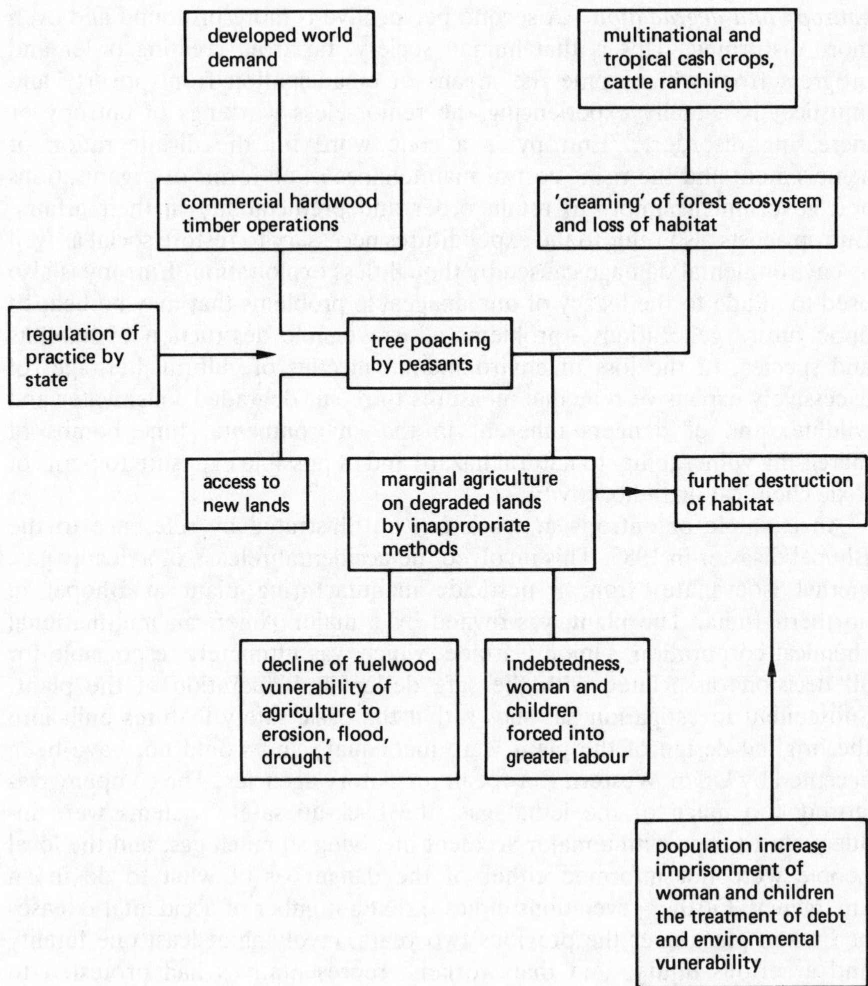

FIGURE 6.2.4 *Loss of entitlement, marginalisation and environmental distribution: the tropical forest case*

cultural devices to impede over-exploitation. We frankly do not know enough to be sure, though in both the tropical forest and dryland situation there is certainly some evidence to suggest that, prior to western contact, many of these societies enjoyed much more room for manoeuvre. Today, as Figure 6.2.4 suggests, that room is severely constrained.

Entropy and degradation A second perspective is more profound and even more disturbing. This is that human society, far from creating order and progress from which come the means of emancipation from poverty and injustice, is actually experiencing the remorseless workings of entropy or increasing disorder.[15] Entropy is a code word for the disintegration of achievement and the rising cost of maintenance of all forms of organisations and government simply to retain order and predictability in their affairs. Entropy costs also refer to the expenditures necessary to restore social as well as environmental damage caused by thoughtless exploitation. Entropy is also used to allude to the legacy of unmanageable problems that may be heaped upon future generations – problems of irreversible destruction of habitats and species, of the loss of environmental niceties of cultural heritage, of excessively expensive remedial measures to repair degraded soils, water and wildlife, and of dangers inherent in the environmental time bombs of increasing vulnerability to natural hazard and of possible exposure to perils of toxic chemical or radioactivity.

An example of entropy at work can be illustrated by reference to the Bhopal disaster in 1985. This involved the accidental release of a deadly gas, methyl isocyanate, from a pesticide manufacturing plant at Bhopal in northern India. The plant was owned by a major American multinational chemical corporation, Union Carbide, which was ultimately responsible for all decisions associated with the safe design and operation of the plant. Subsequent investigation has shown that the basic safety features built into the original design of the plant were inadequate and would not have been accepted by US or Western European regulatory agencies. The company was storing too much of the lethal gas, the back-up safety systems were inadequate to cope with a major accident involving so much gas, and the local people were not informed either of the danger or of what to do in an emergency. Further revelations indicate that a number of accidental releases had taken place over the previous two years, involving at least one fatality and a serious injury, and that workers' representatives had protested to company officials and to the Indian authorities about the dangers. Neither Union Carbide nor the Indian authorities responded. Worse still, in 1983 Union Carbide actually lowered its safety standards at Bhopal because the plant was losing money.

Here is a tragically clear example of an uncompensated technological risk. In this case not only were workers operating in a dangerous environment, but local people were being exposed to perils which Union Carbide was creating 'on the cheap'. The lines of communication between the plant safety managers, the Indian regulatory authorities and the US headquarters of Union Carbide were appallingly bad. The accident was inevitable: the only question was when it would occur and how bad it would be.

In the event, 2500 people died and over 200 000 were injured, some maimed for the rest of their lives. Whole families were wiped out and many children became orphans. Union Carbide will now face damages far in excess of anything it would have spent to upgrade the safety standards to meet existing US conditions. Furthermore, the whole chemical industry will have to pay for a 'post-Bhopal' safety review. This will upgrade standards, will require a lot of expensive retrofitting of safety equipment and will mean that safety levels will have to meet international, not national standards. The price of chemicals will rise progressively and the difficulties of siting new plants will increase. Organisation, communication and management will all become more costly and demanding. And what of the Bhopal people? The plant will probably never reopen, the court cases over liability and compensation will work their endless way through the Indian and American judicial systems and the sufferers will slowly die in much agony while medical people dispute over the correct treatment and small, 'temporary' compensation payments are made.

Bhopal will not be the last major industrial disaster either in the Third World or in the developed world. The problem lies in double standards of safety and management, in the uncritical acceptance of hazardous technology and materials by debt-ridden governments anxious to create jobs and technological development, and in the unwillingness of risk creators and environmental damagers to face up to the true costs of their actions before the damage is done.

Both the marginality (or vulnerability) thesis and the entropy perspective contain two similar lines of argument. One is that most, if not all, individuals are not in control of their actions, even when they know or at least suspect that their behaviour may not be beneficial either to the natural environment or to other members of the global community – present or future. This has an analogy in the 'framing of consciousness' outlined in Figures 6.2.1 to 6.2.3. It also has implications for the debate about determinism and possibilism. We are really considering a form of 'constrained possibilism', where choices are conditioned by agencies and circumstances over which individuals and even governments cannot have complete control.

The other feature of both these explanations is the remorselessness of the process: there almost seems to be an inevitability to the outcome. 'Development' seems to equate not with improvement in well-being, but in an interest-biased assymetry of wealth where only a small proportion gain and an increasing number lose with unpredictable consequences for our descendents. The environmentalist critique goes beyond that offered by Ron Johnston's vision of critical science; it seeks to drive at the very heart of Western society's hubris and optimism, and to develop a new moral order based on principles of *nature's* justice, thermodynamic laws and biogeochemical cycles. The more committed environmentalists are seeking a set of determining conditions based on an ecological imperative of global survival that may dictate social and individual choices. To avoid the accusation of fascism or tyranny, environmentalists hope to persuade through education, enlightenment and consciousness-raising. The emancipated citizen would, they hope, be far more ready to recognise the longer-term advantages of collective self-restraint, and to support what they believe to be necessary radical reforms that would lead to a much more communally oriented politics based on environmentally and socially sustainable self-reliance.

GEOGRAPHY AND THE NEW ENVIRONMENTALISM

To summarise, the new environmentalism is about establishing a more fundamental awareness of the forces and institutions that create environmental damage and social disintegration. That awareness can only come, so it seems, out of conflict, protest, selective use of civil disobedience, critical analysis of the dangers that are in store, and honest experimentation through alternative approaches. The new environmentalism will expect a more radical analysis of society-nature relations, based on the linkage between social schisms and environmental brutality. It will seek to establish an *environmental* theory of value and to produce an alternative theory of development based on the concept of sustainability. A comprehensive theory of sustainable development awaits preparation: this is an area of theory-building in which geographers are well placed to be actively involved. It will open up refreshingly different approaches to project appraisal, where costs and benefits are not just treated as economic commodities but as assets and liabilities with social and environmental meaning.[16]

Geographers will have to widen their definitions of justice and equity to embrace not only class and gender, important though these are, but environmental assets and future generations. Geographers will have to think again about how problems are formed in the minds of different actors and how issues are presented for solutions to be offered. Geographers will have to consider more carefully for whom they are working, what their motives are and in what way they are assisting or retarding the development of a broader consciousness. Geographers will have to be careful about utilising their skills as link-people between the physical and social sciences, through which their analyses and prescriptions may increase the manipulation and alteration of environmental systems and the dependency of social groups upon both these systems and the advice offered. In short, geographers have to become emancipated themselves before they can truly enter the contemporary environmentalist debate.

NOTE AND REFERENCES

1. The Guide to Further Reading lists a cross-section of this literature.
2. For an analysis of environmental issues in centrally planned economies, see B. Komarov, *The Destruction of Nature in the Soviet Union* (Notting-

ham: Pluto Press, 1980); V Smil, *The Bad Earth: environmental degradation in China* (London: Zed Press, 1984).

3. For a summary of the contemporary agriculture and conservation debate, see P. Lowe, G. Cox, M. McEwen, T. O'Riordan and M. Winter, *Countryside Conflicts* (London: Gower/Maurice Temple Smith, 1985).
4. See T. O'Riordan, 'Halvergate: the story so far', *Ecos,* 6 (1984) pp.24–30.
5. For a discussion of environmental groups in the United Kingdom, see P. Lowe and J. Goyder, *Environmental Groups in Politics* (London: Allen and Unwin, 1983) and D. Marsh (ed.) *Pressure Politics* (London: Allen and Unwin, 1984).
6. For an analysis of the lobbying surrounding the Wildlife and Countryside Act, see P. Lowe *et al., op. cit.*
7. The best analysis of the Franklin Dam issue is M. Sornjarajah (ed.) *The South West Plan Disputes: legal and political issues* (Hobart: University of Tasmania Press, 1983). See also G. Bates, 'The Tasmanian dam case and its significance in environmental law', *Environmental Planning and Law Jnl.,* 1 (1985) pp.325–345.
8. See A. V. Kneese, *Measuring the Benefits of Clean Air and Water* (Washington DC: Resources for the Future, 1984).
9. See the report of the Special Committee chaired by Sir Douglas Black, *Investigation of the Possible Increased Incidence of Cancer in West Cumbria* (London: HMSO, 1984).
10. See W. Cannell and R. Chudleigh, *The Gravediggers' Dilemma* (London: Friends of the Earth, 1984).
11. See N. Myers, *The Primary Source: Tropical Forests and Our Future* (New York: Norton, 1984); C. Caulfield, *In the Rainforest* (London: Heinemann, 1985).
12. For two comprehensive and sobering reports of environmental destruction in the Third World, see N. Myers (ed.) *The Gaia Atlas of Planetary Management* (London: Pan, 1985); L. C. Brown (ed.) *State of the World Report* (New York: Worldwatch Institute/Norton, 1985); and IIED/URI 1986 *World Resources* (New York: World Resources Institute, Basic Books, 1986).
13. See also P. Blaikie, *The Political Economy of Soil Erosion* (Harlow: Longman, 1984); cf. A. Sen, *Poverty and Famine:; an essay on entitlement and deprivation* (Oxford: Oxford University Press, 1981).
14. See Corbridge, Chapter 5.3. Two very readable accounts make a good case of how multinationals and aid agencies damage environmental resources: S. George, *Ill Fares the Land* (London: Workers and Readers, 1985) and 'The World Bank: global financing of impoverishment and famine', *The Ecologist* 15 (1985) pp.2–82.
15. The most compelling account of this analysis is J. Rifkin and T. Howard, *Entropy: a new world view* (London: Paladin, 1985).
16. A start has been made by K. Shrader-Frechette, *Science policy, ethics and economic methodology* (Dordrecht: Reidel, 1985).

FURTHER READING

For a cross-section of views on contemporary environmentalism, see H. Stretton, *Capitalism, Socialism and the Environment* (Cambridge: Cambridge University Press, 1976); F. Sandbach, *Environment, Ideology and Policy* (Oxford: Basil Blackwell, 1981); S. Cotgrove, *Catastrophe or Cornucopia* (Chichester: Wiley, 1982); M. Redclift, *Development and the Environmental Crisis: Red or Green Alternatives* (London: Methuen, 1984). A general survey is D. Pepper, *The Social Roots of Modern Environmentalism* (Beckenham: Croom Helm, 1984); my own account was initially developed in *Environmentalism* (London: Pion, 1981).

For more recent literature see D. Lowe and W. Rudig *The Green Wave* (Cambridge: Polity Press, 1988); J. Porritt and D. Winner *Going Green* (Oxford: Blackwell, 1988); J. Elkington and T. Burke, *The Green Capitalists* (London: Gollancz, 1987); M. Redelift, *Sustainable Development: Exploring the Contradictions* (London: Methuen, 1987); R. K. Turner (ed.) *Sustainable Environmental Management: Principles and Practice* (London: Bellhaven Press, 1988).

Epilogue

Bill Mead
University College, London

Bill Mead is Professor Emeritus of Geography at University College, London, where he was formerly head of department. He has been President of the Institute of British Geographers and The Geographical Association and is an Honorary Vice-President of the Royal Geographical Society. His main interests are in the geography of the Nordic countries and his last major book was *An Historic Geography of Scandinavia* (1983). Recently published work has appeared in *Lund Geographical Studies, Geografiska Annaler, Ymer, Fennia, Daedalus, Historisk Tidskrift*, and in Anne Buttimer's *The Practice of geography*. He is a doctor honoris causa of Uppsala, Lund, and Helsinki Universities, and a medallist of the Royal Geographical Society, the Royal Scottish Geographical Society and the Finnish Geographical Society.

This book derives its title from the Greeks. Horizon is one of their splendid words – a concept for the geographer, a metaphor for everyman. During the last generation, new horizons in geography have attracted a larger number of geographers than ever before. Nor have there ever been greater financial and technological opportunities to help them pursue their aims and publish their findings. Some idea of the volume and range of publication is measured by the bibliographies prepared for the successive meetings of the International Geographical Union, and by the fact that the specialist library of the Royal Geographical Society receives some 700 different geographical periodicals annually – a number which continues to grow. At the same time as geographers may be somewhat overwhelmed by the progress of their subject which this explosion of publication represents, they are faced with parallel developments in a range of cognate disciplines. 'The additiveness of human capabilities' – to use the phrase of Peter Medawar – helps in the assimilation; but for some, at least, the volume of material clouds the horizon.

Technological and methodological developments have both eased and complicated the work of the geographer. Admittedly, equipment costs money and, as geography has become an increasingly expensive subject, it has become increasingly dependent upon external patronage and funding. Nevertheless, 'the mass of abstractions and the secondary mechanical world', as Edwin Muir once called it, should liberate more than it binds. Naturally, there are other points of view. Jacques Ellul sees technology acquiring a sacrilegious character, giving rise to aristocracies of technicians, who don mathematical vestments and leave little for the 'sphere of dreams'. Certainly, mechanical – and mechanistic – processes are not enough, but it is past dreamers who have given rise to them and who will refine or replace them.

It is worthy of note that the new technical facilities have made their presence felt, while a 'positivist' phase of geographical thought has asserted itself in the broader contextual field of enquiry. At the same time, the facilities have multiplied and diversified in parallel with increasing specialisation in the subject. Specialisation has transformed the research contribution of geography, but it has increased the risk of fragmentation – fragmentation which can disturb judgement and produce disharmonies.

The days of the seemingly simple dichotomy between physical and human geography, or between systematic and regional studies, are over. Antitheses multiply. Pacts of tolerance are now needed between specialists who live in libraries and those who labour in laboratories, between those who wear white coats and those who are still contented with muddy boots, between those who employ hard data and those who use soft data, those who are purists and those who are popularists, those who deal with surface textures and those who delve into deeper structures, those who stress scientific method and those who abide by the lived experience, those who (as Claude Lévi-Strauss asserted of the practitioners in a related discipline) 'harbour a secret desire . . . of awakening among the natural sciences when the last trumpet sounds' and those who are prepared to leave their fate to the recording angel. Viewed positively, the differing forms of discourse employed by this variety of specialists should sharpen wits and provide evidence in support of William Empson's aphorism 'no grit, no pearl'.

In fact, there are at least two reasons why the consequences are not always as they might be. The first is organisational – and, to a certain extent, pedagogical. In most university departments, the student must select courses from an embarrassment of riches. The choice may result in anything from a somewhat anarchic array of courses to a narrow range of specialist options. Those who go on to teach will then tend to encounter a wide-ranging geography syllabus, much of which they will be unfamiliar with. Meanwhile, the broader economic situation is forcing contraction upon the university system at the same time as curriculum changes create pressures upon the time allotted to geography in the classroom. As university specialists retire, almost all departments of geography will reduce the range of options offered – ultimately, perhaps, to the point where it will be a question of specialisation between rather than within geography departments. A whole series of consortia may be necessary to maintain the existing range of specialisms that geographical institutions support. But, if *plus ultra* continues to be the motto at the research level, perhaps there should be a *ne plus ultra* to the school curriculum. In other words, perhaps the time has come (as in many continental countries) to decide what should be undergraduate material and where the cut-off point should come in the school examination syllabus.

The second consideration is linguistic. In recollecting the revolution that their subject has experienced over the last generation, geographers are inclined to forget the changes in the language that has accompanied it. The realisation that there is a language of geography is nothing new and it has yielded entertainingly discursive texts, not least among the French. But there has emerged a language beyond the vernacular, with professional geographers producing their own private thesauruses and with bigger and better dictionaries of geography competing for limited money even to the neglect of atlases. It may be argued that, just as specificity characterises the living speech of particular places, so vocabulary appropriate to a discipline evolves according to its especial needs. Nevertheless, while attempting to make the language of geography more precise, it must be recognised that language itself is imprecise.

Early in the century, Edward Thomas declared: 'Words never consent to correspond exactly to any object unless, like scientific terms, they are first killed'. This is a dilemma for geographers with their specialisms. Tongues never flame in private and professional languages, regardless of the fact that such languages are unsuitable for popular purposes. Geographers not infrequently complain that, by comparison with other disciplines, their work does not claim the wide attention that it merits. Perhaps they will have to learn to speak in two languages. One language is required to meet the needs of the televiewers (who react so responsively to the 'old Teutonic monosyllables' of Dryden that are employed by the down-to-earth naturalists), the radio listeners (who find no difficulties with the current vulgate of the historians) and for the million subscribers to the *National Geographic Magazine* (much of the profit from which supports primary geographical research). Is a second language enough for the professionals? Perhaps, ultimately, if it be the 'algebraic topological language of structure' as suggested by Peter Gould.

Doubts having been cast upon the trustworthiness of words, faith has been shifted to figures. The phenomena of the real world seemingly too complex for investigation, have had to be intellectually simplified by the employment of theoretical models. It is over a quarter of a century since the Lund Geographical Series published William Bunge's *Theoretical Geography*, disturbing the generally held view that theoretical geography was a contradiction in terms. For rather longer, the statistical and the technical have competed with the actual. Simultaneously, the positivist approach has inclined to dogmatism. Not surprisingly, there has been a generational reaction. The alternative humanistic approach emphasises the real world. While not unsympathetic to theory, it inclines to the opinion of Herman Hesse's *Glass Bead Game* – that it is a matter for masters only. It acknowledges the subjective and, directly or indirectly, has fostered autobiographical reflection. And reflection has underlined at least one important paradox – that the explosion of geographical information has tended to distance the subject from the lay public. Public attention will be claimed by such studies as Alice Coleman's urban utopias, Peter Hall's great planning disasters or Richard Batterbee's acidification of lakes, but not to the same degree in respect of sales as that achieved by *The State of the World Atlas* and *The State of the Nation Atlas*. In the same way as 'environment', that key word of the geographical vocabulary, has been taken over wholesale without acknowledgement, so the methods of cartography have been discovered and popularised by non-geographers who offer through them 'instant accessibility' of information to the public. Ptolemy lives.

So, too, does geography, more than 2000 years after his countrymen invented its name. This book derives its title and the origins of much of its contents from the Greeks. It was the Greeks who conceived the microcosm and the macrocosm – the concept of the locality and the world, and who linked geography and geometry. Theirs are the *Traces on the Rhodian Shore* that laid the foundations for scale and terrestrial measurement – and provided the title for Clarence Glacken's masterly book. Their toponymy, reiterated round the world, recalls their polity and economy. They introduced the word 'theory' which, as Peter Gould reminds us, originally meant the payment of close attention to outward appearances (still a central feature of geographical training). Not least, their *Odyssey*, literal or metaphorical, is the prototype of all those voyages of exploration that draw humankind to the horizon.

Author Index

compiled by Miles Ogborn

Subject Index